Beverly Garland

Beverly Garland
Her Life and Career

DEBORAH DEL VECCHIO

Foreword by Joseph Campanella
Afterword by Peggy Webber

McFarland & Company, Inc., Publishers
Jefferson, North Carolina, and London

ALSO OF INTEREST

*Peter Cushing: The Gentle Man of Horror
and His 91 Films,* by Deborah Del Vecchio
and Tom Johnson (McFarland, 1992; paperback 2009)

Hammer Films: An Exhaustive Filmography,
by Tom Johnson and Deborah Del Vecchio
(McFarland, 1996; paperback 2012)

Frontispiece: Bevery Garland, ca. 1977.

LIBRARY OF CONGRESS CATALOGUING-IN-PUBLICATION DATA

Del Vecchio, Deborah, 1950–
Beverly Garland : her life and career /
Deborah Del Vecchio ; foreword by Joseph Campanella ;
afterword by Peggy Webber.
p.   cm.
Includes bibliographical references and index.
Includes filmography.

ISBN 978-0-7864-6501-9
softcover : acid free paper ∞

1. Garland, Beverly, 1926–2008.
2. Motion picture actors and actresses — United States — Biography.
3. Television actors and actresses — United States — Biography.
I. Title.
PN2287.G383D45 2013   791.4302'8092 — dc23   [B]   2012045586

BRITISH LIBRARY CATALOGUING DATA ARE AVAILABLE

© 2013 Deborah Del Vecchio. All rights reserved

*No part of this book may be reproduced or transmitted in any form
or by any means, electronic or mechanical, including photocopying
or recording, or by any information storage and retrieval system,
without permission in writing from the publisher.*

Front cover image: Beverly Garland publicity shot from the
1957 film *Not of This Earth* (Allied Artists Pictures/Phofest)

Manufactured in the United States of America

*McFarland & Company, Inc., Publishers
Box 611, Jefferson, North Carolina 28640
www.mcfarlandpub.com*

For Carl — this one most of all

Table of Contents

Acknowledgments ix
Foreword by Joseph Campanella 1
Introduction 3

1. Beverly Lucy Fessenden 7
2. The Actor's Life for Me! 12
3. Beverly Campbell 18
4. Beverly Garland 25
5. Somebody Get Me a *Medic* 32
6. The Beast and the Amazon 42
7. Scream Queen 47
8. *The Joker Is Wild* 52
9. *Decoy* 56
10. Return to Gotham 59
11. Coco La Salle, the Lady Pirate 63
12. Where in the World Is Beverly Garland? 68
13. *The Miracle Worker* 71
14. *Stump the Stars* 76
15. *Twice Told Tales* 87
16. *The Bing Crosby Show* 94
17. *Pretty Poison* 101
18. *My Three Sons* 108
19. A Singing Cowboy, Hojo, and the Saga of the
    Freeway Chickens 116
20. The Cowboys 120
21. *Roller Boogie* Mama 128
22. A Star on the Hollywood Walk of Fame 142
23. *Scarecrow and Mrs. King* 154

24. *The Haunted Symphony*, Russia and Roger Corman —
    Together Again After All These Years 161
25. A Hollywood Survivor 170
26. Fifty Years in Show Business 180

Farewell to Television's First Lady 189
Epilogue 191
Afterword by Peggy Webber 193
Appendix I: The Television Credits 196
Appendix II: The Film and Made-for-Television Movie Credits 202
Chapter Notes 225
Select Bibliography 236
Index 237

Acknowledgments

I would like to extend my heartfelt thanks to Joseph Campanella and Peggy Webber for contributing the Foreword and Afterword to this book, as well as Kaye Ballard, Rex Reason, Lisa Stoll and William Windom for sharing their memories of Beverly.

A very special thank you to James Crank for his continued support of this work which I hope will honor his mother as I intended.

I would also like to acknowledge the University of Southern California — Special Collections Performing Arts Library, the Margaret Herrick Library of the Academy of Motion Picture Arts & Science, the Library of the American Film Institute — Louis B. Mayer Library, the Academy of Television Arts & Science, the Museum of Broadcasting, and the Lincoln Center Library where I conducted some of my research on Beverly's films and television appearances.

All of the photographs, advertising artwork and graphics included in this book are from the Carl Del Vecchio Collection.

While every effort was made to provide accurate and definitive information regarding Beverly's film, stage and television work, I could not track down the original television air dates for some of her specials, talk and game show appearances. Any sources cited as "unknown" were taken from news clippings (many from Beverly's personal scrapbooks) that did not have an author credit or newspaper or magazine title for identification. However, this was not due to a lack of trying on my part. If anyone reading this book can supply some of the missing data, please do so in care of the publisher and I will happily include it in the next reprint opportunity.

Many taped interviews with Beverly Garland were conducted over the past 35 years by my husband, Carl Del Vecchio, and myself. Some of Beverly's comments here previously appeared in various issues of *The Beverly Garland Club Journal* of which my husband and I were principal officers. I also made several trips to Los Angeles to conduct additional taped interviews with Beverly and her husband, Fillmore Crank, exclusively for this book. They both fully cooperated and enthusiastically supported this work. My only deep regret is that they did not live to see it in print.

Beverly was totally open and candid when I interviewed her. She shocked me more than once during our long sessions together and I think readers will see a side of Beverly that they might find surprising.

One thing that should become apparent from the very start is Beverly's sense of humor. She will, I promise you, cause you to laugh out loud more than once as you read this book. I wanted my readers to experience Beverly the way she was if you had the opportunity to talk to her face to face. I often thought the best way to "write a book" about Beverly was to point a camera at her and film whatever she said because she was so lively and hilariously funny. It's hard to project that in the written word.

My hope now is that whoever happens upon this book will come to know the real Beverly Garland, both on and off the screen. You will also discover just how special a lady — as well as an actress — she truly was and you will enjoy the journey upon which you are about to embark.

Foreword
by Joseph Campanella

I have so many memories of Beverly. The first time I actually worked with her — although we hadn't gotten to know each other yet — was when she was doing *Decoy* (episode title: "My Brother's Killer") in New York City. I remember how impressed I was with her work.

Then I remember seeing her in one of those B-picture horror movies. She was so real and so good in those pictures — in that one in particular — she actually made me believe in her character. That was how good she was in it. She was no starlet, she was an actress.

Even after I worked with her on *Decoy* I started looking for her on television. Whenever I found a show that she was going to be on, I made it a point to watch it — in those old black & white days. I looked forward to working with her again some time.

That opportunity finally came a few years later when she came back to New York in 1962 to film *The Nurses* (episode title: "The Walls Came Tumbling Down"). In it, we played husband and wife and she was just terrific.

The thing about Beverly was that you didn't "see" her working. She just walked onto a set and seemed to capture the character she was playing immediately, whole and solid.

When we worked on *The Nurses*, that was really something special because we were able to blend together as a couple very easily and very comfortably. I thought the show was very good.

We did a made-for-television movie called *Unwed Father* (1974), although we didn't actually have many scenes together. But we saw each other work. Beverly played the harridan alcoholic mother of the unwed father and she *was* an alcoholic mother! It was amazing! She could just slip into her character so easily.

We didn't get to know each other socially until I left the New York stage and came out to California. My wife and I ran into her in a park. She was with her husband, Fill Crank, who was a wonderful guy. We got to know each other socially and appreciate each other personally. Beverly was true as could be; honest as could be, with no phoniness about her. She didn't have a phony bone on her.

We also appeared together on a religious series, *Human Dimension* (episode title: "And Then They Forgot God"). This particular story took place in the future and she again played my wife. It was a very emotional subject. She was just tremendous and she made me a better actor. She was so real in her reactions. We did every scene in one take.

I also remember seeing her on game shows in which you got to see her real personality.

She has a laugh that could easily be called a "dirty laugh" but it was just wholesome and from the bottom of her heart.

I deeply regret that she's gone now and that we can never work together again in this life. But perhaps we will again in the afterlife. I hope.

Los Angeles, California

Joseph Campanella *is an American character actor born in New York City. With numerous stage and screen credits, he is best known as a television actor, including starring roles in* Mannix *(1967–1972) and* The Bold Ones — The Lawyers *(1969–1972). He starred in the daytime soap opera* The Bold and the Beautiful *from 1996 to 2005.*

Introduction

Beverly Garland didn't set out to become one of televisions most prolific performers. She began honing her craft on the stage, working towards earning her Actor's Equity card. What she really wanted, however, was to be a movie actress. She wanted a career like Bette Davis, whom she admired the most and in whom she felt a kindred spirit. She was born too late to be considered for the Hollywood studio star treatment that launched the careers of many Hollywood "legends" and though she wouldn't agree, it probably was the best thing that didn't happen to her. To be under a particular studio's thumb would have killed this very talented free spirit. Beverly would have hated being tied to a particular type of character, as many of these Hollywood "cookie-cutter" actresses were.

Even Bette couldn't wait to get out of her contract at Warner Brothers. She saw how it stifled creativity. No, the best thing that happened to Beverly Garland was when that Warner Brothers executive told her that she wasn't being considered for a studio contract because she, quote: "just wasn't pretty enough."

When Beverly began her career, television was the great unknown. Movie studios were terrified of it because it kept paying customers home.

But television to the novice actor was a godsend. Here was the perfect venue for the budding performer to be in and to be seen. Many of today's icons were weaned on television in their early days. Beverly found more work on television than in film because there were so many more choices and chances for her on the little screen. She could really show both audiences and television producers just how multi-talented she could be. Not many actors are as good playing both dramatic and comedic roles. Testing for film parts often led nowhere but Beverly was seen by Frank Sinatra in a dramatic television anthology series, *Climax!*, and he insisted she be cast in a co-starring role in his Paramount picture *The Joker Is Wild* (1957). On another occasion, a television producer remembered her comedic performance in an episode of *The Farmer's Daughter* and this led to her being cast as Bing Crosby's wife in his series *The Bing Crosby Show*.

Actor-producer Rod Cameron considered Beverly his "lucky charm" and cast her in every one of his television series pilot episodes — and every one of them sold! In fact, television producers would seek out Garland to appear in their pilots because she was such a strong presence and could deliver a forceful performance that got noticed. She was partly responsible for one of television's most well-known shows, *Dr. Kildare*, having appeared in the pilot episode that sold the series. She even went on an MGM studio-sponsored East Coast publicity tour with members of the regular cast to promote the show.

Beverly often lamented that she hurt her movie career because she worked in television. She was convinced that when she starred in the series *Decoy*, right after her A-picture role in *The Joker Is Wild*, that it forever closed the door to her chance at film stardom. I humbly disagree. I think *Decoy* was the one television appearance that stuck in the minds of more American viewers than any other show or film with the exception of her role as Barbara Douglas in *My Three Sons* and, more recently, as Dotty West in *Scarecrow and Mrs. King*. Many film actors would have loved that kind of exposure. In *Decoy*, Beverly was perfectly cast as television's first policewoman and undercover cop. Countless women joined police forces across the country because of that series and the impression she had made on them. That's power!

Beverly worked so much in television and appeared in so many pilot episodes that sold network series that *Los Angeles Times* television critic Walter Ames dubbed her "Television's First Lady." No other actress can make that claim.

Beverly also made her mark on the big screen — only not, perhaps, in the way she might have intended. During the 1950s, she starred in several films for a young director named Roger Corman. Two of those films would go on to become science fiction classics, *Not of This Earth* and *It Conquered the World*. No one was more surprised than Beverly. Many years later when she was asked to make guest appearances at various science fiction and horror film conventions, Beverly would apologize for not being able to offer up too many stories about those Corman films. "I made them and forgot about them.... I had no idea they would one day become so well regarded."

Part of the reason for their enduring popularity was her performances in them. She was not your typical heroine in *It Conquered the World*, cowering in a corner while awaiting rescue from a menace from another planet. She picked up a rifle, stood her ground and even managed to get off a few rounds before succumbing to her eventual fate. But young people who sat wide-eyed in their seats at local movie houses never forgot. Here was an actress who could handle the situation as well as any man. In *Gunslinger*, a Corman Western, Beverly's husband, the marshal, is murdered and she puts on his badge and goes after the bad guys herself!

She was also always ready to take on new challenges in completely different directions. A decade after her marriage to land developer and builder Fillmore Crank, Beverly and her husband went into the hotel business. Neither one had a clue how to run a hotel, but they bought seven acres in the shadow of Universal Studios in North Hollywood and built a 155-room motor lodge. Beverly could be seen on at least one occasion in the tour bus parking lot at Universal encouraging tourists to stay at her hotel. Not long afterwards, and through more conventional means, the hotel generated enough business that she no longer had to act as a barker for her guests, but she was determined that the business which bore her name would be a success. And it was and remains a very popular destination for tourists and business people. Beverly wouldn't allow it to fail. She explored every avenue opened to her to keep her business viable, from becoming a spokesperson for the National Tour Brokers Association to being installed as the Honorary Mayor of North Hollywood — a title she held for many years.

This can-do attitude followed Beverly all her life. She never let preconceived "norms" dictate who and what she should be. Beverly bucked the system time and again. She was told she wasn't attractive and yet she had legions of male admirers from her film and television appearances. She was short in stature yet she modeled professionally. She worked while pregnant during a time when many actresses in similar circumstances were forced to put their careers on hold. She was proud to show pictures of her children. Her gutsy approach succeeded in getting her a coveted starring role in a television series.

Beverly had no family fortune or connections to help her on her chosen career path. She didn't have the benefit of a family history in the performing arts. In fact, many of her ancestors lent themselves more to military and political careers than acting. Beverly's great grandfather, for example, was William Pitt Fessenden, secretary of the treasury under Presidents Lincoln and Johnson. But that kind of pedigree wasn't going to get her leading roles in Hollywood.

However, Beverly did have her admirers in the print media. *The Hollywood Reporter*, *Variety* and *The Los Angeles Times* almost always found her work laudable, and/or criticized the production in under-valuing her by placing her in unworthy roles. Columnists of the caliber of Hedda Hopper, Sheilah Graham and Louella O. Parsons were fans as well. Hopper named Beverly one of her "Top Film Finds of 1956."

She had the acting bug but very little help in making the right career choices when she first set out. It took her many years to become an overnight success and she had perhaps more slips and falls than most of her contemporaries. Yet these setbacks helped to harden her resolve and in retrospect they were probably what she needed to never give up on her goals.

Beverly didn't admit it, but it is this author's opinion that seeing her father's dream of being a singing star fade and die was probably never far from her thoughts as she jumped back into the fray time and again. And yet, when she married Fillmore and became a stepmother of two and later a mother of two herself, she decided that her career would have to take a back seat while she raised her children.

She continued to work but tried to limit her choices to jobs where she would come home at night. Beverly turned down a starring role in *The Nurses* because it would have meant transplanting her family to New York City and she felt it would have been too traumatic for the children.

Beverly also knew that young marriages were often fertile ground for infidelity — as she experienced with her parents as a child and later in her own marriage. Ironically, Beverly would also learn just how close she came to being a victim of domestic violence as the result of a bad marriage and how being on location at the time probably saved her life!

Beverly's career spanned seven decades. She had over 50 feature and made-for-television movie roles, as well as over 700 television appearances to her credit. She starred in or had recurring roles in nine television series. She performed on the stage on numerous occasions. She recorded a 45 RPM record and even had her own weekly radio show. In 1955, Beverly was nominated for an Emmy Award. In 1983, she was honored with a star on the Hollywood Walk of Fame, and in 2001, the City of Los Angeles proclaimed January 19 Beverly Garland Day.

Beverly also hobnobbed with presidents and former presidents. Her husband built a house in Palm Springs for Dwight D. Eisenhower. Beverly and Fillmore also attended Ronald Reagan's 80th birthday party and made a startling observation.

I think Beverly has much to teach young people who want to pursue an acting career in television or films. Her performances are as fresh today as they were when she originally gave them. Her experiences in front of the camera, on the stage, and off the set are not necessarily unique but they are worthy of review.

I always thought Beverly would have made one heck of a drama teacher but she was always too busy working. She always preferred to be working.

Beverly believed that actors were a special breed and only the very strong of heart should apply. However, while she had numerous opportunities to quit the profession, Beverly kept at it and her body of work speaks highly of her devotion to her craft. Perhaps it will be an inspiration for others on their chosen path.

Beverly Garland was a remarkable woman who had a remarkable life. She was also one other thing as well: She was a Hollywood survivor.

1. Beverly Lucy Fessenden

Beverly always told a funny story whenever anyone asked her about the day she was born. Her parents were living in Northern California when her mother became pregnant. They had gone with some friends on a week's vacation to Santa Cruz, a popular resort town in those days, when Amelia "Millie" Fessenden went into labor. She was promptly rushed to a local hospital and a short time later, Beverly was born on October 17, 1926.

While Millie was recuperating, a major earthquake hit the area. The nurse on duty rushed in with Beverly — her tiny head covered in plaster dust — and hastily threw her into her mother's arms. Her mother took one look at Beverly and tried to give her back. "This isn't mine," Millie said. The nurse was probably more shocked by the woman's response than the ongoing earthquake and asked, "What do you mean that's not yours?" "This is *not* my baby!" Millie insisted. The nurse was quickly losing patience with her and said, "Mrs. Fessenden, this *is* your baby!" All the while Beverly's mother was still trying to give her back. "No! No! *No*! This is not my baby. I didn't have a little girl. I had a *boy*!" The nurse was not going to give up that easily: "I'm sorry but you didn't have a boy. You had a girl." Millie was equally stubborn: "My doctor told me I was going to have a boy. This is a girl. So this is *not* my baby!"

When Beverly's mother demanded to see the doctor, the nurse decided that she had finally had enough. "Mrs. Fessenden," she said, "we're having an earthquake here." During the entire exchange, Millie's bed was rocking back and forth. The nurse added, "I haven't time to argue with you because the hospital is full of falling debris and all the babies have got to be taken out of the nursery. I'm sorry but *this is your baby!*" The newborn girl and her mother were promptly wheeled out of the hospital as the walls around them buckled and swayed with the tremors.

"I was a breech baby so maybe the doctor really didn't see what I was," Beverly explained. "I don't know. It was a tough delivery for my mother. Breech births — especially in those days — were difficult and dangerous. The feet come out first and the baby can choke very easily. That's probably why I'm such a nut — due to the lack of oxygen!"[1]

Beverly's mother finally had to accept the fact that she had a girl but then she didn't know what to do with her. She didn't even know what to name her. She finally decided on Beverly, after a friend of hers. It was really an afterthought, however, since she was supposed to be a boy and Millie had already decided to name her James, after Beverly's father. "So," Beverly said, "that's how I got the name Beverly — a name I've never really been comfortable with because my real name is Jim!"[2]

When Beverly was two or three months old, her parents lived in an upstairs apartment in Oakland, California. "I remember my mother giving me my bath in the sink. Now, how

I remember that, I'll never know. But I remember being in the sink and my mother holding me as she bathed me. The next thing I remember was when she put me in the closet because I had done something bad."³

Beverly's father, James A. Fessenden, remembered Beverly's first public appearance when she was about three years old. "A local theater was advertising a popularity contest for kids with a 'diamond' ring as the one and only prize. For fun, we decided to enter her in the contest. She had no friends in the audience as many of the other contestants had. The contest was judged by the emcee holding his hand over the child's head while standing in back of them and the applause of the audience in response as the deciding factor.

"As he did this, Beverly would look around and with each youngster she would clap her little hands and when he came to her she stood quite still. I don't know what possessed her to do this or how she happened to think of it, but she was so cute doing it that the audience actually went wild and naturally she won."⁴

When Beverly was about four, her family moved in with her grandfather who lived in Long Beach. "My father's parents were divorced." Beverly recalled. "My grandfather remarried after that. I never met his second wife but they had a son, Bill Fessenden. Many years later, while we were living in Arizona, my father got a telegram that his half-brother had been killed during the first wave of the Normandy invasion on June 6, 1944. I remember my dad going into the bedroom and sobbing. My dad had adored his half-brother. He was tall and good-looking and had just gotten married before he went overseas. This was very tough on my father."⁵

Beverly's mother had quit school and became a cosmetologist. "She always said, 'I'm a cosmetologist'— not 'I do hair and nails,'" Beverly said. Beverly had very fond memories of sitting with her mother under the pepper tree at her grandfather's house as her mother did her nails. "She would buff my nails until they shined and I loved it."⁶ "On certain days," Beverly recalled, "the iceman would come up the street and we'd put out our 'ice' sign. While he was busy delivering ice, I would go out to the truck and under the gunny sack there were all these little pieces of ice. It was fun to see just how many pieces of ice I could steal and eat as fast as I could before the iceman returned."⁷

Beverly, age three, enjoying a day at the beach, circa 1929.

After a short stay with her grandfather,

Beverly and her parents moved to a little house in Glendale, California. The house was quite run-down but Beverly remembers her mother saying, "We'll be as snug as a bug in a rug. You wait till I fix it up and we'll be as snug as a bug in a rug." And, according to Beverly, it was adorable when she finished with it. "The only thing I hated about it was that the bathroom had a pull chain toilet. It would scare me when I had to pull the chain to flush the toilet. I would run as fast as I could to get away."[8]

Beverly also recalled that the family had a large dog. "In those days, people used to polish their shoes and then put them outside by the front door so that the shoes could dry over night. The next day, our neighbors would come by and ask, 'Do you have a match to my shoe, please?' because my dog would spend the night stealing anywhere from ten to fifteen different shoes and bring them all home."[9]

Beverly continued, "Then we moved to another house in Glendale, on Cottage Grove. There were a lot of kids in the neighborhood. I had a good friend there named Pat Snow. My parents were very good friends with the Snow family."[10]

There was a big storm drain near the house and Beverly was never allowed to go near it. But one day, Pat and Beverly decided to go into the storm conduit. They walked around in there but it was so dark that they soon became too frightened to stay. They jumped out and ran home, climbing into the huge fig tree in Beverly's backyard which seemed a lot safer to them. Beverly's mother came out a short while later and said to her daughter, "Did you go into the storm drain?" Beverly said, "No." Then her mother asked her friend, "Pat, did you go into the storm drain?" and she said, "Yes." Beverly was dumbfounded: "What the hell is the matter with you, Pat?" Beverly asked her friend. Millie told them to get out of the tree and she promptly sent Pat home. "Then my mother took me inside and broke her hair brush on my behind. Needless to say, I never went into that storm drain again."[11]

Beverly attended kindergarten at Horace Mann Elementary School in Glendale. She didn't remember much about kindergarten except having to take a nap on the floor and painting. "They had great paint," she said. "I hated taking a nap but I loved to paint."[12]

Her first stage performance was playing a turkey in the school's Thanksgiving Day play and recited, "I am a Turkey, for you see, Thanksgiving Dinner must have me!"

"I had a papier-mâché turkey costume that

At age ten, Beverly appeared in a school play as a turkey. She was very proud of that paper turkey costume.

I thought was the most fabulous thing that ever happened to me. To be a turkey in a play was just incredible. Then I think I played a couple of trees and a few flowers and things like that. But I loved to do all that kind of stuff."[13]

What Beverly didn't like was being sick — and she was a very sick child. "When I was in the fourth grade, I had some kind of stomach problem and always had terrible stomach aches. So my mother had to keep me home most of the time. As a result, I had to repeat the fourth grade, which was terrible. To think that I had failed fourth grade," she lamented.[14]

Beverly finally graduated from elementary school and transferred to Roosevelt Junior High School. The family had moved once again, and Beverly was able to walk to school every morning — through a vacant lot and a park — with her new best friend, Edna. ("Edna had lots of brothers and sisters and her house was always a disaster in the morning. But she always got out of the house on time.") Beverly had a bike and would ride all over Glendale on it after school.

At the back of the house there was a huge eucalyptus tree with a swing rope. The idea was to climb the tree and swing down the rope. The first time Beverly tried it, she got so scared that she jumped instead and broke her arm. "I was always doing stuff like that," she said. "I was a great doll player, however, I loved to play with dolls. My father had made me a doll house and I could play with it for hours."

"When she was about seven," Beverly's father James recalled, "her mother had given Beverly a nice little sewing kit. She had more fun trying to make things for her dolls such as cut-out patterns, etc. She loved using those cute little scissors and one morning she arose real early and was very quiet in the living room. She often played by herself and we thought she was perhaps making something for her dolls. But to our surprise when we looked in the living room we were speechless for a moment. Beverly had taken those cute little scissors and had cut the front room curtains and drapes to shreds."[15]

"I also loved to play in the dirt and play with trucks with all the little neighborhood boys," Beverly recalled. "Then, one day, I discovered religion."[16]

Beverly's mother and father never got up on Sunday mornings because they would normally spend Saturday evenings night clubbing. In those days, women wore cocktail hats when they went out for a night on the town. "I would often slip into their bedroom on a Sunday morning," Beverly said, "to find my mother sound asleep with her cocktail hat still on her head. All my school friends' parents went to church on Sundays and I decided that with or without my parents, I was going to go to church, too."

There was a Baptist Church a couple of blocks from Beverly's house and one Sunday morning she attended services there. "I loved it," she recalled. "I especially loved when they would sing 'Onward Christian Soldiers.' That was my favorite song. I just adored it. I went to church there every Sunday. I even spent three months that summer at Sunday School.

"Then, one day, I announced to my mother that I was going to be baptized. 'You're going to *what*?' she shouted. My mother was a Lutheran and my father had been raised Seventh Day Adventists. In fact, my father's sister had been a missionary in India and I also had a cousin who had been a missionary in Africa. My mother was very shocked, but she finally said, 'Okay, if that's what you want.'"

Beverly wore a pink dress on the day she was to be baptized. "I was almost at the church door when I realized that I had forgotten to put on my underwear," she laughed. "I was in a panic because when they baptize you, they dunk you in water and I was terrified that someone would notice. So I had to run home, put on my underwear, and race back.

"At this particular Sunday service I was alone with all these older people. It was very unusual for little girls to go to church by themselves. Pastor Maddox was at the podium lecturing and he said, '...And we don't dance.' I said, 'What? What did he say?' to the lady sitting next to me. She replied, 'We don't dance.' I said, 'What?' She said, '*We don't dance!*' I said, 'We don't dance?' She repeated, 'No, we don't dance!' 'We don't dance ... we don't dance?' I couldn't believe it. Well then, I can't be a Baptist! I left after the service before being baptized and never went back."[17]

Beverly adds, "Then I discovered the Little Theatre of the Verdugos in Glendale."

2. The Actor's Life for Me!

"As a kid," Beverly recalled, "I was always play-acting and would often come home from school and recite some silly little poem I had learned that day for my mother's bridge club. You see, in those days, mothers stayed home and played bridge — at least, that's what my mother did.

"I think my mother was secretly thrilled that I wasn't going to be a Baptist so she willingly took me down to the Little Theatre in Glendale to try out for a role in a play that I had heard they were going to produce. I auditioned for *The Maker of Dreams — A Fantasy* by Oliphant Doron." Beverly was to play the part of Pierrette. To her mother's (and her) delight, she got the part. After the play opened on December 26, 1940, she received her very first review in the town's local paper: "Startling are the performances of two players barely in their teens. Beverly Fessenden as Pierrette and Jimmie Schroder as Pierrott in *The Maker of Dreams* capture much of the charm of these two legendary lovers." "I was so proud," Beverly recalled. "I thought plays were wonderful."[1]

Several weeks later, on February 5, 1941, Beverly appeared in *Dr. In Spite of Himself*, a musical comedy by J.B.P. Moliere, as a "Maid in Waiting" with such memorable lines as "The postman is here, sir." One of her co-stars was a young lady by the name of Gloria Talbott. Years later, Talbott would appear in the motion pictures *We're No Angels* with Humphrey Bogart, *All That Heaven Allows* with Rock Hudson, and the science fiction favorite *I Married a Monster from Outer Space*.

In June of that same year, Beverly had a ten-day run in *Ever Since Eve* by Hollywood screenwriters Colin Clements and Florence Ryerson. In an interview with director Caradoc Rhys by Norman Boyd, Rhys stated that Beverly had "the talent to become an actress if she would like acting as a profession."[2]

This was when Beverly's parents decided that maybe she really could become an actress and introduced her to Anita Arliss. The sister of British actor George Arliss, Anita was well known as a drama teacher in Hollywood. Beverly's father recalled,

As Beverly started school, we wanted to give her some kind of training in the arts and started her with piano lessons. She just would not practice so the piano lessons were soon dropped. The same thing happened with the violin ... and dance lessons. When she was about fourteen years old, we thought she might like dramatics as she was always putting on some kind of an act with her dolls as an audience and then with other kids. So, we started her with Miss Anita Arliss ... with private lessons. Beverly seemed to just love this training and she would practice on her own with no coaxing for hours at a time. This seemed to be *it*. She soon took parts in some of the school plays and then in a small summer theater. For business reasons we had to move and Beverly had to discontinue her lessons, but by this time she had learned many basic rules and principles of the art which have stayed with her. She also had the knack of learning lines quickly and easily which was a great asset in the acting profession.[3]

Beverly recalled that in those days, "Agents were kind of like gumshoes, they did not have the clout. It was the drama teachers who had the clout. They were the ones who knew the studio heads and they could go in there and say, 'Listen, I have a student who I really think is good and I would like to have him or her read for you.' They really had the 'in.' Many studios even had their own drama teachers. They put you under contract and they sent you to school. That's how it worked in those days. So, to take classes from Anita Arliss was really kind of wonderful, I thought. So did everyone else."[4]

Beverly said her father was an incredible salesman. "He could sell your own toupee off your head. He was also a singer — very much in the style of Bing Crosby. My dad was quite good, too. He had performed in San Francisco with various big bands. In fact, my dad met my mother during one of his performances. She had been dating the orchestra leader and started dating my father as well. My mother was pretty wild in her own way. She finally gave up the orchestra leader and married my father on May 4, 1924."[5]

In those days, many people went dancing. According to Beverly, they had Saturday night dances and tea dances at all the big hotels. Beverly's father made a lot of personal appearances and sang on the radio as well. Beverly kept a newspaper announcement from July 1, 1928, that read: "Heard during dance intermission Jimmy Fessenden. Tenor sings from KYA on Tuesday nights from 10 to 11 o'clock." He also sang at weddings, luncheons and private parties. "But after a while," Beverly added, "my mother just wouldn't have it. My mother was a very jealous woman and did not like that my father was at these dances and parties singing with all these very beautiful women around him till three or four in the morning. She had a fit and made his life miserable until he finally gave it all up. I don't know what she said or did but he must have loved her enough to do it. By then, my parents also had me to raise and I guess my father figured his singing gigs might not always be there to support us."[6]

Beverly's father got a job selling Camel cigarettes for several years. He was a good salesman but he was on the road all the time. Then he had an affair and Beverly's mother was going to divorce him. Beverly was devastated.

> I was still in junior high school at the time. I remember him coming into my room and telling me that he was leaving — and then he left the house. I just sobbed and sobbed. It was the most horrible thing. I didn't care about the affair. He could have had ten affairs. I just didn't want him to leave me. I don't think we have any idea what children go through when their parents divorce. I just didn't want my father to leave me. I wanted my parents to stay together. I didn't care if they were unhappy or who my father was sleeping with. I wanted them both with me in our house. It was very important to me as a child and that's all I cared about.
>
> My father was my champion. He was special. Little girls, I guess, are very close to their daddies. My mother and father would argue a lot — they would argue all the time and I always took my father's side. There was something about my father that was so important to me. Eventually, my mother forgave my father and he came back. She really was mad for him. Whether my father had another affair after that, I don't know. I remember I was around twelve years of age and it was during Christmas when my father's "friend" sent me this fabulous bathrobe. It had all these quilted flowers on it and I loved it! But my mother made me send it back.[7]

James Fessenden left the cigarette business and got a new job selling chemicals, waxes and other cleaning fluids. During the Second World War his territory included all the big military bases. Then in the summer of 1941, shortly after Beverly's first few lessons with

Anita Arliss, the family moved to Phoenix, Arizona.[8] "Phoenix in those days consisted of one drive-in, two movie theaters, a Goldwaters Department Store, and the Indians were still selling jewelry outside Woolworths," Beverly said.

> I went to North Phoenix High School. I would sit in my Spanish class and look out the window and there were just fields with horses grazing. That's how it was back then. I think there were sixty thousand people in Phoenix then. Now, there are millions. But it was a tiny town when I lived there.[9]
>
> I remember going to Scottsdale, and all it was then was a big Main Street. The only store there was a launderette with all these washing machines and dryers. The dryers in those days were wringers.
>
> I'll never forget, when we lived in Glendale, my mother didn't have a washing machine. We had a back porch with a big sink. Our local paper was advertising washing machines so she called and said she wanted to try one out. They said, "Absolutely!" and brought one out to the house and hooked it up. My mother then invited everyone in the neighborhood to come over and wash their clothes! We didn't have a dryer, so we wrung everything out and hung the laundry all over the house. Afterwards, my mother called the store and told them that the machine really wasn't what she wanted. They eventually came out and took the machine away. But in the meantime, we had a great time and washed everything in the neighborhood — sheets, blankets, clothes — everything![10]

In Arizona, the Fessendens lived in a tiny pre-fab house that wasn't well-insulated. "Summers in Phoenix," Beverly recounted, "were horrendous because we had no air conditioners then. We had a swamp cooler and that was it."[11]

Beverly's parents were very big on horses. They had two horses and boarded a couple of horses as well. Beverly had a horse named Ginger. Her mother's horse Ginny Lee was a Palomino. "So we rode horses," Beverly said, "although most of our riding was done in the early morning hours or in the evening when it was cooler. We were very big on the 'cowboy thing' in Arizona."[12]

Beverly's parents loved trout fishing. During the summer months they would go camping with another family and pitch a tent. Beverly's dad would cook whatever he caught. "Trout was my favorite fish of all when I was a child but I remember getting terribly car sick and hating the drive out to those camping sites."[13]

Summers in Arizona were spent having barbeques, riding horses, and swimming in the pool. One of Beverly's boyfriends was a lifeguard at a country club, Jim St. Clair, and she was madly in love with him. "Jim ended up marrying somebody else. I was hysterical that he didn't love me and didn't want to spend the rest of his life with me!" Beverly laughed.[14]

Because it was a small town back then, everybody knew each other since kindergarten and if you didn't fit in, you were nobody. "I've always been a loner," Beverly said, "but in high school I was a joiner because I had to be in order to survive. I made up my mind then and there that I would fit in. Freshman year I dated a guy who was not part of the in-crowd and it was not a good experience. Sophomore year, I went with Phil Gates because, not only did I like him, he was also president of the student body and he was on the football team. From that point on, I was very calculating because I wanted to be popular."[15]

In those days, there were sororities and fraternities in high schools. Beverly wanted to be part of that and joined Kappa Delta Kappa in 1943. Dating Phil Gates probably had a lot to do with Beverly getting into the sorority. However, being in a sorority wasn't all about dating "the right people." The house was very much involved in school social events and charities, as well as holding several events to help with the war effort.

By the time Gates left for Arizona State College, Beverly was dating other boys on the football team. She remembered there was one fellow by the name of Fred, the handsomest kid in the school. Fred was part Spanish and nobody wanted to bring him into the clique, so he was a bit of an outsider. However, by that time Beverly had some clout and could date anyone she wanted. "I had dated Fred in my senior year," Beverly said, "but after graduation, my parents decided to move back to California so that was the end of him. In 1995, I went back to Arizona for my school's fiftieth reunion and there was Fred, just as handsome as he was back then," Beverly smiled.[16]

Shortly after arriving in Arizona, Beverly joined the Little Theatre of Phoenix, which had just opened. She had previously appeared in the school production *Rhythm Roundup — A South American Cruise*, a musical comedy put on during the winter of 1941-42. The show was an annual event at the high school and was produced entirely by the students — including writing, acting and directing.[17]

"My first performance at the Little Theatre," Beverly said, "was in May 1942 in *Out of the Frying Pan* by Francis Swann. I played the role of Marge Benson, one of six starving actors trying to break onto the Broadway stage. Just prior to its opening in Phoenix, we put on two performances at Luke and Williams Fields, two local Army Air Corps bases." One local paper reported, "[O]n both occasions, the halls virtually shook with laughter" and that they were a tremendous hit with the troops. It was the first time the Little Theatre Of Phoenix had played to a strictly military audience as part of the war effort.

"It was at the Little Theatre that I met Steve Allen," Beverly added. "He was my friend for years. I would often see him at the Theatre playing the piano."[18]

Then in June, Beverly won a contest on KOY, a Phoenix radio station. She had entered the "Let's Put on a Play" program and won $5 as well as her own weekly radio show which began the following September. *The Community Chest Show — Story Time* usually ran about 15 minutes and Beverly would feature some local family in need of help from the Community Chest organization. "I still have my first pay stub from the station," Beverly recalled, "dated September 26, 1942. I was paid $2.00. $1.98, after deductions!"

Beverly continued to work at the Little Theatre during the war and was in several plays including *Heart of a City*,[19] *The Quiet Wedding*,[20] and *The Women*.[21] "I also recall," Beverly said, "that our junior-senior high school play *Don't Take My Penny* had 120 students trying out for just 17 parts. I played one of three 'model wannabes' in the production and I had to affect a lisp for the part."[22]

Beverly did well in most of her classes but there *was* one class where she had her share of difficulties. "I took a class in shorthand at North Phoenix High School and one day my teacher came to me and said, 'Look, if you are willing to leave my class, I'll give you a 'D.' Otherwise, you're failing." To which I replied, 'I'll take it!' Shorthand and I did not work out. I just couldn't do those squiggly things. I took the class because my mother kept saying, 'You've got to learn shorthand. It's the only way you'll be able to work. You *have* to be a secretary!' A secretary or a nurse — those were the career choices for most girls back then. So I thought I'd better learn shorthand. But I just couldn't do it. Typing and shorthand were the two subjects I really never did master."[23]

Beverly's graduating class that year was about 100 students. "When I graduated, Mrs. Nakowsky — she was Russian and taught history — was announcing the names of the students who were graduating with honors and she said, 'Beverly Fessenden.' I couldn't wait to get home that day to tell my mother the good news. 'Mom,' I said, 'I'm going to graduate with honors!' and my mother turned to me and said, 'You go back and find out whether that was a mistake.' I said, 'But I'm on the honor roll.' And she said, 'Beverly, just ask her.' She had taken all the air out of my ego balloon. So the next day I sought out Mrs. Nakowsky and I said, 'Yesterday, when you read the names of the honor students, did you mention my name?' And she said, 'Yes.' When I got home, I shouted, '*Mother! Yes!*' She still couldn't believe it but I did make the National Honor Roll Society."[24]

In November 1944, Beverly applied for admission to Stephens College Nursing Program in Columbia, Missouri. The following March, she was accepted. Beverly recalls the conversations she had with her parents about her decision to attend Stephens College:

> My father had asked me, "Now, what are you going to do?" I said, "I want to be a nurse," and he said, "A nurse? You're not going to be a nurse!" I said, "I'm not?" And he said, "No. You're going to be a doctor!" I said, "I am?" and he said, "Yeah." I thought to myself, "My God. A nurse I can be. I can empty bed pans and all that. What I can't do is brain surgery. I know that!"
>
> My mother always knew, way down deep, that I wanted to be an actress. She had been the one who schlepped me around to the Little Theatres. She often stayed till 12 or one o'clock in the morning if I wanted to talk with the kids after the plays since I was too young to drive. She was always very much behind me, no matter what path I chose.[25]
>
> So my mother said, "You know, we don't have very much money but if you want to go to Stephens, we'll get you through it." I recall saying to her, "Mother, maybe I should choose a different career because I can't be a doctor. I just can't. But I don't want to disappoint my father." Shortly after I graduated from high school, my family moved back to California and my mother suggested I return to Anita Arliss' drama school and from there try to break into show business. I thought that was a great idea. A wonderful idea. "I'll leave the brain surgery to someone else," I thought.[26]

Beverly called Anita, who said, "Oh Beverly, of course I remember you and I'd love to have you. I know that I can really do something with you. I thought you had talent then and I think you still do.' So I said, 'Okay,' and that summer I wrote to Stephens College to say that I was not going to attend. I had one acting class with Anita Arliss on August 1, 1945, and three days later, she died."[27]

When the Fessendens moved back to California, they lived at 1667 Arboles Drive in Glendale. That summer, Beverly had started dating a fellow by the name of Johnny Mason. By mid–August he proposed but he had just joined the Navy and was going to be stationed out of San Diego. The long distance engagement only lasted a few months and then they broke up. "We just didn't get along," Beverly said. "We were both too stubborn and wanted our own way too much of the time."[28]

With the death of her acting coach, Beverly had to work while she decided what to do next.

> I've always worked my entire life. I like to work. I'm happy working. I like to be busy. I used to waitress in thousands of places because I made good tips and the work was fast. That's what you want. Busy, busy, busy. So that you're not saying, "I hate this job!" Once I became an actress and I started to get roles, I still worked in between acting assignments. Finally, I got enough parts that I could hold myself over until the next role. I had enough money to wait for the next film or television job to come along. So I didn't have to go out and waitress or work a cash register or model any more. I could always make enough to pay the rent. And then I could always collect my unemployment, which was $25 a week back then. So, between my unemployment and a few jobs I got, I finally got to the point where I could make it without being a waitress.[29]

Beverly's first paying job was at Sears Roebuck in Phoenix. "I was the elevator operator and had just been promoted from the stock room. I'll never forget it because I would open the elevator door and announce, *Going Up*! There was always one person who would get into the elevator and then say, 'Oh, I thought you were going down' and would want to get out. 'Jeez,' I would think, 'what's the matter with you people?'"

Not long after Beverly moved back to Glendale, a friend told her she was going to modeling school and that piqued Beverly's interest. "'What are you learning in modeling school?' I asked. My friend got up and walked and then turned. I said, 'Well, heck. That's just a stage turn. I can do that. I can be a model!' So I went to I Magnins, one of the most fashionable stores at that time, and I said, 'I want to be a model.' I told them that I had modeled for a store in San Francisco. I made a stage turn and then another stage turn and I got the job. I hoped that they wouldn't call the store in San Francisco because I never modeled before in my life!"

In those days, customers would come in and buy a $2,000 dress but they wanted to see it on a model first. One day, Beverly put on a dress and modeled it for a customer but the man didn't buy it because she had put the dress on backwards. "Well, that was the last time I modeled at I Magnins!"

Beverly even taught modeling at one time. "I needed a job and I saw an ad for a teaching job at a modeling school. I walked in and said, 'I'm a teacher.' They didn't know. I figured, 'Hell, I can make a stage turn. I can teach these kids how to do that.' You walk and then you turn; walk and turn. Now makeup—*that* I wasn't so sure about. But what the heck. I did the best I could and I taught there till I got an acting role. I worked for the school for quite a while because I would get a role, leave, and then I would come back. I never had any formal training in hair and makeup. I figured these kids didn't know any more than I did. The teachers apparently didn't know any more than I did! Eventually I got enough steady acting work that I didn't have to go back."

Beverly even worked for a Santa Ana endocrinologist who wanted her to stay on because she looked so good in her white nurse's uniform. "I even worked for Bette Davis' husband, William Sherry, who was in real estate in Laguna Beach for a while."

But her most memorable job was at Forest Lawn Cemetery. In the summer, shortly before Beverly was to begin her first semester at Glendale College, she got a job there as a mail girl. "The day I started, my boss showed me around the facility. 'As our mail girl,' he said, 'part of your duties is to drive to the Glendale Post Office to pick up the mail.' Under the cemetery's administrative offices there was a twenty-stall garage where they kept all the limousines, hearses, and other company cars. My boss said, 'Now this is very important, Beverly. Do you see the car in stall 1A? Well, *do not* forget this: No matter what happens, always take the car in stall 1A when you go to the post office.' I said, 'Got it!'"

After Beverly had been working at Forest Lawn for about a month, one day she went down to the garage and got into the vehicle in stall 1A for her daily trip to the post office. "I'm at the post office when there is a phone call. 'Is the Forest Lawn mail girl there?' the caller asks the mail clerk. 'Yes,' he replies, 'she's right here.' The caller then asks, 'Could you get her, please?' I take the call. 'Hello,' I said, 'this is Beverly.' It's my boss screaming, 'Beverly, we're having a funeral and we don't have the body! You took the hearse and the body is in the back!'

"It was so funny because when I was driving down to the post office, I wondered why everybody got out of my way. I had taken the hearse because it was parked in the stall my boss told me to take the car from. Needless to say, that was my last day at Forest Lawn!"[30]

3. Beverly Campbell

In the fall of 1945, Beverly started attending classes at Glendale Community College. She joined the college's radio station — KIEV — as well as the school's Saints and Sinners Club.

Beverly's best friend since junior high school was Rehlein Graupe, who had come over from Germany at the start of the Second World War. Her Jewish father was a very important lawyer in Germany until the Nazis ransacked their home and had taken him away to a concentration camp. Somehow, Rehlein's mother got him out. Fortunately, they had some relatives in Glendale who sponsored them to come to America. But they were only permitted to bring five hundred dollars with them, so most of their fortune was confiscated by the Nazis.

> Rehlein and I were partners in crime. She wasn't as bad as I, however, I was very bad. When we were kids we would arrange sleepovers at her house and then climb out her bedroom window late at night and roam around Glendale together. I was always the one pushing her to do that, saying, "Let's get on our bikes and go to the middle of town and watch the boys — bowling!" It was quite an adventure at ten o'clock at night. Afterwards, we would climb back into her bedroom and go to sleep. We never got caught.
>
> Towards the end of our first semester at Glendale College, we had a free afternoon. We had to come back later that day because we were in a play. We had lunch out with several of our friends and each of us had about three beers. Rehlein and I came back to do the play and someone said, "Those girls have been drinking!" The teacher asked both of us if we had been drinking. Naturally, we said, "No. We only had one beer with our lunch."
>
> We were then informed that we were not going to be in the play, and worse yet, that we were both getting a failing grade. We would have to repeat the entire semester. My father went to the school and raised hell but I was still expelled because I drank beer. I never went back to Glendale College but Rehlein did return and eventually graduated.[1]

Early in 1946, Beverly had auditioned for — of all things — the Earl Carroll Theatre. "This was sort of a West Coast version of the Ziegfeld Follies. I tried out and, oh, there were all these gorgeous women — and there I was. I couldn't dance and so I would stand at the back of the stage and watch the girls go through their routines and try to mimic their steps. And I was chosen!"[2]

Nineteen-year-old Beverly wasn't picked for the theater revue, but for the road show. "I recall coming home quite excited to tell my mother the good news and she said, 'No, you can't go!' I said, 'But Mother, I'm an Earl Carroll girl and over the door of the theater it says, 'Through These Portals Pass the Most Beautiful Girls in the World'! But my mother wasn't going to budge. 'No,' she insisted, 'I'm not going to have you go on the road. You're too young. If you were going to dance in the show in Hollywood, that would have been

Beverly (first row, left) rehearses for a program on the Glendale Community College Radio Station Kiev in the fall of 1945 (other rehearsers unidentified).

okay. But you are *not* going on the road!' So that was the end of my Earl Carroll dancing girl career. It was a national road tour and all the girls were going to dance all over Hell and back! But I wasn't going to be one of them — thanks to my mother!"[3]

Since the Earl Carroll Theatre was no longer an option to help launch her show business career, Beverly joined the Rainbow Players. She had heard that this Hollywood-based playhouse — headed up by George Howard — was a showcase for young talent and that their productions were often attended by agents and motion picture studio talent scouts.

In addition to her classes at Glendale Community College, Beverly appeared in two Rainbow Players productions, *Quiet Wedding* and *June Mad*. In the former, she played Janet Royd, the same part she had previously played in the Phoenix Little Theatre production. She also decided to try out her first stage name: She chose Beverly Blake. The plays were successful.

Then Beverly's father decided that, because he had been a traveling salesman for so many years, he now wanted to be a fisherman. "I don't know why," Beverly said, "but that's what he decided to do!

"My mother had been speculating in the real estate market for years. She had been buying and selling the houses we lived in for most of my life and each time she sold our house, she made a little money on it. Our house on Arbolis Drive was also put up for sale and when it sold, my parents moved down to Balboa Island. They took some of the money they had saved and had this 46-foot cruiser and commercial fishing boat built which they named 'The Fisherette.' It had two ten-ton holds on it to keep albacore tuna, as well as sleeping quarters. My parents were so excited."[4]

While the boat was being built, her parents came up with the idea that they would build a little shed next to the unemployment office, so that when people came out of the office, they (the parents) would cash their checks for a small fee. In those days, people didn't want everyone to know that they were getting unemployment. The check-cashing shed was doing quite well until one day someone opened a shed across the street and charged a smaller fee!

Beverly recalled the day her parents christened their new boat. "When my parents launched the Fisherette, we watched it being slowly lowered into the water — lower, lower, lower — and then it promptly sank to the bottom![5] My parents, however, were undeterred. After they got the boat seaworthy, they quickly gathered their fishing gear and a picnic lunch and headed out to sea. But the further out they got, the more uncomfortable my dad got. 'Oh my God! I can't do this!' he said. My mother said, 'What do you mean, Jimmy?' and my father replied, 'I'm so sick!' Every time they went out on the boat, my dad got seasick. Now, why they didn't check this out before my parents went ahead and built this two ten-ton hold, 46-foot-long fishing boat, I will never know. But they had to hire a captain because my father was never on deck — he was always below in bed."[6]

To add insult to injury, the albacore didn't run that year. It was the first year in memory that the tuna didn't show up. They lost a lot of money and eventually had to sell the boat. "I don't know what happened to the Fisherette," Beverly said. "I think it finally went for scrap."[7]

Although Beverly was living on Balboa and Rehlein was up north in Los Angeles, they still kept in close contact and decided to spend their vacation time on Catalina Island. They stayed at a rooming house with 20 other vacationing students and spent most of their days on the beach or window shopping at all the quaint little shops in town.

"During one of our town visits,' Beverly recalled, "we decided that we would pick up [filch] a few little things as we wandered through the stores. We took items like a pencil or a comb or something like that. Everyone in our rooming house had little things that they had taken. However, as we were coming out of one shop, we were grabbed by the local police. 'What have you got?' the officer asked and I said, 'This 25-cent ring.'"[8]

The police then went to their rooming house. Evidently, shopkeepers had been complaining that people had been stealing all summer and that some of the girls in the house had been responsible.

> They singled out Rehlein, myself, and another girl who was about 15 years old as the culprits. The police questioned everyone at the rooming house and even went through all our belongings. But, naturally, none of the other girls would admit to taking anything. So the police assumed that we had taken everything. To make matters worse, the shop owners were convinced that we were also stealing more valuable items and using the Campbell boys' fishing boat to transport the stuff to the mainland to sell on Long Beach. The stories were starting to get more and more bizarre![9]
>
> Bill and Bob Campbell were brothers. They were both in their early twenties and had a fishing boat. We became friends with them during our stay and I had started dating Bob shortly after we arrived on the island. So the police took us to the station house and called our parents. We were convinced that we were going to be sent to Tehachapi Prison. Of course, we weren't going to go to prison. But we thought we were going there at the time.[10]

Eventually, we were placed on probation for one year in the custody of our parents. Rehlein's mother came and that fall, Rehlein went back to Glendale College. I decided I was *not* going to be under my parents' thumb for one year. So I married Bob Campbell — the man with the fishing boat — instead. That marriage lasted all of three months! I remember going to Burbank to meet Bob's father only to find out that he was a bookie! His house was filled with telephones — all ringing at once — and there were dozens of milk bottles stuffed with betting slips under the telephone tables. I quickly decided I'd had enough and I divorced him.[11]

While living on Balboa, Beverly joined the Laguna Beach Community Players. They opened the 1947 season with *Lady in the Dark*, a musical comedy with music and lyrics by Gershwin & Hart. It was a wonderful opening and Beverly's reviews were quite encouraging. Even the *Los Angeles Times* reported that Beverly "made a hit with her portrayal of a chic but bird-brained female." *The Laguna Beachcomber* said she was "utterly at home on stage." The buzz even landed Beverly an interview with a talent scout from 20th Century–Fox studios.

The Laguna Beach Community Players followed up with a production of *Glamour Preferred* in early June. It was seen by several Hollywood celebrities including Robert Stack, Bette Davis and her husband William Grant Sherry who was a playhouse patron.[12] Beverly will never forget what happened the night of her performance. "I was moonlighting as a

In the summer of 1947, while appearing with the Laguna Beach Community Players, Beverly moonlighted as a waitress at the Castaways Restaurant. That's Beverly, third from the left, with the restaurant staff.

waitress at the Castaways Restaurant at the time. I used to work anywhere I could get a job in order to support myself and be able to perform at the playhouse. I was waiting on tables one night and Bette Davis came up to me with her party and said, 'I saw you in your play and I thought you were marvelous.' I will never forget that as long as I live! I just thought that that was the most marvelous thing that ever happened to me. I mean, to have someone like Bette Davis praise my work was incredible! I must have made an impression on her. I may be wrong, but I don't think she was the type of person to throw compliments around lightly."[13]

Shortly after Beverly filed for divorce from Bob Campbell, she was on a plane to New York. She had decided to try to make it on the Broadway stage.[14] Beverly had a great aunt who lived in Westport, Connecticut. "She was very, very wealthy and had married a bookie—it must run in the family! In those days, bookies were guys who just went around the neighborhood with money in their hands, taking bets on horse races. My great aunt ended up marrying this man when she was about fourteen years old. She traveled with him to racetrack after racetrack because there were no betting windows or off-track betting stores. Later they bought the Westport Inn and she ran it for many years. I will always remember her bookie husband who wore a celluloid collar."[15]

When he died, Beverly's great aunt continued the bookie business. She also had a house next door to the inn. She had rented out the first floor to a woman and her son; the second floor consisted of a kitchen, a bath, and a large room with a huge bed in it. "My great aunt rarely got out of bed except to go to the races. She never read a newspaper. She only read the racing form and kept all the bets for her friends. Her friends would say, 'Oh Miriam, bet on Jacob in the third race.' She would tell them, 'You're darn right I will!' She never did, of course. She'd bet on Loopy Doop instead. Now if Jacob happened to come in, she'd pay it. But she used your money to play the way she wanted to play. That's how she did it. She was a character."[16]

Beverly was given the attic room in her great aunt's house. It was tiny and had no bathroom.

> I was given a bowl and a pitcher of water instead. When I told her that I had to take daily baths, my aunt was shocked. "We don't take daily baths," she said. "It's absolutely terrible for your skin. You can't do that. You can come with me to the baths. Once a week I go to the baths in New York where I get a pedicure, a manicure, and a French bath." The rest of the week she took sponge baths. Well, it was *horrible* living there!
>
> So I decided to get on the train to New York City and become an actress—fast! I got to New York and I was just in awe. "Hello? Here I am in New York! I'm going to be an actress—on the stage!" Now what do I do? Where do I go? How do I even get off this train platform? I mean, I knew absolutely nothing! I knew no one! Nada. I realized I couldn't do this. I was scared to death. I didn't know there was such a thing as *Variety* or a union. I didn't even know how to find an agent. I was in a panic and I had to get out. So I got back on the train to Westport."[17]

Beverly had no money and her aunt wasn't going to give her any. She took a job with a local photographer whose specialty was retouching photos. "He taught me how to take out images and his customers really liked my work. I could take out anything! I could completely erase your ex-boyfriend, or trim a large nose on a face. I could obliterate anything and I was very good at it. But after three months of living in an attic with my eccentric aunt—who only left the house to bathe or go to the racetrack—and wiping out photo people, I was desperate to get out of Westport and go home to California. But how?"[18] She had been married for three months and still had a diamond ring.

I found a huge ad in *The New York Times* which said, "We Buy Diamonds!" Oh boy, they buy diamonds! I can go home. I can sell this diamond and get home!

So I take my ring and I get back on the train to New York. The address on the ad said, "Floor 42, Empire State Building." Well, it's the tallest building in the world so I should be able to find it! The elevator doors open on the 42nd floor and I find myself surrounded by imported Italian marble floors and walls and a secretary seated in front of a pair of floor-to-ceiling carved walnut doors. "Yes?" the secretary inquires. "I'm here to sell my diamond," I reply. The secretary points to the doors and says, "This way, please." I open the door and there is a very dapper-looking man sitting behind an enormous desk way down at the other end of a cavernous room. "May I help you?" his voice echoes. Oh my God! I'm in the wrong place! Ah, hell! He buys diamonds, doesn't he? So I walk the seven blocks it takes to get to the other side of the room and I say, "I understand you buy diamonds" and he says, "Yes." I say, "Well, I'd like to sell this" as I hand him my ring. Now I thought he was going to say, "Where is it?" But he was very nice and didn't. He takes out his little eyepiece and examines the diamond — which is half the size of a pinhead — and hands the ring back to me. "This has a flaw," he says. *"It has a flaw?"* I gasp. My God! It's so bloody little. How do you find a flaw in so tiny a diamond? "I'm sorry," he adds. "I can't buy this." I realized he probably only dealt with precious stones the size of the Hope Diamond. He wasn't interested in my tiny little diamond. I thanked him and once again got back on the train to Connecticut."[19]

In Westport, there were three jewelry stores. At one of them, the jeweler told her there were two flaws. "Two," Beverly exclaimed. "The guy in New York only found one! I go to the second one and he says, 'Nope. It's got a flaw.' I go to the last store and I say, 'Let me tell you something. I have this diamond and I think it might have a flaw. I have *got* to get home. I can't stay here any longer. I need $45 for a Greyhound Bus ticket and five dollars to eat. That's a dollar a day for the five-day trip. I need $50. Would you give me $50 for this diamond?' He starts to tell me that it isn't worth $50 but I tell him that it is all I have and it is the only way I can get home. He looks at me and says, 'Okay.' I take the $50 and get on the next bus heading west. We stop at the worst greasy spoons along the way and the buses back then were horrendous, but I eventually get home."[20]

The year following her disastrous trip to New York, Beverly played the role of Mrs. Cliveden-Banks in the Laguna Beach Playhouse production *Outward Bound*. "During one performance the scene was set on a ship at sea and we're doing our stuff and all of a sudden this cat walks across the stage. Now everything is waves from the edge of the stage to where we are on the ship and we all stop to watch this cat meander across the "water." I mean, she could have tried to swim. At least it would have looked better!

"You try not to get out of character and you try not to laugh. But whatever you do, the audience will go along with you. What we did was just be quiet and wait till the cat walked through and then picked up with the next line of dialogue as if nothing happened.[21]

"I did a play in Hollywood some years later and there was a woman — she played my mother. It was a period piece. I had a big scene with her and she was very bosomy. She wore a corset and the top stay of the corset came out part of the way in between her cleavage. Every time she talked, it moved — from side to side, back and forth — and I was fascinated by that thing. I couldn't take my eyes off it. I tried to look at her face but my eyes always strayed back to the metronome of a stay."[22]

Although she continued performing at the Laguna Beach Playhouse, Beverly was anxious to move on. She knew that in order to have a chance to work in legitimate theater, she would need an Equity card. The Holiday Stage in Tustin was taking applications for their theater group. Young thespian hopefuls who were accepted could work as apprentices — alongside professionals who were also hired — and upon completion of their season tenure, would earn that coveted Actors Equity card. "I applied," Beverly recalled, "and in March 1948 I received a letter from Harold Turney, one of the co-founders, informing me that I could start that summer.

> When I first got there, they looked at me like "Oh, God! Who are *you*?" Then I did my first show and they all fell in love with me. I originally thought I would have to do a lot of scenery painting. After all, I was an apprentice which meant no pay. But then I did several plays and I loved it. It was summer stock but the main thing was getting that Equity card. That was very important. It let everyone know that you were a professional.
>
> I remember when I did *D.O.A.*, my first feature film, I didn't have a SAG [Screen Actors Guild] card. I got a special card to make that movie. But once I made the picture, I got my SAG card. All I had to do after that was keep it up. It was always very difficult to get a Screen Actors Guild card. First of all, you can't work unless you have a card, and you can't get a card unless you work![23]

Beverly graces the cover of the playbill for the holiday stage production *The Spider* (July 1948).

The work at Tustin was tough. Productions ran for an average of five days, Tuesdays through Saturdays. On Saturday nights after the last performance, the sets were struck and new ones were assembled on Sundays. They held two rehearsals on Sunday night and two full dress rehearsals on Monday before opening the next day. Beverly said, "The work experience I gained at places like Tustin and the Laguna Beach Playhouse would help me throughout my career and I would always be grateful to them for the privilege."[24]

"I appeared in five productions at Tustin that season: *She Loves Me Not* [in a co-starring role], *Goodbye Again*, *The Spider* [in her first starring role], *Life with Father* and lastly *I Remember Mama* in which I played Katrin, the eldest daughter. I also doubled as the play's narrator. One reviewer reported that I 'scored magnificently. The role was difficult with a heavy demand on emotion which Miss Campbell executed excellently.'"[25]

Beverly's parents knew someone, who knew someone, who knew someone who was an agent. His name was Ray Cooper. He came down to Tustin to see Beverly, liked her and asked if he could represent her. "Some time later," Beverly recalled, "with Ray's help, I tested and got my first film role as Miss Foster in United Artists' *D.O.A.*—a film that nearly ended my movie career before it had even begun!"[26]

4. Beverly Garland

On October 30, 1948, Beverly began touring with Miriam Hopkins in the National Company production of *Happy Birthday* under the direction of Joshua Logan. "Miriam was the ultimate actress," Beverly explained, "and though I didn't know a helluva lot about her, it was made perfectly clear that she was the star. I had heard that she could be difficult. Just how difficult became all too obvious to the entire production company. I can still see Josh Logan walking up and down the aisle during rehearsals saying, 'I hate chocolate ice cream, I hate pheasant under glass, I hate Miriam Hopkins!'"[1]

"We took the show on the road playing the Biltmore and several other theaters in Southern California. Eric Fleming was also in the cast. Back then, Eric had a weight problem. During the show's run, I never saw Eric eat anything but scrambled eggs and tomatoes for breakfast, lunch, and dinner. That was it! He always wanted to lose weight and, of course, with that diet he did. He was very thin years later when I did several *Rawhide* television episodes with him. I was very happy for him when he got that series because he was a fine actor. He wasn't terribly handsome, but he was a very interesting-looking man, I thought."[2]

Every young actor dreams about the circumstances that will land them their first part in a major motion picture. A tabloid rumor alleged that director Rudolph Maté happened to see Beverly in a performance of *I Remember Mama* and that this resulted in her getting a leading role in his film *D.O.A.* Beverly couldn't be sure if it was true or not. "I can't confirm that but it is quite possible. My agent, Ray Cooper, however, had arranged for me to test for the part. I didn't hear anything from Ray for nearly two weeks and had almost given up on it. Then I got a call at work that I had the part. I was a wreck! It was the most exciting day of my life. Production on the film started in August 1949. I was paid $500 and I was thrilled. I had never made so much money before."[3]

Edmond O'Brien starred in this *film noir* classic as Frank Bigelow. While on a brief vacation trip to San Francisco, he becomes violently ill and is told by a doctor that he has been deliberately poisoned. The poison has no antidote. Bigelow has only a couple of days to discover why he was poisoned and who murdered him.

"Eddie O'Brien was very gregarious," Beverly said. "He loved acting. It was his life. He couldn't get enough of it. He was a very intense actor and very into himself. Everything revolved around him and he came first. I wasn't intimated by his demeanor. I adored the idea that he was so dedicated. You didn't have to waste time making idle conversation with Eddie. You could do what you were hired to do — which was to act. That's what he was doing and I thought that was great!"[4]

Unfortunately, that wasn't the case with another actor on the picture. "He was absolutely, incredibly bad. He was so bad, even I — and this was my first picture — knew he

In the stage play *I Remember Mama* at the Holiday Stage (August 9–14, 1948), Beverly (left) played Katrin, the eldest daughter of the Hansen family (other actress unidentified).

was awful. But I remember the film editor — who I was dating at the time — saying to me, 'Yes, he is terrible. But you don't have to worry about him. He's going to come out smelling like a rose.' I asked him, 'How?' and he replied, 'Because when we cut back and forth, you won't see that he's screwing up. We will cut it a certain way and he will look brilliant. It's all in the way the film is cut. Cut it a certain way and you're perfect.' They did and he looked quite good in the final print.[5]

"Years later, I remember watching a television show that I did and there's a scene where the lead actor comes in and tells me that my husband is dead. It wasn't a very big scene but it was *my* big scene and they kept the camera in close-up on the lead. They didn't show me, my reaction, and I'll never forget that. Whoever cut that show kept the lead's reaction when everyone watching it would have wanted to see my reaction to this terrible news. They waited a few seconds to return to my character, but by then it was too late. That's how a cutter can ruin a scene and all your hard work."[6]

There was some talk that *D.O.A.* was a strong contender for Oscar nominations in several categories. The movie's publicity man took Beverly out to dinner and they were seated at a table with some other people whom Beverly didn't know; one of them asked her, "Do you think that *D.O.A.* will win the Academy Award?" Beverly said, "Well, there are a lot of good pictures up for it this year."

"If I had only known! You *never* tell the truth. You just did not do that in those days.

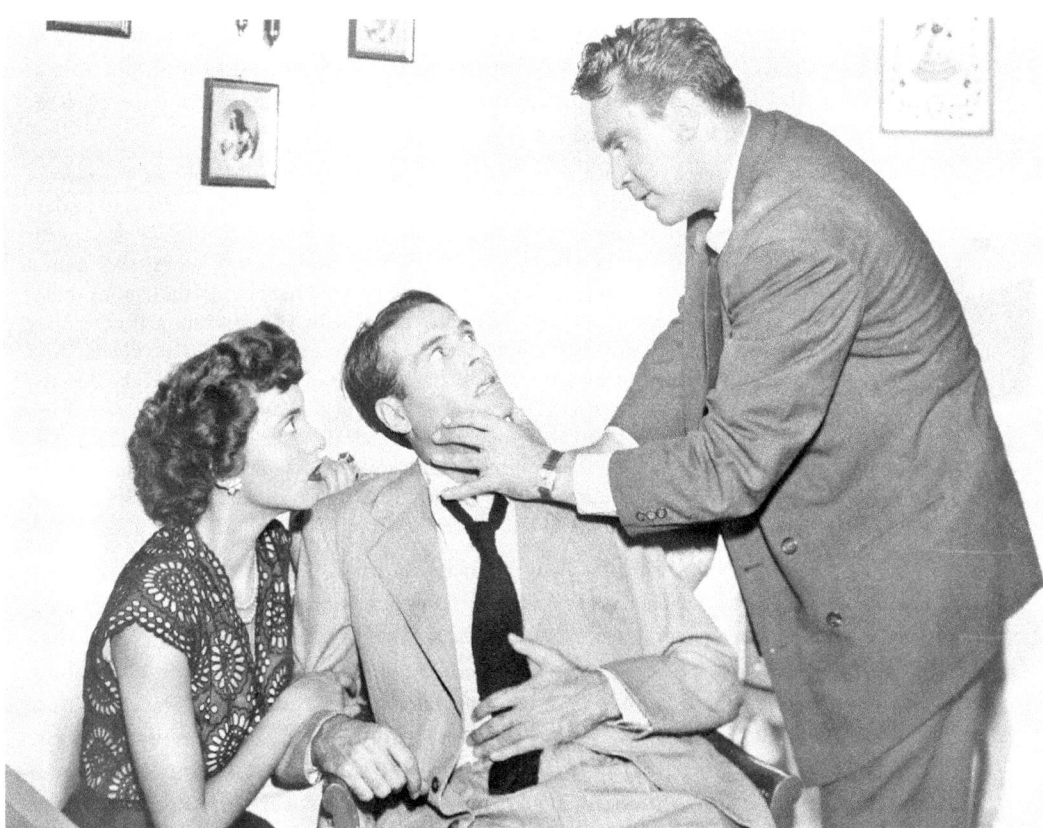

Paul Bigelow (Edmond O'Brien, right) gives Miss Foster (Beverly) and Stanley Philips (Henry Hart) the shocking news that her boyfriend has also been given a dose of luminous poison in this scene from the film noir classic *D.O.A.* (United Artists, 1950).

But I didn't know that. I said, 'I think that *All the King's Men* will probably win'—which it *did*! But I was *not* supposed to say that.[7]

Not long after that night, my agent Ray Cooper contacted the producers of *D.O.A.* saying to them, "I just talked to so-and-so who's doing a picture and I told them to call you so that you could recommend Beverly." That's how they did it back then. He must have called them four or five times and nothing ever happened. Finally, Ray saw the producers one day and said, "You know, I call you and tell you to speak to so-and-so and nothing ever happens." And they said to Ray, "Oh really? Well, someday we'll tell you why." Ray was totally bewildered by their cryptic response. "You'd better tell me now," he insisted. So they said, "Listen. We gave Beverly her first break, paid her a lot of money and she doesn't appreciate it. She doesn't care and is badmouthing *D.O.A.* We have no intention of telling anybody that she's good or recommending her for any role. Period."

Ray immediately called me and said, "You'd better go over there and talk to those people," which I did. I said to them, "I am so sorry. I really am. I made a mistake and did not mean to ever have you think that I was unappreciative about what you have done for me. It was fabulous and I should never have said that. I don't quite know how to tell you how badly I feel about this." And they looked me straight in the eye and they said, "We don't know what you're talking about." That door was permanently slammed shut!

So I left their office and I was black-balled in this town for a good three years! I could not get a job. This industry can be very vindictive at times.[8]

Twentieth Century–Fox was about to film *Pinky* and they wanted a white actress who could play a black girl. Beverly's agent took her out to Fox and they said they'd like to test her. Beverly recalled, "They made me up with these red, red lips and these strange eyebrows. I looked like something the cat dragged in!"[9]

> I made the test with actor Kurt Kasznar. We filmed an excerpt from the movie *Reunion in Vienna*. A short time later, my agent got a call from Fox and they said, "Ray, you have to understand something. This picture is called *Pinky* and it's about this black girl. But we don't want her to really be black and you sent us a black actress. We don't want a black actress. We want a white actress." My agent was at a complete loss. "What are you talking about?" he said to them. They reiterated, "We want a white actress." Ray insisted, "I sent you a white actress!" They replied, "No you didn't. You sent us Beverly. She's black." Ray shot back, "She is *not* black!" And they said, "Well, we saw the test and she sure looks black to us!" Ray called me and said, "Beverly, you have got to go back to Fox and meet the head of casting on this picture because they think you're black." I did go to see them and they finally had to admit, "Well, you're not black, but you sure photograph black." As I left their office I said to myself, "There's no way in hell you're going to get this part!" As it turned out, the role of Patricia "Pinky" Johnson eventually went to Jeanne Crain — who looked whiter than white — and she got an Oscar nomination for it![10]

With *D.O.A.* still several months away from its national release, and before Beverly had made the mistake of speaking her mind, she landed her first television series role on one of the earliest situation comedies, ABC's *Mama Rosa*. "I was in 13 episodes and they paid me $9.25 per show. This was in the days before there was even a union." The show was set in a Los Angeles boarding house run by the title character and Beverly played Mama's daughter Nina who, like many of the show's characters, hoped to break into show business. Anna Demetrio played Mama Rosa, and as the star of the show she was required to do all the commercials for the show's sponsor. Back then, commercials were often done live — as was the show. The show's sponsor was Sun Vista, maker of canned pinto beans. Anna, who spoke with a heavy accent, could never pronounce "pinto beans" correctly. According to Beverly, "During one live broadcast, Anna encouraged everyone watching the show to buy Sun Vista's canned 'penis beans.' It was hysterical. I could never understand why the network insisted on her doing all the commercials because she was so bad at it!"[11]

While Beverly was still working on *Mama Rosa*, her agent got her an episode of *The Lone Ranger* entitled "The Beeler Gang." "My first day on the set was scheduled for 5 A.M., and the studio was out by MGM in Culver City. Unfortunately, I didn't know how to get there. I got in my car and headed east instead of west. It was getting later and later and later and I was still headed in the wrong direction. I finally stopped at a gas station in the middle of Watts and I asked the attendant if he could tell me how to get to MGM from there. 'MGM,' he says. 'Where the hell is that?'"

> I eventually arrived at the studio in tears. I burst onto the set and was greeted with a seething director screaming, "You're *late*! I don't understand why you're so *late*!" That didn't help my condition any, I can tell you! After a very tense and difficult shoot, we finally made it to the final scene of the show. The director said to me, "Okay. Now your little boy says to you, 'Who was that, Mama?' and you say, 'That was the Lone Ranger!' Okay?" Simple line, no problem, I thought.
>
> We were on the fifteenth take, and out of desperation, I finally howled out as loud as I could, "*That was the Loooooone Raaaaaannnnnggggeeeerrrr!*" and the director yelled, "*print it!*" I couldn't believe it. I was so bad but that's what they wanted. I thought, "Okay. I'll give it to you. I'll give it to you just like that. You want it that way? Well, that's the way you're going to get it!" The director came over to me later and said, "I didn't think you'd ever get it." Well, I didn't think I ever would either! They loved it — but talk about overacting![12]

After the *D.O.A.* fiasco, Beverly found herself having to climb her way back up the motion picture ladder virtually from the bottom rung. In early February 1950, she went on a "cattle call" at MGM when she heard they were casting for a party scene in *A Life of Her Own* starring Lana Turner and Ray Milland. "There were 20 to 30 girls who showed up and they lined them up. [Director] George Cukor came out and said, 'I'll take you, and you, and you.' Then they dressed us all up and we were taken to the party scene set. I think I had a couple of ridiculous lines, but I was trying to get myself noticed so a line or two was better than none. I was so proud that I had been selected. I was finally going to be in an MGM movie. I must have said something to that effect because I remember one of the girls saying to me, 'You know, they only pick the girls that they want to date or go to bed with.' Thankfully, nobody ever approached me but I was uncomfortable the entire time."[13]

Not that Beverly didn't have to deal with over-zealous studio executives during her career. "Universal's casting director literally chased me around his desk! I was actually running around his desk! He was such a jerk that I reported him. But, naturally, they never did anything about it. He stayed on at Universal for years. That incident really had me upset. It was the first time something like that ever happened to me."[14]

Working on *A Life of Her Own* also gave Beverly a glimpse into what it was like to be a Hollywood star in those days. "Lana Turner arrived on the party scene set over two hours late with her entourage—maybe fifteen people, including her hairdresser, her masseuse, and her record player. They had set up a big tent as a dressing room for her on the sound stage and she'd play her records while she ate lunch. When we finally started shooting the scene, Lana had six lines and the guy she was playing to had three lines—and it took *forever*! We must have worked on that one party scene—which was very short—for five days and I thought, 'Well, that's what it's like to be a movie star!' Thank God, I never became that kind of movie star!"[15]

Although Beverly was still performing occasionally at the Laguna Beach Playhouse during its 1950 and 1951 seasons, she was fortunate to be one of the first performers to work in a new kind of theatrical experience: theater in the round. In 1947, Ruth and Nathan Hale opened the 100-seat Glendale Center Theatre on Colorado Street. One of their earliest productions was *Persuade Me*, a three-act comedy-drama written by the Hales and starring Beverly Campbell as Lecia, a young mother. In his review of the performance, Jack Gotch lauded Beverly's performance, reporting that it "showed depth, warmth and a sustained naturalness."[16]

Some time later, Beverly joined another center stage theater group at The Players Ring. Kathleen Freeman, a veteran performer, was very active in getting this repertory theater off the ground. She often directed, acted, and wrote music for many of its critically hailed productions. She was a great teacher as well and helped Beverly tremendously.

The Players Ring was the ultimate "go-to" theater for young talent. Many well-known film and television stars got their start there. Lots of press people, casting agents, and directors attended performances in their never-ending search for fresh faces.[17] Beverly's first performance at the Players Ring was in *Once in a Lifetime*, which opened on September 6, 1950. She played May Daniels in this satire about Hollywood in the 1920s, written by George Kaufman and Moss Hart. Her notices were very encouraging. One reviewer wrote that she was "a leading woman with a fine flair for comedy ... in the same category as Barbara Stanwyck."[18]

Hoping that a second appearance in an MGM film might lead to something bigger, Beverly got another small part in *Strictly Dishonorable* starring Ezio Pinza and Janet Leigh.

Costume test for the party scenes in *A Life of Her Own* (MGM, 1950) with unidentified actress on the left, Beverly on the right.

She had a humorous exchange with lead Leigh but her appearance didn't generate too much interest from critics or producers. Beverly headed back to the Players Ring. "My association with the Players Ring continued that summer in an ambitious though frugal production of *Ring Around the Ring* which was presented as a series of 18 old vaudeville skits and sketches. The theater was always operating by the skin of its financial teeth back then, but it forced us to always find creative ways to put on plays with shoestring budgets. And we loved it! Thankfully, the audiences and critics were usually very supportive."[19]

During performances of *Ring Around the Ring* they previewed a scene from their next presentation, *Dark of the Moon* to pique interest and generate advance ticket sales. It worked. The *Mirror* critic, Tom Coffey, reported: "If this bit is a fair indication of what we can expect in the full production, I hope we'll see it soon."

The cast went into rehearsals shortly after *Ring Around the Ring* ended its run. "By mid–August 1951," Beverly explained, "two weeks before *Dark of the Moon* opened with me in the pivotal role of Barbara Allen, I was also married to my co-star, Richard Garland, who played Witch Boy. Richard — his nickname was "Chuck" — and I had only been seeing each other for several months before we decided to marry. Richard was under contract at Universal Studios for about a year. He was signed about the same time as Tony Curtis and could have been a star. He was a fabulous-looking man.

> One of my best girlfriends at that time was Molly Dodd. Her father was an Episcopalian minister and he was known as "a minister to the stars." All the actors would go to Father Dodd, and so, when I went in search of God for a second time in my life, I decided I would become an Episcopalian. In the meantime, Chuck Garland and I decided to get married. However, in those days, you didn't live together unless you were married. That's just the way it was.
>
> Chuck and I had found this tiny apartment up in the Hollywood Hills. The apartment was like a boxcar. It did have a little patio, however. But we loved it and decided to rent it before we married to avoid losing it.

We wanted to have our wedding in a little church in the Valley and we set a date. I went to see Father Dodd, hoping that he would officiate at the ceremony, but he was on vacation. So I had to see another minister and he told me, "You cannot get married. You have to get a dispensation from the church because you were married to Bob Campbell." I said, "But I have to get married because I'm moving into this apartment and I can't live there with Chuck if we're not married!" The minister, however, was not about to be swayed by my morality versus apartment dilemma. "Well," he said, "you can't get married now. You'll have to wait until Father Dodd gets back a month from now." I couldn't believe what I was hearing. "But I'm getting married and moving in there." I cried. The minister only shook his head: "Sorry, but you can't do that."

A few days later, while I was still trying to decide what to do, the church sent me a letter saying that I was excommunicated — but added that they would still like me to pay my tithe. I couldn't believe what I was reading! I thought, "My tithe? I'm excommunicated! I cannot take the sacraments and you want my tithe?" Well, that was the end of my Episcopalian Church! Richard and I ended up having a civil service instead. We celebrated that evening with an intimate dinner at the Vagabond's House.[20]

Dark of the Moon opened on September 5, 1951, and the reviews were wonderful. One reviewer predicted that Beverly and Richard would "both be famous actors one day soon." Well, it wasn't going to happen soon enough for Beverly. She was about to make her third MGM feature film *Fearless Fagan* starring Janet Leigh. Only this time, Beverly didn't even have a single line of dialogue. Beverly's dream of becoming a Hollywood star was fading fast.

5. Somebody Get Me a *Medic*

In March 1952, Beverly made her final stage appearance on the Holiday Stage in *The Moon Is Down*. Then in May, she starred in two productions at the Beaux Arts Theatre in Los Angeles for playwright-director Myron Fagan, *Red Rainbow* and *Thieves Paradise*. Her reviews were quite encouraging, but as a whole the productions were not well received.[1]

Beverly's dad and mom had moved to Hollywood after they sold the boat. Beverly lived with them until she married Richard Garland. Then her parents suddenly decided to move to Riverside. According to Beverly, "Riverside at that time was very rural. There were lots of orange trees. It was a very small, charming town near the Mission Inn where all the movie stars used to go for quiet getaways. My parents bought several acres there. The land was formerly an orange grove and they built a lovely big house on it. My parents raised Poodles and they did very well.[2]

"My father always wanted to be a doctor. He loved the idea of being in the medical profession. When he learned that a Beltone Hearing Aid franchise had become available, my father bought into the business and opened an office in the house. Beltone was the best hearing aid you could buy at that time. So my dad became a consultant and my mother was 'hired' as his assistant. He just adored it, especially when his patients began calling him 'Doc'; it was a moniker that would stay with him for the rest of his life. Later my dad became a volunteer sheriff there. He became very big in Riverside."[3]

Shortly after *Thieves Paradise* ended its run at the Beaux Arts Theatre, Beverly was signed by producers Jack Pollexfen and Aubrey Wisberg to appear in two low-budget indie films, *Problem Girls* and *The Neanderthal Man*. In *Problem Girls* she played one of the "psychopathically neurotic" students at a private school for girls where a lot more than higher learning is going on. In *The Neanderthal Man* Beverly was cast as Nola, one of the victims of a mad scientist who, *a la* Jekyll and Hyde, experiments with a regression serum with predictable results.

Beverly also did a television pilot for Revue Productions, *City Detective* starring Rod Cameron. Her co-stars in this early police drama were Jack Kelly and Lee Van Cleef. The series made quite an impression on the networks when it was sold to a record number of stations (171) nationwide.

Beverly received exciting news while performing in *The Play's the Thing* at the Players Ring.

> I got a call from my agent that I had been cast in an Allied Artists Western called *The Fighting Lawman* opposite Wayne Morris. It was my first starring role in a feature film and I was ecstatic! I had met with the people at Allied Artists before being cast and they had asked me if I could ride a horse. 'Of course, I can ride,' I told them. I would have told them I could rappel down

Mount Everest if they needed me to do that, too! After all, I had had horses when I was a kid in Phoenix, and while I hadn't ridden in years, how hard could it be? Wasn't it like riding a bicycle?

On the first day of the shoot, I drove over to the Jack Ingram Ranch and the director took me over to my horse, saying, "Why don't you get on the horse and just ride it? Get the feel of the horse, okay? Then we'll begin." When I finally got a look at this animal, I began to think that this was going to be a terrible idea. In movies and on television, these horses look like big dogs. However, this particular horse was a behemoth!

I somehow managed to mount the beast at which point it turned its head and looked at me as if to say, "You've got to be kidding? You really don't know what you're doing, do you?" And away it went with me just barely hanging on for dear life. The horse was still in motion when way off in the distance I heard the director shouting, "You can come back now!" I thought, "If I could come back, I would. But not until this horse is ready to come back!" We were out there for quite a while and then he finally decided to return to his wrangler.

[I was thankful that] my first scene didn't have any dialogue because I was still trembling from that wild ride. The director says to me, "In this scene, we want you to ride like hell towards those rocks in the hills. Then we want you to take out your rifle and shoot. Okay?" I nod. The director yells, "Action!" and I'm now riding this horse towards the hills. "*Cut*," the director yells, adding, "No, no, no! This is the end of the movie and you've got to ride this horse —*fast*!" I nod. The horse is moving when my hat flies off. "*Cut*! Beverly, you've got to keep your hat on." I get the horse to move a little faster and we reach the mark. I pull out

The monster (actor unidentified) claims a victim (Beverly) in this posed publicity photograph from *The Neanderthal Man* (United Artists, 1953).

the rifle and I'm about to start shooting when the director starts screaming at me, "Cock it! Beverly, don't you know how to cock a rifle? And I'll tell you another thing, you're not going fast enough!"

So I pull my hat down around my eyes, because it was too large for me to begin with, and that's the only way it would stay on my head. I get that horse to race over to the rocks but instead of leaning to the right side of the horse's head for the rifle, I leaned into the horse's neck and it was at that very moment that the horse threw its head back and hit my nose.

There was a sound man who was on that picture and whenever he saw me he would say, "Do you remember, Beverly, at 6:30 in the morning, when on my sound machine I heard this *crack*? It just echoed from hill — to hill — to hill. *Crack! Crack! Crack!*

I sat on that horse and the wrangler came over and said, "Let me help you...." I tried to stop him, saying, "No. I'm okay. I can do this." He looked at me and said, "Yes, you probably can. However, your nose now extends from the top of your forehead to the bottom of your lips!" My nose had been broken in three places. They took me to a doctor and Virginia Grey replaced me on the picture two and a half minutes later. My nose was such a disaster that I couldn't go on performing at the Players Ring, either. Carolyn Jones had to take over for me while I recuperated.[4]

Beverly had some reconstructive surgery done on her nose. Within weeks of the operation, she was anxious to get back to work, and her agent got her a small part in Universal's *The Glass Web*. It was directed by Jack Arnold and starred Edward G. Robinson and John Forsythe. Beverly's salary was $150 a day. "My scenes were filmed on the first day of the shoot and I was done by five that afternoon."[5]

Universal tried to cash in at the box office by shooting the picture in the new 3-D process but most test audiences found the gimmick more annoying and distracting than entertaining. Universal released it in 3-D anyway.[6]

In the meantime, Beverly's husband Richard Garland's contract with Universal had expired. "They wanted to pick him up for another year, but Richard wanted more money. He felt he was worth more, but the studio refused to renegotiate and he was out. So now he was a freelance actor — as I was — and had to get jobs like everyone else. He had a very good agent and he did work. But he wasn't overly ambitious. Most people who knew him thought he was kind of laid back, but facing the world was very difficult for Richard. He didn't seem to be able to do that well and once he left Universal, his career just did not take off. He started drinking more and more to avoid all his troubles."[7]

Surprisingly, Allied Artists was willing to give Beverly another shot at a western after her first disastrous attempt and signed her to co-star with Wild Bill Elliott in *Bitter Creek*. However, they made sure she wouldn't have to shoot at anyone on horseback during the film. Upon its release, *The Hollywood Reporter* noted that Beverly represented a "refreshing change from the usual oater heroine" and that her "fine acting added interest to the yarn instead of slowing it up."[8]

Immediately following *Bitter Creek*, Beverly got a supporting role in 20th Century–Fox's *The Rocket Man*, a minor sci-fi fantasy about a small boy and his magical space gun. The film is probably best remembered for its comedic bits supplied by co-screenwriter Lenny Bruce. Soon afterwards, she was on a plane to Florida to begin work on Columbia's *The Miami Story* with Barry Sullivan and Adele Jergens. The film was based on a true story about the city's successful attempt to rid itself of organized crime's growing influence and its novel approach at dealing with the problem: Miami citizens hire an ex-mobster (Sullivan) to bring down the town's mob boss (Luther Adler) and his syndicate.

The Miami Story was Beverly's first big part in a feature film. "I enjoyed playing Holly

Abbott and thought she was a well-developed character. It was also 'fun' to be beaten up and to have scenes where I had to have special makeup applied to make my face look swollen after I had been attacked. I loved roles that are offbeat and Holly Abbott was definitely one of those great parts."[9] Beverly next appeared in two Wayne Morris Westerns for Allied Artists, *Two Guns and a Badge* and *The Desperado* and managed to survive both without breaking or smashing any body parts.

Next it was on to deepest, darkest Africa via the Arboretum in Arcadia, California, where location shots for *Killer Leopard* were photographed. The film starred Johnny Sheffield in one of his last appearances as Bomba, the Jungle Boy, and was based on the Bomba book series by Roy Rockwood. Prior to these Bomba movies, Johnny had played Boy in the Johnny Weissmuller Tarzan series for MGM. "Johnny [Sheffield] was such a sweetheart," Beverly remarked. "He was very athletic and did all his own stunts. He was just wonderful to work with, although getting past our first scene together proved harder than I first thought. [In the scene,] he knocked at my door and I answered it. Johnny was wearing his loincloth and had a lot of body makeup to make him look really tan. I asked him who he was and he said, "Bomba!" "Bomba?" was my reply. I cracked up and we had to begin again. "What's your name?" I asked politely. "Bomba!" he replied. I broke up again. It really tickled my funnybone. I had a terrible time trying to open that door without laughing. It was such a silly scene."[10]

Hoping to cash in on his recent success with the release of *The Miami Story*, producer Sam Katzman began production on another of his "city" pictures, *New Orleans Uncensored*. It was filmed on location in the summer of 1954 with Arthur Franz, Beverly and Michael Ansara in key roles. Unfortunately, film critics were all too eager to make comparisons between it and its contemporary, *On the Waterfront*, since both films dealt with dockworkers and the rackets. Needless to say, *New Orleans Uncensored* lost. The film's director, William Castle, would go on to make somewhat of a name for himself in another film genre — horror movies.

Because she was never under contract to a major film studio, Beverly had to look for work wherever she could find it. Television was opening a lot of doors to young talent and she was fully prepared to take advantage of any opportunity she could find.

> I remember my agent called me and said, "I have an interview for you. This role is very important. It's for a very sexy girl. So dress in something really wild." I went on the interview and I had this *fabulous* — I thought — very sexy black dress on and they said, "Aha. Okay. Fine. We'll let you know." I called my agent from the studio and I told him that I looked as sexy as I could. He said, "Great!" adding, "I have another interview for you to go on right now." As I walked into the second audition, I was thinking to myself that I probably wouldn't get this television show because I had this wild, sexy dress on. I decided to keep my coat on during the entire interview. Well, the producer looked at me and he said, "Would you take your coat off and walk across the room?" I thought, "Well, so much for this job!" I did as he asked. I walked across the room and the producer said, "Yeah. You do look like you're dying from leukemia. You've got the part." I was delighted, but I went home and got rid of that "sexy" dress.[11]

The part was for the pilot episode of a new series called *Medic* starring Richard Boone. The series was created and written by Jim Moser, who had previously written over 150 episodes of *Dragnet*— and was interested in creating another reality-based series, this one focusing on the medical profession. The episode was filmed mainly in and around Los Angeles County Hospital. Actors handled the principal roles while, many nurses, doctors, and technicians from the hospital's staff were hired to play supporting parts. (Each episode of the series was to deal with an actual medical problem, and authenticity was critical to the show's success.) Beverly's episode was titled "White is the Color."

> In it, I played a pregnant wife who finds out that she has leukemia. Her one wish is that she lives long enough to give birth to her child. My husband was played by Lee Marvin.
> Lee used to pick me up on his motorcycle every morning and take me to the hospital. We filmed the show on one of the hospital's top floors, part of which was closed off to the public for our use. We had access to some of the patient rooms and operating theaters on the floor, to use as sets. During breaks, we would all go down to the hospital's cafeteria. Rather than change clothes for lunch, I would go to lunch in makeup with my pregnancy padding on. Lee would just love to walk me down the corridor to the areas that were still in use for real hospital patients. He would wait for visitors to arrive at the elevator and then — without warning — he would turn to me and punch me right in my padded stomach. Naturally, I loved to play along and I would groan in "pain." People who witnessed this were duly horrified. We overheard one woman say to her companion, "Can you *imagine* her being married to a man like that? What a horrible husband!" I was amazed that Lee never got arrested! We had a lot of fun with it.
> Richard Boone was the complete opposite of Lee Marvin. He was a very intense man. He almost had a coldness about him. I never got very close to him. He had what I used to call "The Boone Players." They were like a stock company of actors Boone used all the time. Although I knew him well, he was always very aloof.[12]

The series sold to NBC-TV and premiered on September 13, 1954. A few months later, Beverly learned that her performance had been nominated for an Emmy Award in the Best Actress in a Single Performance category. "I walked around on a cloud for days," Beverly said.

Shortly after *Medic* premiered, Beverly made the first of five appearances on *Lux Video Theatre*. "All their shows were done live back then. One of the things that stands out in my mind about those live television shows was that you had to dress behind the set. You'd finish your first scene and had to run behind the set where someone threw your change of clothes at you and you'd dress right then and there. In addition to the wardrobe lady, there was always another woman whose sole job was to check your cleavage. You could never show any cleavage on live television. This lady had little pieces of lace that she would sew into your dress to cover the cleavage!"[13]

Beverly remembered one live show that she did where a murder had been committed in the story. During rehearsals, the guy who was killed crawled out while the other actors were talking because his part was over. "The night of the live broadcast, we were all standing around talking about the murder victim — the camera had him in the shot — when he starts to crawl away! We couldn't believe what we were seeing! All across America, viewers watched as our corpse crawled off the set. That was the fun thing about live television. You never knew what you were going to see!"[14] While Beverly was doing these *Lux Video Theatre* shows, she became one of the "Lux Girls" and began doing some of their live commercials as well.

Then in October 1954, her agent got her the role of Miss Swift in Paramount's *The Desperate Hours* starring Humphrey Bogart and Fredric March. "I was thrilled to be on the picture and was in awe of everyone! Director William Wyler was wonderful to work with and he seemed to like working with me. Bogart and March played chess on the set all the time. That's all Bogart seemed interested in doing. March, on the other hand, was quite a lecher. He came on to everyone. Still, it was a fun picture to do."[15]

Beverly's Emmy nomination was starting to get her noticed by more and more television and film producers. She made her first of four guest star appearances on *Four Star Playhouse* in an episode titled "Bourbon Street," with Dick Powell and a long on-screen relationship with this actor-television mogul developed.

Beverly received an Emmy nomination for her performance as a pregnant leukemia victim in the premiere episode of *Medic*, entitled "White Is the Color" (September 13, 1954). She's pictured here with series star Richard Boone.

Dick Powell was such a talented man. I got to know him very well. He sang and he danced, he produced, directed and acted. He was just a very gifted man. I never felt that Dick Powell was a terribly handsome man, but I felt he was a brilliant person.

I remember going to his house for some reason and June Allyson was there. I was very taken with his big house in one of the canyons — Benedict Canyon, I think. What a wonderful old house, it was so fabulous.

"I don't know what his marriage to June Allyson was like. I had heard lots of rumors that it was pretty tough. He was married to Joan Blondell and I don't know if June Allyson took him away from Blondell, but I have a feeling that she did and I also have a feeling that she played on him. Now, I don't know if that's true, but there were lots of rumors about that. He deserved better if that's true. But I just thought he was a very special guy. He liked me and used me in his shows a lot. He was A #1 class.[16]

Beverly then guest starred on *The Star & the Story* in "The Lie." She also appeared on the enormously popular show *The Millionaire* in "Millionaire Carl Nelson," the first of two guest roles.

Prior to her Emmy nomination, Beverly had a small part in a picture called *The Go Getter*. When the picture was released, thanks to the nomination, Beverly was suddenly elevated by the film's publicity department to the female lead! Beverly was also signed by Warner Brothers for a starring role in *The Steel Jungle* as Frances Novak, the pregnant wife of Perry Lopez. There is a strange story in the film's production notes about a set visitor who was upset over witnessing a scene where Beverly got punched around. The visitor approached the film's writer-director Walter Doniger and asked, "Aren't you afraid that you'll hurt the young lady in the condition she's in?" According to the story, Doniger turned to the visitor and replied, "That's okay, sir. We have permission from the union!" Beverly recalled,

> *The Steel Jungle* was probably one of the hardest pictures to do because Perry Lopez was just not a good actor. I hate to say that about him. He could say his lines but he just could not hit his marks. We would do take, after take, after take before he finally got it right. I knew my lines and I hit my mark, but we'd have to do it again and again because of Perry. [We did one scene] so many times that I just wasn't as good as I was in the first few takes. Suddenly the director said, "That's a print!" I objected but was told, "Yeah, but Perry hit his marks, Beverly. We've got to go with it." That's what can happen to you.
>
> Although it was a good showcase picture for me, Warner Brothers didn't offer me a contract. Years later, somebody from the studio confided to me, "You know, we thought of you so many times for pictures, but you just weren't pretty enough."[17]

On March 7, 1955, the 7th Annual Emmy Awards were presented on NBC-TV. In those early days, the ceremonies were usually held at a restaurant or supper club. This year, the network hosted the awards in its first live coast-to-coast broadcast from Hollywood and New York. Beverly was one of seven actresses nominated in the Best Actress in a Single Performance category; the other nominees were Ethel Barrymore, Dorothy McGuire, Ruth Hussey, Eva Marie Saint, Claire Trevor and Judith Anderson, who had been nominated for her performance in the *Hallmark Hall of Fame* presentation of Shakespeare's *Macbeth*.

"I was in some darn good company, but it probably came as no surprise that Judith Anderson won. I mean, I'm doing a 30-minute show as a dying pregnant woman and she's doing three and a half hours as Lady Macbeth. Who do you *think* is going to win? I certainly didn't have any illusions with competition like that!"[18]

Despite Warner Brothers' earlier opinion of her looks, Beverly was still working steadily in television. She had guest star roles on such series as *The Damon Runyon Theatre, Soldiers of Fortune, Big Town, Frontier, The Lone Wolf, Navy Log, Studio 57* and *The Schlitz Playhouse of Stars*. She made her first of two appearances on the anthology series *Science Fiction Theatre* in an episode titled "The Negative Man." In October 1955, Beverly would film a second episode of *Science Fiction Theatre* titled "The Other Side of the Moon." Her contract was dated October 4, 1955, and she was paid $300.

Her professional career was going strong. However, her marriage to Richard Garland was over and she had filed for divorce.

I was doing a play at the Players Ring with John Crawford.[19] He and his wife Lorraine were very good friends of ours. She was a former Earl Carroll girl. They lived with their children in the Valley and while John and I were doing the play, Richard wasn't working steadily and he and Lorraine would often hang out together at her house. After the play, John and I would come back to the house around 10:30 or 11 P.M. for coffee before Richard and I went home.

One night, we got back and I found Richard and Lorraine in the kitchen and I knew then and there that something had gone on between them, but I didn't know what. I could tell because he was breaking away from a kiss or he was just about to kiss her when I walked in on them. Later, when we got home, I accused him. I said, "Did you kiss her? Are you having an affair?" Richard emphatically denied it. "How could you think that?" he said. "How could you *ever* say that?" He appeared so hurt over my accusations that he made me feel like the most horrible wife in the world. Finally, I practically got down on my knees begging him to forgive me. I recall saying how sorry I was to have accused him of infidelity. I just went on and on. I should have considered the fact that he was a damn good actor.

Some time later, however, Richard said to me, "You know, I have to tell you something. You were right. Lorraine and I were having an affair." I was shocked. I told him our marriage was over and ordered him out. He absolutely would not accept that. He begged me to forgive him, but it was like a door slamming shut. I looked at him and I said, "No matter what you say to me; no matter what you do; whatever feelings I had for you are dead." Those feelings never did come back. I was absolutely through. I ended up going to a psychiatrist because I asked myself how I could be so in love with someone on Monday and be out of love on Tuesday. He said to me, "It's very easy. Your faith and trust in this man — whom you loved — was shattered and you could not accept that." It seemed impossible that something like this could happen to people. That feelings could shut down so quickly. But he confirmed that they did. So I walked out of his office glad to know that I wasn't crazy for feeling this way and that was that. I was finished with Richard and I would never take him back.[20]

Being able to throw herself into her work and block out everything else around her has often been the best therapy for Beverly — especially during traumatic times. She was glad when her agent got her the female lead in Allied Artists' *Sudden Danger*. Then he told her about another feature production that was about to start in Louisiana under the direction of an up-and-coming filmmaker named Roger Corman, *Swamp Women*. Roger had been on the set of *The Miami Story* and was quite impressed with Beverly's performance. In *Swamp Women*, Beverly was cast as an escaped convict who, along with three other cellmates, trek into the Louisiana bayous in search of a hidden cache of stolen diamonds. What they don't realize — until it is too late — is that one of them is an undercover policewoman. Marie Windsor, Carole Mathews, Mike Connors, and Ed Nelson co-starred with her. According to Beverly, "None of us had any idea what we were in for working with Roger Corman!"

Roger found an old hotel that was abandoned and they had not yet taken out all the metal beds and some of the furniture. He rented it. We all shared a bathroom with another cast member. I shared mine with Ed Nelson! At night, after being in the bayou all day with this swamp muck all over you, you couldn't wait to take a bath. You just hoped that whoever was sharing the facilities with you wasn't in there when you got back!

The first night we were there, Marie Windsor and I were sitting in her room talking until late in the night. Marie had just gotten married to Jack Hupp, a well-known Beverly Hills realtor and broker, and she was anxious to tell me all about the wedding. Finally, I suggested we get some rest because we had an early shoot the next morning. I left and was just about to go into my room next door when I heard a scream and a crash and I ran back into Marie's room. By this time Marie was laughing hysterically. Her bed had completely collapsed — with her in it! I don't think the bed ever got repaired or replaced, but afterwards poor Marie preferred to sleep with her mattress on the floor. Thank goodness she had a sense of humor.

Roger wanted to film in a real swamp — and we did. There were lots of bugs and mosquitoes.

Beverly (center) autographs photographs for fans at a Boston theater to promote the opening of *The Miami Story* (Columbia, 1954).

We got chiggers and everybody told us to put nail polish on them. I don't think that's the proper treatment because they all survived and thrived under the polish! However, the worst thing Roger made us do was eat the cold sandwich lunches he would provide! Roger was never big on spending any money on his cast and crew!

Roger also wanted his swamp women to wear cut-off Levi jeans. So we all cut the legs off our jeans and we made these very short shorts. In those days, that was considered to be terribly sexy! Women didn't wear shorts cut that high. At the end of the picture, I'm up in this huge tree and one of the girls throws a spear at me and kills me. I have to free fall out of this tree from some twenty or thirty feet above the ground. Roger said to me, "Don't worry, Beverly, they'll be somebody down there to catch you." I was so naïve — I believed him! Thank God, the stuntman — who was a big guy — really was there and he caught me, because I just went limp and fell dead weight out of that tree! Back then, when you worked in B-movies, you did all your own stunts. Whatever had to be done, I did it!²¹

Corman commended his star, saying Beverly was not only a brilliant actress but was logical as well. He recalled that one *Swamp Women* scene involved a chase through the bayous. His actors were supposed to wade into the swamp and cross to the other side. However, someone remarked that the water was home to some very poisonous snakes. Naturally, the actors were apprehensive after hearing that. According to Roger, "So I jumped into the water, waded around, climbed out and said, "See, that proves there are no snakes in the water." To which Beverly replied, "Roger, that only proves you're an idiot!"

However, according to Corman, Beverly was "the first into the water to play the scene."[22]

Beverly's memories of working with Corman were — for the most part — pleasant, because she got along with him quite well.

> He always was fascinating to me. He is a good businessman and he has such incredible energy. I found that he was a dynamic man to be around. I always knew he was going to be a tremendous success because there was no stopping the man, He just made up his mind that he was going to be a success and he was successful.
>
> Roger could do anything on a picture except act. He could run the camera or do the editing on a film. Roger was also fun to work with. He did these films on shoestring budgets. Many times, his actors were angry with him because he made them work hard and for long hours. And no matter what happened to you, you worked anyway. But that was okay with me because I was that kind of person too. I love to work and I've never liked fooling around. I wanted to get the work done. Roger was very professional, except when it came to paying you a good salary, feeding you on the set, or putting you up in a decent hotel while on location! Of course, you didn't have to work for him. It was up to you, so you couldn't complain about it. Roger made films for as little money up front as possible and has brought in countless really solid B-movies that turned a profit within a very short time of their release. That's been his formula from the very beginning and it's made him a very wealthy man.[23]

When Beverly returned to California, she began a long-term business relationship with the husband of one of her actress friends, Nancy Gates. "Bill Hayes had begun a business management company with another close friend of mine, actor Jeffrey Hunter. I thought it was a great idea, since I was getting more and more work and didn't have the time to pay the bills and invest my savings wisely. Bill took care of all this for me. It came about at just the right time because I was about to leave the United States for South America and would be gone for several months while I worked on my next feature, *Curucu, Beast of the Amazon*, under the direction of Curt Siodmak."[24]

Even after her divorce from Richard Garland was finalized, he continued to call her. When he did, she could tell he had been drinking. "I couldn't talk to him because I wanted him out of my world. Once we divorced, he really started going downhill. He worked enough to keep himself busy, but I wanted a new life and so I just stayed away from him. I felt that was the smartest thing I could do." But as Beverly was to find out a short time later, Richard still wasn't ready to move on.[25]

6. The Beast and the Amazon

In director Curt Siodmak's autobiography, he remarked that Beverly was anxious to do *Curucu, Beast of the Amazon* to get away from her ex-husband, Richard Garland, after a turbulent divorce. That was only one of the reasons. Beverly felt very lucky to get the picture and loved the challenge it presented to her. It was a fun script. It had lots of action and would be filmed completely in Brazil with many fabulous locations. And, yes, there was the added bonus that she would be thousands of miles away from her ex. She readily agreed to do the picture. According to Beverly, "What both Curt Siodmak and I didn't realize was that filming *Curucu* probably saved my life.

> Richard was very unhappy about our divorce and was not handling the situation well at all. He was drinking heavily and would come over to my apartment unannounced at all hours of the day and night and bang on my window. It was frightening. He was also getting more physical and the best thing I could have done at the time was get away from him.
>
> Shortly after I left for Brazil, my best friend, Bunny Cooper, was staying at my apartment when someone tried to kill her! Bunny was sleeping and suddenly woke up to find a man choking her. She managed to cry out and whoever was there ran out when he heard her voice. Bunny, to this day, is convinced it was Richard who attacked her. There is no doubt in her mind. You see, Richard didn't know that I had gone to South America. He assumed it was me in that bed.
>
> Richard always drank a lot and eventually became an alcoholic. He just kept drinking, and drinking, and drinking. He had great potential as an actor, but his career never went anywhere. He thought he was going to be a big star—but that was never going to happen because of the alcohol.[1]

When Richard Kay, one of the film's producers, sent Beverly's agent the *Curucu* script, she thought the role she was being offered, Dr. Andrea Romar, was a wonderful change from the kind of parts she had been playing. Siodmak's screenplay was about a young American medical biochemist who was interested in the way certain South American jungle tribes were able to shrink human heads. If she could determine what plants were used in the process, perhaps chemicals from these plants could be developed to shrink cancerous tumors. When Dr. Romar arrives in Brazil, she meets Rock Dean (John Bromfield). He owns several plantations in the country and is trying to learn why his native workers are suddenly leaving their jobs and returning to their jungle tribes. They team up to find out what is frightening the workers and ultimately make some strange and remarkable discoveries.

Beverly had to take all sorts of clothes with her to South America because she was told that in some locations the characters would dress formal, and in others they would need clothes to wear in the middle of the Brazilian jungle. "When we started to shoot the picture, I found out that there were no changing rooms on any of the sets. I think I wore the same pair of Levis and shirt from the beginning to the end of the picture!

Beverly posed for this publicity photograph to promote *Curucu, Beast of the Amazon* (Universal-International, 1956).

"I had red hair in this film. I always had a different hair color in my pictures. I had asked if I should take peroxide. I was told, 'No. You don't need peroxide. Just bring your red hair dye.' So I didn't, and the only peroxide I could buy in these tiny towns was less than ten percent peroxide, which was what you used to put on a cut. It would only cover my hair for just that day. So I spent all my evenings in the bathroom dyeing my roots!"[2]

When the cast and crew got to Belem, which is located very close to the equator, they stayed at the Grand Hotel, which dated back to Brazil's colonial days. It was right on the shores of the Amazon River. Beverly's room had one light bulb which hung down in the middle of the room from what seemed like a 100-foot-high ceiling. The bathroom had a toilet and a sink and the rest of it was all shower. Beverly recalled, "The shower nozzle was right in the middle of the room so when you turned it on everything got sopping wet. It was really a shower, with a sink and toilet in it, and a drain in the middle of the floor!

"When I filmed a picture on location, I usually got hotel rooms with a single 15-watt light bulb in it. This place was no different. Since there was no makeup man for me on the set, I had to do all my own makeup, which was impossible under a 15-watt light bulb. However, this room had a teeny, tiny little balcony and a hat stand. We usually had very early morning calls. So at 4:30 in the morning, I would take the hat stand out on the tiny balcony and, hanging my mirror on the stand, I would put on my makeup in the light of whatever sun was coming up that day. It wasn't easy — my room was on the shady side of the hotel — but I did it!"[3]

At night, Beverly would have to take off the bed sheets and shake out all the bugs. She had candles which were similar to citronella candles:

> They didn't kill the bugs, they just made them scurry away for a while. My room looked like Vampira's bedroom with all these little candles around it. It was really a kick![4]
>
> As bad as the hotel was, the facilities while on location were worse. If you had to use the loo, you had to go to this old farmhouse. And, of course, we all got sick. You had to get into this truck and the truck would take you to the farmhouse. Anyone who has ever had an intestinal virus knows what you go through. You think you have to go to the bathroom every five minutes. And when you get there, nothing happens. It was a mess!
>
> On the first day of the shoot, a truck arrived loaded with two large tin containers. One of the containers had something which looked like it had rice in it and the other had tea. They also brought tin plates. I watched them dish out this slop and then wipe the tin plates with an old rag when we were finished and stack the plates up for the next day. Well, that was the end of my lunch on the set! Before I left the hotel in the morning, I would put a bread roll in my purse and that's what I would have for lunch. I couldn't wait to get back home and have a malt, a hamburger, and some French fries![5]

Of course, there were a tremendous number of bugs and flies everywhere. The first time Beverly picked up her cup to drink the tea, it was full of flies. "After a while you just drank the tea with the flies. It just didn't make any difference."[6]

> We filmed one scene on the Amazon River on a fishing barge. What we didn't know was that the Amazon at this particular spot was very near the Atlantic Ocean and it had tides that went in and out. All of a sudden we couldn't move. We were stuck on a sandbar in the middle of the river and this river was miles wide! No one would dare chance swimming to shore because of the crocodiles and piranha.
>
> The man who owned the barge said to us, "I'm going to cook up some food. Do you want to eat?" "*No!*" we all said. "We don't want to eat." You couldn't eat anything in Brazil. I mean, you couldn't drink the water, either. We had to drink wine or beer — if you could find it. You had to be very careful what you ate because you could get so sick.
>
> So there we all were on this dingy barge — Curt Siodmak, John Bromfield, another crew member, myself, and the camera equipment — stuck on a sandbar for what seemed like several hours. Finally, another boat came along, but they could only come within a hundred feet of the barge or they, too, would get stuck on the sandbar. They said to us, "You can stay here until the tide comes back in and the boat can get off the sandbar [which could take several more hours], or you can swim over here and we'll take you to your hotel." We all looked at each other and John

and I said, "Well, what the hell, we'll just swim over there to that bloody boat!" John and I got in the water and made our way over to the other boat. When we finally got back to the hotel, I had these little red bugs all over my body that itched like mad! I don't know what was in the water, or what these tiny organisms were, but I was covered with them and it took several scrubbings with soap and water to get them off. It was a very buggy country!⁷

Beverly found Curt Siodmak was occasionally difficult to work with. "I realize now," she said, "that it was because it was such a very hard picture for him to make. He had to deal with a crew that spoke so many different languages — Portuguese, German, English, French, as well as native dialects — and although he spoke most of them, I think it was a very tense time for him. I just knew that it was difficult to understand Curt because of his thick German accent. And — I could be wrong — but I had a feeling that he was coming on to me. I was afraid to spend too much time with him, or have dinner with him, because I thought he would think I was interested. So, I spent most of my free time there by myself."⁸

John Bromfield had brought his girlfriend Larri Thomas — who had a small part in the picture — to Brazil with him and they got married. So they were not interested in spending too much time with Beverly. "I'd knock on their door and say, 'Are you going to be doing anything tonight?' and they would say, 'Oh, Beverly!' They didn't want me hanging around. Everyone else in the crew spoke either German or Portuguese. There was one really cute German guy named Franz, who was the chief grip on the picture. I decided not to pursue that because I didn't understand what the hell he was saying! He might have been saying something horrible to me and I wouldn't know. So I had no one to talk to for the three-month shoot. Just about the only company I had was a little monkey that kept following me around and would never let me go. No matter where I was, he was on my shoulder. I wanted to bring him back home to the United States — he was just a doll."⁹

The production filmed many of the scenes for *Curucu* on coffee plantations. These plantations were also working farms with cows and chickens. "There was this wonderful little man who spoke absolutely no English. His only job during the whole shoot was to carry an umbrella over my head. It was *very hot* in Brazil!

> Now we had this monster costume [the Curucu monster that had been terrorizing the plantation workers in the film] which was made out of beautiful bird feathers. We had brought it out with us from Los Angeles. Well, the costume either got lost or destroyed and Curt Siodmak was furious.
>
> A couple of days later, the man who owned the plantation we were filming at came storming onto the set with his wife after him, and both were screaming their lungs out at Curt. Everybody was shouting in Portuguese. We later found out that the little man — the sweet little man who held my umbrella — realized how upset everyone was that the monster costume was gone, and, during the night he, and a friend of his, had gone to the ranch and had plucked all the feathers from the chickens. When the farmer woke up the next morning, he found all these naked chickens running around his plantation. The little man had wanted to give Curt Siodmak all these feathers as his gift.¹⁰

One of Beverly's *Curucu* co-stars was a boa constrictor that Curt had rented from the Belem Zoo. This boa constrictor was about 16 feet long, the biggest snake she had ever seen. "In the scene," Beverly said, "this snake was supposed to fall out of a tree and wrap around me. I was then supposed to fall to the ground, screaming. Well, they had three native snake handlers off-screen holding its tail and three holding its head. They wrapped the rest of the snake around me. We started to film and I immediately started screaming my head off. Suddenly, Curt Siodmak yelled, 'Cut! Cut! Cut! Cut!' and ran over to me, saying, 'Are you all right?' I said, 'Yes, I'm fine. Am I not supposed to be screaming?' Curt replied, 'Yeah, I'm sorry. I'm sorry. I just wanted to make sure you were okay.' I thought this was very strange at the time.

"Twenty years later, Curt Siodmak came to my house and said, 'You know, Beverly, I wanted to thank you so much for what you did in Brazil with that snake. Because, if the handlers at either end of it had let go, it would have constricted, and you would have been dead. There would have been no way we could have gotten it off you in time to save your life. But we didn't want to tell you that in the middle of Brazil.' I guess he was afraid that if he told me, I wouldn't do the scene. I said to him, 'Well, thanks a lot, Curt. I'm so glad you told me that!' I really wasn't afraid of snakes. But I also really wanted that scene to be over with as quickly as possible."[11]

However, that wasn't the scariest thing Beverly ever did in the picture. "That happened later on in the shoot," Beverly recalled. "Siodmak had had this tribal village built for the scene where the natives bring us after we have been captured. They had built the village about ten days before we were going to film this particular scene. It was constructed of fresh palm fronds which quickly dried out in the intense Brazilian heat. We finished that scene, and in the next one, they were going to burn down the village. We had three cameras filming the fire sequence — thank God!"[12]

In this scene, a native was supposed to throw a flaming spear at one of the huts. However, instead of the hut burning slowly, it immediately exploded, and quickly engulfed the entire village set in flames — with John and Beverly in the middle! "I thought, 'Well, this is it. I'm going to die here.' There was so much fire and smoke, we couldn't see a way out. We both just froze. But as scared as I was, I pushed John and he ran. I made up my mind then and there to try to run through the flames. I decided I had to try to get out of there if I possibly could. It's amazing what goes through your head. You think you're talking to yourself for 25 minutes, but this all happens in a split second! Thank God I got out. My clothes, hair, eyebrows, and eyelashes were all singed. We just barely made it out alive!"[13]

The picture came out about a year later to good reviews and made money for Universal. In his autobiography, Siodmak remarked that he "wanted to make a picture in South America which was a challenge since no studio ever had succeeded in bringing back a completed motion picture." Orson Welles had tried once and failed. Curt Siodmak had succeeded. When Curt's book was published, he sent Beverly a copy with the following dedication: "For Beverly — The greatest and bravest trouper in film and life I've ever met."

Beverly had somehow managed to survive the Amazon jungle and her divorce from Richard. But now, she was about to make another picture for Roger Corman called *Gunslinger*, where her survival skills would be tested once again.

7. Scream Queen

Beverly barely had time to recuperate from her "ordeal" in Brazil when she learned that Roger Corman had suddenly moved up the start date for *Gunslinger* from March to late February 1956. "Years later," Beverly chuckled, "I read somewhere that Roger had changed the film schedule in order to get in under the wire regarding a change in union contract agreements which limited an actor's studio work week from six to five days. Roger hoped to film *Gunslinger* in under a week and no doubt wanted the 'benefit' of that sixth day to avoid the expense of paying his actors for a second week. Leave it to Roger to squeeze the blood out of every penny he spent on his pictures!"[1]

Most of the film was shot on location at the Jack Ingram Ranch in Topanga Canyon. The ranch had a wonderful recreation of an Old West town that was used in countless movie and television Westerns over the years. It was cold and rainy when Beverly arrived on the set. In fact, it rained almost the entire time they were there. The cast was assigned one of the old, unheated wooden shacks as a dressing room.

Gunslinger provided Beverly with another very strong woman's role that appealed to her as *Curucu, Beast of the Amazon* had done. In this film, she played the wife of a slain U.S. marshal who puts on her late husband's badge and vows to clean up the corrupt town and avenge his murder. The marshal suspects Erica Page (Allison Hayes), owner of the local dance hall and saloon. Page has been buying up land in anticipation of the railroad coming through town. She has also purchased the services of a dangerous gunslinger (John Ireland) to intimidate any resistance to her scheme, and his job includes keeping an eye on the new marshal. An unexpected relationship develops between the marshal and the gunman, forcing her to decide whether she'll follow her heart or the law.

> I played Marshal Rose Hood, and I have always considered it one of my favorite roles. I think I was the first woman to play a marshal in a movie western. Roger would often cast against type in those days. I could never resist a plum role like a lady marshal in a genre that would never have considered such a gender reversal like that before. However, working with Roger was always an adventure and this film was no exception.
>
> John Ireland and I did a love scene very early one morning in a tree. I don't know why the hell Roger wanted us in this tree, but there we were! However, this particular tree — which was very picturesque — belonged to a colony of red ants and they were not very happy that we had decided to disturb them at 6:30 in the morning! They were crawling all over us. Here we were having a wonderful love scene and these ants were *biting the hell out of us*! If you watch that scene closely, you can actually see the ants all over me. This happened on the first day of shooting and it went downhill from there!
>
> The day before Allison Hayes and I were scheduled to film a big fight scene, Roger said to me, "All right, in this next scene I want you to come out of the dance hall and then run down the

stairs, leap on your horse, and ride out of town." Of course, I was still doing most of my own stunts in those days. However, I did have a stuntwoman who did any trick riding that Roger required.

Well, I always seemed to have the worst time with horses on my pictures. Something bad always happened to me when I had scenes with them. So I thought, "Okay. The thing to do is to think *high*! If I can do that, I can then run down these stairs, jump on this horse, and ride out of town." I'm thinking high as I run down the steps and at the bottom I jump! A moment later, Roger's cameraman — who was looking through the viewfinder — said, "Well, she went up, but I never saw her come down, she just disappeared!" I had sailed right over the horse.

On my second try, I was running down the stairs when I twisted my right ankle. I couldn't walk. Roger was very upset because now they were going to have to do all sorts of cutting instead of the seamless take he was hoping to get. He had to get me a box to stand on so that they could film me mounting the horse.

When I got home that night, my ankle had swollen to double its normal size. Instead of soaking it in cold water, I put it in very hot water. It felt great at the time, but when I got up the next morning, my ankle had now swollen to three times its normal size! It was so painful that I had to call someone to take me to the studio because I couldn't drive. When I got there, Roger looked at my ankle and said, "Well, let's get to work! We have to shoot the fight scene with you and Allison." You could be dead and Roger would find a way to film around that. When I got over my initial shock at his reaction, I said to him, "What do we do? I can't walk so how can I do this fight scene? I can't even get my boot on!" Roger just smiled.

A short time later, a doctor — at least I was told he was a doctor — arrived on the set with a very large syringe and he put several shots of Novocain directly into the bone of my ankle. The pain was unbelievable. But within minutes, my leg felt great! I could do anything now. The wardrobe lady came and cut my boot up the back so I could get my swollen foot in the shoe. We filmed the fight scene and I did all my own stunts. I worked all day and, let me tell you, we didn't hold back on that scene; we really scratched, punched and pulled each other's hair! Of course, I didn't work again for several weeks after that! I couldn't walk on that leg. But Roger got his scenes shot. That's all that mattered."[2]

One day Allison Hayes was so cold and tired that she fell off her horse, breaking her arm in the process. Roger had her arm bandaged and she finished her scenes. When the director of photography got very ill and left in the middle of the day, Roger took over. "Other than dropping dead during a Roger Corman film," Beverly laughed, "the only way you could get off one of his pictures was to leave the country. Roger wouldn't spend the money it would take to get you back!"[3] In the end, it was Mother Nature who outwitted Corman. His projected six-day shoot turned into a seven-day production due to all the rain.

Gunslinger went into theatrical release in the summer of 1956. In the meantime, Roger was preparing two science fiction features. Roger offered Beverly starring roles in both films and after reading the scripts, she couldn't say no. They were wonderful parts. Little did she know then that these appearances would follow her throughout the rest of her career and that she would be fondly remembered by many for her participation in them. The films were *It Conquered the World* and *Not of This Earth*.

The former went into production in March 1956 and starred Lee Van Cleef and Peter Graves. Roger filmed the picture in under two weeks for about $100,000. They did all the location work in Hollywood on Beechwood Drive and the famous Bronson Caves. Van Cleef played Beverly's husband, a disgruntled scientist who was part of a U.S. Army space satellite project, but left after a disagreement with the armed forces' aggressive policies. He has been secretly collaborating — via satellite radio communication — with what he believes is a sympathetic counterpart on the planet Venus and hopes that together they can find a peaceful solution to the Army's misguided plans. To his horror, the scientist finally realizes that he is actually abetting an advance invasion force whose sole aim is to conquer and enslave Earth.

> I adored Lee Van Cleef but it was difficult to work with him. He used to drive me crazy because he always drank so much. He would arrive on the set on time, but his breath was awful, and he would sweat. He would be wringing wet because of all the liquor he drank the night before. It's hard to work with someone who is always sopping wet! He remembered his lines — most of the time. He was always spending his evenings just running around and he would come to the set the next day — expelling his breath: "Ho-hum. Okay. What'll we do now?" However, if he thought he forgot his lines he would get nervous and the perspiration would begin to pour off him because he really was playing around. But we all forgave him because we loved him so much.[4]
>
> Lee almost gave up acting because of his drinking. Then he went to Europe and made those spaghetti Westerns and became a big star. I had lost contact with him and didn't know what the hell had happened to him until someone told me he had found a new career overseas. I was very happy for him. He was sweating over there now![5]
>
> Peter Graves was terribly shy and stoic. He was not at all demonstrative. But he was very sweet and he was a very decent man. Like his brother, James Arness, Peter was a very quiet man. He was calm and collected and knew all his lines, as always. He was very loyal to his friends.[6]

The house on Beechwood Drive that was used in the film has since been demolished. Beverly recalled that "the house was horrible. I don't know whose house that was. I really hated that house!"[7]

When *It Conquered the World* went into production, Corman kept telling his cast about the Venusian creature he had special effects man Paul Blaisdell make for the picture. However, they never saw it until a day or two before the production ended and they were going to shoot the scenes with it in the caves of Bronson Canyon. "Roger said to me, 'I want you to come out and see this monster,'" Beverly said. "'You're just going to love it!' So I went out to the set with him, took one look at this monster, and I said, 'Well, when it's finished, I'm sure it's going to be just great!' Roger looked disappointed. 'It *is* finished,' he said. 'This is *it*? This is the monster?' I replied. 'This funny-looking little carrot?' It was so small, I could have stepped on it and crushed it. It was small and fat and it kind of waddled. It certainly didn't look scary to me!

"I was never in any scene with the monster because audiences would have seen just how small it really was. I suggested that Roger film me against one wall and the monster against the opposite wall in the cave. Then I said to him, 'When I'm talking to the monster and giving him hell, maybe you could lift it up so that I can look up at it instead of down. The head on this thing was great, but it was a monster without a body. For some reason, Paul Blaisdell forgot to give it a body! But Roger always considered it to be his favorite creature."[8]

Several weeks after they completed filming *It Conquered the World*, Roger started production on his second science fiction adventure, *Not of This Earth*. It was another low-budget, two-week shoot that was filmed mostly in a rented house in Hollywood and in nearby Griffith Park. Beverly's co-stars this time were Paul Birch, Morgan Jones and William Roerick.[9]

Not of This Earth was an interesting movie about an alien from the planet Davanna whose home world has been ravaged by nuclear war. As a result of the nuclear fallout, the aliens have a disease that causes the blood to evaporate in their veins. Daily blood transfusions are necessary to save their race. The visitor from Davanna has come to Earth to determine if humans are compatible donors. If he is successful, the Earth will be invaded and its inhabitants enslaved to keep his race alive.

Beverly played nurse Nadine Storey, assigned by a doctor under the control of the alien to supervise his daily transfusions. "By this time," Beverly said, "I was getting used to the rigors of a Roger Corman production." However, like his previous films, *Not of This Earth* was not without its controversies. Paul Birch walked off the picture in a dispute over the special white contact lenses he was forced to wear for hours on end as the vampiric alien. Contact lenses in those days were very thick and uncomfortable to wear. Fortunately, Roger had already shot most of his scenes, so he was able to bring the film in on time by using another actor with a similar build to stand in for the disgruntled Birch.[10]

> I recall a conversation I had several years ago with my agent concerning Roger Corman. I had just tested for a lead role in a made-for-television movie Roger was producing at that time called *Georgia Peaches*. My agent remarked to me that was a shame Roger had not moved "forward" into really big productions because of his obvious talents. I honestly feel that Roger thoroughly enjoys making pictures for the least amount of money and in the shortest amount of production time. I think he could easily be doing more "important" work. But as far as he's concerned, he really doesn't want to change his formula. His formula has worked for him from the very beginning. Roger's films are targeted at the teenage movie market and whenever he's strayed from that core audience, his films usually haven't done as well.
>
> Even as far back as 1956, Roger was keenly aware of his bread and butter: teenage boys. There were two scenes that I did in *Not of This Earth* that — for its time — were considered quite sexy. The first was when I go for a swim in that skin-tone, very tight bathing suit. The other was when I'm dressing and I put on my stockings. We certainly have come a long way since then! But in those days, these scenes were considered very titillating.[11]

Paul Blaisdell, who created all the fantastic flying creatures and the squat invader from Venus, also recalled Beverly fondly. "Oh yes, I do have remembrances and Bev, ... I want you to know this is sincere. I remember those dark eyes and that shock of blond hair of yours, and I remember how you could project yourself so strongly onto a movie screen. You have such enthusiasm, such 'go get 'em' or whatever you want to call it that it projects itself on film. It's wonderful to watch you and it was surely a hell of a lot of fun to work with you. And I guess I like talking with you best of all — yeah, I can swear too, you know, Bev! And honestly, recalling those ancient movies, *It Conquered the World* and *Not of This Earth*, I think that without you they would have been nowhere!"[12]

The year 1956 saw Beverly making appearances in an astonishing 14 television shows in addition to her six feature film roles. A close look at her work during this prolific year reveals that Beverly made more than one appearance on four different prime time shows; made return appearances on three shows from the previous year; and also filmed two more pilot episodes within this same twelve-month period.[13]

Beverly was being recognized as a very capable actress who could be depended upon to deliver an excellent performance, and who could just as easily handle a live televised show as a taped broadcast. Don Royal, columnist for *The Daily Press*, observed on July 17, 1958, "Miss Garland is one of those actresses Hollywood calls 'useful.' This means she is untempermental and can do just about anything. You can cast her as a siren and she'll attract like the best of them. Tomorrow, you can turn around and have her playing 'Plain Jane Without A Brain' and she'll do that well, too."

Beverly and one of her favorite co-stars, David Niven ("He gave the best kisses," Beverly confessed). Here she is being manhandled by Niven in a scene from "Touch and Go," the April 26, 1956, episode of *Four Star Playhouse*.

Beverly was also working with bigger name stars such as David Niven, Ralph Bellamy, Lew Ayres, Howard Duff, Zachary Scott, and Brian Keith, to name a few. But it was on the big screen that Beverly's heart had been set and she was about to be rewarded for her patience with a plum role in a major Hollywood production. A role that would come from a source that Beverly could never have imagined — even in her wildest dreams.

8. *The Joker Is Wild*

Although Beverly had gone though two unsuccessful marriages, she wasn't yet ready to throw in the towel on finding "Mister Right." Her only mistake was that she started dating actors again.

> Some time after my separation from Richard Garland, I went out to MGM for a reading. They teamed me up with a young actor from Australia whom they were grooming for stardom, named Rod Taylor. We started dating and were seeing each other for quite a while. Then I went to Brazil to do *Curucu, Beast of the Amazon*, and when I came back, we picked up where we had left off. But then I found out that Rod was dating other people at the same time! I wasn't happy about that and we broke up. Oh, but he was gorgeous! He was a doll — as well as a good actor.
>
> Years later, I worked with Rod on an episode of his series *Hong Kong* and it was very pleasant, "Hello," "How are you?" "Goodbye." That was it. It was no big deal. He did his thing and I did mine and that was that. I felt a little awkward at first but then I thought, "Screw it!" Rod was just another actor.[1]

Beverly dated Jeffrey Hunter for a short time, but they were just very good friends. It was the same with David Janssen. "I was more like a buddy to him. Although he was crazy about my friend, Bunny Cooper. Bunny's brother, Ben Cooper, and I dated for quite a while, too. Ben had come out to California after playing one of the children in *Life with Father* on Broadway. He was under contract at Republic for some time and did a lot of films for them. But he just didn't make it after that. Then he got into Amway and he made a fortune! He was a darn good actor, and a good talker. But he was an even better businessman."

Beverly even dated Lew Ayres. "We had done a *Ford Theater* television show called 'Measure of Faith,' and he asked me out. I liked Lew but he was so much older than me and very settled in his ways. He was much more serious about our relationship than I ever was."[2]

Beverly had made up her mind that she was never going to get seriously involved with an actor again. "Personally, I think they're all the same. I mean, they have great egos and they just think they're something. They're fascinating; they are wonderful people and they're funny. They can be charming and most of them are very good-looking. Actors have great personalities. But they are mostly interested in themselves because they have to be. That's fine. That's the way they should be. But I didn't want somebody like that. I wanted somebody who was really interested in me! Actors believe that they come first and you come in a distant second place. That wasn't what I wanted.

"If Richard Garland didn't get a role, he would pout and carry on. I would have stayed with him if he hadn't cheated. I would have tried my best to stroke his ego. But he probably would have cheated on me somewhere along the line. I'm sure there are some actors out there that are true-blue and great. I just never met any of them."

Beverly even dated Roger Corman for a short while. "Roger and I had such a good relationship and we worked very well together, because we were both very professional. I think it could have easily turned into a serious relationship but I really didn't think that's what I wanted."[3] Roger wanted to put Beverly under contract but she didn't want to limit herself to a series of low-budget pictures which was all that he was making at the time. Beverly wanted to do much more than that with her career. "I did make one more picture for Roger called *Naked Paradise*. Roger flew us out to Hawaii for two weeks in early September of 1956. It was filmed on the beautiful island of Kauai." Roger even put her up at the Coco Palms Hotel, which had great accommodations and even better food. Of course, the rest of the supporting cast and crew were put up at an abandoned Boy Scout camp on the other side of the island. "But Roger really splurged on me this time![4] I felt everyone in the cast performed well. Everybody was relaxed. It was just a good movie to work on. It was one of the most pleasant movies I ever did for Roger."

Beverly liked all the characters Roger gave her, but *Naked Paradise*'s Max MacKenzie was one of her favorites. "She was exciting. I really felt that she had some depth. I felt the role had more to it than my just being the girl on the boat. You learned how and why she came to be in that position. Then, during the course of the film, she changes. She rebels and grows as a person. She was an interesting gal." Other than being upset because her hair was too short and being uneasy about going into the water because she wasn't that strong a swimmer, Beverly thought the boat scenes were fun. "We were on this fairly big sailboat. Everybody had their spot on the boat. Cast and crew stayed in their little spot and did their thing. Roger had the positions all worked out.[5]

"After that, Roger and I went our separate ways professionally. But we have always remained good friends. He's married to a great lady who's very high-powered, which is precisely the kind of woman Roger has always needed. She's extremely bright which is another plus because Roger is very intelligent. Together they make a perfect couple.

"What I have always loved most about Roger Corman was listening to him make a deal while talking on the phone. He is a *fabulous* businessman. He is fascinating to listen to and that's what has always attracted me to him. If he could just make deals — 24 hours a day — I'd be madly in love with him! We wouldn't have to go anywhere on a date. Just listening to him wheel and deal was the ultimate in entertainment for me. He is brilliant at it! I mean, this *is* the man who was the first to distribute Ingmar Bergman films to U.S. drive-ins! Who else could have done that?"[6]

Around this time, Beverly had a date that she would never forget. "I had just finished filming *Badlands of Montana* for 20th Century–Fox when I learned that I had been cast in Paramount's *The Joker Is Wild* starring Frank Sinatra! This was a wonderful break for me." Evidently, Sinatra had seen a *Climax!* television episode that Beverly had done, "The Fog," and urged the film's producer to cast her in the role of Cassie Mack, wife of Austin Mack (Eddie Albert).[7] "I had a fabulous dressing room on the set," Beverly recalled, "and Edith Head designed all my costumes. It was all magical!"[8]

Beverly had an interesting time her first day on the set. "I was excited, I guess ... too excited. Well, for this picture I had a small cap that fit over one of my teeth just to fill it out a little. It slipped in place and stayed there, only to be taken out at lunch. At lunch this first day, I sat down, took it off, wrapped it in a paper napkin, and promptly threw it away! My dentist had to send a spare by messenger! Edith Head had designed some wonderful clothes for me. Cassie had a tendency to overdress, being an ex-showgirl, and some of the outfits were really funny.⁹

> It was also on this very first day on the picture that Frank Sinatra asked me out. I thought he was kidding and didn't take him seriously. I had a tremendous crush on Frank. He flirted with me all the time and kept asking me out. One day, he asked me again and I said yes. Well, I was in a panic! I didn't know what to wear. I drove my roommate nuts asking her questions like, "Do you think I should play Sinatra or Perry Como records when he comes to the house?"
>
> Frank arrived and we got into his brand new car — a Corvette, I think. We had been working together for about four weeks but I was so intimidated that I didn't know what to talk to him about. I finally said something really dumb like "Why did you decide to become a singer?" Everything I said to him sounded like it was coming out of the mouth of a two-year-old! It was awful. After about ten minutes, he looked at me as if to say, "Oh my! I'm going to have to spend the whole evening with *her*?" I was just about the worst date you could possibly imagine.
>
> We had dinner and then Frank took me to a recording session.¹⁰ When he brought me home, I was even more of a wreck because he had such an incredible reputation! But he simply kissed me on the forehead and said it was "a lovely evening."¹¹

In spite of that disastrous date, Beverly felt she was now on her way to a major turning point in her career. To have gotten a part in this big a picture was really quite a coup for her.

Working on the picture, Beverly was pleased to learn that Sinatra wasn't the type who enjoyed endless rehearsals. As she recalled, "You'd come in and rehearse so you could figure out where the camera was and then the director would say, 'Let's do it one more time' or 'Let's go through this again' and Sinatra would say, 'No. We already did this. Shoot it! Everybody knows what the hell they're doing!' He hated to rehearse. I don't like to rehearse particularly. I usually do my best thing on my first take. That's what I like to do. Once I get my performance down, I don't change it much. What you see me do the first time is probably what I end up doing. Like Barbara Stanwyck — her first takes were her best takes."¹²

While Beverly's reviews weren't over-exuberant, they proved she was on an equal footing with her contemporaries. Herb Kelly (*Miami News*) reported, "Beverly Garland gives a strong performance as Albert's wife" and *Variety*'s Gene said, "In featured spots are Beverly Garland who works well..."

Beverly completed her scenes on Wednesday, December 12, 1956, and the following Monday morning she was reporting to the set of *Wire Service* at RKO-Pathe to make a second appearance on the series, in an episode titled "The Profile on Ellen Gale."¹³

Just before leaving for New York City on a two-week promotional tour for *The Joker Is Wild*, Beverly met the real Cassie Mack. During the meeting, Cassie was heard to remark,

Portrait of Beverly taken to promote *The Joker Is Wild* (Paramount, 1957).

Beverly and Beau relax in her dressing room between scenes on *The Joker Is Wild* (Paramount, 1957).

"It's frightening as hell to meet someone who plays you on the screen."[14] It's too bad Beverly couldn't have met Ms. Mack before filming her on-screen counterpart; she might have been able to incorporate some of her mannerisms as a result of the experience. However, reviewer Kay Proctor said, "Outstanding also, at least to me, was Beverly Garland. Cast as Cassie, the piano accompanist's ever-present wife, she forcefully emerges, perhaps unexpectedly, as Lewis' [Sinatra] unwelcome conscience."[15]

9. Decoy

Beverly was still in New York City promoting *The Joker Is Wild* when Hollywood columnist Hedda Hopper named her one of her "Top Film Finds of 1956." Her name was listed along with John Cassavetes, Don Murray, Carroll Baker, Gina Rowlands, Jean Seberg and Anthony Perkins. It was a fabulous endorsement of her potential.[1]

According to Sheilah Graham's "Hollywood Today" syndicated column, in New York Beverly was tripping the light fantastic with tickets to some of Broadway's top plays of the season such as: *My Fair Lady* and *Auntie Mame*, and was on the arm of "a different eligible bachelor each night."[2]

Before Beverly returned to Los Angeles, she met with the producers of a proposed series called *Decoy—The Story of a New York Policewoman*. The show would be based in part on the exploits of a female undercover cop. Producers Everett Rosenthal and Arthur Singer needed a strong, attractive and compelling actress to star in this groundbreaking series and Beverly would be perfect. As Beverly recalled, "Somebody telephoned and asked me if I would do a pilot. I went back East and met with the show's producers."[3] Beverly agreed to return to New York City in March to film the pilot show.

No sooner had she deplaned in Los Angeles than she was back filming her fifth starring role in a *Lux Video Theater*. It would reunite her with her *D.O.A.* co-star Edmond O'Brien in an adaptation of Ernest Hemingway's *To Have and Have Not*. Hemingway's book had been adapted for the big screen by Warner Brothers in 1944 and starred Humphrey Bogart and Lauren Bacall.[4] The TV version premiered on January 17, 1957. On January 21, *Variety*'s Kove reviewed the show, noting: "Given a good story, such as this, result was top-notch entertainment.... Edmond O'Brien and Beverly Garland registered strongly."

Movie studio executives may have been terrified that television was on the verge of closing down motion pictures for good, but that apparently didn't stop them from utilizing it to scout for new talent. "Hollywood Today" columnist Sheilah Graham reported on February 15, 1957, "Universal-International executives saw Beverly Garland in the video version of *To Have and Have Not* ... and now they're interested in signing her to a multiple-picture contract with a big build-up. Beverly exudes that kind of sharp appeal which first brought Bacall to notice."

About ten days before Graham's column appeared, *Variety* (February 5, 1957) noted that Beverly was being "paged for the femme lead" opposite Fred MacMurray in Universal-International's *Decision at Durango* (later re-titled *Day of the Bad Man*). Beverly remembers the circumstances very well. "There was a guy at Universal. He was a casting man. He actually chased me around his desk. I reported him to the head of the studio and he didn't lose his job. They denied it. He was a real...! He was there for years. I made up my mind a long time ago that I wasn't going to sleep my way into anything, anywhere, any time and I never did and I never have."[5] She did not appear in the MacMurray movie.

About a month later, Beverly was on her way back to New York City to film the *Decoy* pilot, which went into production on March 28, 1957, and was completed in seven days.[6] "I remember running through Central Park and it was freezing. We worked till about midnight but the cameraman realized there was a problem. 'Beverly,' he said, 'we have to get this one shot but the camera is frozen so let me tell you what I want you to do. I know you're running from this guy just as fast as you can through this park. But this is what I want you to do. You run like this [in *slow motion*]. Trust me, it will look fine in the finished print.' That's what I did and it looked great!

"I knew that they wouldn't let me stop until they heard the tinkling sound of my ear falling to the sidewalk frozen — really frozen."[7]

Returning home in early April (with ears intact), Beverly was soon in front of the cameras once again opposite Brian Keith in the Edward Small production *Chicago Confidential* for United Artists release. Beverly had been offered a starring role in Universal-International's *Amazon* opposite Don Taylor but she turned it down because she would be on Brazilian locations for ten weeks. As she told *Variety* (April 16, 1957), "[W]ith the series *Decoy* on the fire ... I would rather do good TV here." It should surprise no one that Beverly's memories of her last film experience in Brazil (*Curucu, Beast of the Amazon*) were still vivid and that she would avoid going back for more.[8]

According to Hedda Hopper in her syndicated column (May 1957), producer Edward Small had seen Beverly's work on the small screen and signed her without even an interview. *Chicago Confidential* went into production on May 9, 1957. Under the direction of Sidney Salkow, Beverly once again found herself in the midst of union racketeering as she had during the summer of 1954 when she filmed, *New Orleans Uncensored* with mobsters infiltrating the longshoreman's union, and prior to that *The Miami Story* where mobsters attempt a takeover of Miami. Ironically, none of *Chicago Confidential* was actually filmed in the Windy City.

Soon after completing work on *Chicago Confidential*, Beverly was starring in her third *Climax!* drama, acting opposite Michael Rennie, Marsha Hunt, and Peter Lorre in an episode titled "A Taste for Crime."[9] In its June 24, 1957, review, *Variety* said, "*Climax!* parlayed Jekyll and Hyde to *The Amazing Dr. Clutterhouse* for a respectable payoff on 'A Taste for Crime.' For those unfamiliar with the double identities that set this play in motion, it had moments of high drama. That it was well performed and moved with electric pace raised its level of acceptance...." *The San Diego Union* columnist Donald Freeman noted, "The talents of both Mr. Lorre and Miss Garland were permitted to flower fully since the yarn was awash with nasty occurrences, such as murder. Miss Garland wasn't exactly a faithful girlfriend to Mr. Lorre, either."[10]

Many years later, Beverly still couldn't get over her being cast in that show. "I just thought, to be Peter Lorre's girlfriend was the funniest thing that ever happened.... I was so thrilled that I was going to be Peter Lorre's girl. I didn't think Peter Lorre got the girl in anything! I giggled inside the whole time...."[11]

Beverly filmed three guest star appearances between May and July.[12] After playing Theo Van Gogh's wife on a *Bell Telephone Time* (aka *Curtain Time*) and the femme lead in an episode of *The Web* (a summer replacement for *The Loretta Young Show*[13]), Beverly was cast as Ellen in "Silhouette of a Killer" for the anthology series *The Alcoa-Goodyear Theatre*. The episode went before the cameras on or about July 11, 1957, with Robert Ryan co-starring in

Beverly couldn't resist flirting with co-star Robert Ryan during the filming of "Silhouette of a Killer," the September 30, 1957, premiere episode of *Alcoa — Goodyear Theater*.

the drama. "I would just make all sorts of eyes at [Ryan] and come on to him," she joked. "He was so handsome and sexy."[14]

Soon after she completed work on *Silhouette of a Killer*, Beverly received word that *Decoy* had sold in syndication. She was finally going to star in her own television series. However, Beverly had two more commitments before leaving Los Angeles for the mean streets of New York City: a guest spot on *Playhouse 90* with a stellar cast that included Joseph Cotten and Maureen O'Sullivan and a starring role in Universal-International's *The Saga of Hemp Brown*.[15]

10. Return to Gotham

On July 25, 1957, *The Hollywood Reporter* ran the following: "Note from Phil Cowen.... If Beverly Garland thinks she's getting a lot of exposure now with re-runs, wait until she learns that *Decoy* pilot she made while in New York is *hot* with the Westinghouse Group of Stations...."[1]

A few days later, *Billboard* (July 29, 1957) reported, "Westinghouse TV (independent networks in syndication market) placed a whopping six hundred thousand dollars pre-release order with Official [Films] which virtually underwrites half of Pyramid Productions costs on the 39-episode series."[2]

It turned out to be a very lucrative deal considering the failure of the shows' producers to secure a major network sponsor. Colgate-Palmolive had been considering *Decoy* along with several other shows, but a deal never materialized.[3]

Beverly was very pragmatic about the opportunity this series offered her. "With *The Joker Is Wild* I felt I was now beginning to move up. Then someone called me and said, 'Would you be interested in doing a television show called *Decoy—The Story of a New York Policewoman*'? During my career, I did my gig and moved on to the next job. I had to pay the rent. I mean, I worked. If I could work—if you wanted me to work—I worked! If you gave me a job and I could do it, I did it. That's how it was. I didn't know if there was going to be another job. I didn't know whether I could pay my rent next week. I had to support myself. I had been a waitress many, many times. I had worked at Forest Lawn Cemetery. I'd been an elevator operator, and I had worked at 'The Broadway' on Hollywood Boulevard. I'd done it all. If you give me an acting job and I know I don't have to go back and schlep those tables any more, I'll take that job. So *The Joker Is Wild* is over and I went to New York and I did the pilot."[4]

It was decided that *Decoy* would go into production on September 9, 1957, with interiors to be filmed at the Mary Pickford Studios in the Bronx. However, just before production began, the producers leased space in the 26th Street Armory in Manhattan instead.[5]

Beverly reported to Universal Studios' Stage 18 on August 8, 1957, for wardrobe and makeup tests two weeks prior to her first scenes at the Janes Ranch for *The Saga Of Hemp Brown*.[6] Her contract with Universal-International guaranteed Beverly a stop date of September 5 in order for her to be able to begin filming *Decoy* on September 8.

On September 4, after selling her car and sub-leasing her apartment, Beverly left Los Angeles for New York to begin work the following Monday, September 9. She took up residence at 40 Central Park South. The apartment belonged to actress Phyllis Kirk; Beverly had sublet it for the eight months she'd spend filming the series. "I had a great apartment overlooking the park," Beverly recalled. "Rumplemeyer's Restaurant was located next to the apartment building. I remember that there was a dumbwaiter in the apartment. The restaurant would send up a menu. I ate a lot of delicious meals at home."[7] Beverly also discovered several other eateries during her stay. "I found two wonderful places, both in the village. One is called 17 Barrel Street and the other is the Coach House. They both had great food and the prices were reasonable."[8]

The third floor of the 26th Street Armory was turned into a studio where most of the interior sets of *Decoy* were built. Exteriors were shot in various locations in the five boroughs of the City of New York. Beverly thought this was one reason why the show might prove very attractive to viewers: "New York City is such a fabulous background for a series. I can't imagine why somebody hadn't used it sooner."[9]

Beverly's character, Detective Catherine "Casey" Jones, was required to do quite a lot of physical activity. "I do a good bit of running up and down stairs, in and out of bars, deep into basements, high onto roofs," Beverly added.[10] She was even required to learn some basic ju-jitsu moves when one of the scripts required her to throw a six-foot-plus man and lay him flat in moments. "I've had to wrestle all types of neurotics and psychos are strong."[11]

In order to prepare for her role, Beverly met with the real men and women in blue. "I went to a real police station.... I talked to some of the policewomen there and learned how to use a gun. I learned how to draw it out fast to shoot. I talked to undercover policemen about their job." She also received invaluable assistance from the show's technical advisor Margaret Leonard, a former NYPD detective. "All the shows, Beverly explained, "were based on actual cases from police files." Most had to be changed in one aspect or another to make them more dramatic or to fit in better with her character.[12]

One of the biggest surprises of this brave new series was how television columnists recognized that *Decoy* was the first salvo being fired across the bow of a once male-dominated region and most were unsure how to react. Guy Wright of the *San Francisco News* (January 16, 1958) remarked, "The temptation is great to dismiss Beverly's series as just too incredibly far-fetched. But I don't want to do that." An unnamed reporter for *TV News* (February 22, 1958) observed, "As any cop will gladly testify, policewomen are mighty valuable. They're good weapons against juvenile delinquency, wayward parents, molesters and similar small fry eyesores. But when they start setting up Bev Garland against bank robbers, murderers and casual gents who run amok with lethal weapons, they're embarking on a highly dangerous way of doing things."

Working on *Decoy* wasn't easy. An average half-hour show was shot in six days with everyone sometimes working well past midnight to meet deadlines. Each show was filmed with only a two-week window before it aired. Beverly recalled just how hectic the shooting schedule was back then. "We usually had a rehearsal on Friday to go over the script, make changes and have discussions with all the actors. We had two or three good readings and a timing. After that, it was up to all of us to learn our lines for the next day's shoot."[13] But then, Beverly had always thrived in that kind of atmosphere. After all, she worked for Roger Corman and survived! "I loved the series," Beverly said, "although overall, it was very hard work. I did 30 shows without a break."[14]

Beverly got the measles and had to work with the disease. "My face was all broken out and my eyes were swollen," she recalled. The show's makeup man John Hall Jr. had to cover it all. "He had to try to open my eyes so I could look like I had eyes," Beverly smiled. She found out she could work with a body temperature of 105 degrees. "One day I fainted on the set. Someone revived me and I went on with it."[15]

Beverly was given a week's vacation, she remembered with a chuckle. "Actually, they

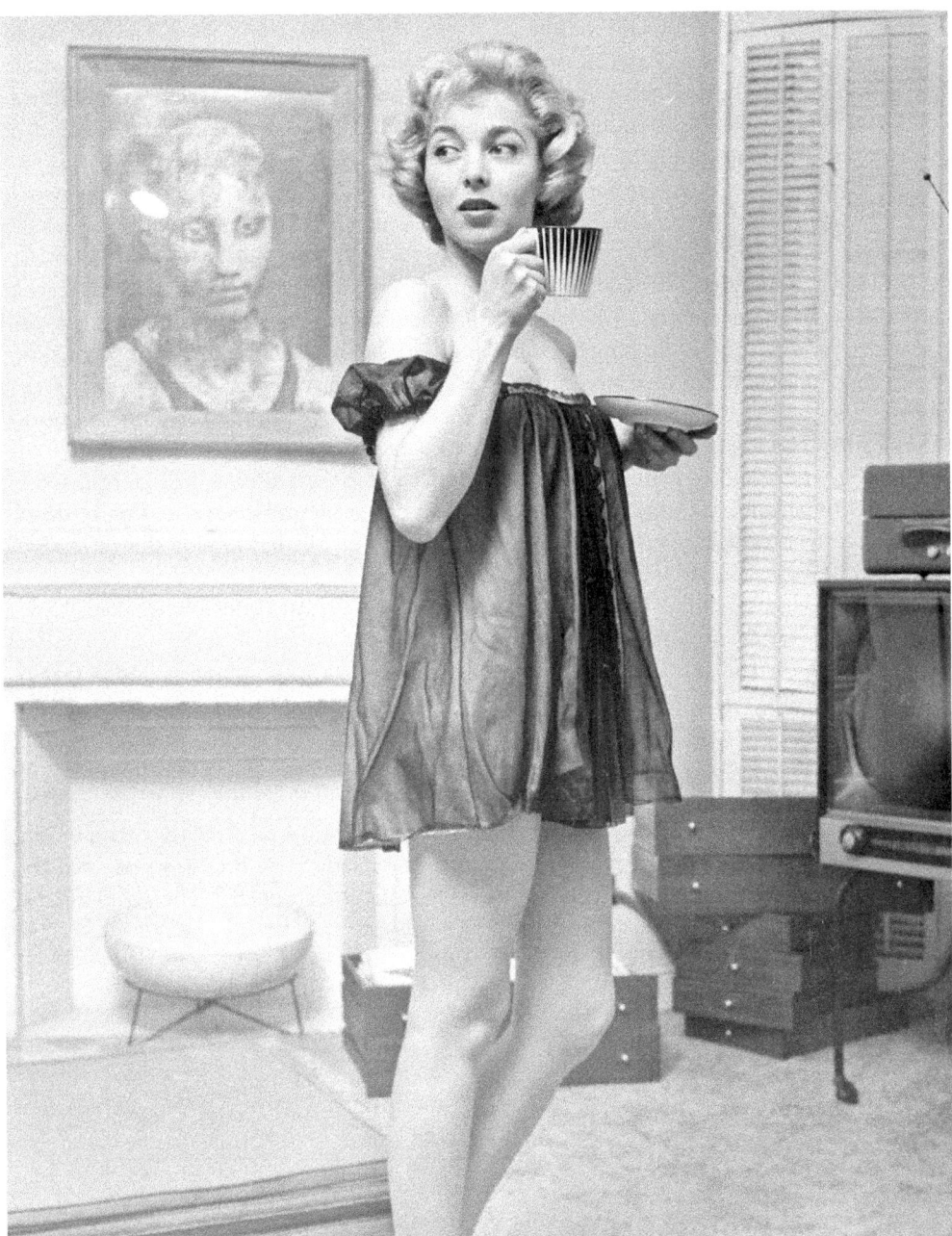

The coffee is hot and so is Beverly in this photograph taken at her New York City apartment in 1958 during the filming of her TV series *Decoy*.

finally let me go home but there was a snowstorm which prevented me from leaving town. So I only had two days in Los Angeles and then I had to get back."[16]

Most of the series was filmed on the streets with hand-held cameras and pedestrian traffic for unpaid extras. Being used to warm California weather, Beverly was uncomfortable most of the time. "We filmed in the winter months and I wasn't used to such cold weather," she recalled. "I couldn't dress for it either. The crew could wear long, heavy underwear and pants, as well as sweaters. I had to dress in character. A big sweater under my coat made me look too bulky on camera. I also couldn't wear boots and my feet froze in the snow.[17] There were no trailers on location, so we were forced to change clothes in area stores or restaurants." The cast and crew took cabs to get from one scene to another. "We did it all by the seat of our pants. It was hard sometimes to film on the streets because people would turn and stare at us. We tried to hide the cameras as much as we could in order to get the feel of the real New York City streets."[18]

Decoy was unique in its day for its documentary-style direction and no-holds-barred approach to its subject matter. *The Independent* (October 14, 1957) reviewer Tom Wade saw the show's potential when he previewed an episode. "Miss Garland has the job of tracking down a strangler with unusual strength. She pretends to be an actress 'between shows' and shortly finds herself trapped by a homicidal killer.... [T]he idea of the program will insure a supply of dramatic situations that have seldom been seen on TV up to now."

Beverly once told a reporter that "being a decoy for the police is a dangerous job — especially for a woman. Casey had to act and a bad performance by her could mean death. Her assignments take her everywhere, into all walks of life. She has to look the part as well as act it. It's an acting job within an acting job."[19]

Decoy ended production on its first season on May 29, 1958. Beverly recalled, "I was worn out but very anxious for a new adventure. So I decided over the Memorial Day weekend to buy a new car and got some maps together."[20] Beverly's route home included driving through parts of Canada, Michigan, Wisconsin, South Dakota, Wyoming, Nevada and San Francisco before reaching Los Angeles. "I put 5,000 miles on my new Chevy before arriving home," she said. "I stopped by Yellowstone Park and was chased by a bear! I honestly can't remember when I've been more frightened."[21]

About two months after Beverly returned to Los Angeles, she received the disappointing news that *Decoy* would not be renewed for a second season, "The producers decided that they didn't have enough money to continue, so production stopped." The series aired in reruns for seven years after being re-titled *Police Woman*.[22]

11. Coco La Salle, the Lady Pirate

After *Decoy*, it took a few months for Beverly to line up work, but then she was back to an almost non-stop schedule of guest star roles.

With *Decoy* still in first run syndication across the country, Beverly made several promotional appearances on local television talk shows and gave numerous newspaper interviews in which she described the show's often hectic and unconventional production routine. During one conversation with Dave Kaufman (*Variety*), she quipped that they had to do takes "between hammering on construction of sets for future [episodes]."[1]

Then on September 11, 1958, *The Hollywood Reporter* announced that Beverly would be co-starring with Tom Tryon in two episodes of *Walt Disney Presents: Tales of Texas John Slaughter* ("Killers from Kansas" and "Showdown at Sandoval"). Beverly recalled meeting the head of the studio on the set. "I met Walt Disney ... and I was a nervous wreck. He was such a sweet man and so very understanding."[2] She also described him as "pixie-like with a lovely smile."[3]

Beverly's role was just the opposite of her recently completed series. In *Killers from Kansas* she played the leader of a gang of bank robbers. In an interview for the Copley News Service, Beverly said, "I was a cold-blooded killer.... There was one scene where I walk up to an old man in his doorway. He is terribly frightened. He pleads with me not to hurt him. Naturally, I pull out my gun and shoot him dead. If you want to know why, I'll tell you. I didn't like the color of his eyes."

A couple of months later, Beverly was offered what would turn out to be one of the most outlandish, yet at the same time charming and enjoyable, characters of her career: Coco La Salle, a Lady Pirate, in the CBS-TV series *Yancy Derringer* (1958–59).[4]

Yancy Derringer starred Jock Mahoney as a former Confederate Army officer, riverboat owner and secret agent for the City of New Orleans Administrator in 1868. Derringer and his Pawnee Indian sidekick do their bit to clean up crime and international intrigue in the Big Easy. Beverly made two appearances on the series, "The Fair Freebooter" and "The Wayward Warrior." Her performances were so well-received that there was a serious effort on the part of the show's creators to put together a new series based on her character.[5]

In a brief interview with Allen Rich, Beverly talked about Coco La Salle. "I recently did two *Yancy Derringer* films in which I played Coco, a pirate girl. Naturally, when I went into New Orleans I had to disguise myself. If they caught Coco they'd have ... hung her or something. One time I was a flower girl; another time a society woman; and the next time, a Frenchman!"[6] Beverly loved working on the show and was disappointed that a "Coco La Salle—Lady Pirate" spin-off series never materialized. "I would have done it," she said. "She was a great character. I loved working on that show. They gave me wonderful things to do on it." She also commented on her co-star, Jock Mahoney. "Jock was just the best. Richard Garland and I knew Jocko for years when we were married. We were friends. He was not an actor. He had been a stunt man.... He was such a good-looking man — especially in that series — so big and tall."[7]

Most of the shows Beverly worked on during her career were professionally handled and, as most actors will readily agree, the business of acting is give and take. Occasionally, however, an actor will run into "a star" who thinks he or she is bigger than their material. One such encounter occurred during the filming of Four Star Production's *Trackdown* series which starred Robert Culp. The episode was "Hard Lines" and Beverly played the wife of a Civil War soldier who, accused of desertion, returns home and is met by an angry mob. The deserter is eventually killed, although Culp's character Texas Ranger Hoby Gilman, tries to save his life.

Beverly was so upset over the way her scene had been butchered when it eventually aired that she didn't hold back when interviewed about it a few years later by Dwight Newton of *The San Francisco Examiner*. "Once on a *Trackdown* show ... she had to react to the shocking news that her husband had just been killed. Beverly gave it her emotional everything. But whose face got the close-up when it was shown on home screens? Robert Culp's. Beverly blew her top: 'Who gives a damn how Bob Culp looks when I've just heard my husband's dead?' she raged. 'By the time the camera got to me, I looked like a complete fool.'"[8]

Years later, Beverly's opinion of Culp had not mellowed. "He was so busy being Robert Culp that he was very difficult to work with. I usually never find that. I usually find people who are giving, but Robert Culp was cold. He wanted you to know that you were in the scene with Robert Culp.... I didn't feel like he gave me anything. He didn't give a damn whether I was there or not. I just did not like that man."[9]

On April 9, 1959, *The Hollywood Reporter* noted, "Lon Chaney, Beverly Garland, Frieda Inescort, Richard Crane, Bruce Bennett and Douglas Kennedy have been cast in *The Alligator People* rolling Monday [April 13] under the API banner for 20th Fox release. Roy Del Ruth is directing..."

Beverly freely admitted that she had more trouble keeping a straight face while making this film than any other. "You have to play these kind of pictures for real — you really have to play them so straight because if you don't, people will not believe you. And that was probably the hardest picture to play straight that I have ever appeared in. When I looked at [co-star Crane] in that alligator makeup and had to say, 'I love you, anyway,' well, I thought I'd die! Oh, I was very good in this picture up until he arrived with his alligator head. I almost lost it then!"[10]

Beverly credits director Del Ruth with keeping everyone focused. "The attitude of the cast and crew was tongue-in-cheek, but Roy Del Ruth did not treat it as a 'quickie' movie. He really didn't. He worked very hard and worked with us all really hard to make it as realistic as possible. This wasn't an exploitation film ... it was a 'B' movie. He didn't laugh much during filming — he didn't think it was very funny. He took it very seriously. Thank God for him because he's really the one that kept our sanity. I must say, there were a couple of times that I just fell apart laughing so hard. If it weren't for Roy, who looked at me as if to say, 'After all, we are doing *Gone with the Wind*,' I think I never would have made it."[11]

One scene required Beverly to walk through a swamp infested with alligators. The swamp was faked but the gators were real. Incredibly, she wasn't bothered about doing the scene. "I have worked with so many snakes and animals of all sorts, that alligators just don't bother me. I worked with this incredible boa constrictor when I did *Curucu, Beast of the Amazon*, which was 20 feet long and it didn't bother me. Alligators, lions.... I can work with them very well. They're just another actor."[12]

As seriously as she tried to play her scenes, there were two occasions where she did "lose it." "I was all right from the beginning of the film up until I found my husband in that wonderful sanitarium and then I just fell apart. That was the end of me. There was that one scene where I had to be a bit romantic and console my poor husband and this was probably the most difficult scene I had to do in the film. This was when he was pretty much an alligator — and I had to say to him, 'I'll love you — no matter what'— which I think took me a good half a day to say! They almost had to film that on the back of my head, but I managed to get through it. That was very hard. Laugh? I thought I'd die. And I'm sure Richard Crane was smirking but you couldn't tell because he had his alligator makeup on. He could snort and giggle and nobody would know it!"[13]

The other occasion where it got so bad on the set that director Del Ruth had to call a halt to production occurred during the scene where Beverly had to go to the clinic to see her husband, who is slowly turning into an alligator. "I walk in," Beverly recalled, "and here they have these guys in these long white robes with this kind of hat thing on their heads, and I tell you, they all looked like they had urinals on their heads! I started to laugh — I laughed so hard that tears came to my eyes. The costume department didn't know how to do this properly because, you see, naturally as you turned into an alligator, your head got quite large and they didn't know what to put over them. So they put these white things on their heads so you wouldn't see the alligator makeup in this particular scene. Well, we did not film for three hours. Every time these things would walk down the hall I would just ... crack up. I couldn't recite a line of dialogue. Then the director began to look at them and it started to get to him too after a while. I guess we must have lost close to half a day of shooting time. Oh, that was so funny."[14]

Although Beverly had worked well with all the members of the cast, she had a particular soft spot for Lon Chaney, Jr. "Lon, I thought, was fabulous, fun and easy. It was fascinating to listen to him talk about his dad and all the things that he remembered about his father's career. He was a favorite person of mine."[15] *The Alligator People* completed principal photography on April 28, 1959, and was released on a twin bill with *Return of the Fly* on August 26, 1959.

"About 20 years after I made the picture," Beverly confided, "I went over to the May Company's pet shop one day. As I was waiting my turn to pay, I noticed there was a little piece of paper on the cash register and on it was a picture of an alligator man and a girl trying to fend it off. The caption under the picture read, 'Oh, the Alligator People always want the same thing!' I took a good look at it and said, 'That's me!' The sales clerk was momentarily startled and said, 'What?' I pointed to the young woman and I said, 'That's me — Beverly Garland. Somebody's taken that from the *Alligator People* ad." The clerk explained that he saw it in a magazine and thought it was very funny, so he cut it out and stuck it on his register. He looked at me and said, 'Gee, would you autograph it?' I said, 'Sure.' and I signed it for him."[16]

On April 30, two days after Beverly left the set of *The Alligator People*, *The Hollywood Reporter* announced, "Beverly Garland has been cast by producer Charles Marquis Warren as femme lead in 'The Incident of the Roman Candles' segment of CBS-TV's *Rawhide*. It would be the first of Beverly's three guest star roles on the series.[17]

Beverly remembered the series co-star Clint Eastwood as having "a great face" and that he was "a cute kid." She also recalled how upsetting it was to hear of Eric Fleming's accidental death some years later. "Eric's death was very, very sad." she said. "I can imagine that Eric — wherever he made that picture in South America — wanted to do his own stunts. He always did all his own stunt work. He got caught in those rapids and that was the end of him. He was very young and talented. He was doing so beautifully, career-wise. It just made you want to cry. Fillmore [Beverly's husband] and I knew him. We used to see him in the neighborhood. He was always barefoot. He was his own man and he did what he wanted to do. Fillmore and I really liked him."[18]

In 1953, Beverly filmed the pilot for Rod Cameron's *City Detective* series. The series sold. Three years later, she was signed to film the pilot for Cameron's next series *State Trooper* and again the series sold. When Cameron began planning his third series, *Coronado 9*, in which he played Dan Adams (a former Naval Officer who opens his own private eye business), he insisted that Beverly be cast not only in the pilot show but in one other episode as well.[19] The pilot was called "The Widow of Kill Cove" and in it Beverly played the wife of an escaped convict who attempts to steal Cameron's yacht and leave the country. Most of the half-hour show was shot on a boat off the coast of San Diego. Beverly recalled that working on this particular show was fraught with problems.

> We did that one show on a sailboat, and everybody got so sick — except me. I took a pill and I didn't get sick at all. But everybody else was so seasick. The sound man was down below moaning and groaning. We tried to film it without the sound man but when we got back, they called me and said, "Beverly, we have to dub everything." I said, "Everything?" They said, "Yes, everything!" You couldn't hear any of our dialogue with the boat creaking and the sound man who was not too well. I'll never forget that we had to dub the *whole show*.
>
> It's okay if you have to go back and do a few lines because a train comes by and you can't hear the dialogue but the whole show — from beginning to end. Dubbing is so hard because you try really hard to do it the same way but it's not the same because you're not as emotionally connected as you were then when you were actually doing the scene. You're just standing in front of a microphone trying to bring it all back.
>
> You watch the film and they play your lines and then they say, "Okay." So you've got the rhythm, and then you hear in your earphones four signal sounds and on the fifth beat, you have to match how your mouth is moving — that your mouth says the same thing that it says up there. You can hear yourself so it's a whole different kind of acting.
>
> So what you are trying to do is copy exactly what you hear on the original soundtrack and make it sound like your screaming and the monster is coming, or you're madly in love, or whatever the heck it's all about. It's now copy time.[20]

Once again, Cameron's series sold. Beverly proved to be his "lucky charm" a third time.[21]

Impressed with her performances in *Tales of Texas John Slaughter*, Walt Disney signed Beverly for two episodes of *Walt Disney Presents: The Nine Lives of Elfego Baca* with Robert Loggia in the title role. Baca was a former gunman who turned to the law, first as a sheriff and then as an attorney.[22] The first of the episodes ("Move Along, Mustangers") went into production around June 18, 1959. Beverly explained what it was like working at the legendary Disney Studios: "Actors used to say that everybody at Disney had gone through analysis because the cop on the beat was nice, as was the guy who let you in at the gate. Everybody was so darn nice that they must have gone through some metamorphosis. Everybody couldn't wait to work at Disney, where people smiled all the time ... where everyone is so kind, fabulous and sweet."[23]

A reporter for *The Sunday Star Bulletin* on the set of *Elfago Baca* witnessed firsthand how far Beverly would go to give her viewers a realistic performance. The eyewitness explained that normally after a film shoot, the scene's props and furnishings were stored away for future films. However, after filming *Elfago Baca and the Mustangers*— Beverly's two-part episode in the series — most of the sets were totally destroyed and that the actress herself was equally culpable. "One of the guilty 'wreckers' was petite, 105-pound ... star Beverly Garland. In aiding the man of her choice, played by Brian Keith ... she is called on to participate ... in a free for all fight in the town's general store. Beverly ... slugged clerks with bolts of cloth and forced them in retreat amidst a barrage of fruit, vegetables, pots and pans, wash boards and saddle packs." Beverly also helped her fiancé pull an outlaw from his retreating horse and fight her way through the streets of the town with "flailing fists and slashing nails." According to the reporter, when the scenes were completed, director George Sherman ordered the rubble that was left be sent to the scrap pile.[24]

Beverly remembered another funny incident while filming a Western:

> In those days, you did all your own riding and all your own jumping and just about everything else too. There was a Western I did — I can't remember if it was a movie or a television show, probably a TV show — and I was the head of a bandit gang. The gang rode up and since I was the head of this gang, I had all these big guys who were stuntmen riding around me. They liked me — all the stuntmen always like me — so they would ride very close to keep me on the horse. And you know they ride so well that one would have his arm behind me and another one would have his arm the other way around me and nobody knew. So half the time I really wasn't sitting in the saddle but my horse was running and we were all riding as a team and I rode right along with them because they were holding me up!
>
> But this one time we were supposed to ride to the bottom of a hill where a funeral was taking place above, and were all supposed to get off the horses — all the stuntmen and myself — and run up the hill as fast as we can to the funeral. And every time we rode up, I was the first one up to the funeral.
>
> Finally the director said, "Why are you always the first one up to the top of the hill, Beverly? I don't understand." So I told him, "Well, when my horse stops, I fall off and I start running. All these other people have to get off one leg at a time. I don't get off the horse, I fall off. I can't just stand there waiting for them, so I run up the hill; that's why I'm always first!" Naturally, when you fall off a horse, you're off very fast! That was so funny. I'll never forget it.[25]

12. Where in the World Is Beverly Garland?

During the summer of 1959, Beverly offered her services as a volunteer at the UCLA Medical Center. "I have been working with sick children," she explained, "helping out in the delivery room and also in emergency. I especially enjoyed helping the doctors in the delivery room. A brand new baby is a delight to behold—every time you see one it is a complete new miracle."[1]

At summer's end, Beverly was given the only female role in an episode titled "The Four of Us Are Dying" in Rod Serling's *Twilight Zone* series for CBS-TV. In it, she would also be making her singing debut. What was startling about that was the fact that Beverly had a range of exactly one note!

It's a rare occasion when an actor receives praise for a performance on the set. Beverly recalled what series creator Serling had to say to her at the end of the shoot. "Rod Serling told me, 'I can't believe what you've done with this part ... you're bringing so much more into it ... things that I really never even thought were in the script. I just want to tell you how fabulous I think you are.' I think that was one of the nicest compliments I ever got about my acting."[2] As far as her character's singing ability, no one made any negative observations about it.

Two weeks after she filmed "Shipment from Kihei" for the ABC-TV series *Hawaiian Eye*, Beverly was flying to the real Hawaiian Islands on the first leg of her "round the world" working vacation.[3] A notice in the October 7, 1959, edition of *Variety* announced, "Beverly Garland has been set for featured roles in two California Studios pilots filming this month in Japan. She'll be featured next week opposite Jerome Thor in 'Rogue for Hire,'[4] then ... Bernard Girard's untitled pilot ["The Man"] starring Neville Brand." (Girard had previously directed Beverly in her Emmy-nominated *Medic* episode "White Is the Color" and she had appeared with Neville Brand in 1949's *D.O.A.*)

In a letter Beverly wrote shortly after she returned from her journey, she said, "On October 13, I left for Japan to do a TV pilot with Neville Brand. I spent four weeks there...."[5] Beverly recalled that California Studios was "going to do a series starring Neville Brand.... But then it just fell apart; it never went anywhere. I don't think they ever aired it.... The funny thing about being in Japan was that when we went into the studio—which was really like an old barn—I walked into what was to be my character's apartment and all of the furniture was scaled down to that of a dwarf! I had to bend down to get to the drawers, because many of the Japanese people are rather short, so they scale everything down to their height. I mean, I felt like a giant in my own apartment with all this funny little furniture—we had to change most of it. That was funny, I thought.

"Then the makeup man came to my room and he had all of these little pots of paint — white, green, blue, pink. I thought, no, I don't see how this is going to work out. He might have been fine but I had a feeling I would look like a painted doll. And he would spend hours doing my makeup, [and] when he ended up, with all the blending of all these colors, it really wasn't too bad. I could never talk to him to tell him anything because he didn't speak a word of English. But it was fun. I loved that location.[6]

The Japanese shoot was covered in the industry papers. *Variety* (October 21, 1959) revealed, "Filming of pilot series tentatively titled 'The Searchers' got under way on Monday, October 19th.... Neville Brand stars in the role of U.S. Treasury Agent looking for control of narcotics in Far East."[7]

The Hollywood Reporter (November 4, 1959) interviewed Beverly during the shoot. "Filming exteriors is murder," she confessed. "Swarms of Japanese crowd around us and the director goes nuts trying to get them to turn off their transistor radios, which have become even more popular than cameras here."[8] Luckily for Beverly, all of her most important scenes were filmed away from the street crowds. Her portrayal of an addict is riveting. The pilot never aired although 16mm prints of the show are known to be in existence.

On October 31, 1959, *The Japan Times* reported, "Having completed her work here, Miss Garland is enjoying a one-week sightseeing tour in Tokyo and Nikko. She will fly to Hong Kong next weekend for a five-day shopping spree before continuing on to Bangkok, Rome, Paris and London."

Beverly had been in contact with her parents all during her time in Japan and later in Thailand before leaving for Rome, where her mother Millie Fessenden was to meet up with her. Beverly's father James Fessenden explained what happened in a letter.

> After shooting was completed, [Beverly] planed to Hong Kong (which she described as "Fabulous") to Bangkok (which she described as "old").
> Millie left California for New York via jet. She was to transfer to another plane which would whisk her off to Rome ... and a rendezvous with Bev. Things didn't work out as planned. Rain and fog forced a Newark [New Jersey] landing and Millie had to take a cab to New York. On the parkway just outside the city, the cab broke down.... After two hours another cab ... deposited Millie at Idylwild [JFK]. Her flight, of course, had departed.... Three hours later, she secured a seat on Air France and was on her way — to Paris, that is. At Paris she had to wait several more hours to make connections for Rome. As you may well imagine, she was pretty tired when she met Bev at the hotel.
> They enjoyed Rome immensely; they were even fortunate enough to have an audience with the Pope. Venice was next. From train to hotel by gondola...[9]

After Rome, Beverly and her mother also toured Florence and Milan. Paris was next. Beverly remarked in a correspondence that she "would have liked [the city] more in the Spring. Then on to Holland — I adored [it] because ... it's quaint and wonderful, then a plane to London. I worked in London doing a half-hour guest spot on another pilot...."[10]

The pilot was Trans-Continental Films Productions' *Dangerman* starring Patrick McGoohan. Beverly remembered her only European production very well.

> When I did *Dangerman* you could not work in England unless there was no way anyone else could do the part. If an English actor could not play the part, you could do it. They don't let Americans come over and work there. (We let everybody come over to the United States to work, however.) My part was a woman that was an American. Everybody who tested had an English accent. They were speaking American but they had an English accent speaking American. It didn't work. So they gave me the part.
> We filmed the show out in the country (I think it was at Pinewood Studios) and they put me

up in this boarding house. When you walked in, there was this huge fireplace with a fire burning and they had this big dining room. The boarding house lady gave me this huge room and I thought it had a fireplace in it but it was one of those things that you turn on and it glows but it doesn't give off any heat. There wasn't even a heater. It was so cold, cold, *cold*! The bathroom had a single 15-watt light bulb. So after a day on the set, I would walk into the boarding house with its roaring fireplace, past the dining room where all these men — there were mostly men who stayed at this house — were slurping their soup, up the stairs to my room where I would put on my heavy overcoat, take off my makeup — which I couldn't see in the dim light — and sleep in front of this "glow" because it "seemed" like a fireplace. I have never been so cold.[11]

Beverly also recalled working on this "very British" set. "They had a cart that would come around with tea, and then they had breakfast, and then they had tea, and then lunch, and then they had tea. So I had more than enough tea!" She also found herself beginning to identify with her cast and crew. As she explained, "On the third day the director came up to me and said, 'I'm going to have to tell you something. You're more English than the people who are English!' My speech was taking on a British inflection! I thought to myself, 'Oh my God! Of course, I knew nobody. I was all by myself and when I would get back to the boarding house I was surrounded by more locals and I had started to pick up on the way they spoke to me. I thought, 'Let me see — James Cagney — how the hell does he talk?' I tried a New York accent. Maybe I could get my American accent back if I talked like a New Yorker. I had the worst time trying to talk like an American. I was becoming 'terribly British' and I was 'so English that we can't really use you unless you talk American.' What the hell is 'talk American'? There were no Americans there. I couldn't hear anybody with my accent. There were only English accents. It was a difficult shoot — trying to talk like an American. However they talk! It was a week in Hell."[12]

The production ended just before the Christmas holidays and Beverly was able to get a plane home in time for Christmas Eve festivities.

On February 10, 1961, *The Hollywood Reporter* announced that *Dangerman* had sold to American television and would premiere on April 5, 1961, on CBS network with Beverly's pilot episode, "Bury the Dead." She had helped sell yet another series with her performance.[13]

13. *The Miracle Worker*

After her return to Hollywood, Beverly was as much in demand as she had been before she left for the Orient. She started the New Year and a new decade (the 1960s) with leading roles on *Perry Mason*, *Zane Grey Theater* and *Riverboat*.[1] She filmed a pilot of Guy Madison Productions' proposed new series *Jericho*. When NBC's *Laramie* premiered on March 29, 1960, Paul Baessler of *The Los Angeles Examiner* previewed the episode ("Saddle and Spur") and wrote, "Even if westerns aren't your cup of Sarsaparilla, look in on *Laramie* Tuesday night and see Beverly Garland, one of TV's finest actresses, in a role that's quite a departure even for this versatile young lady.... [Y]ou may not recognize her in Levis and a scraggly coiffure.... Miss Garland ... can be depended on to give competent — often outstanding — readings to a wide variety of roles."

During the filming of the show, a stagehand was overheard remarking, "Whew! I sure would hate to be married to her!" Beverly was told of the remark and asked director Tommy Carr if she might have went over the top with her character. "Play it your way," Carr replied. "You don't want to marry him!"[2]

After she completed a guest spot on *Tales of Wells Fargo* (the title role in "Pearl Hart"), Beverly was approached about taking the female lead in a proposed series, *The Lawyer*. The show dealt with a group of attorneys handling international cases and sounded quite promising, but Beverly turned it down.[3] In an interview for *Los Angeles Mirror News*, Beverly explained her reasons to Hal Humphrey: "The plan called for me to be in the lead on alternate weeks. But after reading a few of the scripts, it was easy to see I would wind up sharpening pencils for my male counterpart along about the fifth installment...."[4] The producer who offered Beverly the series was Hubbell Robinson, whose production credits included *Thriller*.

On April 29, 1960, Mike Connolly of *The Hollywood Reporter* offered readers the following scoop: "Beverly Garland may slide into Anne Bancroft's starring base when Anne summers from *The Miracle Worker*." To be offered a starring role in a Broadway play was a lifelong dream for Beverly, and yet she declined. Beverly explained why she had to make the choice to stay in Hollywood:

> I was asked if I could go back to New York to do *The Miracle Worker*. Anne Bancroft was going to go to London and then do the movie and Fred Coe wanted somebody to replace her on Broadway.[5] So they called and asked me if I would be interested in doing it. I had never done Broadway. I'd done a lot of theater but by that time my career had been in pictures and on television. I had not done a lot of theater now and at the time that I was debating this, I had been dating Fillmore and he had said to me, "If you go to New York, I won't be here when you come back." I said, "You won't?" He said, "Nope. If you do *The Miracle Worker* then I won't be here when you come

back." And I believed him. Of course he would have been there when I got back! But he had me and so I said I wasn't going to do it.

Interestingly enough, years later, I asked Suzanne Pleshette, who was hired after I had turned it down, about her experience with the play. The story is that Suzie went to do *The Miracle Worker* and it was just hell because they wanted Anne Bancroft and Suzie got up there and she was doing the part her way but the director kept saying, "When Annie did it, it was done like so and so." But Suzanne Pleshette is Suzanne Pleshette and Beverly Garland is Beverly Garland and nobody but Anne Bancroft can be Anne Bancroft. We're not all clones. So Suzie said it was just the worst thing that she ever did.

Patty Duke apparently didn't want Annie Sullivan to be Suzanne Pleshette either. She wanted her to be Anne Bancroft. She was very mean to her. So it was probably the best thing that ever happened to me that I didn't do it.[6]

Instead of starring on Broadway, Beverly headed to Las Vegas—and got married. "I was living in Beverly Hills in a great apartment," Beverly explained, "and my girlfriend Ellen was going with a man by the name of Keller Hausells. One day she said to me, 'Kell has this friend by the name of Fillmore Crank ... would you like to have a blind date with him?' I said, 'Okay. Yeah, that would be fine.'"

Fillmore came over and I walked in and I thought, "Ooh, a nice-looking man." And we went out to dinner and then he asked me out again. He didn't know what to do with me. Didn't know where to take me. We went out to dinner again and that was fine. I loved to hear him talk because he could talk about anything and he was wonderful. I had been going with Hollywood-type men that are sharp and fast—that kind of conversation—and Fillmore was a very slow talker. He was not a jazzy man.

I went out with him three or four times and I remember saying to my stand-in, Lorraine Colway, "You know, Lorraine, I don't know." She said, "You know, Beverly. Come on, he's the best person you've ever met. He's so good...."

So then he asked me if I'd go bowling. "Bowling? I really don't want to go bowling." He didn't know what to do with me. Where to take me. I talked to Lorraine again. I said, "You know Lorraine, I really don't think this is going to work. I mean, I just don't think so."

Fillmore was building houses in Palm Springs and at that point, he didn't want to go out with me any more either. He'd had it with me and I'd had it with him. Not long afterwards, Kell said to Fillmore, "I'm going to have a birthday party for Ellen and I would like you to invite Beverly." Fillmore said, "Well, I'd love to go to the birthday party but I'd like to take anybody but Beverly." Kell said, "I want you to take Beverly because I want Ellen to have everybody that she knows there. I don't want some strange girl coming." Fillmore reluctantly said okay.

In the meantime, Ellen said to me, "Kell is having a birthday party for me and I'd like you to bring Fillmore." I said, "I'll come to the birthday party if I can date anybody but Fillmore." I didn't want to go with Fillmore. She said, "But I want people that I know at the party." I finally said okay.

When Fillmore called to ask me to the party, I said I'd go. The night of the party, Fillmore got caught in traffic. He was one and a half hours late and I was so mad. First of all, I didn't want to go with him anyway and now he was so late.

The party was at this Japanese restaurant. At the restaurant there was this long, long table and he sat by Ellen and Kell and I sat at the other end. We didn't speak during the whole party. By the time the dinner was over, there was just the four of us left and Ellen said, "Let's go to the Little Club and hear some music."[7] So we went and the music was very romantic. I remembered that I had talked again with Lorraine and she said to me, "Beverly, do not let this man go. Don't do this! He's too wonderful." I said, "Okay, I'll take another look at him." So I'm sitting there at the bar and they're playing this very romantic music and I looked at him and I thought, "You know, first of all, he's terribly attractive and ... ah well, maybe I ought to give him another chance. Maybe I shouldn't drop him." So we had a very wonderful evening and I started going out with him again. Three months later, Fillmore asked me to marry him — or I asked him to marry me — I can't remember which was which, and we got married in Las Vegas. Fillmore didn't have the three dollars for the marriage license so I had to pay that. But it was okay.[8]

Fillmore Crank recalled how he met Beverly:

I'd gotten involved with this building project down in Palm Desert and I had a lot of free time at night. I used to watch this show called *Decoy* and I thought she was the sexiest woman I'd ever seen and wouldn't I like to get a chance with her. I had been dating some Hollywood actresses. One of them was Allison Hayes and another was Linda Christian. Allison was a very voluptuous

Mr. And Mrs. Fillmore Pajeau Crank on their wedding day in Las Vegas, May 23, 1960.

girl. She really had a figure — knock you out! We had been out on a date and I was driving her home. We saw a lot of drive-in theaters along the way and I noticed that she was in every picture. I said, "Allison, how come you work so much?" She said, "Because I work cheap." I loved that response. Very democratic — very honest. I liked her. She was a cute girl. She wasn't a phony. Far from it.[9]

I wasn't single for long — about three years after my wife died. I knew this gal named Marilyn. I was one of three or four of us that were "available" and she would arrange dates with these starlets. I don't remember some of their names. All of them, however, were in the movies. All pretty. It was a prerequisite. Linda Christian was Tyrone Power's ex-wife. I had a tough time with her because she was pretty wild. She was a dancer and that didn't go anywhere. But I was going out with her just as I met Beverly.

My oldest friend and partner, Keller Hausells, called me and asked, "Would you like a blind date?" We were going out to dinner on a double date and I said, "I'll take anything. You know, I'm available." And Keller said, "Well, this gal is named Beverly Garland." And I thought, "Ye gods! That's the girl I want!" We went out and I thought that she was a smart-ass — a Hollywood smart-ass. And she thought that I was a dull dimwit. So we really hit if off!

You know, you're able to adjust. I could see something in this girl that I liked and I guess she saw something. We went out a few more times and we got pretty thick. Then why we got married, I'll never know!

I don't remember where I proposed. It was probably down in the desert, because I was down there a lot. We were building there and Beverly had come down with me and she made a crack to my site manager that she decided she was going to marry me. My manager Bob Higgins said, "Look, there's nobody going to marry Fillmore Crank. No way." She tells the story that that's what did it. Since when was somebody going to tell me what I can or cannot do? So I got maneuvered into it.[10]

The first Mrs. Crank was his USC sweetheart Barbara Logan. They were married in 1942 and had two children, Cathleen, who was born in July 1944, and Fillmore Jr., who was born in September 1947. Tragically, Barbara was killed in a car accident in 1957, leaving Fillmore with two young children to raise alone. "During this time," Fillmore said, "I obviously circulated the network of available ladies and then I met Beverly and I'd seen enough. I guess I met her in January and we got married in May."[11]

Beverly didn't hesitate to marry Fillmore even though he was a widower with two teenage children because as she put it, "I was crazy!... I just felt Disney mothers do this and I certainly could be a Disney mother. Walt Disney always did these kind of wonderful stories, so I'll be a Disney mother. I'll just take these children and everything will be just fine. Ha!"

What Beverly failed to remember was that stepmothers in Disney films usually didn't fare well. Happily, though there were some rough patches along the way, the new Crank family handled the transition better than most. Beverly said,

I thought, "I can do this." But it was not easy raising children. I had never raised children, so what the hell did I know? Fillmore had to go every week to Palm Springs because he had these homes that he was trying to build and sell. A lot of them were furnished. So I went with him all the time and our housekeeper stayed with the children when I stayed in Palm Springs. Then I came home and found that the kids were climbing out the window at night and doing all these things. I said to Fillmore, "I can't come out with you any more. Somebody's got to watch these kids." I added. "Maggie is a sweet lady but she's a housekeeper. I'm the stepmother, so I have to be the one that stays."

I tried to raise his kids. I look back on those poor children and they had such a really terrible time. It was not easy for them. It was probably the hardest thing in the world for them to have a stepmother who was an actress, for God sakes! It was hard. They had lost their mother at a very early age ... and it was terribly traumatic.

Fillmore was young when he became a widower and he just didn't know what to do. He said to me many years later, "If I had only handled things similar to the way Fred MacMurray did on *My Three Sons*. But I didn't know."

Fillmore was a very good friend of Ward Bond and Ward was going to help him get through all of this. Ward said, "You know, I think you should send Cathleen to a boarding school and sell your house." Fillmore had a big, big house with horses. "Get out of there because it brings back memories of Barbara, and send Cathleen to a very prestigious school (which he did down in La Jolla) and then send Fillmore Jr. to a military school...." Fillmore sent Fill Jr. to one way out in the desert some place and the boy just cried all the time.

They had it tough and Fillmore just didn't know how to deal with this. The kids were troublesome but when you look at teenagers today, they weren't troublesome at all, really. But it's all relative. However, when I look back on their lives then, I think "Those poor babies. They didn't know how to express how hard it was for them."

When I think about that time with them, I think I never expected them to be my friend. I really treated them like they were my children. I was very much a disciplinarian — which was probably the right thing to have done. Oh, they tried to test me all the time, pitting me against Fillmore and that kind of thing. I think I could have done a much better job with those children if I had understood them more. Now we're into so much more physicality and more understanding of children than we were then. I really feel I failed them. I think Fillmore always thought that he failed them.[12]

Fillmore did credit Beverly for keeping the family together. "It worked out pretty good," he said. "We really never had any great friction. I think they resented the fact that I remarried — we got married. But I think that that got absorbed slowly but surely. I don't think children ever get over losing a parent. I don't think they ever get over divorce, either. My parents were divorced in the 1930s during the Depression. It really bugged me as a kid. My parents — I don't think they spoke to each other much for many years and that hurts.

"But at this time, Beverly has done so much for this family. She's contributed her vitality; she's contributed her integrity and respect, and that has to help. There was a lot of trouble when Cathleen was around 16. There were some problems with discipline — trying to keep these kids in line. It's not exactly *My Three Sons*. I always felt bad that I never did that. I didn't know. I didn't know. I thought giving the kids an education was important — which it wasn't. It didn't do any good. They should have been home. But nobody got in any trouble. We never had a drug problem or drinking problem, or anything like that."[13]

Not only did Beverly try to keep her new family from falling apart, she also had a vibrant acting career to maintain. And, to top it off, Beverly's very next job was a guest spot on *Hong Kong* in an episode called "Freebooter" with ex-boyfriend Rod Taylor.

14. *Stump the Stars*

On October 6, 1960, Beverly was back in Westerns, this time playing a murderous bank robber in Four Star's *Stagecoach West*. The episode was "The Storm" and starred Wayne Rogers and Tom Drake. The series was produced by Vincent Fennelly and this particular episode was directed by Tom Carr. Under any other circumstances, this would not set off alarm bells but Beverly clearly recalled what happened the last time she had worked for Fennelly and Carr. Both men had been behind the camera on her first Western film, *The Fighting Lawman*, back in 1953. That's when, on her very first day, during the filming of her first scene, Beverly broke her nose in three places.

Well, on her very first day on *Stagecoach West*, during the filming of her first scene, Beverly fell and split her knee wide open! However, this time the trouper was not about to be replaced, and she hobbled her way through the shoot. Beverly finished up the year with stints on *Michael Shayne* and *Thriller*.

Beverly's husband Fillmore was kept busy supervising his housing development in Palm Springs, Desert Bel Air, a forty-acre community of single family homes, across from the Eldorado Country Club.[1] Someone once asked Beverly what Fillmore thought of the golf course and she replied, "I don't think he's ever seen it. He's always out in the trees and the weeds."[2] The golf course location did attract one buyer of note, however. Fillmore built a $150,000 hacienda for avid golfer and U.S. President Dwight D. Eisenhower, who planned to move in directly after the inauguration of his successor, John F. Kennedy.[3]

Beverly was equally busy in Hollywood filming "Between Two Guns" for CBS-TV's *Checkmate* and pilots for several proposed series. The first was the Fess Parker vehicle *Russell*, based on the American Old West artist Charles Russell. Arthur Hiller directed the Borden Chase teleplay titled "Night of the Wrangler."[4]

On February 5, 1961, Hank Grant of *The Hollywood Reporter* noted that Beverly was being sought for several new shows: "Beverly Garland ... guested 11 pilots, none of which failed to sell, resulting in a flock of 'insurance' bids from producers. Currently on MGM-TV's *Dr. Kildare* pilot, same studio wants her for *Darrow for the Defense* ... *Beverly Hills Is My Beat* pilot ... and Goodson-Todman wants her for their *Medical Detective* initialer."[5]

But it was Paul Baessler of *TV Weekly* who put it best when he noted, "Bev has participated in almost as many launchings as Helen of Troy."[6]

The day pre-production began on the *Dr. Kildare* pilot "Twenty Four Hours," Beverly was told to report to MGM at 3 P.M. for wardrobe fittings. Upon arrival, she was told to wait and someone would come for her. By 4:30 no one had appeared and Beverly stopped one of the wardrobe employees to ask if someone would look for the supervisor on the show. The woman was clearly annoyed and replied, "My dear, this is a motion picture studio. When we have time to get to you television people, we will."[7] Fortunately, the rest of her time at the studio was much more amicable by comparison.

Beverly recalled a rather strange request by the production team when she began filming *Dr. Kildare*. "Someone asked me if they could take my blood. I said, 'What?' and they said, 'It's never been done on television before but we want to show it all so everybody knows that we are taking this girl's blood in one continuous shot. We'd like to do that.' I said,

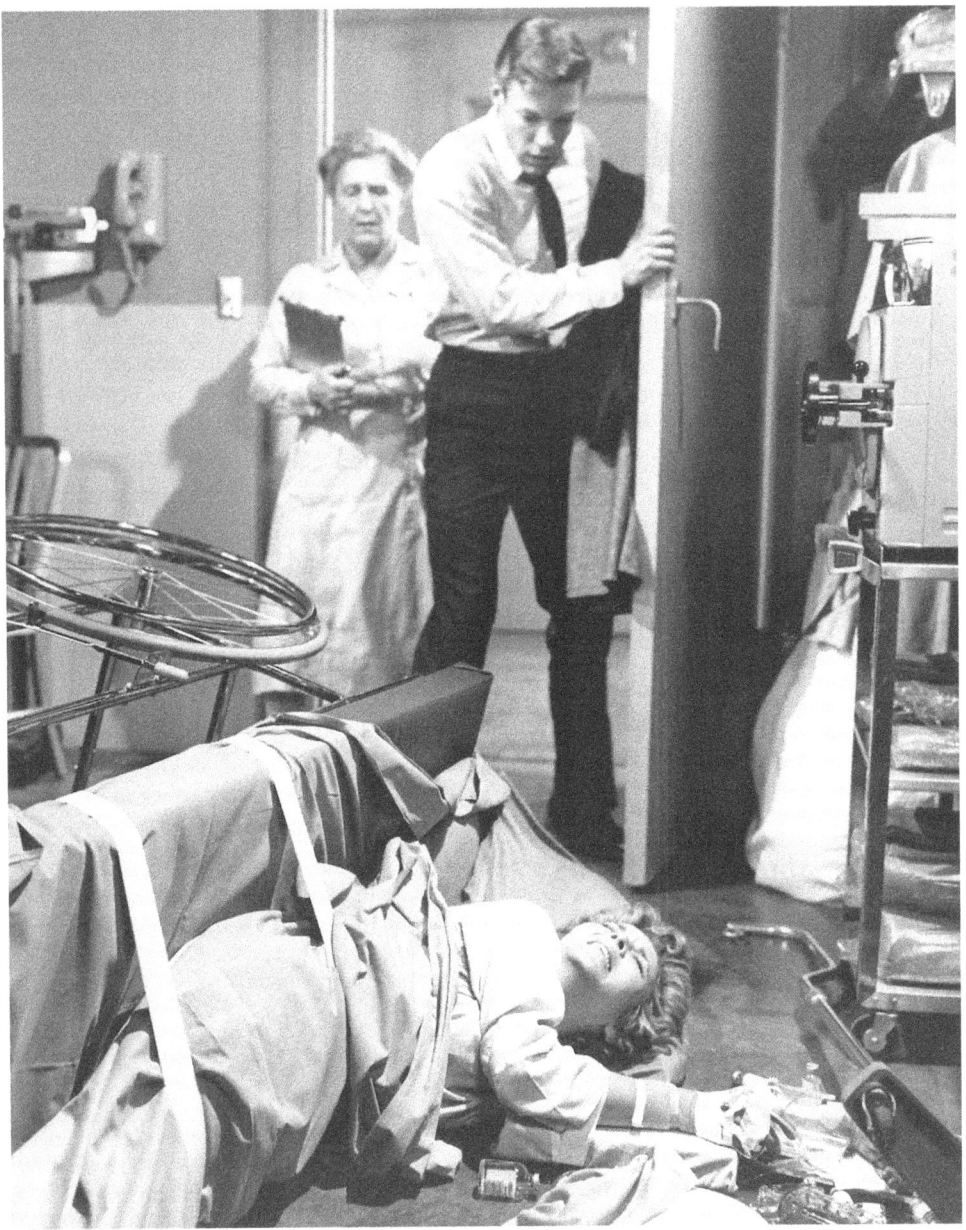

Beverly's strong performance as a suicidal alcoholic in "Twenty-Four Hours" (September 28, 1961), the pilot for *Dr. Kildare*, helped sell the series. (Pictured: Richard Chamberlain, unidentified, Beverly on floor.)

'Well, okay. You can.'" Perhaps it was a lucky thing for Beverly that the story didn't involve her character having open heart surgery![8]

She was, however, involved in a minor emergency while filming. Beverly's character was supposed to attempt suicide by slashing her wrists. She got so carried away that when the makeup man removed the liquid chocolate that substituted for blood in those black-and-white television days, there was real blood underneath and Beverly had to be taken to a local hospital for treatment by a real doctor![9]

About two weeks before *Dr. Kildare* premiered on NBC-TV, Beverly went on an East Coast promotion tour for the series with appearances in New York City and Boston. She described what those promotional tours were like: "You go to a hotel. They have lots of different people who go to these events who are promoting a picture or a television show. They have rooms set up with newspaper people and some of them bring cameras. They tape an interview with you. It's like a book tour except you are promoting a movie or a television series. They are fun because you know what you will be talking about. I went on a similar tour for *The Joker Is Wild* and *New Orleans Uncensored*."[10]

Dr. Kildare premiered on September 28, 1961, to excellent reviews for both the series and Beverly's performance. Hank Grant of *The Hollywood Reporter* (October 2, 1961) wrote, "A smash guest performance by Beverly Garland, whose role of an alcoholic threaded the main plot of the opener." Charles Denton of *The Los Angeles Examiner* (September 28, 1961) noted, "The debut show also offers Beverly Garland an opportunity to deliver one of her most impressive TV performances as an hysterical alcoholic whose child has been taken from her."

Beverly had nothing but praise for the star of the show, Richard Chamberlain: "He was tall and cute and charming. He was just as sweet as he could be. He got one of his first breaks on *Dr. Kildare*. I always felt that he was very, very good. He did very well with his career since. I think he could have done more, but I felt he had a whole other life that prevented him from doing more with it. Although Richard Chamberlain was a star, he could have been a much bigger star. I thought he was a wonderful person. I liked him."[11]

Adjusting to her marriage and instant family was sometimes difficult when old habits have to change, as Beverly explained: "I used to get up at 3 o'clock in the morning and do my housework because then I had the whole day to do what I wanted to do. I remember Fillmore coming in the kitchen one morning and saying, 'Do you have to vacuum at three o'clock in the morning?' I said, 'But Fillmore, that's a good time for me because then it's over and I don't have to think about it all day.' He said, 'But I would like to sleep!'

"I'd been vacuuming for years at three in the morning and nobody bothered me about it. I looked at him like — it bothers you? When I was by myself, I did all my vacuuming and all my dusting. I did everything. I cleaned my house early in the morning and it was done. That had to stop. It was so hard because I didn't have the whole day any more. I should have gotten him a pair of earplugs."[12]

The day before her *Dangerman* episode ("Bury the Dead") premiered on CBS-TV, Beverly began work on "The Nine-Twenty Hero," an episode of MGM-TV's *The Asphalt Jungle*. About six weeks later, Beverly's unsold *Jericho* pilot starring Guy Madison ("A Rope for a Lady") was the final episode aired on CBS-TV's *Zane Grey Theater* (May 18, 1961). On May 21, just before Beverly and Fillmore left for Las Vegas to celebrate their first wedding anniversary, *The Asphalt Jungle* aired on ABC-TV.[13] After their return from Las Vegas, Beverly appeared on another prime time cop show, *87th Precinct*, created by popular novelist Ed McBain and starring Robert Lansing and Ron Harper.

Someone once said that "the road to Hell is paved with good intentions." Perhaps this is a fitting appellation for the movie *Stark Fear*. What began as a very intriguing idea by a group of amateur filmmakers quickly turned into a debacle—a torturous, misguided affair that slowly unravels before the viewers' eyes. But what is truly sad is the fact that all three of its principal players gave excellent performances in a film that deserved far less. Beverly's co-stars were Skip Homeier (who had recently appeared with her in *The Asphalt Jungle*) as her psychotic husband and Kenneth Tobey as her sympathetic boss. In true trouper style, none of these fine actors compromised themselves or tried to take the easy way out—even though one could hardly blame them if they did.

Stark Fear started out as the brainchild of three men: director Ned Hockman and screenwriter Dwight V. Swain (both faculty members of the film and journalism departments at the University of Oklahoma), and Joe S. Burke, a local businessman who owned his own public relations and advertising firm.[14] The trio had delusions that they could produce their own shoestring feature along the lines of *Marty* (1955) or the more contemporary *Never on Sunday* (1960), and make millions as these highly acclaimed films had done for their producers. They formed their own production company, B.H.S. Productions, Inc., and, according to one contemporary newspaper source, collected over $150,000 in the form of stock options which they had sold to several local businessmen.

They earmarked approximately $100,000 for the film, and production began on July 5, 1961, in Norman, Oklahoma, with a five-week shooting schedule. Most of the interiors were done in cheesy fraternity houses on campus, while exteriors were shot in and around Norman, as well as Lexington, Oklahoma, Eureka Springs, Arkansas, and at the Will Rogers Airport in Oklahoma City. Unfortunately, even the scenery that surrounds the action is pathetic with nothing but dust, nondescript main streets, oil rigs, cattle pens, and more dust! Not even the backdrop of what was once mystifyingly called "the little Switzerland of the south," Eureka Springs, is anything to wow the folks back home with picture postcards. At least *Marty* had New York City for a backdrop, and *Never on Sunday* had the beauty and charm of the Greek Isles![15]

This is only the beginning, however. What is more confusing is the actual premise of the film. Advertised as a psychological melodrama, *Stark Fear* is more about the horrors of spousal abuse. Ellen Winslow (Beverly) tries to help pay the household's mounting bills by taking a secretarial job. When hubby Gerald (Skip Homeier) discovers that she will be working for rival oilman Cliff Kane (Kenneth Tobey), he explodes with unjustified anger, and falsely accuses his wife of having an affair with Cliff. When he physically threatens her, Ellen flees the house and moves in with a friend (Hannah Stone).

Deeply upset and confused over her husband's aberrant behavior, she tries to smooth things over by going to his office. To her surprise, Ellen learns that Gerald hasn't been seen for several days and is now in danger of being fired. Ellen talks his boss into giving her some time to locate Gerald and sets off in search of her missing spouse. Ellen soon realizes that the man she thought she knew and loved has quite a disturbing past, and a very dark side to his personality.

While it makes an attempt or two at credibility, *Stark Fear* eventually stops short of committing itself to its own moral and social objectives and quickly sinks into the muck of the typical, shallow, sexploitation quickie of its era. Ellen's continued misguided loyalty to her hateful, brutal, and sadistic husband borders on the near pathological itself. Modern viewers will find themselves shouting warnings at their screens from the get-go, finally throwing their hands up in disgust when the victimized heroine continues to blame herself for her miscreant husband's deteriorating mental state.

Scripter Swain attempts to drive his points home with alternating sledgehammers and feathers, often using Ellen's friend (Stone), and on occasion even total strangers, as his pulpit to both pontificate and soothe the beleaguered heroine. Eventually, even he bites off his own tongue in this verbal diatribe.

Director Hockman fares even worse. His inexperience as a director is agonizingly obvious here, and at some point Skip Homeier took over the reins no doubt out of total frustration, and tried valiantly — though in the end, unsuccessfully — to salvage this mess.[16]

Beverly had plenty to say about *Stark Fear*. "Oh my God! Isn't that the worst thing you have ever seen?"

> The guy that ran the drama department of the University of Oklahoma decided he was going to make a movie and somebody told him about me and he came out to California. He told me that he had this script and they wanted to make a movie at the college. He was going to direct it. I read the script and I said, "It doesn't really make any...." And he interrupted, saying, "Don't worry about it. We're going to take it to the Cannes Festival. Scripts don't have to make any sense." I said, "They don't?" He said, "No, no, no, no, no.... The way it's filmed...."
>
> Now they paid me a lot of money. I had nothing to do that summer so I figured with that kind of money, why not? So Skip Homeier and I went out. The first day, it took about five and a half hours to set up the first shot. Skip looked at me and I looked at Skip and we said, "Well, this man doesn't know what he's doing. He has no idea."
>
> We sat down with the writer and tried to work on the script in an attempt to make some sense out of what the hell this was all about. Nobody would listen. We didn't know anything. They knew it all. Finally, it got so bad that Skip ended up directing the last part of the movie himself. It was just a fiasco. It was the worst thing that I have ever been in. I just took my money and left.[17]
>
> A couple of years later [1963], when I was pregnant with Carrington, a theater somewhere in Westwood played it and I called and asked, "You're showing *Stark Fear*?" The theater owner said, "Yes. I'm going to play it one more night. It opened last night and it was so bad that I'm playing it one more night ... then I'm never playing it again." I think it played only one night in every theater in the country and that was it.
>
> They had tried to do something along the lines of *Psycho* but they just could never get it right. Everybody in Norman, Oklahoma — from used car salespeople to the town's dog catcher — put money into it ... and it was a complete disaster. I wonder if he still has a job there at the college, that poor man ... and the writer — you couldn't talk to this writer. He was also a professor at the university. He taught journalism or something. You couldn't talk to these people. They wouldn't listen to you. They had made up their minds *exactly* what they were going to do ... and we were committed. I mean, we couldn't leave. So we did it and went home."[18]

Shortly after Beverly's return from Oklahoma, there was talk in the trades about the startup of a new independent film production company, Garmore Productions — a combination of Garland and Fillmore. Their first project was tentatively titled *Okai*, about an Apache Indian on the run who takes refuge in a mission. However, the project never went anywhere.

About a week after Beverly returned from Boston and her successful *Dr. Kildare* promotional tour, she received the devastating news that her beloved father, James A. Fessenden, had been killed in an automobile accident by a drunk driver.[19] Beverly recalled what happened that terrible day. "Fillmore and I were just married and my father had been on his way back from seeing a Beltone client in Palm Springs when he was hit head-on by a 27-year-old drunk driver — killing him immediately.

> My mother had come up to visit me. We had lunch and then we had gone to Orbachs on Wilshire Boulevard for some shopping. She then drove home to Riverside and I had decided to stop at a local food market. When I walked into the market, the manager who knew me said, "Beverly,

the butcher wants to speak to you for a minute." I thought it strange but I found the butcher who said, "Fillmore wants you to call him." I said to myself, "Jeez, It's 5:30 and I've got to get my stuff for dinner. I've got to get home. What does he want to talk to me for?"

In the meantime, my mother had arrived home and found that the dogs had not been brought in from their run. It was strange that Daddy hadn't brought in the dogs. All of a sudden the phone rang and the dry cleaning man my parents used said, "Mrs. Fessenden. I'm so sorry." She said, "Why?" He said, "Oh, that Jimmy has been killed." Of course, she had no idea. She had just walked in the house after having stayed with me for three days.

I went to the store pay phone and called Fillmore in Palm Springs and he said, "Honey?" and I said, "I'm at the Stop & Shop and I'm trying to get home." He said, "Are you okay?" and I said, "Yes. I'm okay ... what is it?" I knew something was wrong. (He told me later, "I just didn't know how to do this.") And then he told me what happened: "Your father has been killed." I screamed into the phone, "*Oh my god*!" I got in my car and I screamed all the way up the canyon. You don't believe what you've been told. It's not true. It's just not true. I have to see it.

I walked into the kitchen and my neighbor, who had heard me screaming, came over to ask me what was wrong and I said to her, "They say my father was killed and I've got to go. I've got to go!" My sweet little neighbor said, "okay," and we got in my car and she drove me all the way over to Riverside. I don't know how I would have done it without her.[20]

Beverly returned to work at the end of November with a powerful performance in "Summer Lightning" for the series *Bus Stop* under the direction of Robert Altman. In a cruel, ironic twist, Beverly's character Janie meets her end when the car she is driving careens off the road.

The following year started in Midland, Texas, when Beverly was asked to help work the phones for the annual March of Dimes Telethon, produced by Tom King. She worked over eighteen hours. On March 26, 1962, *The Hollywood Reporter* noted that Beverly had "landed her second singing role at MGM-TV. She'll play a night club songstress in the *Cain's Hundred* episode 'The Left Side of Canada.' Her first part as a warbler was in *The Twilight Zone*. Funny thing is, she can't sing." The premise of the show was an interesting one. Mark Richman starred as a former mobster lawyer who turned crimefighter and whose mission was to apprehend the 100 most dangerous gangsters in America. Unfortunately, the series only lasted one season so only about a third of those mobsters were actually pinched.

Once again, Beverly's talent for selling television series was proved when producer Elliot Lewis cast her in the premiere episode of *The Kraft Mystery Theater*. The pilot was titled "In Close Pursuit" and co-starred Jan Sterling and William Windom. Once again, Robert Altman was hired to direct. Sold as a replacement series for *The Perry Como Show* (the singer was on his annual 16-week vacation), the series opener featured Beverly as a waitress falsely accused of a murder.

Another star of the episode was a feline named Rhubarb whose salary was $100 per day. The script called for the cat to awaken Beverly so that she could discover the dead man in her kitchen. The animal's trainer, Glenn Smith, placed a piece of cloth under Beverly's pillow. Apparently Rhubarb was trained to find the cloth no matter where it was hidden. On cue, Rhubarb jumped up on the bed. While it looked as though the cat was trying to rouse Beverly from her sleep, all he really was trying to do was to get her head off the pillow so he could retrieve his favorite patch of cloth.[21]

Reviewer "Art" of *Variety* (June 20, 1962) panned the episode, noting, "Because of the way it was written, this putative mystery was not worth pursuing very closely. Misses Sterling and Garland were remarkably patient in acting out inferior roles." *The Hollywood Reporter* (June 15, 1962) concurred: "The A.A. Roberts plot strained viewer credulity in an opening scene by involving a murderess in a bit of unexplained stupidity which inevitably was to damn her. Characterizations, however, by Misses Sterling and Garland held the show together."

Beverly's worth to the industry continued to prove itself, time and again. *TV Time* (June 5, 1962) reported, "Beverly is one of those rare actresses who believe in playing her roles realistically." The columnist cited one instance when Beverly told her makeup man *not* to try to make her glamourous: "I'm supposed to be a dissolute, unhappy drunk. Put some lines in my face and some creases on my forehead...." She also insisted that hair stylists not fuss with her coif in other roles. "Who is going to believe my heart is breaking if I look like I just stepped out of a beauty salon?"

TV Time went on to say that Beverly's roles are "invariably difficult and demanding." and that when a part called for an actress who could "run the full emotional gamut," Beverly was usually on a very short list of actresses producers had to choose from.

One (unnamed) producer who had hired Beverly many times in the past was quoted in the column: "Beverly can be counted on to give everything she has to a role. When the script calls for her being slapped or mauled, she insists that her antagonist pull no punches." The producer added that it was a good thing that she was a "one-take artist," otherwise she would land up more in the hospital than on the screen.[22]

Beverly didn't land in the hospital as a patient but as a guest star in a medical television series. On June 14, 1962, *Radio Television Daily* ("Coming & Going") reported that she had arrived in New York City that day to start rehearsals for *The Nurses*. The episode "The Walls Came Tumbling Down" also featured Joseph Campanella (whom she had previously worked with during her *Decoy* series). Beverly and Joseph "meshed," and made such a positive impression on the show's producers, that both were offered recurring roles in the series. Beverly turned it down, but for a reason that had nothing to do with the show. "I felt I couldn't do it. I couldn't live in New York. I was just married to Fillmore for about two years and I wanted to be with Fillmore. He was very busy trying to put his life together with his building business so I just couldn't do it. Once I got married to Fillmore, my whole outlook on my career changed. My marriage and stepchildren came first — and later my children with Fillmore. That was my priority and it has always been my priority. If work came along and fit in with my marriage, my children, and my home life, I would accept it. That's how I did it.

"Now a lot of young actresses don't do it that way, but I felt I had to make one or the other more important. I thought about it and decided that I was going to have to make a choice and that I was going to have to live with my decision."[23]

Nurses producer Herb Brodkin liked Beverly so much he even tried to tempt her with guarantees of guest star spots on his other shows such as *The Defenders*. Beverly would not be swayed. "Whatever choice you make," she said, "is the way it has to be. You can't change your mind later on. Once you make this choice, you've got to stick to it."[24]

The summer of 1962 saw Beverly returning to the stage for three performances of *Say When Again* at the campus theater of San Fernando State College to benefit the Valley Home for Women. Beverly's co-stars included John Agar, Pat Buttram, and Bob Crane. She also co-hosted a summer television series *Summer Story Time* on KABC-TV Los Angeles, a weekday show for children. Through the use of puppets, music, art and films, the hosts related stories from the Bible. Beverly's co-hosts were Linda Leighton and Nancy Gates.

While still co-hosting *Summer Story Time*, Beverly made a guest appearance on *Stump the Stars* as it was making its transition from New York to California (and at the same time changing its name from *Pantomime Quiz*). The show aired on July 23, 1962. About a month later, Beverly was signed as a regular. Other regular cast members playing charades on opposing teams were Ross Martin, Jan Clayton, Diana Dors and Sebastian Cabot. After Clayton and Dors left the show, they added Richard Long, Hans Conreid and Stubby Kaye. The premiere episode, which aired on CBS-TV at 10:30 P.M., featured Jayne Mansfield and Jerry Lewis as guests.

> I remember going to interview for that show with Mike Stokey. I went and I tried out and when I came home, Fillmore said to me, "What is the show about?" I replied, "Well, it's a show that's like charades. This is what you do," and I got up and explained, "They give you a card with a song parody or riddle, phrase, etc., written on it and you act it out." So I showed him. Fillmore said, "Oh, you're awful! Just awful! They're not going to hire you!" and I said, "They're not?" Fillmore said, "Oh God, no! They're not going to hire you!" I said, "Oh, well. Okay."
>
> But I was hired and I appeared on every show.[25] However, I'd get up and read the card and I'd run over to Mike Stokey and say, "What's this word? What does it mean?" He'd whisper what it meant and I'd run back and Ross Martin would get so mad because Ross knew words and he was as bright as could be. He was a painter and a writer as well as a fabulous actor. Here he was doing *Stump the Stars* with stupid me. He would get so mad that I didn't get the clue or if I didn't give the clues correctly. Then he would be furious with me. Oh, God. It was awful. But I did the best I could. Someone once said to me that I was the comic relief and I think he was right. I was the comic relief. I was so funny. I used to get so involved and I'd get in their face and yell at them because they weren't getting it. But I loved that show. I loved it. It was so much fun.
>
> Mike Stokey would have us come in early and then he would field us sample stumpers and we'd have to get up and do it. They were not the quotations that we were going to be doing on the show. But we were Mike's team and we were the main stars of the show so we had to know what the hell we were trying to do and so Mike had us go through our paces twice — everybody had two stumpers — and rehearse so that we could master the hand signs and such. We got pretty good at it. We were good. We played in front of a live audience and we dressed up. It was like a cocktail party. Later they had popular TV series guests like the casts of *The Dick Van Dyke Show* and *Rawhide*. It was a very popular show.[26]
>
> All the clues were given to cast and guests cold. They had no idea what the subject matter was going to be. No idea what it was going to say. That was what was so scary, especially if you were a guest star. You were scared to death that you were going to make an ass out of yourself.
>
> I remember when I went to New York to do the pilot for *Decoy*, Mike Stokey was doing the show in New York. It was called *Pantomime Quiz* then. They asked me to do a show and I was scared — oh my God — I was so scared. But I did it. I got [a stumper that was] pretty simple so I was okay.
>
> Certain actresses would come on and be so "actress." You know, "Here I am!" and their whole personality changed because you can't be "on" when you've got to get down and dirty. So this star attitude they came in with all just went to hell in the two minutes you had to pantomime the clue you were given.[27]

The show was so popular that *Stump the Stars* books were published so that people could play it at home. They also came out with a *Stump the Stars* board game. After the series ended, Stokey tried to revive the show with a new crop of young actors but it didn't last. Beverly said that Stokey owned the rights to the show so no one else could ever do it. "I think somebody could have taken it over and gotten six really sharp people to do the show again. But because he owned the show, nobody but Mike could do it."

> Beverly appeared in all 58 televised episodes. However, there were supposed to be 59 shows. Beverly explained why one of the shows never aired.
>
> I had taken a seven-day cruise to Mexico with Sebastian Cabot and his wife, which left on January 28, 1963. It was supposed to be a brand new ship but it turned out to be the oldest ship

still afloat. As you walked along the promenade deck and looked at the lifeboats, you saw that the paint was so thick from numerous applications that there was no way they'd be able to pry them from the deck to lower them in an emergency. It was just *awful*. It was really *bad*.

To make matters worse, the ship was so slow that you'd throw an orange peel overboard and you could still see it for a long, long, long time. Terrible!

I don't think Sebastian realized that when you're on a cruise, they give you a menu and on it they have eggs, bacon, sausage, ham, omelets, French toast, Eggs Benedict, and pancakes. I guess Sebastian figured that you order one of each because that's what he did — he ordered one of each of the items on the menu. He went home 100 pounds heavier than when we started."

Anyway, it was one of the first cruises that went down to Mexico and back. But the ship started to have engine problems and it got slower, and slower, and slower. The smokestack was clogged and there was soot falling everywhere.

Well, we couldn't get back to San Pedro where the ship was supposed to dock, and Sebastian and I were scheduled to appear on the show that night. CBS was going to send a helicopter to take us off but they couldn't get Sebastian Cabot off the ship because he weighed so much. The helicopter couldn't lift him up in the chair lift. So they ended up canceling the show that night because CBS was not going to broadcast the show without us.[28]

Beverly offered more observations about Cabot: "You would invite Sebastian Cabot to your house for dinner and if the conversation wasn't revolving around Sebastian Cabot, he was bored to tears. If the conversation was about Sebastian, you had a wonderful time. He was very into himself and he really wanted to be the center of attention no matter where he was. Maybe that was one of the reasons why he never lost the weight, because he was such a heavy man that you certainly noticed him and he certainly wanted you to notice him. He certainly wanted to talk about Sebastian Cabot — constantly — which was fine but there are times when you have to say 'Hello!' to other people, too. But I honestly did like him."

Beverly also shared her recollections about another co-star on the show. "Diana Dors fascinated me. She had white, white, blond hair, this wild figure and she came from England. I was really awed by her, but she was a real broad. She was a good girl and she was fun. But when you looked at her, you couldn't decide if she was sophisticated or trashy. She was one of the originals on the show and then she left and went back to England. She had this white blond long thick hair that I would have given my right arm for! She wasn't with us a long time but she gave the show a certain glamour that it certainly didn't have with me! So it really was kind of wonderful to have her there. I thought people would certainly tune in if Diana Dors was there and I'm sure they did!"[29]

While on summer hiatus from *Stump the Stars*, Beverly was once again reunited with her *D.O.A.* co-star Edmond O'Brien when she was cast in the episode "Image of a Toad" in MGM-TV's *Sam Benedict*. Filming began on Friday, August 12, 1962, in San Francisco before the show returned to the studio for interiors.[30]

Beverly reunited with her *Medic* husband Lee Marvin when the two appeared on a game show called *By the Numbers*, hosted by Jay Stewart. A second *By the Numbers* appearance — this time with her *Checkmate* co-star Anthony George — followed in November of 1962.[31]

Beverly was on the *Rawhide* set on September 19, 1962, to film her second appearance on that show, "Incident at Sugar Creek." She made a third guest star appearance on December 17 in "Incident of the Gallows Tree."

On October 2, 1962, Beverly hosted the start of the annual Christmas Seals Campaign at the association's headquarters in downtown Los Angeles.[32] Three days later, she was cast

Stump the Stars **host Mike Stokey (seated) welcomes in the New Year of 1963 with series regulars Sebastian Cabot, Diana Dors and Beverly.**

by producer Joe Connelly opposite Richard Conte in an episode of *Going My Way*. Gene Kelly starred in this TV adaptation of the Academy Award–winning Bing Crosby film. The episode was titled "A Saint for Mama" and it was directed by Joseph Pevney.

Beverly found Gene Kelly "fascinating, because I remembered all the films he had done. But I remember being very disappointed in him because he wouldn't tap dance. I kept hoping that he would tap dance in or tap dance out of his scenes — but he never did."[33]

While Beverly didn't have any religious visions as a result of her appearance on the show, she did have a terrifying glimpse of the power of Mother Nature a few weeks earlier when a brushfire threatened her Laurel Canyon hilltop home. In an interview for *The Detroit News*, she recalled how upset she, her housekeeper, and her two stepchildren became as the flames approached the house. "If [the flames] get really close," Beverly told everyone calmly, "everybody grab a pillowcase and stuff as much as you can in it. Then each of you grab a cat and we'll be on our way." Beverly went on to say that since they had four cats at the time, it worked out. When asked about her valuables, Beverly was quick to reply, "I learned long ago not to attach importance to objects that can be replaced."[34]

15. *Twice Told Tales*

It had been about three years since Beverly had appeared in a science fiction–horror film, *The Alligator People* with horror icon Lon Chaney, Jr. On November 7, 1962, *The Hollywood Reporter* announced that Beverly would be paired with yet another horror film cornerstone, Vincent Price in United Artists' *Twice Told Tales*, based on three tales by Nathaniel Hawthorne. In the film, she would have love scenes with one of her favorite co-stars, *Naked Paradise*'s Richard Denning. The film's producer Edward Small and director Sidney Salkow were old associates as well.

Price appeared in all three stories, "Dr. Heidegger's Experiment" (with Sebastian Cabot), "Rappaccini's Daughter" and "The House of the Seven Gables." Beverly appeared in the latter with Vincent and Denning. It told the story of a tragic love triangle and the fulfillment of a family curse.

Of Price, Beverly said, "He was the most marvelous human being. Just kind and sweet and fun. He made you feel at home. You just want to bundle him up and take him home with you and keep him forever! I don't know anybody that does not like Vincent Price. He was just a very special man. And he always remembered you, remembered who you were. He was fun to work with and just a love!"[1]

December 1962 found Beverly devoting many hours to the Christmas Seals campaign as Honorary Chairman. On December 5, a booth opened at the corner of Hollywood and Vine where Beverly Garland–autographed Christmas Seals were sold.[2] She also made seven radio and television appearances to help the drive, including *The Steve Allen Show* and *The Bob Crane Show*.[3] Beverly's help contributed to the drive exceeding their previous year's campaign goal with a grand total of $680,000 in sales.[4]

Back on the promo junket, this time for *Stump the Stars*, Beverly left Los Angeles on a five-city publicity tour. She paid visits to Baltimore, Boston, Milwaukee, Minneapolis, and Washington, D.C.[5] Part of the reason for this promotional tour was to explain that several of the show's original panelists were going to be dropped and that the show's host, Pat Harrington, Jr., was also leaving. As Beverly explained to the *St. Paul Pioneer Press* (December 16, 1962), Pat's departure was by mutual agreement. "Pat is a stand up comedian and there was no place for that kind of comedy on the show. It's the fastest-moving show on TV so the originator of the program, Mike Stokey, has taken over."[6] While in Wisconsin, Beverly told Wade H. Mosby, "I love this show. It's given me my first opportunity to smile in six years." As she explained to the reporter, her television appearances of late were all very heavily dramatic. Her two appearances on *Dr. Kildare* found her an alcoholic in one and a hysterical woman on the other. She played a blackmailer on *Sam Benedict* and "the other woman" on *Going My Way*. She operated a saloon in one episode of *Rawhide*; in

Beverly, Jacqueline deWit and Vincent Price in a tense moment from "The House of the Seven Gables," a segment of *Twice Told Tales* (United Artists, 1963).

another, her false testimony nearly hung an innocent man. "When I got *Stump the Stars* I could just forget it all and have a good time."

Beverly also mentioned that she was starting to be recognized when she was out in public. "It's sort of a nice feeling," she told Mosby, "after all these years of being so 'disguised' in TV and movie roles that my own mother wouldn't recognize me."[7]

After spending New Year's Eve in Palm Springs with the Eisenhowers, Beverly appeared on *Stump the Stars* with guest star Vincent Price. The show aired on January 14, 1963. The same day, Beverly left for a second round of promotional tours for *Stump the Stars*. This time she visited Cincinnati, Detroit, Oklahoma City, and Phoenix. Before returning to work on *Stump the Stars* (and shortly *after* that disastrous Mexican cruise with the Cabots), she made a surprise visit to the set of Seattle, Washington, kiddie show host J.P. Patches the Clown, in disguise as his girlfriend Gertrude. She wasn't sure who made the arrangements with her public relations people, but she recalled that she had "a wonderful time" and that she was "always game for anything like that." The show aired on February 4, 1963.[8]

In an unusual move, the *Stump the Stars* show and cast returned to New York City for ten days in mid–February to tape six shows, taking advantage of Broadway stars as guests. Two of the first to be cast were Joseph Cotten and his wife Patricia Medina, who were starring in *A Calculated Risk* on the Great White Way.

Beverly was interviewed extensively during her promotional tours for the show. One important observation she made to a Boston paper concerned the fact that "*Stump the Stars* tests your ability to be yourself; to think on your feet without a script. People who try to preserve their public image, to act the way they think the public expects them to act rather than as themselves, aren't for this show. In concentrating on their public image, they lack the spontaneity and spirit the program requires.[9]

"Hedy Lamarr did the show," she said, "and she was just a wreck! I never saw anyone so panicked in my life. And they would always give the guest stars something very simple to do so that made it easier for them."[10]

Upon her return from New York, Beverly reported to the Warner Bros. set of *The Dakotas* to guest star in "Chooser of the Slain" in the role of Katherine Channing.[11] Beverly, perfectly cast, showcased what she could do with a character who was pure evil. In a teleplay sometimes reminiscent of Dürrenmatt's 1956 play *The Visit*, she plays a wealthy woman who wants deputy marshals Del Stark (Chad Everett) and Vance Porter (Mike Greene) brought to trial and hung for the death of her husband. As the owner of the town's only industry (a cannery), the vengeful widow threatens to close the business and put everyone out of work if she doesn't get her way. An otherwise familiar tale is saved by Beverly's masterful performance and an ironic twist ending. Another anomaly is the unusual addition of a Chinese sheriff! Beverly's episode aired a few weeks before the series was suddenly cancelled.[12]

Beverly and Fillmore had been married for almost three years. Beverly had wanted to start her own family but as of their third anniversary, she still had not conceived.

> When I married Fillmore, what I wanted more than anything else in the world was children. But Fillmore really didn't want any more children. He had two children. I said, "But Fillmore, I want a child." So we tried but I couldn't conceive. Finally I said, "Okay, I think you better get tested." He said, "*Me*? I've had two children." I said, "Well, I still think you ought to get tested."
>
> I remember I was taping *Stump the Stars* and Fillmore called me and said, "Well, I went and got tested—and it was not much fun, I can tell you that! But the doctor said it was not me. There's something wrong with you, Beverly. I don't know what."
>
> So I had my tubes blown out. I tried everything I could to get pregnant. So I went to another doctor and he said, "I think we ought to open you up and see why you can't get pregnant." Of course Fillmore, being raised as a Christian Scientist, said, "Well, you're not going to open my wife up!" I said, "I'm not going to do that!" It ended up that this doctor did do that to some lady and she was pregnant and the fetus had to be aborted. Fillmore said, "No, we're not going to do that!" He really was against doctors. I said, "We'll have to adopt!" Finally he gave up and said okay.
>
> Now at that time, we had bought a lot of property in Palm Desert and we had built a community there—lots of houses that we were selling. Fillmore had built a huge house for us, a wonderful Spanish house. However, many of the houses didn't sell. Then some adjacent property owned by an Indian tribe opened up for development and all the builders came in to build on that land. We finally ended up going under. We still had this magnificent house and I still had not conceived, but we built a room which we called the Phantom Room because we didn't know what sex the adopted baby was going to be.
>
> During this time we traveled a lot to Palm Desert so I went to the county adoption agency there. I went through all the interviews and finally they called me to say, "We'd like to come and look at your house and see where this baby is going to live." At first I said, "Okay." But then I said, "No, you know what? I have to tell you something. I could be wrong but I think I'm pregnant!" The agency representative said, "Well, that's great. But you can call us if you aren't." I was, and nine months later Carrington was born.[13]

On April 1, 1963, *The Hollywood Reporter* noted that Beverly had been cast in "The Odyssey of Jubal Tanner" for *Gunsmoke*. The series had been on the air since 1955 and it seemed strange that it took this long for Beverly — who had appeared in numerous big- and small-screen Westerns — to make her debut on this enormously popular series. This was her first of four *Gunsmokes*.

Having worked with both brothers James Arness and Peter Graves, Beverly revealed,

> They're both just good men. Both are handsome men — Peter was the more handsome of the two, whereas his brother is much more rugged. And, as *Gunsmoke* went on, James became more and more rugged. He didn't give a damn how long he was out in the sun or how many wrinkles he had. But always introspective — very contained men.
>
> I'll never forget during one episode of *Gunsmoke* ["The Victim," January 1, 1968], Jim Arness knocked at the door — we must have done this scene ten times — because I would open the door and say, "Yes?" and then I'd say, "Oops! So sorry! You're not there, you're way up there!" Jim was so tall — he must have been 6'6". I could never make direct eye contact. Every time I opened the door, I'd find myself staring at his chest. I could never get my head high enough!

Beverly added that James was "such a love. I did a lot of *Gunsmokes* and he always treated me so great. Jim Arness is like a wonderful, comfortable chair." Beverly's affection also extended to the series' crew and other cast members: "They were all so good to me, I just loved them all."[14]

Beverly not only rated high in law enforcement circles due to her *Decoy* series (which at this time was still in syndication reruns), but on May 18, 1963, she was crowned Queen of Armed Forces Day. As official hostess of the March Air Force Base, Beverly also participated in the groundbreaking ceremonies for its new Air Force hospital.[15]

At March Air Force Base in Southern California, Beverly was crowned **Queen of Armed Forces Day** on May 18, 1963. No doubt she passed inspection.

15. Twice Told Tales

The following week, Beverly was working on the set of another MGM-TV medical series, *The Eleventh Hour*. The episode was titled "What Did She Mean By Good Luck?" and it was helmed by one of her favorite *Decoy* directors, Don Medford.

Just as television studio productions were in full swing for the 1963-64 season, Quinn Martin Productions announced that Beverly was signed as a guest on a new dramatic series that would prove to be one of the most popular in TV history, *The Fugitive*. The series starred David Janssen as Dr. Richard Kimble, whom Beverly had dated during his earlier

What a catch! Beverly and David Janssen on a 1958 date at Marineland of the Pacific. Beverly got to wear a mermaid costume used in the Aqua Show.

Richard Diamond days. Beverly spoke with *TV Guide* about her relationship with Janssen during that period. "David was having his troubles at the time. Something about whether his *Richard Diamond* series would be on or off. I was right there to comfort David. But I think he thought of me as a kind of Mother Superior, which ended that."[16] Her *Fugitive* episode was originally announced as "Fire in the Mountains" but the title was later changed to "Smoke Screen."[17]

At the end of July, Mike Stokey got the okay from CBS-TV for another season of *Stump the Stars*. He was glad to have Beverly back on board again. "The truth is," he said, "Beverly made the show. This is that rarity, a girl who can be funny and sexy at the same time."[18] Beverly admitted that she sometimes got carried away when giving clues on the show. As she explained to *The Philadelphia Inquirer*'s Harry Harris, "I've slapped Sebastian Cabot twice—he thinks I'm going to kill him! I cracked Tommy Noonan's glasses and almost broke Stubby Kaye's nose. I get over-exuberant, yell and carry on. I throw myself into it.[19]

"There was an actor I worked with once. I can't think of his name and I've never seen him since, but we worked on a television show together. Well, I was the 'heavy' and I had to slap him—it was in the script. Well, I slapped him and he got so upset because I hit him! Most men, when you have a part where you have to slap them, they'll say to you, 'For God's sake, don't fake it. You're not going to hurt me. Just slap me because my reaction will be so much better.' Most actors are big guys and taking a slap is all part of this business. That's what most actors think and I feel the same way. So I slapped this guy, never dreaming that he would have a fit about it! He went to the director and said, 'I can't have her slap me in the face, it's terrible. I don't want it done that way. She'll have to fake it.' Which I did after that, I faked it, but he was a real cry-baby! I got a real kick out of him. I think he was afraid I was going to ruin his face or something."[20]

Beverly was four months pregnant when she filmed an episode of *The Farmer's Daughter*, "The Stand In." In it, she played a pregnant Congresswoman who doesn't allow a little thing like giving birth to deter her from affairs of state. Her outstanding performance would land her a very important starring role in a new television series within the year.

In fact, producers would go to extraordinary lengths to get Beverly for their shows. When she appeared in the pilot episode of Jackie Cooper's proposed series *Calhoun*, Cooper was willing to have scripts revised to change her character's profile from a mother of three to an expectant mother of two with subsequent stories to coincide with the actual birth of Beverly's baby if the series sold.[21]

Unfortunately, the series didn't sell. However, Beverly did give birth to her daughter Carrington on January 27, 1964. Beverly recalled what it was like for someone of her age at that time (37) to be pregnant:

> I'm pregnant with Carrington and the hospital calls me and says, "We're having a get-together of all the mothers-to-be and we're going to show you the nursery and talk to you about what's going to happen." I said, "Oh, good! I can't wait. That'll be great for me."
>
> When I came back [from the get-together], I said, "Fillmore, never again! I mean, these girls are 15! I'm 37 years old! I'm an old lady! I'll never do that again! People were looking at me like, "*you're pregnant?*" God! That wasn't one of the happiest things I ever went through. I thought it was going to be so great. But I didn't realize that everybody there was 12 and I'm 37!
>
> People were not having babies when they were that age. Now, they're having children at 79! However, then it was pretty old.
>
> I remember my doctor saying, "I want you to come every week and I want you to take these pills. Because, you know, we have to be very careful—you're not a young woman." So he really

had me on all sorts of things — diet and exercise, etc. And with Carrington I must have gained 12 or 15 pounds![22]

Beverly was also made painfully aware of her limitations once Carrington was born.

I had this baby but I was still working. I worked all the time I carried Carrington. I did a lot of shows and Carrington did them with me. But I realized when I was still working after Carrington was born that I was leaving all sorts of written instructions for Fillmore on how to care for her. It was getting tougher to leave for work at five in the morning and writing, 'This is what she takes at three o'clock and this is what she takes at five minutes after three. And if she has a little cough you give her that, but if she has a runny nose you give her this.... I mean, the list was yards long!

So I said to Fillmore, "I can't do this every morning. I have to have somebody who lives here and who I can trust so that I can go to work at five in the morning and have someone who gets up then to take care of the baby. I have to have someone here who knows what to do."

We ended up having live-ins, but nobody ever cooked dinner for Fillmore except myself. Fillmore used to say, "I always knew when you were working because I could smell those onions at three in the morning 'cause you were making a casserole before you left." But I had someone to bathe the baby and put her to sleep if I didn't get home in time to do it myself.

When I got home, I made dinner for Fillmore but then I had to learn my lines. It was a lot of work, but then I had a tremendous amount of energy. I have always had a lot of energy. I am the kind of person who does it. If I have to do it, I do it! And if I'm tired, I do it anyway![23]

16. *The Bing Crosby Show*

Two months after Beverly gave birth, she was back to work filming *Charlie, He Couldn't Kill a Fly* for yet another Perry Como–Roncom Films Inc. anthology series, *Kraft Suspense Theatre*. This new show was a follow-up to the 1961–62 series *Kraft Mystery Theatre*. Beverly co-starred with Richard Kiley and Keenan Wynn under the direction of Bernard Girard.[1] Beverly also made a guest appearance on *The Steve Allen Show*. She had known Allen since they both worked together in Phoenix at the Little Theatre and at KOY Radio.[2]

For several years, television network executives and producers had been trying without success to entice one of the entertainment world's most beloved performers, Academy Award winner Bing Crosby, to the small screen to star in his own weekly series. In fact, Bing himself had expressed interest in appearing in a situation comedy that would complement his multi-faceted talents as a singer and thespian. However, a series with just the right combination of song and sophisticated humor continued to elude the otherwise eager star.

Crosby was no stranger to television and headed his own production company, Bing Crosby Productions, which in the early 1960s produced the dramatic prime-time series *Ben Casey* and *Slattery's People*. BCP president Basil Grillo felt that "wacky comedies" were peaking and that the trend was moving in favor of more refined humor. He hoped to find a vehicle for Crosby that would emphasize this alternate approach.

Producer Steve Gethers (a former actor and lead player in the long-running soap *Love of Life*) agreed with Grillo and pitched a character to Crosby. In an article for *Showtime* (September 1964), Gethers told Edgar Penton, "In this half-hour situation comedy Bing Crosby plays 'Bing Collins,' a consulting engineer who couldn't make the grade economically as a singer in his post-college days. He and his college sweetheart-wife are deeply in love after 20 years of married life and they share the joys and problems of their two daughters in a spirit of camaraderie. In Bing Collins we have the antithesis of the typical television father who is stupid until the end of the play. Our television father will start out smart and wind up the same way."

Gethers' sitcom family lives in a comfortable rambling stone house at 717 Meadow Drive, Any Town, USA. Bing Collins is an intelligent, articulate man who has varied interests and likes to sing on occasion. Gethers also added a fifth member to the household: an old wartime buddy, Willie Walters, who came to dinner one night and, ten years later, was still there. Willie is a handyman by trade and also lends a hand tutoring the Collinses' daughters in manners and learning to play various musical instruments.

Crosby was happy with the concept and gave Gethers the go-ahead to begin his search for writers. But, unlike other series producers who normally turned to comedy writers for scripts, Gethers enlisted the talents of some of the most distinguished dramatic playwrights of the time—writers such as Mayo Simon, Jerome Ross, Loring Mandel, and Irving G. Neiman, among others. This was a tactic which was previously unheard of in Hollywood writing circles. Gethers, a writer himself (he scripted many of the teleplays for the first season of *The Farmer's Daughter*), explained in an interview for the *Los Angeles Times* (July 6, 1964), "I didn't want jokes. I wanted comedy built out of character, and I went to men who'd written brilliant dramatic character studies. They said they weren't comedy writers but these scripts prove they're wrong."

Gethers also engaged the talents of Academy Award winners James Van Heusen and Sammy Cahn to write two new songs for the show's opening and ending credits. He then hired Bing's long-time friend and business associate, John Scott Trotter, as the show's musical director. Trotter had known Crosby since the late 1930s when he took over as orchestra conductor from Jimmy Dorsey on Crosby's *Kraft Music Hall* radio show. Trotter also arranged and conducted Crosby on his Decca recordings for the next 17 years.

Another unusual move was the hiring of James Sheldon as the series' sole director. Sheldon, whose extensive television credits include *The Twilight Zone, The Alfred Hitchcock Hour, Studio One, Gunsmoke, Alcoa Theatre, Perry Mason*, and *M*A*S*H*, would helm all 28 episodes. His experience would come in handy when a threatened television actors strike in mid–July 1964 forced many series to speed up production in order to avoid having the shows pre-empted in mid-season if the actors "walked." *The Los Angeles Times* (July 6, 1964) reported, "James Sheldon shot the final scenes of one Crosby show in the morning and segued effortlessly into the opening scenes of another after lunch. The threat of a TV actor's strike [for more residual money] has even the stage where the world's most relaxed man, Bing Crosby, [working] at a fever pitch to get at least the initial five episodes in the cans before the strike deadline."

Of all the unorthodox moves Gethers had made in getting the series off the ground, it was the casting of the show's lead actress that raised the most eyebrows around Hollywood. On June 2, 1964, *Radio Television Daily* reported, "Basil Grillo, president of Bing Crosby Productions, announced, 'Der Bingle's [Bing Crosby] new situation comedy series rolls the middle of this month at Desilu-Gower Studios with Beverly Garland cast as Bing's TV spouse."

Gethers remembered Beverly from her guest appearance on *The Farmer's Daughter* ("The Stand-In") and was quite impressed with her performance. He showed the episode to Bing and he agreed to call her in for an interview. Beverly recalled her first meeting with Crosby in an interview with Hedda Hopper (*Los Angeles Times*, March 28, 1965): "When I was called for an interview, I'd never met Bing and I didn't know what to say; it was so silly to introduce myself. So I whipped out pictures of my baby [Carrington] and said, 'Do you want to see the most adorable child in the world?' Then Bing showed me pictures of his children and we hit it off." Beverly was signed for the role of Ellie Collins two weeks later. She was the only actress tested.

"One of the most difficult experiences I had being cast for a role was *The Bing Crosby Show*," Beverly recalled, "because Bing was very concerned about who was going to play his wife in the series. I had to do a test with Bing. I had always admired Crosby. I remembered him in such big pictures as *Going My Way* and *Holiday Inn* when I was a young girl so I was really petrified when I tested with Bing. I wanted it to be so right. It was wonderful that he liked me and I was cast in the show. But that was very difficult because we did a film test on that one and usually you don't do film tests on television shows."[3]

Los Angeles Times reporter Cecil Smith, while interviewing Beverly years later about her role on *My Three Sons*, recalled his surprise when he learned that she had been signed for *The Bing Crosby Show*. Smith said, "[I]t shocked the town. The Garland image had always been heavy drama. She played psychopaths, murderous females, dope addicts, and alcoholics. She had the most blood-curdling scream on the soundstage."

A few days after Beverly was cast in the series, she learned that a fire had completely destroyed Paul Levitt's Players Ring theater on June 12, 1964. The theater, which had helped jumpstart the acting careers of many stars such as Carolyn Jones, James Arness, Michael Landon, Robert Horton, and Beverly, would not be rebuilt.[4]

Rounding out the cast were veteran character actor Frank McHugh as Willie Walters, Diane Sherry as Joyce Collins, and Carol Faylen as Janice Collins. McHugh started out in vaudeville and appeared in some 150 features since 1930, including *Going My Way* with Crosby. Carol Faylen is the daughter of actor Frank Faylen, who played Dobie Gillis' dad in *The Many Loves of Dobie Gillis* (1959–63). She also had several guest stints on *Leave It to Beaver* before landing the role of Bing's boy-crazy teenage daughter. Diane Sherry is probably best remembered for her roles as Lana Lang, Clark Kent's high school sweetheart, in *Superman* (1978) and as Charity Bromley in *Hawaii* (1966).

The Bing Crosby Show went into production around the 15th of June on Stage 7, where Desilu-Gower Studios had soundstages they had leased from Paramount. Crosby, an avid golfer, could often be seen practicing his game using a steel-framed net sent over by his thoughtful "landlady," Lucille Ball. He also had a bicycle parked just outside the stage door so he could ride over to Stages 8 and 9 where his other two productions, *Ben Casey* and *Slattery's People*, were shooting. As part of her contract, Beverly received $5,000 to decorate her dressing room on the set.

Set visitors would often find Crosby and Frank McHugh using the time between scenes to play an improvised game of trivia where each would try to outdo the other recalling obscure or famous vaudeville performers and the songs they performed in their acts. Beverly marveled at Bing's photographic memory, "He was the kind of person who could sit down and look at a script in the morning and he would memorize all the lines. He was a great sports buff and he also remembered every star, every actor, just about everything from the 1920s and 1930s because that's when he started in the business."[5]

She also recollected that Crosby was always on time for rehearsals and she never saw him lose his temper. "He's quiet on the set," she recounted to Charles Witbeck during an interview for King Feature Syndicate (February 14, 1965), "but knows what is going on all around him. Bing doesn't play the star bit. You never hear the phone ring for him or see secretaries come running out with papers to sign. If he wants something, he goes and gets it himself."

Beverly told Lydia Lane (*Los Angeles Times*, January 31, 1965), "Bing takes things so easy, but he has tremendous control. The only way you can tell when something is bothering him is that he doesn't sing or make jokes. You never know if he is elated or depressed. Bing hides his feelings. He's not an extrovert. He doesn't particularly like small talk but his mind is shooting along."

The only thing Beverly found really strange about the show was the on-screen couple's sleeping arrangements. "Bing absolutely would not have a double bed or even twin beds together on the set. So the master bedroom had beds where one bed went up against one wall and the other bed was placed along the adjoining wall with a table where the heads of the two beds met. I don't know anyone that sleeps like that, but that's what Bing Crosby wanted, so that's what we had. But I thought it was kind of crazy."[6]

The cast from *The Bing Crosby Show* (1964–65): left to right, Carol Faylen, Frank McHugh, Beverly, Diane Sherry and Bing Crosby.

One of the show's most enjoyable components was the inclusion of at least one song during each half-hour episode. The tunes were carefully chosen to reflect some aspect of the episode's plotline. "When I was a young girl, I wanted to be a singer like my father," said Beverly. "He loved to sing and wherever we lived my father could always find people to sing harmony with. I wanted to sing with him but my father would say to me, 'Don't you hear yourself? You are so off-key. Don't you hear it?' Then when I did *The Bing Crosby Show*, John Scott Trotter said, 'You have a range of exactly one note!' I thought, well, between John Scott Trotter and my father, I guess I will never be a singer."[7]

Beverly never forgot what happened during the filming of "The Christmas Show" (December 21, 1964). "Throughout the whole show, I'm supposed to always want to sit down at the piano and play a Christmas carol and nobody wants me to do it. Finally, at the very end, I do sit down and I'm supposed to play 'White Christmas.' I'm not only supposed to play it, I'm supposed to sing it, too! Well, I realize it's a comedy, but to have Bing Crosby, who is 'Mister White Christmas' himself, standing in the wings—I just could not do it. I just tightened up. Eventually, I just did it and it was supposed to have been funny. But even if I did it straight, it was still funny."[8]

One very often hears harrowing tales about the pressures of working on a weekly television series. However, this was apparently not the case on *The Bing Crosby Show*. Reporter Eleanor Roberts noted that during her set visit, she immediately noticed a "camaraderie that was rarely found on Hollywood sets." Bing would often be seen doing a time step or singing up a storm at the end of the work day.[9] It was also widely-known that the show's work schedule called for a two-week break after every four or five episodes were filmed, to give Crosby a chance to take care of his other business interests, spend time with his family, and/or play golf. The cast and crew were required to work 12-hour average days, five days a week, to make up for the time lost during these frequent hiatuses.

During one of these breaks, Beverly and her family took a well-deserved vacation in Newport, California, a favorite summer retreat of the Crank family for many years. Beverly recalled those family trips:

> There was about three years where we [rented] the same house. We loved this house. They had a big bedroom but they only had a double bed in it. Fillmore said, "You know, we have some spare beds at the hotel. I'm going to bring down a king-sized bed and put it in there for them. We'll give them this bed"—and we did. We brought it down on a truck and set it up and we put the old double bed outside on the back balcony. Well, the owners were so mad, they never rented the house to us again. We could never understand why. They had gotten a brand new bed. But I think they were mad because we left the other bed outside on the balcony. Maybe it was a family heirloom and they didn't want anybody to take that bed outside.
>
> Summers in Newport were great because you can just let your kids run and do what they wanted to do. That was our big summer down there. There was just so much to do and so many kids. You could walk to everything. In those days you didn't have to worry about your children and they could have the whole island to themselves.
>
> Usually my friend came down with her little girl and we always invited other kids down. We'd go down in the station wagon. When the kids were little, we brought their cribs and playpens in addition to everything else. When we got there, Fillmore had to put the crib together and the playpen and everything else that had to be assembled. We were so happy when the kids were old enough to just sleep in a bed and we didn't have to have cribs and changing tables and high chairs! I'm just glad we didn't have six! I don't know how we would have done it.[10]

Never one to let an opportunity to work pass her by, Beverly also made a guest appearance on the premiere episode of NBC-TV's *What's This Song?* with *Bonanza* star Lorne Greene. This show was the precursor of the long-running game show *Name That Tune*. In December of 1964, Beverly was the recipient of an award from the Radio & Television Women of Southern California during a Sunday brunch at the Beverly Hills Hotel. Other awards were presented to Carolyn Jones, Dorothy Malone, Kathy Nolan, Connie Stevens, and Yvonne De Carlo during the ceremonies. On January 16 of the new year, Beverly made a guest star appearance on *The Hollywood Palace*—another Bing Crosby production. Among the other guests were the King Family. Daughter Carrington, whose baby pictures helped her mother to be cast in the show, celebrated her first birthday on the *Bing Crosby Show* set on January 27.

Beverly usually reported to the studio around 6:45 A.M. every morning for hair and makeup and often didn't return home until well after 7:30 that evening. The work was hard, but as Beverly explained to Allen Rich in an interview for *The Valley Times* (October 15, 1964), "Who's to stop Bing? He owns the show. This doesn't happen on any other series."

The Bing Crosby Show premiered on Monday, September 14, 1964, at 9:30 P.M. It preceded Crosby's other network series *Ben Casey* on ABC, and *Slattery's People*, which also held the 10 P.M. time slot on rival network CBS. *The Bing Crosby Show* had a regular sponsor, Lincoln-Mercury Ford Motors.

The series opening episode "A Fine Romance" was an appropriate set-up piece. When Joyce Collins (Sherry) observes her father Bing (Crosby) routinely setting up his food-laden TV tray in front of the family television set to watch his favorite baseball team (he's wearing an official Pittsburgh Pirates cap), she casually mentions to mom Ellie (Garland) that the romance seems to have gone out of their 20-year marriage. Ellie sets out to rekindle their marital flame by telling Bing that they need to re-establish "date night"—which results in some very funny situations. In the end, the couple realizes that they didn't have to prove they still loved one another; their love was obvious all along, even in the everyday, mundane things they did. What was important, however, was that they did these things together.

Hank Grant of *The Hollywood Reporter* (September 16, 1964) praised Beverly: "As Bing's wife, Ellie, Beverly Garland projects as a perfect choice; she's a combination of wife, sweetheart, and mother that's mighty soothing on the nerves. And she has sexy appeal without pushing for the effect." *Variety* (September 1964) proclaimed: "Miss Garland pairs well with Crosby; it's an ideal TV mating." Al Salerno of the *New York World-Telegram and Sun* wrote on September 15, 1964: "[Bing] had the considerable support of Beverly Garland, who played his wife as if she were an old hand at it."

Bing Crosby Show guest stars included both up-and-coming performers and well-established Hollywood names. Among those who lent their talents to the show were Frankie Avalon, Macdonald Carey, Vikki Carr, Dennis Day, Glenda Farrell, Joan Fontaine, George Gobel, Thomas Gomez, Phil Harris, Ruth Roman, James Shigeta, Mel Torme and David Wayne. Crosby's wife Kathryn Grant and son Gary also had guest roles.

Beverly had fond memories of working with most of the guest talent, recalling one incident in particular that occurred during the filming of *One for the Birds*. The story involved a sudden rash of jewelry heists in the neighborhood after the arrival of one of Bing's former show biz buddies, Barney Jenks (Phil Harris), and his talking bird Blackie. Jenks is arrested for the crimes, but Bing suspects Blackie and sets out to get evidence to nail the crafty bird. According to Beverly, "Phil Harris' character brought along his pet mynah bird. The bird was trained to fly out of its cage and land on someone's head. During one scene, the bird flew on Bing's head. Some loud noise off-camera spooked the bird, who dug its claws into Bing's hair and flew up into the soundstage rafters with his toupee."[11]

While most new television series fall into familiar ruts, it can be forgiven if the show provides a clever new slant, or if the main characters endear themselves to their viewing audience. *The Bing Crosby Show* had both these sought-after qualities and more, yet it only lasted one season. Production stopped due to poor ratings.

A Sunday or Monday night time slot has traditionally been the most highly prized in the television industry since it was usually the time of the week that had the highest number of viewers. *The Bing Crosby Show* held a coveted time slot of 9:30 to 10 on Monday nights. Of all the shows it was up against, its only real competition was *The Andy Williams Show*, a weekly variety series on NBC.

"[P]eople were more into lawyer shows — dramatic series," Beverly said about possible reasons for the low ratings. "I don't think situation comedies were doing very well and it was, maybe, just the wrong time. I think that if [Crosby] could have stayed with it, the show might have succeeded. But then I suspected he thought, 'Well, I'm not making it' and he didn't want to be a loser. I think Bing Crosby was not as popular as he used to be. He was getting older and I don't think he wanted to go out with something that wasn't a big hit. I think at the end of the last show we did for the season — which was the Christmas show — I believe he had already made up his mind that he wasn't going to continue...."[12]

With the cancellation of *The Bing Crosby Show*, Beverly was free to look for jobs. But building up a steady work load once again was going to take time. On June 30, 1965, *Variety* noted that she was signed for the premiere episode of ABC's *A Man Called Shenandoah* starring Robert Horton. The episode (written by Norman Katkov, based on a story by E. Jack Newman) was initially titled "The Ordeal" but that was later changed to "The Onslaught." Directed by Paul Wendkos, it premiered on September 13, 1965. Three days later, Beverly appeared in "Lazyfoot, Where Are You?" the premiere episode of yet another western, *Laredo*, starring Neville Brand, Peter Brown, William Smith, and Philip Carey.

While roles for women in westerns were limited, a very interesting possibility presented itself. According to the November 17, 1965, edition of *Variety*, Jack Sher (the associate producer of *The Bing Crosby Show*) had written a screenplay called *Mary Monday*. The article went on to say, "[I]t's a comedy dealing with the adventures of an internationally famed woman photographer, *a la* Margaret Bourke-White, who inadvertently becomes involved in a plot to rob the Tate Galleries." Sher wanted Beverly for the title role and also claimed to have been actively seeking Alec Guinness for the male lead. Like many of these proposed series, nothing ever came of it.

Beverly ended the year with yet another guest star appearance in a Western — but this one was a horse of a different color, because the series was created by none other than Rod Serling, known to audiences worldwide as the creator of *The Twilight Zone*. Beverly shared the screen with star Lloyd Bridges and yet another Bridges, Lloyd's 12-year-old daughter Cindy, in *The Loner*. It was not a happy experience for Beverly. "[Lloyd] was more preoccupied with her [Cindy's] performance than his own. It was very upsetting and distracting — for me, anyway."[13]

The year ended with Beverly filming a week-long appearance on Jan Murray's new NBC game show *PDQ*, which started on January 3, 1966, as well as a week on another quiz show, *You Don't Say*, which began the same day.

17. *Pretty Poison*

"One day," Beverly recalled, "my mother came to visit and I noticed that she was wearing a new watch and some other trinkets. I'll never forget it. I said, 'Hey, that's a great watch!' and she said, 'Well, let me tell you how I got it...'

My mother had a brother. His name was Julius. My grandmother was very fond of him. She adored Julius. Although he was not an attractive man, he finally got married. Unfortunately, his wife was later killed crossing the street by a driver who ran the light. After his wife's death, Julius came out to California and lived in downtown Los Angeles in a courtyard bungalow development. He became the caretaker there. He watched the bungalows and would repair the plumbing and little things like that and I guess he got his rent free.

One day, my mother got a call that Julius had died — he apparently died in bed of a heart attack — and the development owner asked if she would go down there and take care of all his things. My mother came up from Riverside and stayed with us and then in the mornings she would go down to the bungalow. The first day she was down there from seven in the morning until after six o'clock at night. When she finally arrived back, I asked her, "Why were you there so long?" "Oh," she said, "there's a lot of stuff." I said, "There *is*?"

The next day she goes and she's there till six o'clock again, and when she got back I said, "Mother — what...?" My mother insisted, "Beverly, he's got a lot of stuff!"

Well, by the third day, my mother said to Fillmore, "Fillmore, I'd like you to come down with me," and I thought, "Gee, that's good. Maybe he can help her."

Little did we know but my uncle was into pornography and in those days porno was an underground industry. My mother had figured out how to operate his slide projector and his little movie projector and she was spending hours down there watching all this pornography and having a ball!

So my mother gathered all this up and she would go into a jewelry store and say, "Oh, I'd love to have this watch!" and the jeweler would say, "Well, the watch costs so and so...." My mother would take out a roll of film and ask, "Would you like one of these movies? I'll trade it for the watch." You couldn't buy pornography anywhere back then. Of course, the man would say, "Yeah!"

My mother got a lot of stuff this way. She was a rascal. She did this for a long time until pornography became big business. This was in the '60s after my father died. She'd find something she'd like and trade pornography — slides and movies — for it. Men loved it. They thought it was great. Now, you can see porno on the Internet.

My uncle had very little. He didn't have *anything*— we thought! We later found out that he had been selling this stuff to collectors in Europe and that he had an extensive collection of European pornography! My mother was just having the best time with it!"[1]

Beverly made three guest appearances on *The Gypsy Rose Lee Show* between January and April 1966 when the former striptease performer had her own talk show out of San

Francisco. The Arthritis Foundation added Beverly to their list of participating stars for their annual Telethon on KTLA-TV over the March 5 weekend.[2]

On April 26, *The Evening Outlook* announced, "Beverly Garland portrays a modern-day Mary Magdalene in 'A Thief Named Dismas,' a two-part show of *Insight* series which is being aired as a special on KHJ-TV. First part will be seen at 9:30 tonight, final half at 9:30 P.M. Wednesday." Beverly was hesitant to do the show mainly because she only had a very limited amount of time to learn the entire script before taping began: "Initially I turned them down. It was so difficult because it was primarily two characters and the dialogue went on and on. I was in every scene. I really didn't think I was going to make it.

> The show was done live on tape. *Insight* had such a small budget — you didn't get paid for any of the plays. You just did it for the hell of it.
>
> We did the show in two days and it was a lot to do. I didn't think I could ever memorize it. I did it with John Dehner. There was no rehearsal time. You just had to come in and know it. We went through it once and we taped it. It was so hard.
>
> If someone really screwed up, they could redo it but they really didn't want to do that if possible. They wanted it to "look" more like a live stage production with no edits in the tape.

Beverly was being too modest. Her performance was in a word, amazing. She once again proved what a consummate performer she truly was.[3] She went on to do several episodes of *Insight* and became good friends with the host of the series, Father Ellwood E. Kaiser. Just before his death, he called her and said, "I'd like to see you." Beverly said, "Oh, we haven't seen each other for so long. That would be so great."

> Father Kaiser came over and I took him to Le Petite. We had dinner and we talked. He had cancer but he didn't tell me. He was just saying goodbye to the people he loved and I had no idea. We had a lovely dinner and we talked about a lot of things. He'd always been one of my really close friends. I always knew that Father Kaiser was there. If I had a problem, I could always go to him and talk about anything. I had tremendous respect for him. I did quite a few *Insight*s for him and I'm sorry he is gone. He was such a good man.[4]

Insight had 190 station outlets during its fifth season. Beverly worked with Brian Keith in "Don't Elbow Me Off the Earth" and "The Dog That Bit You," with Efrem Zimbalist, Jr., in "The Day God Died," with Robert Lansing in "Why Don't You Call Me Skipper Anymore?," with Dick Van Patten in "The Day Everything Went Wrong" and with Steve Forrest in "Man in the Middle."

Although it was originally reported that Beverly would have a regular role on Disney's new frontier drama *Gallagher Goes West* with Roger Mobley in the title role, she actually only appeared in two episodes of the twelve-part serial.[5] The series, set in the late 1880s, was based in part on the short story by Charles Dana Gibson and dealt with the exploits of a newspaper copyboy who aspires to become a reporter. Beverly's episodes were "Tragedy on the Trail" and "Trial by Terror." "The director on this picture was so negative with me," Beverly recalled, "that I had a tough time. It was not an easy thing for me to do this picture. He and I just didn't click right. I was made to feel that I was not right, or I didn't do it right, or it didn't look right. It wasn't a happy picture for me."[6]

In mid–May, Beverly was asked to narrate the Santa Fe Springs Parade for KTLA-TV and on June 20, 1966, she was appointed the Honorary Police Chief of Studio City at a dinner party given at the Sportsmen's Lodge. Her long-time friend Nancy Kulp (*The Beverly Hillbillies*) was honored at the same event.[7]

In between family trips to Arrowhead and Sun Valley, Beverly made an appearance on the *Pistols 'n' Petticoats* episode "The Ross Guttley Story" in the title role. The *World Journal*

Tribune (November 5, 1966) noted, "Beverly Garland has a lot of fun with the part of a cliché female bank robber who decides to go straight in this farcical episode. All the ladies — Ann Sheridan, Garland, and Ruth McDevitt — enjoy a tongue-in-cheek romp." Production on that episode began on September 7, 1966. Five days later, Beverly and Fillmore were contestants on Chuck Barris' *The Newlywed Game*. "Everyone on the show were newlyweds except us — we'd been married six years already — and we couldn't answer one question! *Not one*! We were the longest married and a question like, 'What does your husband like to eat?' I couldn't get right. We were awful!

"They said, 'We can't believe it! You're the oldest married couple on this show and you don't know anything about each other!' And we said, 'No we don't. That's why we've been married as long as we have. We leave each other alone. It's always a mystery!'"[8]

Beverly was offered a role in 20th Century–Fox's *Pretty Poison* and filming began in August 1967 in Great Barrington, Massachusetts, where both exteriors and interiors were shot. Based on the novel *She Let Him Continue* by Stephen Geller, the screenplay was adapted by Lorenzo Semple, Jr., and it was directed by Noel Black. Beverly recalled, "I can't remember reading for that part. Someone had seen my work on something else I had done and felt that I would be very good as Tuesday Weld's mother."[9]

Beverly was cast as Mrs. Stepanek, mother to Sue Ann (Weld), with Anthony Perkins completing the top three in the cast as Dennis Pitt.[10] "I loved the part," Beverly said. "Mrs. Stepanek was a marvelous character. Great Barrington, Massachusetts, was a fabulous place to work. Beautiful countryside."

Many people wonder about their family's history and there are a myriad of ways to search out your distant ancestors. Beverly, however, learned about hers when she arrived in Great Barrington to begin working on the film. In an interview for *The Contra Costa Times*, Beverly told Margaret L. Lesher, "When [I was] in Massachusetts for a picture called *Pretty Poison*, the woman who owned the inn where we stayed invited me to go antiquing. When I mentioned that my real name was Fessenden, she nearly came unglued. She was well aware of the old Mainline Family, the Fessendens. There is a Fessenden College, Fessenden Street, etc. It was the only time that being a Fessenden really paid off."[11]

Most of Great Barrington was turned into a movie set and cast and crew stayed at every motel, hotel, inn and boarding house not only in town but in the surrounding area as well. Townspeople were hired as extras and residents were also recruited as stand-ins for Perkins and Weld. The Stepanek home was also a real location; the house was owned at the time by the Boyer family. During an interview, Mrs. Boyer said that 20th Century–Fox had rented the entire house. The family was put up in a motel in town for the duration and they were paid quite a handsome fee for the use of the house. Mrs. Boyer added that the film crew had turned the front yard and inside of her house into a jungle of wires, cables, lights and other necessary equipment. One day she returned to the house to pick up more clothing while the crew was setting up for the day's shooting but couldn't even climb the stairs to her own bedroom due to all the heavy cables and wires. They even built a small platform outside an upstairs window so they could film at the proper camera angle. Despite all the mess and confusion, Mrs. Boyer said that the crew was very careful not to damage any of her property. She remembered that she had met Beverly on the first day of filming and then on several other occasions during the shoot. She commented on how friendly Beverly was, and said her whole family had thoroughly enjoyed being in Beverly's company. The manager of the town's only movie theater said that *Pretty Poison* had its world premiere there in 1968.[12]

Beverly thought Weld was marvelous. She had her own house during the shoot and had brought her baby with her. Beverly recalled that Tuesday had her over for dinner on more than one occasion. "She was a joy to work with on the picture," Beverly said. She also recalled the scene when she was required to slap Tuesday. Evidently the slaps weren't faked. "Yes," Beverly explained, "Tuesday and I really slapped each other around. I think really good actors like to be very physical when something like that is called for."[13]

Doing her own stunts also required Beverly to fall down a flight of stairs after she is "shot" by Weld. "The stairs were very steep and they wanted me to fall down all of them. I said I thought I could do it, but they did look awfully steep. So Tony Perkins said, 'Let me try it. If I can get down the stairs without hurting myself, then we'll let Beverly try it.' I really thought that that was marvelous of Tony. So he tried to go down the stairs and he said there was just no way — I'd break my neck!

"They originally wanted to put the camera way at the bottom and therefore see me rolling down all of the stairs. What they actually did was put the camera halfway up the stairs and I was shot at the head of the stairs and then I fell, but I fell on a mattress that you couldn't see. That way I could do the fall but I didn't have to go down to the very bottom."[14]

Looking back, Beverly said she enjoyed the project very much. "I thought Noel Black was a very good director. I worked very hard on this film. I just worked constantly on that. It was not a very big part but I worked really diligently and very, very hard on it and I think it showed. As small as the part was, it was outstanding, I believe."[15]

Critics agreed. *Variety*'s Murf wrote in September 1968. "Miss Garland [is] excellent in her portrayal of a casual but not unloving mother...." *The Boston Herald*'s Alta Maloney reported that same month, "The portrayal of the mother by Miss Garland is outstanding, just suggesting caricature to the right degree." Overseas critics also appreciated Beverly's approach. According to Marjorie Bilbow of Britain's *Today's Cinema* (March 7, 1969), "Beverly Garland provides striking support as waspish mother."

Pretty Poison opened nationwide on September 18, 1968. That December it won the New York Film Critics award for Best Screenplay.

No sooner had Beverly returned to Los Angeles than she went back to work on *Judd for the Defense* starring former *Donna Reed Show* co-star Carl Betz. Next she made the first of two guest star appearances on *The Wild Wild West*, another very popular series starring Robert Conrad and Ross Martin. Beverly had co-starred with Martin on *Stump the Stars*. Her first episode, *The Night of the Cut-Throats* also starred Bradford Dillman and Jackie Coogan.

Beverly had this to say about her former *Stump the Stars* team player Ross Martin:

[He] used to get so mad at me on *Stump the Stars* because maybe I didn't understand a word or didn't act it out right. He was a perfectionist, a wonderful, brilliant man. You just couldn't help but love him even though he was a very intense man. And yet he had a wonderful way of coming over and giving you a big hug and a compliment that would just make your head spin. He was a really fascinating person because he was probably one of the brightest people I have ever met in my life.

I think his intensity is probably what killed him more than anything else. But he was a charming man and I loved him. He always let everybody know that Ross Martin was very good but yet he had a wonderful, childlike way about him.... [H]e was a very special person.[16]

Soon after, Beverly made her second appearance in a *Gunsmoke* episode. This time her co-star was James Gregory and the show was called "The Victim." This was during the show's thirteenth season on CBS. After the shoot ended, Beverly was on a trip to Northern California when she noticed that something wasn't right. "We went to Sun Valley," she said, "and I borrowed my girlfriend's ski clothes because I didn't have any ski outfits. As I was putting on the clothes, I thought to myself, 'My God! I have got to stop eating up here. I am eating and these clothes are getting tighter and tighter on me. I'm skiing but apparently I'm not losing weight.' When I came home I decided I'd better go to the doctor and see if I'm okay. So I did, and my doctor said, 'Let's take a test,' I did and I was pregnant with my son, Jimmy."[17]

Once again, Beverly continued to work throughout the pregnancy. She made a two-part *Mannix* called "Deadfall" which starred two of her dearest friends, Mike Connors and Joseph Campanella. She also worked on an episode of *The Mothers-In-Law* which starred Eve Arden, an actress she had always adored, and an old friend and colleague since their Las Palmas Theatre days, the multi-talented Kaye Ballard. Ballard had high praise for her co-worker in an interview for this book: "Beverly Garland was a wonderful professional actor whom everyone admired. I worked with her in a stage play and on television. A true professional. That's the highest compliment in our profession."[18]

On April 27, 1968, *Record World* gave a four star rating to Blue-River–BMI Records for their 45 RPM release "A Letter to My Runaway Child"/"Tempest in a Teacup." In their review, it was noted, "Top TV actress does lovely job of reading." The actress this review was referring to was Beverly!

> Our neighbor across the street was a violinist — he played for all of the movies and played lead violin for almost every film soundtrack. He was also a conductor. His name was Harry Bluestone, and at one time when the whole hippie movement was going on and kids were running away from home and nobody knew where they were, Harry wrote this song. Actually, it is more on the line of poetry than song, about a mother saying something to the effect of "Where are you? What have we done? Did we do something wrong?" I don't know, it was kind of a maudlin thing I guess.
>
> Harry wrote it and he did the background music.... I think it was really something that Harry just wanted to experiment with.... So that's the closest thing I ever did to doing a record.... A lot of other [actors] came out with the same kind of thing around the same time...."[19]

Originally scheduled to go into production early in 1968, *The Mad Room* was delayed until May. The delay proved to be somewhat problematic for Beverly.

> I was pregnant — I was *very* pregnant! Actually, when they were going to do this movie, they asked me and I was three months pregnant and I didn't show. By the time they got around to me, I was six months pregnant and I did show. So they kind of had me in A-line dresses with lots of ruffles and things like that. I think I did pretty well for being six months pregnant. I didn't think I showed as much as I thought I was going to show. With Jimmy, I think I only gained about 11 pounds anyway.[20]
>
> During one *Gunsmoke* ("Time of the Jackals") I was carrying Jimmy and in one scene I get shot and I had to fall down. "No, no, no!" they said. "What?" I said. "I can fall down." "No. Absolutely not! You might hurt the baby." The fall was shot with a stunt double.[21]

The Mad Room co-starred Stella Stevens and Shelley Winters and was written and directed by Bernard Girard, the director Beverly always said was the one she loved working with the most.[22] However, Girard had an uphill battle after the film was completed. According to Beverly, "The editors went in and just destroyed that movie. Barney threatened to take his name off the film. It was an absolute mess."

> Apparently Bernard Girard wanted to shoot it one way and then the studio wanted him to film it another way. But Bernard did shoot it his way. Then, when they edited it, they wanted

to cut certain things. Bernard wanted certain things in and he got very upset with the cutting. So I think that he decided that if they were going to cut it the way that they were going to, that he would like to have his name taken off the film.

The result is that some of the things in the film don't make any sense to me. I think that some scenes were cut very badly. Bernard filmed certain scenes that the studio decided they didn't want and then it didn't cut together the way it should have.[23]

Some directors have the first cut in their contracts, hoping that by the first cut when editors took it over they could see where the director was going with it and maybe they would just refine it. But then what sometimes happens is, the editor says, "No, I don't like what he did. I'm going to cut it myself." All the director's work goes down the drain. Now many directors cut the whole movie themselves.[24]

Most of Beverly's scenes were shot without a problem. However, there was one scene that had to be re-shot numerous times — not because of Beverly's performance but because of an uncooperative special effect.

It was during the scene where I'm supposed to kill myself. It was incredible. They had this tube rigged through my dress up through my bra, down my arm to pump through fake blood. The scene took place in the bathroom and I'm supposed to look in the mirror over the sink then take a drink from a bottle of liquor I brought with me, break the bottle, and then I'm supposed to slash my wrist and scream ... and the "blood" never came out.

"Okay, let's do it again." So they have to re-rig it all over again. They have to take out all the tubing, clean it all up and put it back in again. I must have been there till nine o'clock that night trying to get this blood to flow correctly and every time it would squirt out, Barney Girard would say, "It isn't enough blood." "My God!" I thought. "Just what do you want, a fountain?"

Then they'd have to wipe the dress off and then get me ready for yet another take. I tell you, I never went through such a mess in my life. I thought we'd never get that scene right. Finally it squirted out but it took a long time to get it just right."[25]

The Mad Room went into general release on April 30, 1969. Although it was another relatively small role, Beverly made the most of it and critics did take notice. John Goff of *The Hollywood Reporter* said, "There are minor sub-plots in the film which fit very nicely, such as Beverly Garland's drunk character searching for her husband who she feels has run off with Miss Winters. Miss Garland is as fine an actress as there is around and draws a gem of a performance." *Variety*'s Brad noted, "Beverly Garland, wife of a masseur who 'services' Miss Winters, has one good scene where she shows up drunk at a party and tells everything she knows." *The Independent Film Journal* called the film "a better-than-average evening of gruesome entertainment ... and Beverly Garland is pretty good...."

On August 6, 1968, Beverly gave birth to a 6 lb., 12 oz. boy at West Valley Hospital in Los Angeles. Beverly and Fillmore named him James Fessenden, after Beverly's father.

It was the best. I mean, I loved being pregnant and I'm so sorry that I didn't have 20 children because I would have loved to have been pregnant all the time. I had no trouble at all. I got a little sick in the morning and ate lots of crackers. But I had absolutely no problem. I just loved it. I couldn't wait to see the baby. I loved the maternity clothes. I just loved the whole experience.

I remember when I went into labor with Carrington. It was about 2:30 in the morning when my water broke and I yelled. Fillmore flew out of bed yelling to Cathleen and Smoke — who still lived with us at the time — "We're on our way! Hospital!" and the kids shouted back, "Okay!" It was so funny. We got to the hospital and Fillmore stayed with me until the doctor said, "It's time." In those days they gave you gas at the very end — just a whiff of gas — and you went out like a light.

They never gave you the newly born baby and I didn't see the cord. I didn't have any of that stuff because I was out of it. Everybody was so modest in those days. I mean, when Carrington had her baby there was a crowd yelling, "Oh look! The head's coming! Oh, boy!"

In those days you stayed in the hospital for a good seven days. The hospital staff was wonderful to me. Back then you could smoke in the hospital and I smoked. The nurse would bring the baby and I had a cigarette here, a breast here, and a baby there. I loved it! I thought it was the most wonderful thing in the world. Then they took the baby away and brought it back at feeding time. It was just the best vacation I ever had!

With Jimmy, Carrington was with me and I had Fillmore's niece Charlotte here as well. She was going to do some kind of a play. She wanted me to help her with the play, to run through her lines and how to walk — that kind of thing.

I had said to Charlotte's mother, "Okay, bring her over I'll work with her" but I felt a little funny at that time. A short time later I could really feel those contractions and I said to Charlotte, "Would you take Carrington home with you tonight and let her sleep over? Because I think this baby is coming."

Fillmore came home and we started for the hospital. Well, the traffic was unbelievable. We finally got there and I could barely get out of the car. I just made it to the front desk and I had to sit down. I just sat down on the floor. I kept thinking, "I'm just not going to make it." The nurses got excited and quickly found a room for me. I think I was in the hospital three minutes before I gave birth to Jimmy. It was that fast.[26]

Once again, Beverly was back to work within weeks. Her first job was another guest spot on *The Wild Wild West* in "The Night of Bleak Island" and soon afterwards another CBS-TV show, *Lancer* with Joseph Campanella, Noah Beery, Jr., and Arthur Franz.

18. *My Three Sons*

On May 23, 1969, Don Fedderson Productions issued the following press release:

Beverly Garland, petite film and television actress, will be Fred MacMurray's wife on Don Fedderson's CBS television series *My Three Sons*, which commences filming its tenth year of programs June 2nd.

Following weeks of searching, producer Edmund Hartmann yesterday signed Miss Garland for a co-starring role in the popular television series.

Hartmann announced that MacMurray and Miss Garland will "meet" in the first show of the new season, followed by seven weeks of dating, courtship, engagement, and marriage, for what will be the first "seven-part segment" in television history.

Casting director Virginia Martindale told *TV Guide*'s Arnold Hano that she had "collected more than fifty names, including those of Rhonda Fleming, Joanne Dru, Joan Caulfield, Pippa Scott and Mala Powers."[1] Martindale was surprised when MacMurray made his final selection. She told Hano that she was sure he would have selected someone similar to his wife, June Haver.

However, Beverly's name wasn't originally on the list. Fillmore Crank explained what happened. "I thought *My Three Sons* was an interesting turn of events. Through a friend, Beverly heard that Fred MacMurray was going to take on a wife. But when she asked her agent about it, the agent said, 'This is not your role!' Beverly said, 'What do you mean, this isn't my role?' She made the agent call Don Fedderson or whomever they talked to and they hired her. And to think the agent collected ten percent used to bug me. Terrible."[2]

Beverly recalled that her meeting with MacMurray went pretty smoothly although he threw her a momentary curve when he started to talk about baseball. Beverly admitted that she knew very little about the game but pretended that she did. She felt very comfortable with Fred because he was a lot like Fillmore — a very straight and conservative man. Beverly felt that this did the trick.

My Three Sons producer Hartmann was apprehensive about the change in the show's focus. "The essence of this show as conceived by Don Fedderson, our executive producer," said Hartmann, "is the idea of a man trying to raise three boys without the help of a wife. Let a woman come into the house and we have no show."[3] But the other networks had begun to saturate the airwaves with similar shows featuring single-parent households — widows and widowers — no doubt as a result of *My Three Sons*' consistently high ratings.[4] When that happens, audiences tire very quickly of copycat scenarios.

Wisely, the producers decided to add a tempting new subplot now that the boys were older and didn't require Dad's constant attention. It allowed Steve Douglas (MacMurray) the luxury of a mid-life love affair and, once remarried, the opportunity to have someone else take over some of the responsibilities of parenthood that Steve had shouldered.

Barbara (Beverly) is a bit jealous of Steve's (Fred MacMurray) old girlfriend (the ex–Mrs. Ronald Reagan, Jane Wyman) in this scene from *My Three Sons* episode "Who Is Sylvia?" (January 31, 1970).

The addition of Barbara Harper (Beverly) and her daughter was a sorely needed boost to an otherwise male household. No doubt the show's writers were also starting to run out of script ideas and the addition of a mother and young daughter would allow them to mine new ground and revive a sagging premise.

Beverly made her first appearance on the show on September 27, 1969, as Barbara, a young widow with a six-year-old daughter named Dodie. Barbara also happens to be Ernie Douglas' teacher. She and Steve Douglas meet when Steve is called to the school to discuss a problem with Ernie.[5] Seven weeks later, Steve proposes. The wedding episode aired on November 22, 1969. According to the Nielsens it was the top-rated show for that week. Subsequent shows also figured high in the ratings. It seems that viewers were happy with the addition of a wife.

Although Beverly had been accustomed to tight movie filming schedules and even live television broadcasts, nothing prepared her for the piecemeal, jigsaw-puzzle filming schedule that was the norm on *My Three Sons*. MacMurray only worked for three months every season. Beverly would be given anywhere from a half-dozen to 15 scripts at a time to take home and memorize bits and pieces. The next day, they would rehearse, do a timing, shoot Fred's close-up and then the master shot for each and every scene scheduled for that day. It was like a fully automated factory.

After MacMurray left on his vacations, Beverly would film the rest of the shows with the cast. Beverly did all her close-ups with a tall stand-in who happened to be a woman.[6] When "Fred" asked her to marry him, Beverly said "yes" to this woman. Fred was on vacation.

One day on the set, Beverly was coming down the stairs and looking very sad. The director yelled, "Cut!" and reminded her that this was her daughter's birthday party and that she should be happy. Beverly apologized, explaining that she thought this was the show when Dodie had the measles. So many shows had scenes where Barbara Douglas went up and down the stairs that it could get very confusing.

According to Beverly, "*My Three Sons* had a wonderful wardrobe man and he would go shopping to all the stores and find what we felt would be right for Barbara Douglas. He would buy all the clothes at one time for all the shows that we were going to do that season, if at all possible, because we filmed so many different shows together at one time that we had to have all the clothes there. So we really did a tremendous amount of shopping. It would take us something like three or four days just going from 9 A.M. until 3 P.M. to shop until we could finally find everything we felt was right for Barbara. At that time, miniskirts came out and of course I wanted to wear them.... But they said no, only Tina Cole [the actress playing Katie Miller Douglas] could wear them. But by the second season everyone was wearing them, so even Barbara Douglas got to wear kind of a mini-skirt."[7]

Because of the strange shooting arrangement, Beverly had to keep the same hair style for the entire season. If she started a show with (say) a ribbon in her hair, it had to stay on for the entire shoot as well.[8]

During the first season of *My Three Sons*, Beverly learned of the death of her former husband, Richard Garland. "Richard never really did well. He worked enough, I guess, to keep himself busy. He married a girl whose parents owned a Mexican restaurant and were very well-known. I think they had a child. He would come and see me sometimes when I was doing *The Bing Crosby Show*. Every now and then he'd show up. He was still drinking a lot and then he got ill. There was a problem with his legs. I don't know what it was but they were going to amputate them, but then he died."[9]

Most people believe that movie and television actors make an enormous amount of money. The star of a television series can command more and more money if the show is a great success. However, the co-stars often make a fraction of the money the star makes. On *Decoy*, Beverly got $1500 a week. "Many years go by and *My Three Sons* comes along and the pay was $1500 a week. I said to Don Fedderson, 'Fifteen hundred dollars? My God, ten years ago I got that for *Decoy*! You can't pay me that kind of money. That's ridiculous! I just can't believe that you're offering that. I really feel it isn't fair.' And Don Fedderson said to me, 'I'm going to tell you something, Beverly, that's what we're paying. There's a line of girls behind you that will take it in a split second. So if you don't want it, I can certainly understand and I can hire somebody as soon as I hang up.' I needed to work and it was a good show so I took it.

"Interestingly enough, about ten days into the show, I got a check from Don Fedderson for $5000. Just as a gift. I never told anybody that because I don't think it was something he wanted to have blasted around. But I think he felt that I deserved something more and he sent me a $5000 check. He certainly didn't have to do that but it was a wonderful 'thank you' for coming on board. I never forgot that. But then, I just kept getting $1500 no matter what."[10]

Of course, Fedderson was probably aware of the quality of actress he had when he hired Beverly. Her experience in the craft and her range were worth far more than what he was paying. "I usually got paid crap money because I wanted to work ... I want to do it,"

Beverly said. "That's the important thing. I don't turn things down because you're not paying me good money. I turn things down because I think they're crappy."[11]

A side benefit of working on *My Three Sons* was that, due to the frenetic shooting schedule, MacMurray's co-stars were free to work on other shows for the months in between seasons. For Beverly, there was one unexpected appearance when Lucille Ball asked her to fill in for a bit part actress who failed to show for work on the day her scene was going before the camera. Like the trouper she always was, Beverly readily agreed to help out and took the part of an Air Force secretary in "Lucy Goes to the Air Force Academy — Part 2" on CBS-TV's *Here's Lucy*.[12]

Then, one night, Beverly got a phone call. It was the beginning of a nightmare. "John Mantley called me," Beverly recalled, "and told me he was doing a new series and that it was going to be like *Gunsmoke* only it was going to star John Gavin." Evidently, Gavin had wanted his girlfriend to play the part but with her English accent she didn't fit the part at all. Mantley let Gavin bring in one or two others but these women weren't any improvement. Eventually Mantley had had enough and told Gavin that he was going to find someone who would be good in the role. Gavin wasn't happy because evidently he had been promised the right to choose his female lead.

Mantley was really in a bind and knew a competent, proven actress of Beverly's caliber could easily handle the part. Beverly knew Mantley from *Gunsmoke* and was willing to help him out and film the pilot movie *Cutter's Trail*, but she had one requirement: "I said I would do it if it would be all right if Jimmy could be brought down to the studio so I could nurse him a couple of times a day."

John Gavin was very upset that they had chosen Beverly over his girlfriend. "Not that he didn't think I was a good actress or anything like that, but he wanted the choice to be his," says Beverly. "Anyway, he was very rude to me, he didn't speak to me on the set. Luckily, I only had a few scenes with him."

Twice a day for each day of the week that Beverly worked on the film, Jimmy was brought to Republic Studios by the housekeeper so Beverly could nurse him. Beverly soon found out just how petty Gavin could be. "I was told that he had threatened to report me to [the Screen Actors Guild] saying that it was the most disgusting thing and that I was unfit to be working because I was nursing my child on the set. As if I was out on the middle of the sound stage breast-feeding my baby! I took Jimmy to my dressing room each time where no one could see anything and nursed him in private on my breaks for all of ten minutes!

"Gavin claims to this day that this isn't true but the producer came to me and said that is what he did and I will never forgive him. He never spoke to me; never said one word to me about it on the set but complained to the producer. Now I doubt the producer was trying to pull some kind of funny stunt. Okay, so he didn't want me. Too bad. I mean, they asked me to do it and I did it as a favor."

Just before *Cutter's Trail* aired on CBS, Mantley called Beverly and said they were going to cut it down to fit a ninety-minute time slot. "I watched it anyway," Beverly said. "and there was one tiny little place where they left me in! I walk up to John Gavin, who is on horseback, and say goodbye to him. So you don't know who I am or what I am or why I am there — it was ridiculous. I was just furious. They had cut all of my scenes out and they left this little tiny segment. So here is Beverly Garland in the movie saying goodbye to John Gavin as if I'm an extra! That's the only time I have been cut out of a film."

Gavin was later appointed U.S. ambassador to Mexico. If it were up to Beverly, it is certain she would have wished to place him a lot further south than that.[13]

With filming for Beverly's second season on *My Three Sons* completed, Beverly hosted a March 1970 March of Dimes benefit at the Biltmore Hotel in Phoenix, Arizona. Also representing the show was Barry Livingston and Beverly's on-screen daughter Dawn Lyn, who played Dodie. "Dawn was nine at the time playing a seven-year-old. But she was so tiny. She looked like she was five. She had that tiny little body so she always looked younger. Dawn had a generic deficiency — her hormones are all screwed up. She never grew. She still looks the same today. She grew mentally which helped her catch on faster than a child of that age so she got a lot of work.

"[*My Three Sons* director Fred De Cordova] had a very sharp wit — very sarcastic — that cut like a sword. You have to have known him. He's funny, but you have to understand that kind of personality in order to get along with Fred. That poor little girl could never understand him. I understood him fine; he didn't bother me. But Dawn didn't get his personality. She had a hard time because he certainly was not a cuddly man in any sense of the word."[14]

Beverly's daughter Carrington was in a couple of shows. "There was a scene in the schoolyard. I thought it would be fun to have Carrington play one of the children. That was the episode where Dawn got her head caught in the fence. Carrington was in that one and also in a birthday party scene in another show. Jimmy was in an episode after the triplets were born."[15]

Carrington and James may have been lucky enough to land "roles" in a top-rated television show, but for the most part they were in the care of the family's housekeeper and then, a short while later, their own English nanny. According to their father Fillmore, "We always had help. When my wife Barbara died, out of the blue came a lady named Margaret Burbridge. She was my housekeeper for five or six years. Then she worked for Beverly and me. Then when Carrington was born, we brought a girl over from England named Shirley Richardson. She finally got tired of this and went to work at the hotel. She was a desk clerk for several years, met this guy and they got married and moved to Colorado. She was a great help to us."

"Shirley used to say, 'I finally got Jimmy off the bottle' and I'd go away for a weekend and [Beverly] would give him the bottle back!' Beverly would smuggle the darn bottle into bed. All the work I did was undone by his mother.'"[16] Beverly confessed,

> I spoiled Jimmy and he loved his bottle. My girl Shirley and all my friends said, "He can't have a bottle any more. You've got to stop it!" Now by this time he's in the first grade! I said, "I know that when he gets married he's not going to go down the aisle with his bottle in his mouth. I know that!"
>
> Shirley said, "He cannot have a bottle any more." I said, "Okay." So when I was here at the house I would let him have a bottle and when I went out she took the bottle away. But Jimmy and I had a deal that a bottle was hidden in his clothes drawer. As soon as Shirley put him to sleep, he got up and went and got his bottle. She was so mad at me.
>
> When Jimmy's friends would come over, I'd say, "You want a bottle?" and they would say, "A bottle? Can we have a bottle?" So I had all these bottles and I would hand them out, "Here's your bottle and here's yours." The little kids would spend the night with Jimmy and I'd say, "Here's your bottle. You've got to have your bottle." They loved to come to Jimmy's house because "We get to have a bottle." I'd get calls from their parents saying, "Susie wanted a bottle! What's that all about?"[17]

Beverly recalled that Jimmy was about one month old and Carrington about three and a half when Shirley was hired. "She was this wonderful young English girl who decided to

Filming the made-for-TV movie *Cutter's Trail* (CBS, 1970) was a horrible experience for Beverly thanks to co-star John Gavin, pictured above.

come and live here and Carrington said to her, 'I don't want you. I don't like you. I wish you would just leave!' Poor Shirley just cried and said she was going to go back to England. I said, 'You mean to tell me that you're going to let a three-year-old tell you what to do? What's the matter with you?' I told Shirley to tell Carrington, 'Stop that. I'm here and I'm staying here!' Shirley said, 'I don't think I can do that,' and I said, 'Yes, you can; you can do that.' Carrington was just going to wrap her around her finger. So Shirley did and Carrington ended up adoring her."[18]

Fillmore had built a guest house behind the main house and that's where the live-in help stayed. His oldest son Fillmore Jr.—nicknamed "Smoke"—lived in that house for a long time. According to Fillmore, "Smoke lived there before he left to go into the Air Force during the Vietnam War. Of course, it was very traumatic for all kids at that time. They were faced with this call to go over there. Smoke was a technician on the F-14 and he did go to Vietnam for a year. But then he came home and went to work for me. Smoke got married to this girl from high school but that marriage didn't work and the marriage finally disintegrated. He divorced her and got involved with my secretary."[19]

Beverly explained:

> Fillmore had this secretary and she had a wild figure and blonde hair down to here. She was a good secretary, though. I remember taking her to the *My Three Sons* set and I said to Fred MacMurray, "Fred, I want you to meet.... This is Fillmore's secretary," and Fred said, "You don't believe that, do you?"
>
> I got a little jealous of her.... She'd sit on his lap or give him a hug. I didn't throw her head-first out the window because that's not how I am. But I didn't like it too well. Then I told my mother and, of course, my mother said, "Well, I'm sure that he's fooling around!" In the meantime, little did I know but my son Smoke was fooling around with her! In fact, they moved into an apartment together. They had separate phones because they didn't want anyone to know that they were living together. He lied to us. He didn't tell us.[20]
>
> I grew up where you didn't cheat. I'm a very jealous person. If you ever want to get rid of me, just cheat on me because I'll be gone. I will not put up with that. It's just how I am. Somebody asked me once, "If you ever found out that Fillmore cheated on you, what would you do?" If Fillmore had cheated on me, I probably would have made his life absolutely miserable but I probably would have stayed because he was such a wonderful person and I would have said to myself, "Do you really want your marriage to go down the drain because of this? I have two wonderful children. They need their daddy." I'm not so sure I would have divorced him.
>
> I don't think he ever cheated on me. But then how the hell do I know? Men will never tell you. They keep it all to themselves. They wouldn't tell you the truth if their life depended on it and sometimes it does. They would rather die than tell you.
>
> I get a lot of that from my mother, because my mother really didn't like men. She felt they all cheated. Well, of course, she lived with my father and he cheated. So there you see. I get this from my family. You trust them until they prove otherwise.[21]

Fillmore was vindicated but he was not happy with the deception. He explained,

> Everybody accused me of playing around with my secretary when it was my son! She was something else. I remember this little girl, I hired her right out of high school. She was eighteen years old, cute as a button and a real live wire. She wanted to visit Beverly on the set of *My Three Sons* and she goes there wearing a velvet dress that was cut so high.... Beverly introduced her to Fred MacMurray as my secretary and Fred took one look at her and said, "You're out of your mind!" to Beverly, and another thing which is really an old story, "Does she type?"
>
> But sure enough, my son comes back from Vietnam and sees this.... He came to me one time when he was working at the hotel. He's sitting at my desk and he pulls out this diamond ring. He's got it in his hand and he says, "What do you think? Do you think I should marry...?" I said, "Well, let me tell you something: If you have to ask somebody, especially me, you shouldn't do it. But you do what you want to do." And he put it back in his pocket and said, "Well, so much for that."[22]

In a letter dated February 14, 1971, Beverly related the family's status in the aftermath of an earthquake. "Just to let you know we are all well and safe.... But there really was some terrible damage — we looked at it today. Freeway looks like papier mache. People with no water, sewers ... lights still out. Hope we do not have another...."[23]

On May 26, 1971, Beverly wrote to say, "We start shooting *My Three Sons* on June 14. I'm looking forward to it. I do love the show and I miss not doing it. I think it will be a fun season." It was Beverly's third year on the show and the last for the series. Beverly said it was due to the hiring of Fred Silverman as vice-president of programming at CBS.[24] She was proud of the show and her participation in it. She believed that Fred MacMurray would have stayed with the series. But when Silverman came in, he moved the show from their long-held Saturday night 8:30 time slot in a deliberate attempt to kill the series.[25]

"Silverman said, 'We're going to change your time slot to Mondays at 10 P.M.' Fred MacMurray kept saying, 'You know it's our time slot. Why do you have us in this awful time slot? We're a family show.' And this was Silverman's reply: 'Well, Fred, the ratings are just going to hell.' Fred kept saying, 'Yeah, but if you hadn't changed our time slot....' Silverman had come on board and he wanted his shows."[26]

Silverman had moved *My Three Sons* to put in place his Saturday night lineup which started with *All in the Family* at eight and *The Mary Tyler Moore Show* at nine. Sandwiched in between these two programs was *Bridget Loves Bernie* in the *My Three Sons* slot. *Bridget* lasted one season but by that time, *My Three Sons* had been cancelled after a 12-year run. The last episode "Whatever Happened to Ernie?" aired on April 13, 1972.

Beverly was once again show-less but a new and more lasting opportunity was about to present itself. Beverly did perform one more small duty for *My Three Sons*: She was asked to hostess CBS's 1971 Thanksgiving Parade Jubilee which covered the four biggest parades in North America (New York, Philadelphia, Detroit and Toronto). The Philadelphia parade was sponsored by Gimbels and Beverly's co-host was Bob Crane.[27]

19. A Singing Cowboy, Hojo, and the Saga of the Freeway Chickens

When the American West was being settled, the Weddingtons, a pioneer family, settled in the San Fernando Valley and bought lots of property. They developed much of their holdings, but there was one seven-acre lot in North Hollywood that remained untouched as a freeway was built nearby and a flood control wash was added on its other border in the ensuing years.

The property was up for sale and Gene Autry decided to buy it. He was planning to build on the land. But he also had other properties in Hollywood that he eventually decided to develop instead. Once again, the property was put on the market.

Fillmore Crank had been interested in this lot before Autry had bought it. He had plans to put up an apartment complex on it, envisioning the buildings amid a park-like setting with trees, streams, and places for residents to sit and enjoy the scenery.

Having decided to purchase the property, Fillmore went to the Valley National Bank for a loan. Fillmore's friend (Casey Stengel's brother-in-law) owned the bank. Fillmore used to have an office in the same building. The Cranks had also befriended the baseball legend, Casey Stengel. But before the bank consented to the loan, they said to Fillmore, "Let Casey go over and talk to you about this property." Beverly recalls what happened next.

> Casey Stengel came over and asked, "What are you going to do here?" and Fillmore said, "I'm going to build an apartment house with wonderful streams and benches so people can sit down and enjoy." But Casey said, "I think you ought to build a hotel." Fillmore said, "Oh, Casey. I don't know anything about running a hotel!" Casey said, "It's easy! You just hire a manager, collect your coupons, go to Europe and live happily ever after!" Fillmore came home and said, "You know what Casey said?" and he told me and I said, "Listen, Fillmore — don't pass go, don't collect $200 — do it immediately!"
>
> Well, that was our joke. Fillmore thought about it and he said, "You know, maybe that's what I ought to do. Maybe I should build a hotel."[1]

The bank was willing to give Beverly and Fillmore a loan to build a hotel but they told them they would need a "flag" — a major hotel chain — to bring people to the hotel. The Howard Johnson Company was in the East and during this time it was interested in expanding in the Southwest. Beverly said,

> We contacted them and they said, "We would really like to start out there and become part of Southern California. So yes, we would like you to have our flag."
>
> We signed a contract to be a Howard Johnson Hotel. We had to pay a certain amount of money every year to use their name and it was very expensive. But if you don't have that, you

can't advertise because one advertisement in *Sunset Magazine* would cost you a fortune. And they do all the advertising worldwide.²

So we signed the contract for 20 years. We really didn't know what the hell we were doing, of course, and we built a 155-room motor lodge which opened in 1972. We had an architect. Fillmore, being in the building business, had to have an architect. Howard Johnson wanted the orange roof with the turquoise bottom. Fillmore was very into early California architecture. He loved the mission style and that's what he decided he wanted to do. Howard Johnson said, "No. You can't do that!" Fillmore said, "Oh, well. Okay," and he just went ahead with his original plan. They kept saying, "No. No. No. You have to have the orange roof" and Fillmore kept agreeing while he kept building with the traditional slump stone and the tile roof—all done in earth colors. He built a cement block building which nobody had built. He continued to do it his way and when it was completed Howard Johnson came out and said, "Wow." They called people who were going to build Howard Johnsons in Southern California and said, "You might want to look at Fillmore's property because it is really outstanding."

"The motor lodge opened with a Howard Johnson Restaurant that had a Friday All-You-Can-Eat clams and a counter where we served Howard Johnson's Ice Cream, which was a big, big thing. In fact, in our first brochure, we had Jimmy sitting outside the restaurant with an ice cream sundae. He was about four years old."³

Then there were the chickens. After Gene Autry bought the property, he never did anything to improve it. There were no trees but there were a number of chickens. It seems a poultry truck had overturned on the nearby Hollywood Freeway and all the chickens ran over to Autry's property and, according to Beverly, "set up housekeeping there."

All during the time the motor lodge was under construction, the chickens remained on the lot. When the lodge opened, Fillmore built a fence between the freeway and the greenbelt and the chickens remained there. Beverly recalled one guest who told her, "I really love this hotel because it reminds me of home. You see, I grew up on a farm and when I stay at this hotel, at four o'clock in the morning I hear that rooster and I love it." Beverly added that, of course, a lot of people didn't like it at all!

"There was a little old lady—she was quite old—and her daily routine was to feed the chickens. She would walk over and put the feed under the fence. When she passed away, the restaurant took over feeding the birds. Eventually, the ASPCA came out and took the chickens away to—they said—a lovely place in the country."

Outfitting a 155-room hotel is enormously expensive. Just before the motor lodge opened, Fillmore found out that somebody had ordered drapery fabric for a hotel that never opened. Beverly described the fabric colors as "wild oranges and greens—wild stuff. When Fillmore was told he could have it free, he said, 'We'll take it!' Just before the hotel opened, someone came in the middle of the night and took every drape in the hotel—every drape out of every room. Someone also took every television set and using the rooms' bed sheets, lowered the sets from the balconies and took them away."⁴

After the hotel opened for business, the funny and not-so-funny stories started to accumulate over the ensuing years. According to Bev,

> I remember somebody hung himself in the bathroom from the shower. Then one guy jumped off the fifth floor balcony and hit the grass. He wanted to kill himself but he didn't. He was very upset.
> Somebody came in and painted their room red—people do that. They get upset. We've had people take bleach and rub it into the walls and the carpet all the way down the hall. Well, you can't get Clorox out of a carpet. It's unbelievable what people do. There was a couple with two children and every morning they would come down and pay cash. This went on for six days.

Then on the seventh morning they didn't come down. So we went to their room to see if they were all right. Well, they had taken everything that wasn't nailed down!

Lana Turner stayed at the hotel while she was filming *Falcon Crest* up at Universal and she asked for three rooms — one to sleep in and two for her clothes.

Beverly also recalled that Turner wasn't happy with one of the paintings in the room and asked for it to be removed. "Sorry, Lana," Beverly replied, "it's bolted to the wall. Just throw a towel over it."[5]

Beverly and Fillmore stayed with Howard Johnson through all the years the corporation was bought and sold because they still had a good reservation system and they were still under contract with them. However, the Cranks eventually decided to rename it the Beverly Garland Howard Johnson — and pretty soon people began to call it simply the Beverly Garland. Beverly recalled, "One time Fillmore got into a cab and the driver asked where he wanted to go. Fillmore started to say, 'There's a hotel on Vineland...' and the cabbie interrupted, saying, 'Oh, yeah. You want the Garland.'"[6]

When the contract with Howard Johnson ended, Beverly and Fillmore tried to operate the North Hollywood hotel as an independent business but eventually had to apply for another franchise and signed with the Holiday Inn chain. As of this writing, Beverly's hotel is still named the Beverly Garland Holiday Inn. She did manage to get top billing after all.

With debate heating up just before the 1973 U.S. Supreme Court decision on Roe vs. Wade, Hollywood was quick to weigh in — both pro and con — on the explosive subject. One of the programs to do so was ABC's medical series *Marcus Welby, M.D.* starring Robert Young in the title role. In "A Fragile Possession," Beverly was cast as the domineering mother of a pregnant daughter, forcing her child to have an abortion in the show's fourth season opener. *TV Guide* advised potential viewers that the show would explore "the physical and emotional damages of abortion...." *Variety* said that the episode was "one of the actress' best performances." If Beverly wanted to prove that her days as one of television's perfect mothers was behind her, she couldn't have picked a better role. Years later, when asked if she had a TV role that she considered a favorite, "A Fragile Possession" immediately came to mind.[7]

Nielsen-wise, *Marcus Welby, M.D.* was the top-rated show of that week, even beating out the television premiere of *Goldfinger* on the opening night of *The ABC Sunday Night Movie*.

Beverly followed this performance with an *ABC Movie of the Week* role opposite the Oscar-winning actress Susan Hayward. *Say Goodbye, Maggie Cole* was the second of two pilot films Hayward made, and a series based on this film was being considered as a mid-season replacement or a new fall show for the following year.[8] Hayward played a recently widowed research doctor who takes a residency in a Chicago clinic in an attempt to rebuild her life after the death of her husband.

Hayward was another of Beverly's favorite actors and she was thrilled to work with her. "She gave so much," Beverly recalled. "You loved doing scenes with her. It was give and take. I wish I could have worked with her more."[9] This would be Hayward's last performance. Within three years of her appearance in this film, she would die from brain cancer.[10]

On October 11, 1972, two weeks after *Say Goodbye, Maggie Cole* premiered, Beverly wrote to say she had just finished an *Owen Marshall — Counselor at Law*. In it, she plays the mother of a child who was sexually molested. Marshall wants to reopen the case of the molester, who insists he was wrongly convicted. It's in emotionally charged dramas like this that Beverly shines particularly bright. Arthur Hill plays the counselor and his real-life daughter Jenny Hill plays the now adult key witness.

While the type of roles that Beverly played were beginning to narrow, she worked steadily. However, she was also very aware that her age was going to factor into what she was going to be offered.

> When I got a job, I said, "Oh boy. I got a job!" That's the big thing in my life. I got a job and I didn't care. Why get upset? I'm working. The first time I was the mother for something, I thought, "Well, I'm now going to be the mother." But there are young mothers and older mothers and ancient mothers.
>
> You reach a certain age and you know what Hollywood is like. It's the youth capital of the world and from 25 to 30—maybe you could stretch it to 35—that's it. That's the time when you transition. Then when you're 80, it's another transition. There are not a lot of parts being written for women who are older and there are a lot of us who are older. I'm not the only one who aged! Everybody else is in the same boat.
>
> You've seen it yourself. You look at the shows that are on television. Almost everyone is 18 to 22. "Who cares if I can act? I've got long blonde hair and I'm in *Playboy*." You have to weather that as you weather everything else.
>
> I must say, before I got *My Three Sons* I hadn't worked for a while. So when I got *My Three Sons*, it was the best thing that ever happened to me. I really was thrilled that I was *not finished*! I just feel that I've been around so long, I can't believe I would fade away into nothing. Every now and then somebody calls and says, "Come and read—oh, gee, you look good!" What did you think I'd look like? It's only been 20 years since you've seen me, that's why! I'm not 185 yet! I walk in on an interview and this is what these people say. When I hear that I say, "You should have called me 20 years ago—I looked even better then!"

Anyway, there's enough interest and enough things happening. Something will pop. It always does.[11]

20. The Cowboys

For the next two years (1972 and 1973) Beverly worked in a number of television series such as *The Mod Squad, Temperatures Rising, The Rookies, Cannon, The Match Game* and *Love, American Style*. She also had starring roles in two made-for-television movies, *The Weekend Nun* and *The Voyage of the Yes*. There might have been even more had a writers' strike not closed many productions for several months as Beverly indicated in a letter dated May 24, 1973: "Work is slow—writers' strike and all. But things will soon pick up...."

Beverly made a second appearance on *Mannix* in an episode titled "Little Girl Lost." Aired on October 7, 1973, it was unique for this series because it was the only case Joe Mannix was unable to solve. However, this particular case would be reopened many years later on a different TV series with more successful results and became a first in television history.

On November 16, 1973, Beverly was installed as the honorary mayor of North Hollywood—an honor she would hold for many years. Beverly described her duties:

> As honorary mayor I would go to the opening of a new bank or new business in North Hollywood. I'd go to many of the breakfasts for the Chamber of Commerce as well as whatever functions the COC was involved with in North Hollywood. Whatever parties they gave or whatever functions they had, I would go and represent them.
>
> For many years, we had a "North Hollywood Night" at Dodgers Stadium and I would either throw out the first ball or be the pitcher or the catcher. The duties vary but most of it involved being a master of ceremonies or a guest or just being a representative. Usually, it's getting up and saying a few words at these various events.[1]

Beverly was still considered by producers a very important component when trying to sell a new series. Warner Bros., hoping to cash in on the success of their John Wayne movie *The Cowboys*, ordered a pilot for a possible television series with some of the original *Cowboys* cast members reprising their roles. Beverly was cast in the role of Wayne's widow, Mrs. Anderson.

Beverly filmed the pilot, the series sold to ABC-TV and then executive producer David Dortort—the former executive producer on *Bonanza* and *High Chaparral*—said that Beverly "didn't quite convey the qualities of John Wayne's widow left to run the ranch." So Dortort replaced her with Diana Douglas. He also added Jim Davis as a marshal.[2]

Well, that may not have been the whole story. Beverly believed that it had more to do with black co-star Moses Gunn. According to Bev,

> There was a wonderful thing between Moses and the widow and I don't think they liked that. It was so comfortable and it felt so good between us. [A friend] later told me that he thought I might have been too pretty. The actress who later played the role on the series was Diana Douglas,

who is Michael Douglas' mother. She was a very competent actress, but she was not as attractive as I was. I was pretty in that. It was one of my good days! They might have had a problem with a Black man and a younger White woman back then.

Now Douglas was a little older than I was. I felt that they couldn't have any hint of a possible romance here with this black man and this woman. But yet we had this kind of wonderful rapport-chemistry when we worked together on this and I just think they weren't comfortable with that.

I think my friend might have been right. I don't know because I certainly was good in it. I didn't do anything wrong. I loved it. It was fun. I could feel that wonderful rapport between Moses and myself. We had this good give and take. It was very good and they were afraid of that.

So if they hired someone who wasn't as pretty and a little older, you wouldn't see that there could be anything there. Absolutely, you wouldn't see that at all. But you did see it because I felt it. Moses felt it. Not that we flirted. But we felt at ease with each other. We felt that connection and I think it came over on the screen. In those days — this was back in 1974 — you just couldn't do that.[3]

The Cowboys premiered on ABC with a new episode to replace the pilot on February 6, 1974. After six months, it was pulled due to poor ratings.

Beverly made a TV appearance that same February evening but on *Doc Elliott*, in an episode titled "A Small Hand of Friendship," playing an unwed schoolteacher who becomes pregnant. The community wants her dismissed when her condition is revealed. The series starred James Franciscus in the title role of a doctor who leaves a major New York City hospital to set up a practice in rural Southern Colorado. About three weeks later, Beverly starred in another made-for-television film, ABC's *Unwed Father*. The very talented cast also included Joseph Campanella, Joseph Bottoms, Kim Hunter and Kay Lenz. Beverly considered her role as the title character's mother to be the type of role she relished. In an interview with Steve Tinney, Beverly explained why this role appealed to her. "I played a real beer-guzzling slob.... My hair looked like it had never been washed. I wore a tattered old robe and dirty baggy slacks at least five sizes too big. I loved every minute of it. What a challenge."[4] Beverly had praise for the unwed mother, Kay Lenz. "She is a tremendous talent ... such great potential.... [She has] much more depth. Kay Lenz is not a beauty but her beauty comes through in a different way because she is just a beautiful little girl inside."[5]

Beverly's performance did not go unnoticed by critics. Sue Cameron of *The Hollywood Reporter* (February 27, 1974) praised her: "Beverly Garland turns in a great performance...." *Daily Variety* (February 27, 1974) agreed, noting, "Beverly Garland turns in a solid performance."

On May 7, 1974, Universal, riding the *Airport* gravy train, began principal photography on their follow-up *Airport 1975*. The all-star cast was headed by Charlton Heston. In a letter dated October 7, 1974, Beverly cautioned, "Don't take your eyes off *Airport 1975*. The scene is short, short, short! You may miss me if you turn your head!" *The Los Angeles Times* (October 18, 1974) reviewer Kevin Thomas noticed enough to give Beverly a nod: "Others prominent are Dana Andrews whose fatal heart attack causes his plane to strike the 747; Beverly Garland, his distraught wife, back in Salt Lake."

Beverly had nothing but praise for Heston: "I found him a very pleasant man to be around. He didn't seem to be 'star conscience' of himself ... a very sweet ... kind man."[6]

A role in the unsold pilot-telemovie *The Healers* followed, prompting *Variety*'s Bok (May 1974) to say, "Anthony Zerbe and Beverly Garland are too skilled not to make something of the scraps the script threw them — but the whole effort was in vain." Beverly then signed to star in the ABC Circle Films–Bobby Sherman Enterprises teleflick *The Day the*

Earth Moved.[7] Although *TV Guide* promoted the offering, promising that "special effects" were the highlight, a superior cast once again enacted a weak storyline, playing second fiddle to Mother Nature's fury. William Windom, who played Beverly's husband, recalled what happened during one scene. "We were escaping from this earthquake zone by a small 12-passenger plane and there were a lot of takes, retakes and double-takes of us scrambling to get into the plane and then scrambling to get out again. Then we had to do it all again from another perspective. We were in and out of that small plane a lot! At one point, Stella Stevens sat down on a barrel which had some water on the top of it just before she was called in to do the take. Beverly did not let her get away with that. 'How do you like that?' she said. 'Goes and sits on that water just so she can have a clingy dress for this next scene!'"[8] Windom also credits Beverly with introducing him to his soon-to-be wife Patricia on that picture.

Shortly after Beverly finished work on the film, the Crank family left Los Angeles on August 5 for a week in Lake Tahoe, followed by another trip down to Newport Beach on August 16.

On October 30, 1974, *Where the Red Fern Grows* opened in Los Angeles. While Hollywood seemed convinced that moviegoers needed constant doses of sex and violence in their pictures, producers G. Ellis Doty and Lyman Dayton believed that most Americans wanted to see more family-oriented fare. Beverly thought it was a "wonderful, wonderful show."

> We did this in author Wilson Rawls hometown of Tahlequah, Oklahoma, and when they told me we were going to Tahlequah, Oklahoma, I said, "Okay. You're so cute. Where are we really going?" They said, "We're going to Tahlequah...." I said, "There is no Tahlequah anywhere! You just made that up!" But we did go to Tahlequah, Oklahoma, and the production coordinator on the picture took me downtown in Tahlequah and bought me some shoes — the most god-awful shoes I've ever seen — which I loved. They were wonderful but the toes went up.
>
> We filmed in this gully next to a river and they built the house exactly like the house that author Wilson Rawls lived in. Of course, there were no facilities; there was no bathroom at all! I always seem to get these films! Nobody seems to think I have bodily functions and I do. I walk and I talk and I pee!
>
> The director wanted me to make my hair dark and I had to have long stringy hair. They put a wig on me and it looked awful so I said, "Let me just play it with my own hair." What I did was wear no makeup. I just washed my face in the morning. I washed my hair and it was just straight as a string. I had these awful clothes that were more like flour sack dresses. I loved the part! I like these kind of parts were you don't wear any makeup and you look like the wrath of God. It's like being insane — I like that, you know. I loved this. It's my kind of role.
>
> We worked out there in Tahlequah, Oklahoma, and it was just wonderful. I loved playing that woman. I just didn't have enough. It was like the mother in *Pretty Poison*, it wasn't enough.
>
> The writer came — Wilson Rawls — and he was fascinated by seeing the house just the way it had been. He was thrilled with all the actors and the dogs. He said it was just the way it had been when he was a boy. He just loved it all. They really tried to be as faithful to the original story as possible. I think they achieved that. Rawls certainly thought they did. We were on location for about eight weeks, although some scenes with Stewart Petersen were shot in Hollywood afterwards.
>
> James Whitmore, who played my father, was such a sweetheart. We never saw him because he went fishing all the time. He loved to fish. They gave him a car and he went fishing. When he wasn't working, he fished.
>
> They had rented a motel for all of us so the cameraman was there. Some of the grips stayed at the motel, and the rest of the crew stayed at Tahlequah College which was nearby. At one point, there was a big problem because none of the crew got their paychecks. We decided that we weren't going to work if the crew wasn't getting paid and so we went on strike. Eventually,

the producer got some money someplace. I don't know how the hell he got it, but he paid the crew and we went back to work.

Stewart Petersen played the little boy. He had never acted before but he was really, really good. He did a great job. The two little girls were Oklahomans that they had found. I don't know if they had tested, but they read and one of them had this high-pitched voice that drove me crazy. "Tell me about the Red Fern, mamma!"[9]

Beverly's mother Millie wasn't happy with Beverly's on-screen persona. Beverly said, "[She] saw the film and wanted to know why I didn't look better than I looked. I told her, 'This is the way I'm supposed to look.' She wanted me to look like a movie star. She wanted me to look pretty. But I didn't look like a movie star, I just looked like what I was supposed to be; a lady who was trying to get an education for those kids during the Depression when there was no money. They lived on this crappy farm and my character was not going to look like Lana Turner. But my mother wanted me to look like her."[10]

Because *Where the Red Fern Grows* didn't have a major releasing company handling it, the film took quite a while to make its way around the country. But according to Beverly, there was another reason for the hold-up. "It opened in Los Angeles and Dayton didn't like the way that they distributed it. So it opened for three days and then he yanked it. Then, apparently, he got a new distributor and he reopened it in Los Angeles. He was going to blanket the market with the film.[11]

"I know it opened in London and they mentioned in *Variety* that they sold the film in 22 countries. It's even sold in Japan. I'd love to hear me dubbed in Japanese. I did an *Insight* and it was on the Spanish-language station and somebody called me and said, 'You must look at this' and there I was speaking perfect Spanish, which I cannot speak. I was fascinated with myself, thinking how well I spoke Spanish."[12]

That fall, Beverly had a guest star role on one of television's most unusual dramatic series, *Planet of the Apes*, based on the enormously popular series of films from 20th Century–Fox. Beverly played Wanda in the episode "The Interrogation."

Beverly explained that before shooting began, she had to go out to the studio for some special training. "They taught us how to walk. We had to get up in front of everybody and walk. They showed us the *Planet of the Apes* movie and they said, 'Now, this is how you have to hold your body.' You couldn't just walk out there and be an ape. We had a kind of choreographer show us how to walk because apes do walk differently than humans and you have to be able to walk that way; there is a kind of gait that you have to get. They wanted everyone in the cast to look the same way when they walked. Apparently, you had to go to Ape School."[13]

Beverly recalled the ordeal involving the makeup. "Makeup started at 5 A.M. for an 8:30 A.M. call. It was not uncomfortable if you reminded yourself to stay calm. It took a good hour to take off the makeup."[14] On her last day on the show, Beverly didn't want to wait to have her makeup removed, but got in her car and drove home. She said she got a kick out of seeing the looks on people's faces as they pulled up next to her car at traffic stops.

> I took my children Carrie and Jimmy on the set. Jimmy was about six years old and he was fascinated with the apes, absolutely fascinated! One of the apes played with Jimmy, and Jimmy just thought that that was the best thing ever! But Momma — no way — he'd have nothing to do with me! I told him we'd go and have our picture taken together, with me in my ape makeup. No, no, no — he wouldn't do it! The other people he believed, I guess, were apes but that could not be Momma behind that mask. He was very scared of me.
>
> After we finished shooting for the day, I said to him, "Come on, Jimmy. Come with me to the makeup room and I'll show you how they take this makeup off." It was a big process to take

off this makeup. Finally, about the fourth day of shooting, I just ripped the makeup off at the end of the day. They kept telling us to be careful when we took it off because it could hurt your face — but by the fourth day you're so glad to get it off, you don't care how much it hurts your face.

So anyway, we went into the makeup room. Jimmy sat there and the makeup man started to peel away the face and Jimmy finally said, "I think I'll go sit in the car." That really scared him. I think he thought my face was coming off. I never really did find out what was going on in his mind then, but he wasn't very pleased with Mommy being an ape. But I had such fun. I loved wearing the little glasses. I loved everything about it. I would have enjoyed being a running character on the series.[15]

In the episode, Beverly is a delight to watch. She played the role for all its worth and seemed right at ease as Wanda, the chimp scientist, despite the cumbersome makeup. Beverly said *Planet of the Apes* was the most fun she ever had working on a show in her career.

Beverly's last appearance that year was on *Ironside* starring Raymond Burr. She had previously worked with Burr on his *Perry Mason* series ("The Case of the Mythical Monkeys"). Also in her *Ironside* ("The Over-the-Hill Blues)," was Leslie Nielsen, whom she previously worked with on *Gunsmoke* and *Judd for the Defense*.

Beverly laughed when asked about working with Burr. "I got along very well with Raymond Burr," she said. "The last thing I did with him was *Ironside*. By that time, he was using cards. He read all his lines and he did it very well. You're standing there and he's looking slightly off to the side — where the cards are — reading all his dialogue. He never looked at you. You had to pretend he was looking at you. He had no eye contact with you at all.

"During *Ironside* I said to him, 'Raymond. I have a great idea for your next series.' He said, 'What?' I said, 'You should play your series in an iron lung. Then you can lie down and have your line cards taped to the mirror of the iron lung. I personally think that would be fabulous. You used to stand, now you're sitting, next you could be lying down!' Raymond even thought about it. I think he was considering a new series, *The Detective in the Iron Lung*. I mean, now you don't walk and you read your lines, you might as well lie down and read!"[16]

Nineteen seventy-five began well enough with Beverly filming another made-for-television movie for *ABC's Wide World of Mystery*: In "Deadly Volley," she plays the owner of a tennis team who is attacked and nearly killed. The police, however, find they have numerous suspects with sufficient motive — including one ghost of a tennis pro who also had a reason to want her dead. She also made a second appear-

Beverly loved playing Wanda, a chimp scientist, in the *Planet of the Apes* episode "The Interrogation" (November 15, 1974).

ance on CBS-TV's *Medical Center*. In this episode, "The Invisible Wife," she plays the neglected wife of a senatorial candidate (Ed Nelson); she develops a bleeding ulcer which is complicated by the onset of pneumonia. However, when she checks into the hospital, she insists that her husband not be informed.

Beverly and Fillmore spent Mardi Gras that year in New Orleans with their good friends Ed and Patty Nelson and were able to watch the show in their hotel room at the Royal Sonesta and critique each other's performance.[17] Beverly had met Ed Nelson in this very city back in 1954 when they both worked on *New Orleans Uncensored*. They had been very good friends ever since.

Beverly always believed that actors gave their best performances when they worked as a team and not when they tried to upstage each other:

> We're actors and we have a thing together. We stick up for one another — not that we wouldn't like to get that part over another actor — but when we work, by God, we work together because you cannot work by yourself. If you don't act as a team — as a group — you'll never make it. No matter how brilliant you are in saying your lines, if you don't say them back to me with that same intensity, my performance is gone and your performance is *really gone*! So you must work as a team. Otherwise, you can be brilliant but if you don't have brilliant people around you, ultimately you are not brilliant.
>
>   This is why people care about who they work with if that is at all possible, because good actors want to work with good actors. It's like tennis — you don't want to go out there and play with some kid who doesn't know how to hit the ball. Where are you going? Nowhere.[18]

Beverly had one other guest appearance that February, co-starring with David Carradine in his *Kung Fu* series episode "Battle Hymn." The show also guest starred blind singer Jose Feliciano in his dramatic debut.

On August 2, 1975, a letter from Beverly announced, "I just finished a *Marcus Welby, M.D.* called 'To Live Another Day' and a Glad Wrap commercial which will start playing in October. We shall be going to Puerto Vallarta, Mexico, October 5 and to San Francisco on November 1 for the USC-Berkeley Game." In the *Marcus Welby, M.D.* episode she plays a Jewish mother whose child has spent most of his eighteen years in the hospital fighting a disease that almost exclusively attacks Jews.

On September 22, 1975, the *Los Angeles Times* announced, "Executive producers Allan Burnes and Jim Brooks have set Beverly Garland to guest in 'Lou Douses an Old Flame' episode of *The Mary Tyler Moore Show*." Fans of Moore's series all have their personal favorite episodes, but this is one show that has to be on everyone's Top Ten List. When asked what it was that Ed Asner actually poured on her head in the final scene, Beverly answered, "They made a real Cherries Jubilee — ice cream, brandy, cherries — and let it melt. I wore a wig in case anything went wrong. It didn't and we did the scene in one take."[19]

Normally, some actors would find appearances in four prime-time series and a feature-length television movie a good year. Beverly, however, felt as though she had hardly worked at all and at the time had this to say about her situation: "I was up for about five series that year and each one of them is now finished. Gone. Dissolved. Never made it. I was up for *Joe and Sons* and they decided to go a different way and that fell by the wayside. So very few of them were any good. They were all just so bad. Parts for women were very scarce. I think it's going to change though. I hope so.[20]

To someone as dedicated to her craft as Beverly was, work was like breathing air. "I need to work," she said. "It's part of my life. It's part of me. I don't know what I'm like when I'm not working. My family will say that I'm horrendous when I'm not working. But

Lou Grant (Ed Asner) believes dinner with his ex-girlfriend Veronica (Beverly) will rekindle the flame; she just wants to borrow money to run off with her boyfriend. A scene from the *Mary Tyler Moore Show* episode "Lou Douses an Old Flame" (November 15, 1975).

when I am working, I'm a different lady and that's probably very true. It gives me so much inside of myself or puts me out there or whatever it does for me. I've never been able to figure it out but I need it. I know that."[21]

When asked about the importance of networking in Hollywood, Beverly had to agree that she was not a self-promoter.

> I've never been a pusher. I'm the kind of person who is laid back and if it happens, it happens. If I had just a little 'moxie' in me, I'd go out and do it.
>
> Fillmore likes show people but he's not the type of person who likes to give or go to parties where there are actors. He says he has nothing to talk to them about. He stands in the corner. He's very funny and he has a wonderful personality but he doesn't know that. He's uncomfortable so we don't go to parties. When I drag him, he usually has a good time. For years I dragged him. He used to say to me, "I go to these parties with you and everybody talks about this movie or that movie or what script they're writing or what show they're directing. They ask me what I do and I tell them I'm a builder and they walk away to talk to somebody else."
>
> People I worked with were not usually the people I invite to my house because Fillmore wasn't comfortable in a cocktail setting with these people. Yet we did have some good friends who were actors but I didn't encourage that particularly.
>
> Then one day we went to this party at a house of a neighbor up the street. I'm very funny at parties. I go in and say, "Hi!" Then I go to a corner and drag Fillmore with me. I talk to him

and then I want to go home. I'm not that comfortable mingling around and doing that. I'm comfortable mingling around if I'm "on"—if I'm supposed to be there to hostess for something. I can make the rounds and talk and do that. I'm on—that's my job. But when I just go to your house for a cocktail party, I'm terrible. I just want to sit in a corner and go home. So I really can't blame Fillmore very much because I was worse than he was.

So we went to this party. We walked in and Fillmore got me a drink. We sat in the corner as I always did. I just didn't care whether I was there or not. We started out the door very early—practically before everybody got there. I used to do that—everybody was still coming in and I was finished. So as we started out the door, some people came in and I said, "Oh, hi! I'm the neighbor down the street. I'm Mrs. Crank and this is my husband, Dr. Crank." Fillmore glared at me and a woman said, "Oh, he's a doctor?" I said, "Oh yes. He's a psychiatrist—a child psychiatrist." Well, she pushed me aside and said to Fillmore, "Let me ask you something. My little boy...." They forced us back in and Fillmore, who never had much to say because he's a builder, had the best time. Everybody wanted to hear what he had to say about their children's problems. Of course, he loves to talk about something and so there he was telling them all the things he wanted to tell me about how I should raise children. We must have been there for four hours and everybody was talking to Fillmore. I said to him, "From now on, that's what I'm going to do. I'm going to introduce you as a psychiatrist and you can talk." I was just as fascinated about what he was saying as everyone else was. I had a great time, too. I said to myself, "Why didn't you think of this before? What a great idea." Nobody knew us. They thought it was fascinating. I might have said I was Beverly Garland the actress but my husband was the child psychiatrist. So Fillmore is responsible for screwing up the lives of a lot of Hollywood kids. But we had a wonderful time![22]

21. *Roller Boogie* Mama

Without a constant flow of customers, any hotel will fail. Even though they had a franchise for the Beverly Garland Howard Johnson Motor Lodge which was a great help, Beverly and Fillmore soon found that it wasn't enough to keep their business afloat.

We were trying to get people to come to the hotel when it first opened and Fillmore said, "At Universal Studios they have all those sightseeing buses — rows of them. So you've got to go up there and convince them to come." I said, "What?" He said, "Convince them to come to the hotel." So I did.

I went up there and knocked on the windows of the buses and shouted, "Hi! Can you roll down your window?" The drivers would reluctantly roll down their windows and say, "Yeah, what?" and I would yell, "I have a hotel right down here at the corner. So why don't you tell all your people they can come down and stay at my hotel!" The drivers would say, "Yeah. Thank you very much," and quickly roll up their windows again.

I said, "Fillmore, I don't think that's the way you do it. It seems to me we should have a salesperson who goes out and does something like that. I'm not making any progress." Fillmore could talk me into doing anything. I can't believe I did that. But I thought Fillmore could do no wrong. I figured, well, if he thinks that's the thing to do, I'll go and knock on the windows of the tour buses. However, I only did that for one day — no more.

We somehow found out about the National Tour Brokers Association — they put together tours all over the United States. Fillmore said, "I think that we should join," and we did. It was a very small organization at that time. I think the first meeting we went to was in San Diego. At that time, the association didn't have many people. Now it is a huge organization.

The convention consisted of people who put together tours so they encouraged people who had restaurants and hotels to come down and show the convention attendees what they had to offer so that if a bus tour was starting in San Diego, for example, and they needed a place to eat or a hotel to stay overnight, they would listen to what your business had to offer — the amenities, rates, facilities, etc. And that's what we did.

One year, I think it was the second convention we attended, Fillmore and I were given colored badges — mine was pink and Fillmore's was blue. One person was allowed to go in to talk to the tour representatives. At the meeting, they announced that all the people with pink badges would now be admitted to sell to the tour brokers. I said, "What?" They said, "Everyone who has a pink badge can go in and be the salesperson for your hotel, or attraction, or restaurant."

I turned to Fillmore and said, "Fillmore, I have the pink badge," and he said, "We'll just exchange badges." I said, "Okay, because I'm not going in there. I don't know what the rates are or anything else about the hotel." Fillmore said, "It's okay. I'll go in." But when we got to the door, Fillmore was told, "No. We have you down for a blue badge. Only she can go in." We tried to explain, but they insisted. "That's the way it is."

So Fillmore and I went back to our room and Fillmore tried to explain all the rates and specials the hotel offered. I told him that I'd never be able to do it but Fillmore told me, "You've just got to do it. Believe me, I'll get it settled."

The doors opened and everybody rushed in. You have so many people to see and they have it all mapped out for you. You have only three minutes to talk to this person and then a bell sounds and you move on to the next tour broker. This goes on until everybody has talked to all the tour representatives. This is how we did it back then and, you know, I loved it! I thought it was so much fun. I said, "Fillmore, I'm going to do it from now on."

A lot of people own their own tours or tour buses and motor coaches. There are a lot of hotels in the Los Angeles area so you go and talk to them. They get the best rate. They look at your slides. They figure out whether they're going to use your hotel or someone else's depending on where your hotel is located and the rates. Fillmore was glad to let me handle the representatives because he didn't want to do it.

Eventually, people began to recognize me as an actress and they asked me to be on a committee and that led to them asking me to be NTBA's spokesperson. So, twice a year, I would go to different parts of the country. I'd appear on television and radio shows to talk about the National Tour Brokers Association. I would explain how much more comfortable touring the country by motor coach was and that these coaches were air conditioned and had screens for movies. I would try to show people that instead of driving all the way out to California or wherever you were going, you could take a tour on one of these motor coaches and have a comfortable, carefree trip. Now, of course, there are motor coach tours going everywhere. But back then there weren't. This was something new. The motor coach industry really worked with the NTBA people at that time. So that's what I did. I became their spokesperson. I was still acting and I did this, too. Fillmore and I attended four meetings a year for the NTBA. We went everywhere from New Orleans to Canada — and everywhere in between.

Later, they asked me to join the board of the Los Angeles Visitors & Convention Bureau and I was a spokesperson for them, too. In fact, Fillmore and I went with Mayor Bradley to Australia for one month to visit our sister city there.[1]

A hotel owner's work is never done! Beverly lending a hand — sort of — at her North Hollywood hotel, circa 2003.

During the months of February, April and June 1976 Beverly made appearances on the popular game shows, *Cross Wits* and *Break the Bank*. "On *Cross Wits* there was a word on the board that began with the letter E and they said, 'What is it that Queen Victoria and Queen Elizabeth have in common?' Then they said, 'Beverly?' and I said, 'Oh ... E ... ah ... *enema*!' They said, 'Oh my God!' The writer later said to me, 'These are the kind of words they won't allow me to put in, but I'm so glad you said it!' Two of the contestants got up and said, 'Well, if this is the kind of show it is, we're leaving!' I just couldn't think of a word that started with an E. I couldn't. Of course, the correct answer was *empire*."[2]

A letter from Beverly's secretary Shirley Richardson, dated May 14, 1976, advised that Beverly and Fillmore had just come back from a vacation in Mexico. She also mentioned that Beverly, "in her capacity as honorary mayor of North Hollywood, ... is extremely powerful in her role ... against the massage parlors along Ventura Boulevard in Studio City. These places are really something else — not only that, but just a few blocks away is the school her son Jimmy attends. So she is really up in arms!" Beverly's fight took her to the steps of Los Angeles' City Hall where she made an impassioned speech in her fight to rid North Hollywood and Studio City of massage parlors and pornographic book stores. This is Beverly's speech:

> As a woman and a mother, I find the entire subject of pornography, of obscene acts, films and publications as an assault on my human dignity. Yet this nation is so immersed in this sea of mental pollution that I feel it is time I speak out. I am a realist and I am concerned.
>
> A short while ago, I was in Philadelphia. I walked those hallowed halls where the Declaration of Independence and the Constitution were worried over and composed. I began to see again that our forefathers, who were no different really than you or I, were well aware of pollution, crime, congestion and the moral problems of a nation. They gave us guidelines so we could grow morally and spiritually.
>
> Our choice, now 200 years later, is to decide if we will soar to new heights or if we will walk in the gutter. Do we say to our children, 'Go ahead, litter, defecate on the street corner, pollute, become morally illiterate, unthinking, mean, and it's every man for himself.... God be damned!' Or do we say, 'Listen. Let me take your young mind and teach you to care, to love, to grow'?
>
> To me, pornography is like smog. It clouds the beauty of love and compassion. It is the cheap moral degrader, the polluter. People say, "Leave it alone ... let it be ... how can it hurt?" Well, I ask, "How can it help? Does it uplift our children? Does it inspire? Does it teach love, kindness, compassion, goodness, or any quality that is worthwhile?"
>
> Some say it is freedom. But to me, freedom is taking charge of your life with dignity, reaching out and becoming a more loving human being. Pornography has nothing to do with love!
>
> I don't think we have time to be complacent or to fool ourselves that it is sophistication. It is time to care. To act. To become involved. For when the crisis of today is ignored, when faith becomes an heirloom, when the voice of decency becomes irrelevant ... then the forces of evil will prevail.

July 4, 1976, was the bicentennial of the United States of America and Beverly, as honorary mayor of North Hollywood, hosted a huge event from July 2 through 5. Much of it was shown on NBC-TV's broadcast *What's Going On America* live across the country. The events included a stage show, a fireworks display, an arts and crafts show and a carnival. All the festivities were held at the Valley Plaza Park in North Hollywood and it was reported that over 50,000 people attended.[3]

Beverly also filmed an episode of *Switch*, "The Argonaut Special," which starred Eddie Albert (Beverly's husband in *The Joker Is Wild*) and Robert Wagner. In the episode, Beverly played Albert's friend and business partner in a ranching enterprise. Beverly asks Albert to help her and her fellow ranchers thwart a ruthless land speculator. Beverly knew that she would be spending a lot of screen time on horseback and, since it had been a while since she had ridden, she borrowed a friend's horse for a few days before filming began and practiced riding until she felt comfortable in the saddle again.

When asked about her *Switch* co-stars, Beverly said, "I think Robert Wagner was one of the sweetest people I've ever met. I never worked with him before and he was just kindness itself. He really was a lovely person. I loved working with Eddie Albert again because it was like 'old home week.' I understood him and I always liked him."[4]

Beverly also mentioned that some scenes from another episode of *Switch* were filmed at her hotel. "They've also done a *Six Million Dollar Man* and *Police Woman* [at the hotel]. In fact, they're done just about all the big shows here.

"They have filmed everywhere in the hotel—inside at the desk area, around in the back, jumping off of balconies—and the guests just love it. Of course, it is a mess when they do film because they've got cables running everywhere. They've done commercials around the pool and the tennis courts. We always put a sign up saying, for instance, "Universal is filming *Six Million Dollar Man* here today" so that our guests will know that sometimes they would not be able to get to the front desk for a while or do certain things that they'd like to do. And yet they get a kick out of that. Most people enjoy the fact that they are in Hollywood and that the studios are filming here at the lodge. And it's good publicity for us and we like it!"[5]

The Crank family spent another month at Newport Beach, and then Beverly and Fillmore headed to Salt Lake City for the National Tour Brokers Association. Two months later, the family spent a day at the beach. In a letter dated October 18, 1976, Beverly explained what happened when they returned home: "We were robbed while we were at the beach. You remember my lovely mink coat—gone. All my silver and television sets. Thank God I have my jewelry. The times we live in are not the best."

The letter went on to say that she was about to do a two-part episode of *The Six Million Dollar Man*: "We are now doing comic strips here in Hollywood only with real people—it's sad. Does anyone out there have a good script for a woman? My agent said the only way women will get good scripts is to write them themselves. I know I can act but I never thought I would also have to take up writing! There are not many parts for women and there are a lot of good women actresses for every one part. Men are just not sure how to write for women—so they have solved the problem—they just don't! So I take what comes along as exercise. It's always better to do something then nothing. But it makes you want to cry."

In *Six Million Dollar Man*'s "Death Probe" (part 1), she briefly plays an American-based Russian agent who tries to recover a Soviet space probe that has accidentally landed in Wyoming instead of its original destination—the planet Venus.

In January 1976, a new Norman Lear show, *Mary Hartman, Mary Hartman*, premiered in syndication on about 100 independent networks across the country. This satire on soap operas, wildly popular in New York and Los Angeles, starred Louise Lassiter in the title role. A year later, on January 31, 1977, a new character was introduced on the show: Cookie La Rue. Cookie is the personification of a "tough broad"—chain smoking, gum-chewing, braless and wearing her hair in a gigantic blonde Afro. She was like nothing ever seen before on television. "I told the hairdresser that I wanted an Afro," Beverly revealed.

> She was a black hairdresser and she just had fun with my hair. I didn't wear a wig. When I first came out, the producers looked at me and said they didn't like the really cheap clothes and long earrings that the wardrobe people had selected for me. But they liked my hair. It was terrible to comb out, I must say. But I thought it was great for the part.

> I did pretty much what I wanted to do with the character. I think I could have done more with her. I wasn't pleased with Cookie. I didn't think she was rounded enough — I missed her somewhere, I just don't know where.
>
> Nobody said anything for the most part on that set — the producers, the director. But then after about three days, the writers came to me and told me how pleased they were. Well, then that really made me feel better. I guess as an actor you always need that — you need someone to pat you on the back. Actors are very insecure people and they need people to tell them that — it's very important to them. When no one gives you feedback, you start to think maybe you'd better change your performance. The director doesn't want you to change anything — but he hasn't said anything to you, so you think he doesn't like it. I go though that all the time. That's just how actors are — they want so hard to please, to do it right. They try very hard. (At least I think really good actors do that.) So when the writers on *Mary Hartman, Mary Hartman* said they were pleased, that really made me feel good.
>
> I liked doing the show. It was difficult for me, however, because on the show they were very quiet — they never talked to you. I mean, you'd rehearse and then you'd do your thing. Afterwards, you'd go to your dressing room. You wouldn't see anybody and no one would come over and talk. It was just a strange set for me. Some sets are very friendly. This one was not very friendly — at least I didn't feel that it was.[6]

Beverly made several subsequent appearances on the series between February 1 and the 17th, during which time Cookie escapes from jail. By the last show she finds herself being returned to her cell. Her appearances were a delightful interlude and Cookie proved to be one of the most memorable characters of Beverly's career.

On April 9, on the eve of Easter Sunday, NBC-TV premiered *Where the Red Fern Grows*. *TV Guide* reviewer Judith Crist noted that it featured "a very good performance by Beverly Garland...."

The following week, Beverly made appearances on two shows on the same night. In NBC's *Lanigan's Rabbi* ("Say It Ain't So, Chief") she plays the widow of a murdered man who was having an affair with the prime suspect. The episode also starred John Astin and Jackie Coogan, both veterans of TV's *The Addams Family*. On ABC, Beverly was a traveling carnival owner whose workers are suspects in a large jewel theft on *The Nancy Drew Mystery* (episode title: "The Mystery of the Fallen Angels"). Two of its co-stars, Robert Englund and Jamie Lee Curtis, would meet their own destinies on Elm Street and Halloween night, respectively.

Beverly and her family were several thousand miles away at the time these shows aired, on vacation in Hawaii. However, not all vacations to paradise are pleasant.

> Yes, we went to the island of Maui and when we arrived it rained, and we stayed there for 11 days and there was a small black cloud that never left our hotel — it rained 11 solid days! It never stopped! There were a few days that it rained everywhere, but every day it rained where we were at the hotel and every day we got into our rented car and took our hamburgers and hot dogs and whatever else we had and went down the road to get some sun. And every day it blew like there was a hurricane. So you would sit on the beach with this wind and the heat, and the sand would blow to the point where you were just covered! And then we would get back in the car and go back to the rain at our hotel. For 11 days we did that! We had a good time, though! The kids liked it — but they could have done without the rain! The kids wanted me to cook, and I didn't mind that, it was just going to the store in the rain all the time. It just never stopped. And, of course, it was one of those marvelous things where everyone says, "Well, it never rains at this time of the year." You know, I always go to places where they say it has never rained or there has never been a hurricane, and it always rains or there is always a hurricane! Despite it all, I think we all had a good time![7]

On August 22, 1977, Beverly's good friend and former *Stump the Stars* teammate Sebastian Cabot died of a stroke.

> I spoke with Sebastian's wife Kay who had phoned me. She told me that he had had a toe amputated because he was a diabetic and he had developed gangrene in a toe that he had somehow injured. So it had to be amputated and she said it was just healing and the whole family was so pleased — and then he had a massive, massive stroke.
>
> He had had a stroke previously which impaired his speaking so he did not speak the way we remembered. His voice was completely different. Kay and the family could understand him but his way of speaking had changed. He had taken voice therapy lessons to try to regain his speech pattern. But Kay said that his melodious voice was gone.
>
> Kay told me something that I thought was really rather moving. It seems in Canada where they were living, someone from a charity — the March of Dimes or Muscular Dystrophy — asked Sebastian to participate in a television fund-raising drive. Well, of course, he could not speak well enough, so he did a walk-on. The announcer introduced him and mentioned Sebastian as being one of the stars of *Family Affair* and also the star of *Checkmate*, which was a very popular show. Kay said that the people there in the audience gave him a standing ovation — for three solid minutes! Kay said that Sebastian was just so thrilled. She thought it was the most glorious moment of his life.
>
> Kay said that for three years she had given him everything she could — she really babied him and tried everything she possibly could to get him well. I just guess it was his time. It's so very sad though. I'll miss him. We all will.[8]

In November 1976, Beverly and Fillmore were on vacation in Mexico when word came from her agent that she had been cast in the female lead in director Christopher Cain's production *Sixth and Main*. Her co-stars were Leslie Nielsen and Roddy McDowall. The Cranks were back in Los Angeles the very next day. The film went into production on November 8 and finished on Christmas Day, with locations in and around Los Angeles. Originally slated for a March release, it was finally in general distribution though National Cinema on August 31, 1977. Beverly described her character, Monica Cord, as a very wealthy woman "who has nothing to do with her life, particularly, so she's always doing something. One week she's a painter, the next week she's going to be an authoress, the week after that, a sculptress. She's loaded with money and bored with life.

> Because she can buy her way in and out of any situation, plus the fact she has no qualms about anything, she goes "where angels fear to tread." She figures if she gets into some kind of a jam, she can buy her way out of it. She's tired of just the cocktail and the luncheon kind of thing, and she wants to get into something fascinating.
>
> She picks up strangers — she's not afraid of them. She's not afraid of picking up a bum or picking up somebody that she doesn't know and find out about them. She could get herself into a lot of trouble because of this — which she does in this movie.
>
> She's always had money, it really doesn't mean anything to her — except for control. She's a very shallow woman and has no real convictions of her own. Monica is like a butterfly — she goes from one thing to another. She can change her thinking in two minutes or allow someone to change it for her.[9]

Normally Beverly would do her own stunts if at all possible. But in *Sixth and Main*, she recalled, "We did a scene where Leslie Nielsen throws me around a room and we had some stunt people do that because the director wanted it to be really hard. When the stunt man threw this girl, he threw her right against the wall!"[10]

When asked to describe her frequent co-star Leslie Nielsen, Beverly said, "Leslie had always been a good friend of mine, but I just didn't get his sense of humor. I just didn't. He came from a different angle than I came from. I couldn't just sit and talk to Leslie. He had a very quirky sense of humor. I liked him but he'd talk and I wouldn't know what the hell he was saying. I must be really dense! But he became so popular. I couldn't believe what happened to him. It was all comedy. He's an incredible dramatic actor but I don't think he'll ever play anything serious again even though I know he could. I don't know if anyone will ever give him a chance. I'm glad of his success, though, because he deserves every second of it."[11]

In his *Hollywood Reporter* review, Jean Hoelscher wrote that *Sixth and Main* "plays like a Frank Capra movie sprinkled with four letter words.... Into the midst of these basically good-hearted people comes a stereotyped, domineering, neurotic, rich woman. Beverly Garland has the thankless task of playing this rather despicable character who seems to have no redeeming qualities. To her credit, Garland manages to soften the character somewhat...."

Beverly offered her own review of the picture. "I think my performance is good. The picture is kind of a strange one — it's almost like two pictures in one. Leslie Nielsen is a bum and I pick him up and bring him to my house. I'm going to rehabilitate him. So it has to do with his life when he's down at Sixth and Main and it has to do with his life once I meet him. Leslie is marvelous in it — he really is so good. Roddy McDowall is great in it too."[12]

Beverly wrote to say that she tested on September 13, 1977, for *The Harvey Korman Show* "and will know by next Monday. If you don't hear, I didn't get it and so will be off to Europe for 14 days. Home October 3, 1977." A subsequent note, dated October 3, confirmed that she wouldn't be filming the show. "We leave today for Paris — what a good time I think we will have!"

When she got back, Beverly had this to say about her adventures in France:

We stayed at the airport here trying to get on this plane from 8 A.M. till almost 8 P.M. — but we finally got on the plane and when we landed in Paris we rented a car. We got there early in the morning — we had flown all night and we were so tired that we were "dingy" and we didn't know it! So we got this little car with the gear shift that Fillmore decided he wanted. So now we're in Paris and we didn't know which way we were going and we had this tiny little map that someone had given us and Fillmore kept saying, "Where are we?" and I kept saying, "I don't know where we are, I have no idea where we are." I didn't know whether I was on the Left Bank, the Right Bank, or where I was! Well, we must have driven past our hotel 40 times — and then we got stalled in traffic and all the Frenchmen were yelling and screaming at us! I thought Fillmore was going to have apoplexy and have a heart attack right there! And I thought, "My heavens, if he does that, what'll I do" — you know, with all the red tape and everything! "I think what I'll do is just stuff him in my suitcase and get back on the plane and bury him when I get home!" Anyway, we finally got to the hotel, and that night we went out with a friend of mine who lives in Normandy. She was an old friend from school. We had a great time!

Then we started off for the country. We stayed in all these quaint chateaux — we stayed in one where Napoleon had lived for a while. And all these chateaux have the most magnificent food I have ever eaten. And I ate everything! I always thought that truffles would be the most exciting thing in the world to eat — they're just awful! But anyway, we really had great food. And I did all the driving. I've never seen anything so charming as the French countryside. We saw castles and villages and towns and old churches and old forts — things that I just never believed were there. Forts that were way up on the tops of hills that have been converted into funny little hotels and shops. We stayed one night in an old church which had been run by an order of monks. The history in the French countryside is overwhelming. We always tried to stay away from the big cities. We went to Nice but we didn't actually stay there, we stayed in Monte Carlo. We tried to stay in the countryside and most of the chateaux we did stay at were high on hills where only the birds go. Many of the places we stayed in were converted castles. It was so much fun. I think the only hard thing was that until we got to Monte Carlo, we packed and unpacked every single solitary day — but when we got to Monte Carlo we spent three days there so that was fun and we really kind of unwound there.

It's really hard driving like that. I remember one day I drove almost seven and a half hours — that's a long time. We enjoyed the whole trip though — we enjoyed the people. We would go to the outdoor markets and get chicken and fruit and cheese and a bottle of wine and we would go find a little stream where we'd sit down and have our lunch. Every day we'd buy fresh baked sourdough bread.

Our trip was exciting. Many times I drove the wrong way on the wrong side of the street and did all sorts of terrible things — and then Fillmore would drive! Well, I really thought that when I finally got home my hair would be white but it wasn't. It's amazing that it isn't. Driving over there is incredible![13]

In 1977, a news item announced that Fred MacMurray and Shirley Jones would be reunited with their television families for an ABC-TV special titled *The Partridge Family, My Three Sons Thanksgiving Reunion*. Ads for the show slated for November 25, 1977 (the Friday after Thanksgiving), said, "Two of America's favorite television families are back for a special celebration. Join Shirley Jones, Fred MacMurray and their clans as they share hilarious, heartwarming moments from their past shows ... enjoy special songs by David Cassidy ... and a full hour of festive holiday fun." Tone of *Variety* (November 25, 1977) said, "It's pleasant to see Fred MacMurray back with TV wife Beverly Garland." Beverly enjoyed it very much and remarked, "That was great because we hadn't seen each other for a long time. It was fascinating for me to see and talk to everybody and find out what everyone was doing. Fred MacMurray had that cancer scare and he was shaken by that, but now it's in remission and he looks marvelous. The show was really fun — we all enjoyed it. It was a highlight of the year to be with everybody again."

The last show Beverly filmed that year began on November 8 when she started work on "Case: The Sylvia Needleman Experience" on *The Tony Randall Show*. In it, Beverly plays a flashy real estate agent "who tries to dazzle Randall into selling his house."[14]

Beverly always felt that comedy was more of a challenge. "I think comedy is much harder to do because your timing has to be perfect. Actually, you have to play comedy exactly as you do drama — you have to play it very straight. You can't try to be 'funny.' I find that the certain way you have to read lines and the timing make comedy much more difficult. I'm very funny if I'm just meeting and talking to people. But naturally when you have lines, your whole timing has to be perfection. I don't think it's as easy to do as drama.

"I love comedy. I started off as a comedienne — a young Eve Arden type — when I started in theater many years ago. I never did go into much serious drama really until I did *Medic* — that was probably one of my first big dramatic roles. Then I appeared in mostly dramatic shows until *The Bing Crosby Show*. But I find that serious drama is easier to do than comedy — definitely."[15]

Beverly found Tony Randall "tremendously talented, he is very bright; he has a tremendous positive attitude. He is a non-smoker and you couldn't smoke anywhere near him. At the time, I still smoked and when I did the show, Tony could smell someone on the other side of a door smoking and he would get terribly upset over that. Anyway, he was just a charming man — he knew where he was and what he was all about. He was a very positive kind of man. He was so very positive — he had come to grips with himself; with who he was and what he was.

"Tony Randall was so self-possessed in some ways but not in others. He was just a charming man — full of energy and full of life. He was kind of opinionated at times but that was his right. He was very good with me, very good to work with and I thought his comic timing was marvelous."[16]

Surprisingly, Beverly found working in front of live audiences somewhat intimidating. "I did a lot of live television in the 1950s. It was fun doing those live shows then. I get in front of an audience now and I just get scared to death! I'm just not used to it. I started on stage and I did live television, but then I got spoiled. I got into film and there isn't anybody there but the crew and you're kind of contained in your little area, and for some reason now live audiences get to me!

"When I did *The Tony Randall Show*, that live audience scared me silly. Now that's ridiculous. I've got to get out of that. Especially when I was trained with audiences. It's funny, when you get away from something for so long, it's hard to get back again."

Thinking back on those early live television shows, Beverly had this to say: "Those were great days and they were fun scripts. The wonderful thing about them was that you had a long time to rehearse — much longer than you do today. Now when you do a program like *The Tony Randall Show*, you don't have time to rehearse. When we did *Lux Video Theatre* and *Playhouse 90*, we had a tremendous amount of rehearsal — a tremendous amount of thinking about our parts and being able to move and do scenes over and over again. But you don't have this today in these half-hour shows. But anyway, I loved doing live shows back in those days."[17]

The New Year began for Beverly and Fillmore with a week-long trip to Florida and the Bahamas for some deep sea fishing. The Cranks did manage to catch some large gamefish. When she returned to Los Angeles, Beverly filmed two television commercials, the first for Polaroid Cameras and the other for General Mills' Buc Wheats breakfast cereal.

Beverly explained what filming a typical commercial entailed: "It takes a day to go to the interview and then you're called back if they like you. Then if you do get the commercial, you are called back in to go over wardrobe and to talk about the commercial — that is, what they want you to do. The day that you film, you're usually there at 6:30 or 7 A.M. and you finish anywhere from 6:00 to 8 P.M., depending on how long it takes. They try to do the commercial all in one day if it is at all possible."[18]

Beverly and Fillmore were also busy planning an addition to their North Hollywood hotel and adding a second hotel in Sacramento.[19]

> When we built the North Hollywood hotel, Fillmore got antsy and he decided that he wanted to have a string of hotels. He wanted a hotel for every child — four hotels — and maybe more! So we went to Sacramento and we bid on a piece of property downtown which we lost. There was another piece of property out further in Sacramento which he bid on and won.
>
>   At the time, we felt Sacramento was just going to burst open. It's the capital of California and it was a small town then. But lots of new people have come in and lots of people from back East have come. It was poised to burst and they really did not have a lot of hotel space. So Fillmore got the plans together and he broke ground on the 260-room hotel in the fall of 1978. Then interest rates went through the roof. But by this time we had ordered the building materials and we had the workers hired. Fillmore was trapped. He said, "I can't stop. I'm in too deep. I've got to do it. I've got to finish and hope to God I can make it work." Well, we opened that hotel so much in the hole, we just could never recoup it. We finally ended up losing that hotel. It was impossible.
>
>   Having the two hotels was wrong because Fillmore needed to be right here in North Hollywood and to concentrate on this hotel. But he said to me one night when I asked him why he was so unhappy, "You know, I really want to build that hotel in Sacramento." I said, "Oh, Fillmore. I don't think that's a good idea." He said, "But I really want to do that." And I said, "You really

want to do it? Okay, do it!" Which I should never have said. He did and we lost it. So that was the end of Sacramento.[20]

Fillmore had even begun to build a house for them in Sacramento so they would have a place to stay. Beverly described it in a letter dated October 25, 1978: "It is a tract house ... 1,518 square feet; four bedrooms, two baths, cathedral ceilings and it's for me to play with, decorate, stay in when we go up and then sell. What fun!"

The Sacramento hotel was originally going to be called Beverly Garland's Pointe West Motor Lodge but someone on the East Coast had named their motor lodge "Pointe West" and had registered that name. To avoid a lawsuit, Beverly and Fillmore renamed it the Beverly Garland Motor Lodge. "They made a big thing about it," Beverly remarked, "and they got their lawyers involved and wanted to take us to court. We just said, 'Oh, well.' We probably could have fought it, maybe, and gone ahead and left it but then we thought everybody calls it the Beverly Garland Pointe West anyway, so why don't we just name it the Beverly Garland? So we changed the name. But the restaurant is called 'The Pointe' so we figured we'd leave that. I was very pleased with the hotel — it was a pretty place."[21]

The hotel was designed with the gold rush era in mind; the restaurant even featured a house wine under Beverly's own label. Although the Cranks couldn't make their second hotel venture a success, they were right about the growth in Sacramento. In 1980, the population was approximately 275,000. By the 2010 census, the population of Sacramento had jumped to over 454,000.

She said in a taped letter dated February 1979, "I have a new agent and a new personal manager and I'm very pleased about both of them. I decided to get a personal manager because I just felt that my career was going down the drain and I have to revive it. The manager is also Joe Campanella's manager and he's done very well with him.

"I stayed with the same agents I had and I finally realized that this was a big mistake — I should have left them years ago. So, in the meantime, I talked to a new agent and I like him so I've signed with him now. I'm going to see what happens with this new arrangement."

Beverly admitted that she should have been more vigilant. "I started off with a very good agent," she confessed, "and I'm somebody who usually stays with an agent for a long, long time. I don't change agents, that's not what I do. But then, I would have a great agent and then he would leave or the arrangement would fall apart. So I guess I've had maybe in my lifetime six or seven agents, which is not too bad. Then if I wasn't working, I would say, 'Ah, you know, I'm not working. What do you think?' and my agent would say, 'Oh, but Beverly, you *will* work!' You know, I don't believe one thing agents say to me. So I would go with another agent.

"My first agent, Ray Cooper, was wonderful. He wasn't very big, he was very small, and he did very well with me. But then it got to the point where my career began to take off and he just couldn't keep up. He didn't have the contacts and he wasn't big enough. So it was always the same thing — should I go with a big agent or a small agent? Should I go with a big agent and get lost or should I get a small agent and not meet the producers? It was always very difficult to find the right agent that would be good for me."[22]

Fillmore had an outsider's viewpoint about Hollywood agents and producers. "I wouldn't say she's had trouble with her agents," Fillmore said. "She just finds that agents don't produce and she had to look for new ones — new blood. These people are hard because you work with them for a time and finally you realize you haven't worked. So what good are they? And what good does it do them? After all, they're not making any money either.

"She'll go out on an interview and you never hear another word about it. You go out for an interview and they won't call back. That's another thing that's crappy about this business. I always think that a person who sits down and talks to you about a job should be acknowledged like, 'I'm sorry, but you win some and you lose some.' Say whatever you can say, but you've got to let them know. In this business, they interview and that's it. They haven't got time to tell you. You just don't get a call back. So if you don't get a call back, you're out!"[23]

Beverly did start to work again. She got a guest star role on *How the West Was Won* in an episode titled "The Slavers." The series starred James Arness and Bruce Boxleitner. "I took it because I really felt that I should start working again. My character is Hannah and she was an old friend of Jim Arness' character. I loved working with him. He just got married about three days before I started working on the show."[24]

Beverly then filmed a segment of the NBC-TV series *The Greatest Heroes of the Bible*. Beverly said in a taped letter she sent shortly after completing the show, "It's called 'Abraham's Sacrifice' and it's being produced by Schick-Sun. I play Sarah, Abraham's wife, who is 99 years old. They did a fantastic makeup on me. I mean, it's incredible. Gene Barry plays Abraham and Ed Ames is also in it. We really had a good time. It was very interesting for me.

"We went to Page, Arizona, because we were supposed to be in the desert. But it was a very difficult location because it was so cold you could have died. I wore four pairs of underwear and a jogging suit that [Barry] gave me. I also wore a cashmere sweater and a vest under my costume as well as boots over four pairs of socks and I was still cold! But I wore a wig so that helped my head."[25]

Despite her discomfort, Beverly always thrived in shows where she had to deal with harsh environments. "I love working when it's rainy and stormy," she confessed. "I love to work in the elements. I like it when they say, 'Now the rain is going to come down in torrents'—*I love it*! 'Now the snow' (when those tiny bits of paper fall)—*I love it*!

> I like anything that is physical in movies. I did a movie once when I had to go across the desert and I was dying and it was hot. We made it when it was hot. We looked like the Wrath of God and *I loved it*!
>
> I loved going through the swamp. I love anything that has to do with disasters. I think most actors do like to work in the muck and the mire; the rain and the crap. I just think that's fun. Maybe they don't. Maybe a lot of actors like drawing rooms and being dressed up. I like to be grungy and I like to play a character that wears no makeup; that wears dirty old clothes. I loved *Where the Red Fern Grows*. I didn't put on any makeup; my hair was stringy down my back; I wore these crappy old dresses that were made out of potato sacks and those old squishy shoes and I just loved it. That's the kind of thing that I like to do. I'm really not comfortable being dressed and furred. I act better and I am better when I play a pioneer woman. That's the kind of part I really love.
>
> I can remember *The Joker Is Wild* and we were all so dressed. It took two and a half hours for makeup and wardrobe—and the clothes were just so special. Edith Head did all the clothes and the fittings. You walk around like you're in your party dress and you can't relax because you have to look perfect.
>
> I really just like to work where you can be grungy. I think what I'd like to do more than anything else in the world is a Western. I mean, the covered wagons and the dust. I would really like to play a pioneer woman with no makeup and lots of kids; lots of problems and Indians.
>
> The Donner Pass—I really would love to do a movie like that. I just think that would be fascinating. I would be the old lady on the wagon train going west to Sacramento.[26]

Beverly also tested for another show, *Skag*, which starred Karl Malden with Peter Gallagher and Craig Wasson as his sons. Beverly explained what transpired after she read for the part of Malden's wife, Jo Skagska.

The network just said no. Piper Laurie has done this and done that so let's have Piper Laurie. I think Piper Laurie is an incredible actress and she's an old friend of mine. She was absolutely wrong for *Skag*. This is one of the reasons why *Skag* didn't last. You had no conception that Karl Malden and Piper Laurie ever went to bed. That they had this wild sex thing. She looked like his daughter. She's very ethereal. She wasn't the down-to-earth broad that was the truck driver's waitress and that's where this lady came from. Karl Malden met her and she was the fanny pinching gal who could handle these guys. I mean, he's in construction and works in the steel mill. You didn't see that in Piper Laurie at all. She had more breeding. It just didn't work. It would have worked with me. You would have had that feeling of these two people and you would have known that they dug each other. You would have seen that immediately; that's what was written in the script and it never came over. They had to re-write it out because it didn't work. Of course, the whole damn thing didn't work. But that's one of the big elements of the story that didn't work.[27]

In the *Greatest Heroes of the Bible* episode "Abraham's Sacrifice" (August 15, 1981), Beverly played Sarah, the aged wife of Abraham.

Fillmore found it just as perplexing, "You just have to deal with rejection and Beverly does it very well. When she was in the high point of her career, it bothered her a lot depending on how far it went. They deal pretty poorly in this town. You know, they lead you down the primrose trail that you got the job and then they dump you....

The one I remember was with Karl Malden. She had the role and everything was set. Then they hired Piper Laurie. Piper was a good performer; a good professional but she just didn't carry it off. Instead of it being a series, it ran for only six shows. The character was a tough woman. Piper Laurie was not. I knew it was a blow to Beverly.[28]

Perhaps all they saw was Piper's Oscar nomination for *Carrie* and thought that alone would attract viewers. It might have, if it were a televised version of *Carrie* and it might have very well attracted viewers for an episode or two of *Skag*. But it would have become obvious to any viewer that proper casting is the key to a successful show — awards on the mantle withstanding.

On April 30, 1979, CBS-TV had a live broadcast of the Miss U.S.A. Beauty Pageant from Biloxi, Mississippi, with host Bob Barker. Beverly was one of the judges. Then, in a letter dated August 7, 1979, Beverly imparted the following news: "I'm doing a picture with Linda Blair called *Roller Boogie*. Carrie and Jimmy are extras in the picture. Carrie has the acting bug and is having the time of her life."

The press generally savaged this movie, with the *Los Angeles Times*' Charles Schreger reporting, "The compelling reason to rush out the door and pay four dollars or five dollars to catch *Roller Boogie* is the chance to prove — once and for all — that there is no tie between excellence and profit in the movie business." *Variety*'s Cart predicted, "Box office prospects are dim unless a miracle occurs," and coined a new phrase, "Discoexploitation," to describe this new film subgenre. It was harmless fun for the undemanding teenage masses.

Beverly recalled how she got the part of Lillian Barkley:

I went in and saw the producer. He had seen me at a party and invited me to his home. He's a film buff and we talked. He then set up a meeting with the director [Mark L. Lester]. I wore a hat and I looked really chic that day, I really did. I got all dressed up because the part called for that type of woman.

So we went and met the director — and he didn't know me from Adam! He said, "Gee, I'm sorry I never watch television so I don't see any of these shows. I don't know what you've done." So I rattled off all the television that I've done and some of the pictures that I've made. But he was a very young director and he hadn't seen any of the work I'd done on television or any of the movies.

He asked if I would mind taking the script into the other room, looking it over and reading it. So I said, "No, I don't mind." I went into the other room, looked it over, came back and read through the script. There was a casting woman there that had helped the director and producer cast the film and she said, "You're it. You've got the part. I think you're perfect."

So that's how it happened. I wish it would happen that way all the time.[29]

[Lillian Barkley is] a woman who is very rich — kind of a "Pasadena Woman." She is married to a man who really thinks she is a dumb bunny and he is always telling her to shut up. She lives in her own world of shopping and having her hair and nails done, and going to luncheons. She pays very little attention to her child. She trusts her daughter and thinks she knows what her child is doing. She's very superficial with her little girl. Lillian is very into her own world and half the time she doesn't know what her little girl is doing — although she doesn't distrust her. She loves her in her own way, but she really doesn't have much time for her. Lillian feels that she gives her daughter a lot of time but she really doesn't give her a lot of time at all. This is really what her character is all about. She is dominated by her little girl, in a sense, and she is dominated by her husband. She is in many ways a completely shallow woman and can do very little on her own — or has not had to do much on her own. Her husband rules the roost and whatever he says, goes. That's what she's like.[30]

Roller Boogie was shot in Los Angeles and Venice Beach, California. They took over an old dance hall and turned it into the Roller Boogie Palace. Outdoor scenes were also filmed at the Hilton Mansion. According to Beverly, "They didn't allow us to film in the house but we did shoot the garden scene there — the grounds are just so beautiful. The swimming pool is decorated in tiny mosaics; it must have cost a fortune! There is a lovely gazebo in the garden with a full kitchen. And the most incredible rose garden I think I have ever seen. Most of the scenes you do today are not done on a sound stage. Almost everything is done on location now."[31]

Reviews gave Beverly a nod for her performance. Cort of *Variety* wrote (December 6, 1979), "Beverly Garland is on target in her caricature of a desperately with it Bev Hills matron." Ron Pennington of *The Hollywood Reporter* (December 10, 1979) noted, "[P]erformances are acceptable with Beverly Garland taking top comedic honors for her hilarious portrayal of Blair's mother.... Overall, the film has a prevailing innocence that is reminiscent of the old 'Beach Blanket' movies. These kids do not drink, smoke or take dope, they're just out for a good time on their roller skates." (Most reviewers never picked up on that simple fact. They were looking for something more and missed the entire point of the picture. It was sort of like *Saturday Night Fever* on skates with Cher doing some of the honors on the soundtrack; and it made a lot of money.)

Beverly's year ended with a guest spot on another very popular, long-running series, *Charlie's Angels*, in an episode titled "Cruising Angels." In it, Beverly plays the love interest of series regular David Doyle but was secretly involved in a robbery using Charlie's yacht to transport illegal gold.

On December 22, 1979, Beverly's stepson, Fillmore Crank, Jr., married Tina Cole. In a letter sent a year before, dated December 1, 1978, Beverly broke the news "I'm very excited about the engagement. If you remember, Tina Cole played 'Katy' in *My Three Sons* and she's the one who had the triplets. She's also with the King Family and has been on the road with the King Cousins. So we're very excited about this new addition to our family. It's kind of one of the highlights of the year for us. We're looking forward to their getting married."

Beverly was certain that this marriage was going to work. Unfortunately, it didn't.

> Smoke [Fillmore, Jr.] went with a girl in high school. Then he went into the Air Force and after a year, he was so lonesome and so homesick that he married her. They had a wedding, then he went to Vietnam and after that he was sent to Germany. So Smoke was gone for about four years. He'd come back every now and then to see her and that was it. It was a happy marriage because they hardly saw each other. About a year after he came home, they got a divorce.
>
> At that time, Fillmore had finished building the hotel down here in North Hollywood. Fillmore decided to build in Sacramento. So he turned to Smoke and Smoke said he'd build it. He's very much like his father — he can do anything with plumbing and construction — he's good at that. So Fillmore turned the building of the Sacramento Hotel over to Smoke and he built it.
>
> Smoke stayed in Sacramento and he married Tina Cole. He fell madly in love with Tina. She had a little house here in Los Angeles — a darling tiny little house. She also has a son named Volney. But Smoke was building in Sacramento. So he talked her into moving up there.
>
> I don't know what happened to that marriage but it just fell apart. I talked to Tina all the time and I just think that Smoke was the culprit. Tina's the sweetest lady that you could ever meet. She's the most absent-minded lady — she drives out of the gas station with the hose still in the gas tank — she does things like that, but she's just the best.
>
> Tina is one of the King Family and is very, very family-oriented. She's a very good Mormon. But something happened to that marriage. I don't know if Smoke started to play around and she caught him at it. I guess it finally just didn't work for them and they got divorced. Smoke has since met someone else and they got married.
>
> Tina's not married. Tina and Smoke had three children together. Tina stayed in Sacramento. She's a drama teacher at a modeling agency there. She's a great teacher. She takes whatever acting jobs she can get. Tina has a great personality and she's cute as a button. I hope she meets somebody because she's a good lady. She's a great housekeeper, funny, full of life. She's really had it tough — really, really tough.[32]

Fillmore was also very unhappy about the divorce. "To this day I don't know what happened to that marriage. She is a lovely girl and he is a good guy and they've got three kids. This was a big disappointment to us because we thought that was a marriage made in Heaven. She never wanted the divorce at all. He had had it.

"Beverly reacts to it because she favors Tina. Of course, there was another woman involved — in my opinion — and Beverly doesn't like that. She has a thing about men playing around. I tell you, I wouldn't dare. I don't dare! I just think that if I started fooling around, I don't know what she'd do. She says she's got pinking shears!"[33]

22. A Star on the Hollywood Walk of Fame

A news item in *Variety* announced the start of Rastar Productions' *The Perfect Circle*, which went before the cameras on January 28, 1980, under the direction of Claudia Weill. The item went on to say that interiors and exteriors would be done in Los Angeles and New York City. Heading the cast were Jill Clayburgh, Michael Douglas, Charles Grodin, Steven Hill and Beverly Garland.

According to Beverly, "I play Steven Hill's bride, Emma. He is a widower who gets married to a woman who his daughter [Clayburgh] feels is not right for him at all. But she finds that the woman is a very sensitive, very sweet woman. Emma is somebody who is very much in love with the father, and has something that maybe Jill Clayburgh's character is looking for but doesn't have herself.

"You can see that this woman has wonderful facets, she is young at heart, and yet, I think, she's an 'old soul' on top of that. She's had a very unhappy marriage before, and now she meets Steven Hill and she marries him. There's a wonderful scene in the movie where Emma gets up and jitterbugs with her son [Michael Douglas] which I hope they still have in the movie — I'm sure they will leave it in. It was good working on that movie because the stars were probably the most talented people around."

Beverly was terribly conflicted working on this particular picture as she revealed during an interview shortly after it had completed principal photography.

> I don't like myself in that picture. I wish I'd never done it. I don't know. I don't want to talk about it. I want to wait and see it. I feel this way about it — that even at my worst, I'm not too bad. So let's hope that that happens. But I have a feeling that this might have been my worst. Good God!
>
> I didn't have time for preparation because they called me on Monday and said, "We're going to shoot tomorrow." I read for this picture and they hired someone else. I can't think of the actress' name. She got very ill and she couldn't do the picture. They called me and they said, "She's very ill. They're having a doctor for her Friday and Saturday. If on Friday night they decide she can't come — she's got pneumonia — you'll shoot on Tuesday. Wardrobe is on Monday." Well, it's a big picture and I was just not prepared!
>
> First of all, psychologically, it was very difficult because, well, "We really don't want you. We really don't like you — goodbye!" Then, "Yes, well, now that the lady we want can't do it, so now we would like to have you." I'm not sure that they did want me. I'm sure there were probably people who said, "Oh, I think we ought to have Beverly" and then made up their minds. But psychologically it was very difficult for me. I wasn't tuned in correctly in my mind. So that was hard. To be fair, they did replace other people in the cast, so I really can't be upset about that. It was difficult for me to handle, for some reason.[1]

And then I went and I saw the rushes and I died because the man who shot it shot it with bounce lighting so that you have these tremendous deep lines — sort of like the Grand Canyon — on your face which, again at my age, psyched me out. It just destroyed me. So that was very difficult.

Though all this I'm working and I couldn't do anything right. I mean, I had a block — a mental block. Now, all I'm hoping is that through the mental block, it all comes through; that I come through. I figure, as bad as I was, I still would be okay. I'm good enough that as bad as I am in it, I'm all right. That's my feeling. So I'm just hoping. I'm sorry. It's such a big picture. I just hope it comes out well.

They have a tremendous editor on this picture. He's an artist. He's the kind that can take a movie and cut it like a fine diamond. I hope with his tremendous perception, I will be saved. I also know Ray Stark is not some slouch so I know it's going to be done with great finesse.

From what I understand, everybody was very pleased. Somebody called my manager and said, "Everyone loved her and she was great." The one who wrote it must have said it to me a hundred times; the director said it. But I don't believe anybody. I'm very bad at that. I don't believe anybody who tells me anything. I just don't believe anybody. I guess all my life people have said that. That's how I am. I don't believe it. "You're really great!" "You look good!" "You look pretty!" Yeah, s—, I don't believe you. Thanks a lot but I don't believe that!

I think probably because you work so hard and try so hard and everybody says you're so good. You look at your watch and you say, "Yes." And I've worked every second of my life. I've been put down; so many times I've not gotten the jobs. So many times have I read for the job and I don't get it. So many times has somebody said, "No, we don't want you."

You have built a wall. You survive, my dear, by building this wall with solid concrete. I have this wall and it's very difficult for me when someone says, "Gee, you're pretty" [etc.]. I listen and I should say, "Thank you. It's very nice." But I don't believe any of that. First of all, I'd rather you didn't say it because it's very difficult for me to handle it, and second of all, I don't believe it. It's a nice thing to say and "Isn't that sweet of you to say that." I'm getting worse now when people begin to compliment me. I completely change the subject as fast as I can. "And how's your lawn? Is it green? I had a terrible time with my plants!" I want to hear it but I can't handle it. I just can't. Isn't that strange?

I see myself completely different than anybody else. That's my hang-up. So it was a very difficult thing for me doing this film. My hang-ups came out and they took over. But I have survived it. As Fillmore said to me, "You've got to use your science and know who you are and what you want." I can do this quietly in my own little closet.

Oh, I can give the impression that I'm a very positive woman. I can give one that impression. But on the inside, I'm a churning bundle of nerves. It's earthquake time! But nobody sees that. I don't ever give that impression. Even when I'm not positive, people think I am. That is also part of the wall, you understand. It's good and that's what makes me a survivor. I can do it. I can get up and do my thing. But there are times when it destroys me inside. This was one of them.

I hope that when I go to see it that I find I was wrong. It was more about how I looked. I was not happy with the way I looked. It destroyed me. I know it was the rushes that I saw and I made up my mind then and there that I would never, never, ever go again. I know that the rushes are not what you are going to see on the screen. It's very difficult. It's hard to see yourself on the screen looking like that. You're saying, "Oh my God!" You don't say to yourself, "Well, that's not how it's going to be in the final print." You don't see that. But I've made up my mind. I now have a new rule and it will never be changed. Unless someone tells me, "You have *got* to come and see this because I don't think the makeup is right and I want you to look at it." [Then] I will go. But until someone says, "I'm the producer and I want to show you something that I think we ought to look at together," I will *never go again*! That is an ironclad rule that I made three months ago and I will never change it![2]

Beverly wasn't surprised when the film's title was changed (to *It's My Turn*). "When we were doing the movie, they said to me [that the title would be] *The Perfect Circle*— we think.' That was the first inkling that I thought it might not be released under that title. That it might be changed."

It's My Turn was the first time Beverly worked with a female director. "I'm not sure but I think I like being directed by a man better. Not that Claudia isn't a very good director, she is. There's an easiness in being directed by a woman because you feel that a woman understands a woman. There's also kind of an interesting rapport being directed by a man. Maybe it is easier being directed by a woman because you feel that she understands where you're coming from. Also, you can say things to her that maybe you couldn't say to a man. Yes, maybe I'm going to have to take my first statement back. I enjoyed being directed by a woman. It's an interesting experience and one that I'm certainly glad I had. I wish there were more women directors. I think they know more of what they want from a woman on the screen than maybe a man even does. I don't know — there's two ways of looking at it. It's hard to say but I enjoyed the experience."[3]

Beverly was surprised to see the screenwriter on set for most of the time she was filming. "Eleanor Bergstein was there every day and she worked very closely with the director. She was there to help us with any interpretation or for any line change. The only problem with that was that I found she sometimes had a completely different interpretation of what she wrote then what the director wanted us to portray on the screen, which was kind of interesting.

"When the author and the director are both present on the set and they see things differently, then you are torn. You cannot listen to the author — you must listen to the director. The director is boss. Whether or not the author of the screenplay wants it that way, if that's the way the director sees it and wants it, then that's it. You never do a scene the way the writer wants it if there is a conflict."[4]

Beverly's reviews should have dispelled all of her doubts about her performance. Robert Osborne of *The Hollywood Reporter* said. "Beverly Garland is especially good as Clayburgh's new stepmother" and *Variety*'s Berg noted, "Beverly Garland and Steven Hill provide a healthy dose of old-fashioned romance as the middle-aged newlyweds."

Just prior to the national release of *It's My Turn*, the producer of *Roller Boogie* wanted Beverly for a role in another film he was preparing, *The Seduction*. He sent Beverly the script but when she read it, she was amazed that he would even consider her for what appeared to be barely disguised pornography. When she told him that she wasn't interested, he became very angry and made threats.

> I guess he's upset with me. That'll be the end of me, I'll never work in this town again. [He] was the one who wanted me for *Roller Boogie* and [he] is the type who never "forgets" and who gets very dramatic. I know he'll talk about me. I just know that. It's the kind of person he is. I can just hear it. Well, that's the way it has to be. I'm anxious to see the picture. I'm anxious to see who does it. I'm anxious to see what they think of it.
>
> When you talk about the really good people in the industry, I don't think I have to worry about [him]. But I know him well enough to know that he will not shut up about me. But I also know that there are enough people who know what [he] does and they will just ignore his gossip.
>
> It's an exploitation movie and it'll make money. But it's a copy. I mean, didn't Lauren Bacall just make a movie called *The Fan*— which is about a Broadway actress who is stalked by a man? It's exactly the same thing. It's a rip-off. This gal is a TV newswoman — a Barbara Walters type — and the guy stalks her. It's the same thing, the same movie. So I just said no, I'm not going to do that. I'm not going to compromise myself. I would have been so embarrassed. I just don't want to be that woman. I hate it. I don't want to be embarrassed.[5]

Just for the record, Beverly did make two black & white short films in the late 1940s (*The Fishing Lesson* and *Fanny with the Cheeks of Tan*) that contained no nudity but had narration that was filled with double entendres. If either were viewed today, one would find them no more titillating than most prime time television commercials.

Beverly recalled that many years ago she was filming a Western in the desert and during one break many of the cast and crew stopped at a local bar. The bar had a Movieola machine and one of these films began to play. When one of the crew noticed Beverly's resemblance to the "star" of the film short, he confronted her about it. Naturally, she denied it was her. "That's not *me*! I didn't do that!"

"But I did do it," Beverly confessed many years later. "That was my bad past."[6]

On Friday, June 27, 1980, syndicated stations across the country participated in a two-hour special called *A Time for Love* which focused on Children's Village, U.S.A., a residential care facility for abused children in Southern California. The co-hosts were Mike Connors, Florence Henderson and Beverly.

Beverly and Fillmore were on vacation in Washington, D.C., and Virginia when they had to get back to Los Angeles in time for her to begin work on *Trapper John, M.D.* ("Girl Under Glass") which was due to go into production around the middle of July. The day Beverly reported to 20th Century–Fox, her union went on strike! She eventually did complete the episode, which was the show's second season two-part opener on November 23 and 30, 1980. In a letter dated July 1980 she wrote, "It's a fun part! I'm very anxious to do the *Trapper John, M.D.* show. It's about a mother who has a young girl who is in the hospital. The girl is having a problem with her heart and has to have another operation. The mother gets very upset because one of the doctors is fooling around. This lady is really kind of a 'psycho,' which is fun for me because she really has some good scenes. I'm not in the show a lot, but what I am in I feel is something you'll remember. It's kind of like the old Beverly—a wild part! I really like it."

In November, Beverly attended the National Tour Brokers Association's convention in St. Louis where her promotional film, *C'mon Along America, There's a Better Way to Go* premiered. Beverly starred in the 15-minute, color, 16mm film with Tina Cole. Also featured were Jimmy and Carrington Crank as Tina's children. The film was lensed and directed by Julian Cole. Beverly plays a travel agent. The film contrasts a self-driven trip and a fully planned tour by motor coach. Beverly was also the executive producer on the film.

> It was fun to be an executive producer, fun to be on the other side of the camera and figure out time schedules and places and all the problems that the production side faces on everyday shooting.
>
> I think it is probably more fascinating than acting. I had a whole new experience open up for me and I would really like to be an executive producer or a producer. I just think it is fascinating to put something together from the beginning and see it cultivate and work on it and see it come to the end result.
>
> I know actors think that they are really everything that matters in a production, but I've found that they really aren't. There are so many things that go on behind the scenes that actors and actresses don't know anything about.
>
> I think an actor must know his craft and do his best with a sense of humor and be on time and do his job. That would certainly make everybody else's life easier. When you are on the other side of the camera, you really realize all the tremendous problems — money problems and location problems and technical problems — that you run into that just absolutely destroy you. So if you have an actor who has a sense of humor and is on time and knows his lines and is a professional — you couldn't ask for anything more. This experience has taught me a lot. As an actress,

I have always been a professional, I believe, but this has taught me to be that way even more so than I've ever been before. It was a good lesson and I'm certainly glad I had the opportunity to do it.

The film will be shown to travel agents and tour brokers all over the United States. It will be shown in clubs and in places where people are trying to sell motor coach touring. It will be used as a sales tool for the tourism business and for tourism bureaus.[7]

In the thirty years Beverly had worked on television, she had never appeared on a daytime soap. On January 29, 1981, that changed when she made her first appearance on CBS's *The Young and the Restless* in the role of Kay Thurston (later Chancellor). According to a press release, Beverly was taking over the role temporarily while her friend Jeanne Cooper was recuperating from an illness. However, that was only partly true.

Working on *The Young and the Restless* was really an experience. You actually film two or three shows in one day — that is, you film little segments for each show. My anticipation of how terrible it was going to be dissolved when I got down to CBS and started working on the show.

I found it interesting because there are many people on daytime television who learn their lines but I also found that there are many people who don't learn their lines at all! They just read off a cue card! It so happened that a few of the people I worked with knew their lines fairly well and it was much more fun working with them. I also found that on daytime television, or any kind of television work like that, you are very isolated. By that I mean, most of the time when you are on a set doing a TV show, most of the actors say, "Do you want to run lines?" So you run lines with them and you work out the scene and you get eye contact. You get a feeling as to how the other actor is going to work. On daytime television, nobody communicates, nobody runs lines — at least nobody ran any lines with me! Maybe if you really get to know one of the other actors well or if you had a very important scene it would be different. But on *Mary Hartman* which was filmed the same way as daytime television, nobody paid any attention to me, nobody wanted to run any lines. The same thing happened on *The Young and the Restless*. You just sit in your dressing room all by yourself and go over your lines by yourself. And I think that's rather difficult. I think actors must work together to make the scenes pay off. Apparently daytime television does very well and they feel it's fine the way it is.

I worked with an actor on *The Young and the Restless* who had the cue cards behind my shoulder and he never once looked at my face, never once knew if I was looking at him! When I gave him some kind of a reaction to his lines, he played the part in such a way that he had no reaction to my reaction. That, to me, is not acting. I resent it. If you're working with an actor who is doing nothing but reading over your shoulder, you can soon find yourself saying, "To hell with it. I guess I'll just read over your shoulder, too!" You can fall into that pit if you are not careful. To me, that's not what acting is all about. I guess I'm from the old school, I think really good pictures are made when the director takes his time and you do scenes over and over again so you can "get into it."

The networks are making a lot of money with daytime television. The scripts are loaded with sex, abortions, and every crazy thing you can ever think of. And the people at home really love it, but as far as I'm concerned, it is really not acting. Soaps are very difficult to act in because there are actors that you work with who care and there are actors that you work with that absolutely do not care. I found that if you ever did a soap and wanted to just read your cue cards, it would probably be the easiest money that you ever made. And I guess maybe you could resign yourself to do it that way. No doubt, there are actors on daytime television who read cue cards so well that you can't even tell they're doing it because they've done it so long.

Anyway, once my initial fears about a soap were gone, I found it was pleasant and fun and I really enjoyed it. Maybe that's because I enjoy all kinds of acting. I don't think it is "pure acting" but I certainly think it was enjoyable. Filming a soap involves a lot of time — I don't think most people realize that. You get to the studio early, you block your scenes in a room, then you go over it again, then you go down on the stage and block it for the camera, then you go over it again, then you go into makeup, then you go over the scene once more and then you shoot it. And finally, you learn your lines for the next day. So it's a long day, involving a lot of time — but it is enjoyable! Of course, the part I played on *The Young and the Restless*, Jeanne Cooper's role, is a fun part because the woman is an alcoholic and she's kind of nuts! I got a kick out of that part.[8]

As it turned out, Beverly's real reason for taking over the role was a ploy on the part of the show's producers to scare Jeanne Cooper straight. "Jeanne Cooper started to drink off-camera and they kept asking her not to drink. She kept drinking and so finally they decided that they would scare the living hell out of her. They called me and asked if I would play her part for a couple of days. I did and Jeanne said to herself, 'I could lose this because they brought Beverly in here. So I'd better straighten out.' She did straighten out. She's a good friend of mine. I like Jeanne Cooper. I did it because they asked me and they explained that they only wanted me for a week. But I had heard later that they would have offered me the role if she hadn't straightened out. But they didn't tell me that at the time."[9]

The Cranks had planned to go to Russia for the 1980 Summer Olympics. However, due to the political tensions at the time, the United States decided not to participate in the games.

> So the Russian Embassy gave us — because we had already paid to go — a half price tour if we wanted to go the following year. We thought since we had already paid that we would go then.
> In the meantime, Carrington was a member of the YMCA and they were going to Japan with a group of students and she wanted to go to Japan so we said, "Okay. You go to Japan and we'll go to Russia." So that's what we did. We took Jimmy and left for Russia on August 6, 1981.
> Russia was still under Communist rule back then and there were certain places where you couldn't go. You couldn't take any money. There were certain things you couldn't buy. It certainly was not the Russia you see today, of course. The only thing you could really buy were Communist posters.
> It was the longest trip and I remember Jimmy, he had long hair then, going through customs. The officials looked at him for ten minutes. I remember thinking, well, they've got to let my kid through. Eventually, they did.
> Then we went to this old, old hotel in Moscow and we got there so very late. On the beds in our rooms were a sheet and a blanket — you had to make up the bed yourself. Then Jimmy got very, very sick. Of course, you had a guide with you all the time; you didn't go anywhere without the guide. She got some kind of pill for him and she made me give him these pills. He couldn't eat anything but rice for three days.[10]
> A lot of people go to Russia and feel that they're being watched and their rooms are bugged. Maybe this is true, I don't know. I certainly never felt that we couldn't say whatever we wanted to say. I thought our tour guide was wonderful but I felt that she was programmed to tell me the kind of answers that I wanted to hear. "Russia does not understand why the Americans don't want peace. Russia certainly doesn't want to have an arms race. Russia has 12 or 15 countries bordering her, so naturally, she has to have an army and she has to be prepared because these countries have a whole different way of life than Russia has, so it is much more difficult for Russia than it is for America, who has only two countries on her borders, Canada and Mexico."
> We had one strange thing happen that bothered me. We would go to the restaurants, and the food was all set out. You couldn't order anything, it's just set out when you go on a tour in Russia. You walk in and are assigned a table and you eat what's there. I found that everybody else was eating wonderful eggs and caviar and we weren't having anything like that. Our group was eating cold meats and bread. I kept asking our guide why we were getting this type of food and she said, "Well, you have a different tour than anybody else." Well we didn't have a different tour — that was one excuse. Then it was, "The cook decides what you are to eat." That wasn't true either. It was just that they make excuses for everything and you can never get the truth out

of them. That's how I felt about it anyway. I never knew whether she was telling me the truth or not. But I accepted everything because I was in their country and I enjoyed seeing everything.

We went to the Kremlin and saw the jewels of the czars that made the jewels in the Tower of London look like you bought them at Sears, Roebuck & Company. I have never seen such incredible riches in my life.

I certainly would never want to live in Russia and be a Russian. I feel there is very little freedom to do anything. You're watched constantly. But as a tourist, I felt it was fascinating to go and see how they lived. We stayed at two terrible hotels that were very, very old. Clean, but old. And very difficult. You know, beds that were tiny and terribly uncomfortable and rooms that were no bigger than a small bathroom. They certainly were not comfortable. We did stay at one magnificent hotel in Leningrad which was built by a Swiss. It was just beautiful. Lots of marble is used because marble is very easy to mine in Russia.

The fascinating thing was the subway. Subways are decorated with crystal chandeliers and mosaics. The trains run every three seconds, it seemed. It costs twenty cents to travel all day on the subway, that's all. There is no advertising; you don't see any signboards or advertising of any kind because everything is run by the government, naturally.

But Russia is not a beautiful place. It's rather ugly, I think. They don't take a lot of time to grow flowers, there are not a lot of trees, nobody keeps up anything as far as that's concerned. Apartments are just great big, huge 40-story buildings that look awful. Around them is very little grass. There was some semblance of growth and flowers here and there which had been done for the Olympics because they were going to try to make Russia look beautiful for the Americans when they came. But otherwise, I didn't see anything terribly attractive that I really liked. However, I was fascinated by the place.

There is nothing really to buy — there is a tourist marketplace just for tourists. You cannot buy items in the regular market or in the other places where the Russians shop. Gums Department Store has nothing to offer. Prices are very, very expensive. Clothes are abominable.

I found the Russian men were quite attractive — tall and good-looking. Russian women were nondescript. The Russians have a very stern look on their face and they'd just as soon bump into you as not bump into you. I don't feel that they're the kind of people to say "Thank you" or "You're welcome" or "Excuse me" at all.

Jimmy kept a diary and he was a terrific little traveler. He never complained and he did everything he was supposed to do. He really enjoyed it. He came out of Russia and he said when he got home there was one thing he wanted more than anything else, and that was the American flag hung up outside of our house. Which is what we have now. It really brought home to him how much he loved America after having been to Russia. That, I think, was very interesting. Taking Jimmy at that age [13] was very good for him."[11]

That fall, Beverly filmed a one-hour pilot called *Judgment Day*. The production cost $1,300,000. The teleplay concerned a heavenly courtroom headed up by Barry Sullivan and with advocates from above and below and with such imaginative names as Mr. Heavener and Mr. Heller (played by Victor Buono and Roddy McDowell respectively). Beverly plays Vicki Connors, a madam. Needless to say, the pilot didn't sell.

Beverly also made a very brief appearance on *Hart to Hart* in "The Hart-Break Kid" which starred Robert Wagner and Stefanie Powers. "It was such a crappy part that I didn't tell anyone about it. I was hoping nobody would see it. Fifty million people came up to me and said, 'Saw you on *Hart to Hart*! Gee, it was great!' You never know what people are going to think or what they like."[12]

Shortly after filming a guest spot on *Flamingo Road* with her *Mad Room* co-star Stella Stevens, Beverly added another line to her résumé as hostess aboard the *Silver Circle Cruise Line* to Panama. "When you're a hostess for the Silver Circle, what you have to do is go to all the cocktail parties and greet all the people. You are the hostess — it's as if you gave the cocktail party. And then, once a day, you should try to go around to see everybody in the Silver Circle group and engage them in conversation. It's very easy. You just have to show up at all these functions and be gracious and nice. The guests like it and it's fun to do!"[13]

Perhaps nowhere in life is the past more likely to come back to haunt you then in show business. This is what happened to Beverly when she was up for the CBS-TV daytime television drama series *Capitol*.

> They had already hired Constance Towers as one of the female leads. Constance apparently knew the producer for fifteen years. They decided that they wanted her because her husband, John Gavin, was the ambassador to Mexico. They thought it would be very good for an ambassadress to do the show.
> So I tested for the "Bitch" part and they said that I was incredible — just incredible.... They just "adored" me! It was just fabulous!... So, of course, I felt magnificent about it and I just couldn't wait to start. Then my agent called me and said I didn't get the part. They said that I was too strong for Constance Towers and that there was no balance because I was just too good! Isn't that cute? Too good and too pretty! So I didn't get the part. CBS decided that people would watch me and not Constance Towers. Do you believe that? So that's how it went. I could have killed them all! But that's what happened. I was very depressed.[14]
> This was the only thing that I ever tested for that I really wanted. They told me that I had the part. I went to the interview and they told me, "Listen, you don't even have to test — it's in the bag. Well, maybe we'll have you test for the other part."
> So they ended up saying, "No, we're going to have Connie Towers for this part but we'll have you do the other part — the kind of bitchy part. That'll be great." Then they said, "You don't have to test, it's fine!" Then they called and said, "You're going to have to test!" I said, "Test? I thought I didn't have to test." They said, "Well, you're going to test and so is another actress."
> I thought, well, they're going to test me, but I've already got the part. They already told me that I've got the part. When I arrived at the studio, there was Carolyn Jones. I had not prepared as well because I knew I had it. Don't *ever* do that, kid! Carolyn had cancer but had not told anybody. I think Aaron Spelling knew it and I think Spelling made a phone call and said, "I would like to see Carolyn get this. She needs the money. It would be good for her." It was the best thing that ever happened to Carolyn. Her cancer — she was able to live with it and suffer through it because she was working. She was a viable person in herself with this cancer. I could be very wrong, maybe Aaron Spelling never did this but I just think this might have been what happened.
> So when I get there I really did not do a great performance. I really had not prepared well because I didn't think I was even going to have to worry about it. And, of course, I did not get it, and it destroyed me.
> I was irate. I thought I had gotten it and I was miserable. Everybody in the family knew that Mother was not good — she felt awful. I was hurt and very upset. That was in the bag and it wasn't in the bag. I believed it because that's what I had been told.
> What can you do? Carolyn did a great job and in the long run, she needed it a lot more than I needed it. Not money-wise or anything, but to be a working actress when that horrible thing is happening to you was good for her. She worked through hell and she gave 100 percent. In the end, she even worked in a wheelchair. She would come in and she was so sick. I've got to give her a lot of credit for that.[15]
> I didn't know for a long time that she had cancer. She hadn't told anyone except her agent — who ultimately became my agent — although I didn't keep him very long. I think Aaron Spelling definitely knew. He had been married to Carolyn Jones, although by then they had been divorced for some time. I just don't know whether he did that but he could have done it. He could have said, "Do this as a favor to me. The girl needs to work and I'd like to see her get the part." I don't know if that ever happened. That's just my feeling. But it could have happened that way. He and Carolyn had remained very good friends after their divorce as far as I knew. I think he would do something like that for her. Where the hell did it come from? I mean, for me

to walk in and have an interview with this man that's producing the show and telling me "You've got it but we don't know which part to give you" to losing both parts. It was a done deal as far I was concerned. So where did Carolyn Jones come from? It just didn't make sense any other way to me. If they had said to me, "Listen, we're going to test a couple of girls and Carolyn Jones is one of them," then okay. But there was none of that. That's why I think somebody stepped in.[16]

Capitol ran for 1270 episodes between March 29, 1982, and March 20, 1987. It revolved around the power struggle of two political families in Washington, D.C., the Cleggs and the McCandless. Jones played Myrna Clegg for less than one season and was replaced by Marla Adams for the remainder of the first season. Adams was replaced in 1983 by Marj Dusay who continued in the role through 1987. In 1986, a new Clegg family member was introduced for the final season, Angelica Clegg, played by Teri Hatcher.

Jumping back onto the Hollywood guest star bandwagon, Beverly made an appearance on *Magnum P.I.* starring Tom Selleck. The episode, "Three Minus Two," also featured Jill St. John. "Selleck is wonderful," she said. "He's not movie-starrish. He's just a really down-to-earth, great guy. He has a maturity about him that people like. I think he's come up the hard way and you can't help but like him. Tom has a wonderful sense of humor and I don't think he's going to get into this whole kind of Hollywood mentality and become a smart aleck."[17]

After a guest spot on *Matt Houston*, Beverly made an appearance on *Remington Steele* in an episode titled "Thou Shall Not Steele." Beverly played Abigail Holt, Stephanie Zimbalist's on-screen mother, and it held the promise of more episodes to follow.

On November 3, Beverly pulled off the surprise party of her husband Fillmore's life when she threw him a "Farewell to 59" Birthday Party. "It was the end of his 59th [year]," she explained, "so we threw his 59th year a wake! We had all his childhood friends from grammar school there, friends that he had known 40, 50 years. We had a casket. The casket had huge roses over it and on the satin pillow we had in brass the number '59.' Everybody was dressed in black like the Addams Family and a lot of people made up their faces. I was dressed as the Merry Widow with my dress cut way down to my bosom and slit way up the side. Everybody was in costume.

"It was also a 'roast' for Fillmore. Everybody got up and talked about him. The tables were all done in white with black napkins and black candles. The placemats said 'funeral.' We had huge bouquets of flowers that said 'Rest in Peace' and things like that."

Fillmore was in shocked disbelief. "He thought he was going to a party for some Canadians who were interested in staying at our hotel in Sacramento. When he came into the room, we were all around the casket saying, 'Here lies Mr. Fillmore Crank—the end of his 59th birthday.' Fill Jr. played the minister. Well, Fillmore almost ran out of the room! It was an incredible party, one that he would never forget. His cake was a grave marker and it said, 'Here lies Fillmore Pajeau Crank's 59th Birthday—May It Rest in Peace.' It was marvelous."[18]

In Hollywood, there probably isn't a more recognizable site than the Hollywood Boulevard Walk of Fame. Motion picture and television luminaries as well as singers are immortalized by having their names engraved in a star encased in cement running up the center of the sidewalks along Hollywood Boulevard. It's a status symbol for those who have finally "made it" in the business.

For many years, it was fan clubs that usually got their honoraries these coveted stars. In many cases this is still the practice. But the rules had changed in the early 1980s when

Beverly's fan club decided to nominate her for this honor. "I broached Beverly on the subject around 1980," recalled Carl Del Vecchio, president of the Beverly Garland Club. "Would she mind if I contacted the Walk Of Fame officials to see how to go about getting her a star? Beverly was delighted over the prospect."

It seems the Hollywood Chamber of Commerce, who sponsors the installation of the stars on the Walk of Fame, had recently changed the nominating rules. Before, just about anyone could be nominated and would receive their star. In order to conserve space and to make the dedications more of a prestigious event, now only 12 new installations would be made each year. And, not only did the nominees have to be well-known performers, they had to be active in civic and charitable affairs as well.

I requested the necessary applications from the Chamber of Commerce and proceeded to compile a complete list of Beverly's acting credits and numerous civic and charitable activities. After conferring with Beverly and Fillmore, we decided to nominate her for her work in television. Nominations had to be made for the performer's work in one area only — motion pictures, television, or recording.

That first time around we learned that there were over 200 nominees for the 12 stars to be awarded. Needless to say, we didn't make it that year. In writing to me of this, the Chamber of Commerce stated that it would probably take a few years before a new nominee would receive a star due to the vast number of applicants, and therefore not be discouraged, to continue nominating the performer each year.

Not one to be discouraged, the following year I updated the lists and nominated Beverly again. This time there were over 300 applicants for the 12 stars. It was obvious that more "drastic" steps were called for. Fillmore and I had a telephone conversation on the matter and it was decided an all-out effort should be made by the two of us for the next nominating period.

Fillmore got to work securing a number of letters of recommendation on Beverly's behalf from some very influential Californians.[19] I, too, wrote to the president of the Walk of Fame Committee. Then Fillmore came up with a grand idea: How about getting Beverly's *My Three Sons* co-star Fred MacMurray to actually sign the nominating application for her star? With Mr. MacMurray being the "official" sponsor and with everything else we were doing, we felt confident Beverly would receive her star this time. Mr. MacMurray agreed most willingly.

Several weeks later, I received a telephone call from Fillmore and the wonderful news when he said, "Well, Carl, we did it. Beverly's getting her star!" Fillmore and Beverly had just received word of the committee's favorable response and called to share the good news. After Fillmore and I mutually congratulated each other, Beverly got on the line. It was very apparent just how happy she was over the news. This was something she'd wanted for a long time and now it was going to be a reality. It did my heart good to hear the excitement in Beverly's voice and to know that I had a hand in making it possible.

Something I found quite interesting is that the performers have the right to select the location of their star from all the available spaces. Beverly's star is at 6801 Hollywood Boulevard — at the time, it was directly in front of the Los Angeles Visitor's Information Center and Pacific Federal Savings, just a few paces from the intersection of Hollywood Boulevard and Highland Avenue — one of the busiest sections of Hollywood. Now it is located in front of the Kodak Theater. The new 3,332-seat theater which opened in November 2001 is the new permanent home to the Academy Awards.

Credit must go to Fillmore for selecting the perfect site. Fillmore spent the better part of a day walking up and down Hollywood Boulevard and Vine Street inspecting various locations for Beverly's star. After discovering that Marilyn Monroe's star is now located in front of a rather seedy fast-food restaurant, Fillmore wanted to make sure that Beverly's star would be in a well-kept and highly visible area.

Echoing Fillmore's thought on the careful selection of the star site was William Demarest, Beverly's co-star on *My Three Sons*. His comment when he heard Beverly was to receive her star: "Beverly, don't let them put your star near a tree or a fire hydrant!"[20]

Beverly at the January 26, 1983, dedication ceremony for her star on the Hollywood Walk of Fame.

Beverly became the 1,759th star on the Walk of Fame. She had her star installation on January 26, 1983. Among those in attendance that day were Fred MacMurray, Dawn Lyn, Tina Cole, Don Grady, Stanley and Barry Livingston, Beverly's children and her mother Amelia "Millie" Fessenden, Marie Windsor (who was also getting her star that year), Jeanne Cooper, Charles B. Griffith, Beech Dickerson, and Ed Nelson's wife and daughter. (Ed Nelson was filming *Capitol* that day and couldn't attend.) Beverly's club president and vice-president were also in attendance.

When she was asked if she visited her star since the dedication, Beverly replied, "Yes, I did go down there. In fact, we had a whole bus load of people who are partners in the Howard Johnson Company, and we took them all to a very famous place to eat. We were all dressed up and we took a motor coach touring bus and on the way we stopped and all got out and saw my star. I cleaned it off and polished it up a little bit.... It looks in pretty good shape. It looks as though people are walking all over it — but at least it's there and that's great!"[21]

23. *Scarecrow and Mrs. King*

They say that when one door closes, another opens. While Beverly was terribly disappointed that she wouldn't be on *Capitol*, she held out hope that something would come along to make up for that lost opportunity.

In March 1983, Beverly once again filmed a pilot episode for a new proposed series, *Scarecrow and Mrs. King*, which co-starred Kate Jackson (*Charlie's Angels*) and Bruce Boxleitner (*How the West Was Won*). The series sold to CBS-TV in May of that year. Beverly's character was Dotty West, mother of Amanda King (Jackson).

Beverly had filmed a second episode of *Remington Steele* ("The Sting of Steele") and there was talk at the time that she would probably be called back for two or three more. But, as Beverly explained, "Since I've gotten *Scarecrow and Mrs. King*, I haven't heard from them. So I'm not certain if they're interested in doing that or if it would even be right. They are, however, two different characters — two different women completely."[1]

Being selected for the *Scarecrow* role was not easy.

When I interviewed for *Scarecrow and Mrs. King*, they asked me to come in and read again. I didn't know Kate Jackson that well at all. I had done a TV show that she was in but I don't think she and I worked together on it.[2] In fact, I was surprised that she was in that show. "Oh, you were in that show? So was I!"

They picked two women — I can't remember who the other actress was — and we had to go to CBS and read in front of all the executives. Kate Jackson was going to read with us. We had to sign the contract — both of us — before we got the job. The other actress had hair like Kate's with bangs and I thought, "Oh well, I know she's going to get it because she's got Kate Jackson's hair."

We walked into this huge room and all these executives were sitting around in a circle. There was a big stage in this huge room and they were all talking. Kate and I stepped onto the stage and one of the executives signaled for us to begin. But before we started, I saw some of them making gestures and they were looking at us. I thought, "Oh shit! Is my slip showing?" or "They don't like my hair." They probably were saying, "Would you like to meet for cocktails after this?" But I felt they were talking about me.

We did the scene — a short, little scene. Oh God. I mean, you are quaking in your shoes with all these people who were sitting there with absolutely no expression on their faces; never cracking a smile; never saying anything. Then the man at the end said, "Well, that was very good, Beverly. I'd like you to do it again and be a little more down or a little more up," or whatever the hell he said. I thought, "Oh, I just screwed this up so badly!"

We did it again and then they asked me to leave and then the other actress — who I knew had the right hair so she was going to get it — went through the scene and that was it. I said, goodbye to Kate and she said goodbye to me. You have no idea what it's like. It's so hard with all those people staring at you and you know they're talking behind your back and at the very end, they say, "Thank you. We'll call you and let you know."

Your contracts are already signed so if you got it you couldn't re-negotiate it; everything has

Efrem Zimbalist, Jr., Beverly, Pierce Brosnan (who would later play James Bond) and Stephanie Zimbalist from the April 5, 1983, Remington Steele episode "The Sting of Steele."

to be negotiated up front and that's it. So that was the scary part. I think I only waited a day or two and they called and said, "You got the part!"

On June 18, 1983, Beverly made an appearance at ShadowCon VII in Los Angeles and was one of the guests on their *Twilight Zone* panel. Other panelists included George Clayton Johnson (who wrote Beverly's episode "The Four of Us Are Dying") and directors Douglas Heyes and Joe Dante. This was the first of many genre convention appearances for Beverly.

According to Beverly, when *Scarecrow and Mrs. King* went into production,

We used to have big meetings with the writers, and I kept saying to them, "I wish the mother could have something that sets her apart. For instance, she always cooks; she always knits; she always exercises. She does something so that in every show you see her doing this and you say, 'Oh yeah, there's Dotty, she's doing her thing.' You know, kind of a theme that would be a recurring thread throughout the season because I thought it would help the character and give her something to do. Dotty had no idea what the hell her daughter was doing.

I also used to say to Kate, "You know, we have no money in this house. We've got these two little boys and you walk out of here in a $3000 gown. Where the heck did you get the money? Are you soliciting on the side? What is happening here?" But, you know, they just ignored me. I used to think that though. How can people believe this thing? How could they believe that she could walk out in a $3000 gown and we can barely afford spaghetti for the kids? But they paid no attention to me.

Then one day we went to a meeting and Kate was there, of course, because she was also the producer of the show—she owned part of *Scarecrow and Mrs. King*. She had all these wonderful "hats" and she got paid for every "hat" she had on. She said, "Now in this episode we're going camping and of course you love to go camping...." I said, "No, Dotty doesn't like to go camping. She goes because you want to go and the boys want to go. But Dotty is not a happy camper. She doesn't like to go camping. That's not Dotty. That's not what she likes to do." "Oh," Kate said, "that's wrong. That's what she likes...." and I said, "No. I'm sorry, but she doesn't." I had my own character, that's who I was. Kate wasn't the mother, I was the mother and I don't like to go camping!

Kate didn't speak to me for almost a week. I sent her this huge bouquet of balloons. We were going to the Emmys that night, I remember. She didn't speak to me for a week because I didn't like to go camping and I dared to disagree.[3]

I would imagine that Kate had to give her approval for me to be hired because she was one of the producers on that show. She also directed a couple of those shows. She was excellent. She really did her homework. She knew what she was doing. She was a very good director. I must say she put on that hat and she wore it well. I was proud of her.[4]

Beverly's workday on the *Scarecrow and Mrs. King* set usually started at six in the morning with two hours for makeup and hair. They usually started work around eight in the morning. Normally, the workday ended between 7 and 7:30 P.M. "So far on *Scarecrow and Mrs. King*, Beverly said in a letter, "I've only had to work maybe two or three days a week, so that makes it very easy and I can do the other things that I'm involved in. If they write more things for Dotty West, then I'll work more. But the past shows have averaged two or three days."[5]

Hairstyles and clothes were flexible but, as always, the producers had the final word:

This year [1984-85], my hair will be short for the show but next year it will be a little longer probably. I've cut it recently and I like it. I'm not so sure everybody else does, however! You do have a say in the hair styles you wear on the show. But you are working with studio hairdressers and they are a strange breed! No matter what you do with your hair, they've got another idea. I wear my hair just kind of windblown and it's a much lighter type of look than Dotty's hairstyles. Dotty wears her hair a lot differently than I do.

We have a new wardrobe girl on the show this year. In the first four or five shows I have not been very pleased with the clothes. I'm going to see if I can do something about changing Dotty's wardrobe. You can pretty much have your say in these matters but when push comes to shove, it's really up to the producers as to whether they like a certain look or whether they don't. They can be the ones that say, "No, sorry, we're not going to buy that idea." Unless it is written in concrete in your contract that you can do exactly what you want regarding these matters — forget it! You just have to hope that you can convince them.[6]

Scarecrow and Mrs. King premiered on October 3, 1983, to mostly favorable reviews and sixth place in the overall ratings for that week. According to Richard Hack of *The Hollywood Reporter* (October 6, 1983), "There is an honesty at work here that creeps around the edge of the plot and slaps at the heart with an innocence that enchants as it entertains. An example is Beverly Garland's portrayal of Jackson's mom, a woman who watches a TV cook for inspiration and worries about runny noses and why her daughter is spending all these late nights away from home...." *Variety*'s Tone noted (October 3, 1983), "One of the better ideas is having Beverly Garland as Jackson's live-in mom. If some of her lines are predictable in the first outing, the character should mold itself into something fresh and lively with a few innings."[7]

Once the series got underway and the actors got to know one another, Beverly had these observations about her co-workers: "Kate Jackson has a good head on her shoulders.

She is a hard worker. She loves her work and just adores acting. Bruce Boxleitner is a sharp, sharp young man. He is excellent. I think we've got two very good people. People who are really hard workers and really care about the business. I really feel that everyone connected with the show — makeup people, hairdressers, cameramen, the entire crew — are just top-drawer."[8]

Admitting that her character had her limitations, Beverly tried her best to develop Dotty West as much as she could. "Naturally the character is written a certain way and I have brought what I feel is the right way to do it.... I think she has a wonderful sense of humor. She's not a demanding mother. She's a sharp lady. I've taken what they have written and I've worked around that to make her a very full-bodied character with what I have to do on the show. I'm hoping that as we go along, there will be more things for Dotty to do. I think I've gotten the character down to the point where it's comfortable for me and comfortable for everyone else. Let's hope that's true, anyway."[9]

The show did have some plotting problems which Beverly observed.

> Kate loved that show *Moonlighting* and that show came on the night before our show. She would come in the next day and change the script because she really wanted us to be doing *Moonlighting*. We said, "But Kate, that's not what we're doing. We're doing *Scarecrow and Mrs. King*." But she loved the way *Moonlighting* was written and she wanted everything changed. Kate took all the lines away from Bruce: "You just say 'Yes' and you just say 'No' or you just nod your head." Bruce said, "Yeah, okay." I mean, he was so easy. I'm sure he wasn't thrilled but he went along. He just didn't make waves. He was very good. I gave him a lot of credit because it was not easy.
>
> Then the edict came down that you couldn't change any lines because she'd change everything. Then, of course, if you change lines, by the time you get to the fourth scene, it didn't work with the first scene any more. It finally got to be the same throughout the television industry that directors and producers would not allow you to change the dialogue at all. It got to be ridiculous. You had, for example, the director saying, "Beverly, there's an 'A' there" and I'd say, "A what?" It got so that you had to say the line *exactly* as it was written — word for word — which was very hard. You could never ad lib anything. All the producers and directors got to the point of saying, "This is the written word and that's the way it has to be." It became tougher, I think, because you couldn't transpose anything; you're saying the same thing, it's just that you said it in a way that worked better for you. But you couldn't do that. Television got to that point because so many actors were changing the dialogue the way they wanted it and the script was not working the way it should. But you can't keep changing things in a script, it just doesn't work that way. There's a structure to a script and that's the way it has to be.

Beverly had this to say about her "grandsons" on the show, Paul Stout (playing Phillip King) and Greg Morton (playing Jamie King). "The boys who played Kate's sons were okay. I don't think they were the best actors who ever came down the pike. But they were young and they were fine and we didn't give them a lot to do. What they did, however, they did well. The thing of it is, when you work with a child or a dog you might as well forget your part because everybody wants to see what the child does. So the best thing, as every actor has said from time immemorial, is, 'Don't work with children or animals if you can help it.' Everyone is fascinated with kids and animals, and you end up being part of the scenery."[10]

Because Beverly's *Scarecrow and Mrs. King* role only required her on set for two or three days a week, she was free to appear in other programs. On November 1, 1983, *This Girl for Hire*, a CBS-TV movie, made its debut with Beverly making a guest appearance as a suspect. The telemovie was an updated version of the popular private eye movies of the 1940s.

During the first season of *Scarecrow and Mrs. King*, Beverly also made an appearance on ABC-TV's *Woman to Woman*, a daytime talk show with Angela Cartwright, Barbara Billingsley and Virginia Mayo. The topic was "Life After Stardom" with Beverly representing *My Three Sons*. However, it was a bit of a cheat since she was currently co-starring in another series when she made this appearance.

By the end of the first season of *Scarecrow and Mrs. King*, two of the show's creative team were out. Brad Buckner and Eugenie Ross-Leming claimed that the rumors about them being unable to withstand the show's fast pace and high pressure were untrue. Ross-Leming, a former *Second City* writer, said, "The pressure was fine as long as everyone's supportive. But there were a lot of raw nerves on the set. When people get vituperative, it's not fun and everyone had strong opinions and we decided life was too short."[11] The blame was being laid at Kate Jackson's door. Judging from what Beverly experienced when she tried to make minor points about her character, it's not surprising that others found the situation intolerable and as soon as their contract was up, they bolted.

On July 31, 1984, Beverly was appointed to serve on the California Tourism Corporation's Board of Directors. Her job was to help the corporation continue to promote California tourism and maintain its place in this competitive market. Beverly also became a spokesperson for the S.O.A.R. Project (The Spirit of the Appalachian Region) in Kentucky. The project's aim was to unite volunteers in the region to provide better assistance for the area's underdeveloped communities.[12]

The week of November 12, 1984, Beverly went to Washington, D.C., on behalf of "Toys for Tots" and while there met President Ronald Reagan.[13] She also appeared on several syndicated talk shows, including *Together* (hosted by Pat and Shirley Boone) and *People Are Talking*, and was a judge on *Dance Fever*, as part of a promotional tour for *Scarecrow and Mrs. King*. She made other promotional appearances including *The Today Show* and *The Merv Griffin Show*.

With season two of *Scarecrow and Mrs. King* underway, Beverly made an appearance on ABC-TV's *Hotel*, a series based on the novel by Arthur Hailey. The Aaron Spelling–Douglas S. Cramer co-production featured Beverly as Alice Korman in an episode titled "New Beginnings" which also starred Patty Duke Astin, Robert Stack and Vera Miles.

Beverly and Vera Miles' careers had begun around the same time and they had been friends. Beverly recalled that not too long after their appearance together on the show, Miles gave up acting. "Vera went to Big Bear," Beverly said. "and she just didn't want to work any more. She kind of disappeared. Her son lived up there.

"Fillmore and Ward Bond were very good friends with Vera so she and I became good friends. We worked during the same time and back then if it wasn't Vera Miles, it was Beverly Garland — that kind of thing. But then she just decided to give it up and she certainly didn't have to because she would have worked. People really liked her."[14]

During the second season of *Scarecrow and Mrs. King*, the cast and crew filmed shows in London and Munich. In a letter, Beverly explained, "*Scarecrow and Mrs. King* is going to Europe and Kate Jackson and Bruce will be going. They'll film two shows and then they'll probably send for the rest of the family. We'll probably shoot a show but it will look like we've been there through about three shows. They're thinking about going to Munich or to Amsterdam or to London.

"We all went to Europe because the Olympics were going to be held in Los Angeles and we thought it would be so difficult to film here. Of course, nobody came to the Olympics because nobody could get tickets. So the Olympics were really for Los Angeles that year

23. Scarecrow and Mrs. King

Photograph from a *Scarecrow and Mrs. King* cast party in Munich, Germany. (Several of the opening episodes for the second season were filmed in Europe.) Back row, left to right: Martha Smith, Beverly, Bruce Boxleitner, Kate Jackson. Front row: Paul Stout and Greg Morton. Summer—1984.

and we all just had a lovely time—all by ourselves. So we didn't have to worry about that after all. I thought it was wonderful to go with the show to Munich. I was there about two weeks during the summer."[15]

Beverly made yet another guest star appearance in another Aaron Spelling Production, *Finders of Lost Loves*. In the episode "Surrogates," her co-star and "lost love" was Kevin McCarthy. "Oh, what a doll," Beverly exclaimed. "He's such a good-looking and sweet guy. He's one of my secret loves! I like him so much—and such a good actor. You'll [also] see him on *Scarecrow and Mrs. King*. I did not work with him, unfortunately, but he does have a part on an episode ['Over the Limit,' aired on October 7, 1985]. He started off with a Scottish accent, just as a lark, but they made him drop it—I don't know why. I wonder whether they know what a Scottish accent sounds like! Anything Kevin does has to be good. So you'll see him on *Scarecrow and Mrs. King*—but he won't have the Scottish accent!"[16]

Always ready to lend a hand when it came to local civic events, Beverly gladly accepted the title of grand marshal of "Burbank on Parade" in 1985. Other personalities of note that year included Sandy Dennis, Miss Burbank 1985, Sandahl Bergman, *Days of Our Lives* cast members Macdonald Carey, Elaine Prince, John Taylor and Andrew Masset, as well as regulars from *Capitol* and *Santa Barbara*.[17] In November, Beverly ran for president of the Screen

Actors Guild representing the more conservative faction of the membership. Beverly finished sixth with over 4300 votes; the winner was Patty Duke.[18]

Beverly also accepted an invitation to lecture her friend Nancy Kulp's (*The Beverly Hillbillies*) students at Juniata College in Huntingdon, Pennsylvania. Kulp was the college's "Artist in Residence" for the winter and spring terms in 1986.[19]

On August 15, 1986, Beverly was one of 13 honorees to receive a Golden Boot Award for her work in Westerns (both motion pictures and television). Bruce Boxleitner presented Beverly with her award.[20]

Despite its poor ratings, CBS gave *Scarecrow and Mrs. King* a go-ahead for a fourth season. However, the show lost its coveted Monday night slot and was moved to Fridays at 8 P.M.[21] Beverly revealed that the last *Scarecrow* season was stressful, but not because the show was in jeopardy of being cancelled.

> Kate Jackson had a scare that she had breast cancer and she had some tests and it looked like she did have it. She panicked about the whole thing and she just didn't want to continue. I think she ended up having an operation but I just kind of lost track of all of that.
>
> At the very end of the show there were times she never came to the set and so they had Martha Smith playing Kate's part. Martha's role was expanded because Kate just didn't want to work any more. The fans of the show would have given anything to see it continue, but Kate had made up her mind that she wasn't going to continue with the show and she didn't. That's how it was.
>
> Strangely enough, *Scarecrow and Mrs. King* had a reunion every few years and the fans who put this together invited all the people who were on the show. We all tried to attend, but Kate never came. They'd email her asking that she just give them something — a handkerchief or something — so that they could auction it off for charity, but she wouldn't even do that for them. She had stopped working for awhile and then she came back and did a couple of things — movies for television or something like that. I don't know what her problem was. I have no idea.[22]

On July 30, 1987, the Garland Center, a $2,500,000 addition to the Beverly Garland Hotel in North Hollywood, broke ground. Slated to be completed by the spring of 1988, the new center included a 175-seat theatre, five banquet and meeting rooms, a large ballroom and a physical fitness room. There were also plans to add new executive offices, to expand the hotel's main lobby and to add a gift shop.

On April 14, 1988, Beverly left for a one-month tour of Australia to promote travel to California. Later that year, she took a cruise up the Mississippi River from New Orleans to St. Louis on the *Delta Queen* to promote the new river cruise line. Unfortunately, that year the states along the river were going through a terrible drought and at one point the paddleboat got stuck on a sand bar. The Mississippi sank to its lowest levels since the Civil War and, in fact, some soldiers' bodies were recovered from their watery graves as a result.

Between 1986 and 1990, Beverly filmed guest star roles on *Crazy Like a Fox* and *Heartbeat*. She also filmed another pilot, *Beanpole* (1990), which didn't sell, and a Showtime Cable Television short, *To the Moon, Alice* (1990), about a homeless family that sleeps on a TV production stage at night, while looking for a job during the day when the stage is in use. In the fall of 1990, Beverly had a starring role in the made-for-television movie *The World's Oldest Living Bridesmaid* as the mother of the bridesmaid, Donna Mills.

The highlight of the year for the Cranks was the wedding of their son James on May 27, 1990, at the Franklin Marshall College Chapel in Lancaster, Pennsylvania. The wedding was held a week after the bride and groom graduated. The couple then honeymooned on Bora Bora. That union was soon to unravel, but not for the usual reasons.

24. *The Haunted Symphony,* Russia and Roger Corman— Together Again, After All These Years

Without a script, an actor has no part; without lines, an actor has no voice. Memorizing lines and remembering them is an actor's job. Beverly claimed she always had difficulty learning her lines.

I usually lock myself in my room and go over them 75,000 times! Learning lines is not easy for me and I have to take a lot of time doing it. I make up my mind that if I have to stay up all night, I learn them before I go to bed—no matter what! I really work at them. I go over them, and over them, and over them. I read the script maybe three or four times and then I take it scene by scene by scene until I have it. Then after I have it, I go over it again.

I hate learning lines. I wish there was a simple way to do it. Bing Crosby used to be able to look at a page and he would have it memorized. He had a photographic mind. I wish I had that ability. I don't, so it's just work! I think that the more you work, the more you're into memorizing lines and so it's easier. Every day you have lines, lines, lines when you have a television series and it becomes a much easier routine. Lines, then, begin to come much easier, but it is work for me and I have to just sit down and do it. It's like anything else, it's like cramming for a test in school.

I usually study my lines in my bedroom. I close the door and everybody in the house leaves me alone. I yell and holler and scream. I like to be my myself. I like to be where it's quiet. Sometimes, when the hotel was first built, I used to go there and they'd let me have a room. I'd just pace up and down that room where there wasn't anybody to bother me—no telephone calls, no nothing! Now, I just sit in my bedroom until I've got them down and go over them till I finally have them.[1]

Now, imagine that whatever you do, you keep forgetting your lines. Beverly went through this and it was one of the most difficult times of her life.

It was right at the beginning of *Scarecrow and Mrs. King*. I couldn't remember. I'd go over my lines, "Hello. How are you?" over and over and then I'd say, "Okay, what's the line? I don't know. What is the line? Oh I don't know." I got so panicked.

There's an actor—I did a couple of shows with him—but he got so bad he couldn't remember anything. We did a scene on the beach and they had cue cards for him. He had to have everything written out for him. I thought to myself at the time, "Oh God. I hope that never happens to me." But it did happen to me and I had such a hard time remembering.

I would work and I would go out on an interview. I usually got the job and I would get through it. I would say to myself, "You are such a good actress that even when you are so bad, you're okay." This panic grew from *Scarecrow and Mrs. King* to everything I did from that time on. It was very hard for me—very hard. It got to the point where I hoped my agent would never call me and ask to go out on an interview because I just panicked.

An actor said to me once that he went through something like this. He was driving home and was on a bridge and all of a sudden he couldn't remember how to drive. He stopped his car in the middle of the bridge. Then it got so bad that he couldn't go to work — he couldn't remember his lines. He was having panic attacks and it nearly ended his career. He couldn't even handle the cue cards — he was just scared to death. But he got help and got over it. I guess a lot of people in the business go though it, but nobody knows it. They keep it to themselves.

I went to several analysts. In fact, one analyst — he charged me something like $250 — he said to me, "Well, if you can't do it, then don't do it. If you want to do it, do it. If you don't want to do it, then don't do it!" But that analyst's advice was the only thing that stuck with me. "If you don't want to do it, then don't do it!" makes sense, okay. "Well, I *do* want to do it!" "Oh, you do want to do it?" "Sure! I can do it if I want to do it." What the hell are you talking about? No wonder you charge so much! No one can understand what the heck you're talking about!

...But of all the people I went to, that's the only thing that stuck in my head that anybody ever said to me. I don't know why, but because he said that, I didn't give up acting. Okay, I'm not going to not do it. Strange.

Now I go on interviews and nothing bothers me. I go and I do it and I'm fine. It's okay. It's all right. There are still times that I panic a little, but that's okay.

Fillmore used to tell me so many times that if you are working every single solitary day, your memory is like a muscle that you use constantly. A typist who doesn't type for a long time can't remember where the "A" key is on the machine. I mean, you're not ready. When I was doing *My Three Sons*, I could go to my trailer at the end of the day to change and read over the next day's scripts. I would go home that night, cook dinner, do my thing, and then come back the next morning and I knew my lines perfectly. It was easy because I was doing it every day and using that memory muscle.

Anyway, I've gotten over that, but boy, I had it for a very long time. It was very hard for me. I just went out there and nobody ever knew it except Fillmore and my kids.

That's why I returned to the stage and did *The Gin Game* in New York — because I was afraid that I couldn't remember my lines. I thought if I could do *The Gin Game*, then I could do anything. It didn't really help me but I did it because I thought I could never do a two-person show.... So I made myself do it and I did it. I don't know whether I did it very well — I have no idea. But that's why I did it. It was something I had to work out.

On July 11, 1990, at the Catskill Actor's Theatre in Highland Lake, New York, Beverly and Ed Nelson starred in D. L. Coburn's *The Gin Game*. The Catskill Actor's Theatre (or C.A.T.) had opened there years earlier with *Inherit the Wind* and the following year they produced *Death of a Salesman* and *On the Verge*.

The Gin Game ran three weeks and ended on August 4, 1990, after 19 performances under the direction of Chris Nelson, Ed's son, who owned and operated the theater. The play took place at the Bentley Nursing Home where Walter Martin (Nelson) and Fonsia Dorsey (Garland) believe they are two of the more alert and lucid residents. Walter teaches Fonsia to play gin, his favorite game. When Fonsia starts to win, Walter writes it off as beginner's luck. But when she continues to win game after game, Walter's mood turns ugly and the budding friendship deteriorates.

Beverly was determined to defeat her fear. "I thought, 'I've got to do the play — two people — and I'll be on stage every second. I've got to see if I can do it." I went over those lines. I went to sleep going over those lines. They hired a young girl for me and that's all we did every single solitary day was go over those lines, over and over. There were still times that I forgot things, but that does happen and nobody knew because you can always ad lib. Sometimes I would say to Ed Nelson's wife, 'You know, we really screwed that up.' But she said to me, 'But nobody would know. You'd never know. Nobody's read the play, Beverly!'" In the end, Beverly had to admit it was great fun.

Beverly and Ed Nelson in makeup for their roles in the stage play *The Gin Game* at the Catskill Actors Theatre (July 11–August 4, 1990).

The building was a converted Catholic church that Chris Nelson had purchased and turned into a charming theater. Nelson also purchased the house next door, which used to be what they called a retreat. "Years ago," Beverly explained, "wealthier people would come up from New York City to these retreats for the summer in touring cars with their children and then their husbands would go back to the city. These retreats were all around the lake and in the evenings they would get into these small boats and they would row from one house to another. They would stop for dinner and drinks. It was all very laid-back.

"These retreats would have one or two bathrooms on each floor that you shared, with a big old tub and a big old sink and no showers. Chris Nelson bought one of these retreats. The rooms were rather small. Everybody had a sink in their room so that you could wash your face and brush your teeth because you couldn't get into the bathroom all the time. Then, Chris rigged up a shower outside because there were no showers in the bathroom and no one wanted to take baths. All the cast lived in this big house. It was absolutely charming."

Unlike Broadway playhouses, rural theaters sometimes have "special added attractions." Beverly recalled, "During one performance we had to contend with a bat. We had some other animals up in the rafters that used to make a lot of noise. All of a sudden you'd hear the strangest sounds — growling and stomping around. "Jeez, what the hell was that?" It was raccoons up there, of course. They had nests in the church attic and they would all of a sudden move around. You had to hope that the audience wasn't paying too much attention. Nobody could get them out of there. It was so funny."[2]

Beverly was offered one of her next jobs while on an airplane.

> Carrington and I had gone to the south because somebody wanted to do a film about ghosts. We went to this Southern mansion which the filmmaker said all these ghosts were supposedly haunting. An Australian film company was going to film there, so they asked me because I was a good screamer. They did this kind of documentary about this house and we did some screaming. Then we ran around and did a few things. They went back to Australia and I never saw what they put together.
>
> We were on the plane back to Los Angeles and the producer of *Stallions* came up to me and said, "I'm going to do a movie and would you like to be in it." I said, "Well, send me the script." He did so and I did it. We filmed it near Lake Tahoe. We all stayed at a motel up there. It was kind of a strange script. It just never worked. Carrington had a little part. She played one of the bartender girls.
>
> The script was just not right. It never was right. Good actors in it—everyone was good in it. But the script was wrong. It just didn't work. It was like *Stark Fear*, it was vague. They used to tell us, "When people see it, they'll put it all together in their head and they'll understand it." Well, I don't think so. It just ends up bad cinema. Bad script. Bad movie. They re-cut it and it was released but it's a whole different story, from what I understood. I mean, they cut the living hell out of it.[3]

Stallions disappeared for several years and then it went direct-to-video, re-titled *Death Falls*.

During her career, Beverly had worked with Lucille Ball and, later, Lucy's son Desi Arnaz, Jr. Next she made a guest appearance on Lucy's daughter Lucie's new series *Sons & Daughters* ("Throw Mama from the Terrain," January 25, 1991), in which she played Marcy, the absentee mother of Lucie and her siblings. It was a wonderful, intense role and Beverly was in top form.

In November 1984, Beverly had been invited to the White House to meet President Ronald Reagan on behalf of her fund-raising efforts for Toys for Tots. Seven years later, in February 1991, she attended the former president's eightieth birthday celebration.

> I don't know how many of his nearest and dearest friends were invited to this party. Laird Cook, who was president of A.R.CO [Atlantic-Richfield Co.], married a girl named Carol and Carol was Lorraine Colway's daughter. Lorraine Colway was my stand-in for many years. A.R.CO was a huge oil company and Laird Cook was very close to the queen of England, very close to the Reagans — very close politically because that's what he did.
>
> The Cooks invited Fillmore and me to go with them to Reagan's eightieth birthday at the Ronald Reagan Library. Margaret Thatcher was also there. So we had our picture taken with them. They had built a replica of the Oval Office so everybody who came had their picture taken in front of the desk at the "Oval Office" with the Reagans. That took quite a while but they had cocktails going and later dinner. Afterwards, Margaret Thatcher got up and spoke very glowingly about Reagan because they had been very close during his two terms in office.
>
> Then Ronald Reagan got up to speak and he said something and then he was looking down at his notes and he said, "And I really think that England and the United States were wonderful together and that's what I believe." And he paused and looked down at his notes again and said, "And I really think that England and the United States..." and everybody was stunned. I looked over and saw that Mrs. Reagan didn't flinch. She didn't do anything but she knew. We all knew — that was *not* Ronald Reagan. He would have said, "I just said that, didn't I? Ha! I lost my place!" He didn't know that he had done that. He didn't know that he had repeated himself at all.
>
> Later, when the news announced that he had Alzheimer's, I thought back to the night of his eightieth birthday. That was when it began, I believe. Margaret Thatcher and Nancy Reagan stood like statues and no one gave any indication that anything was wrong.... But I think that it was probably the beginning of the disease.
>
> So it didn't come as a surprise to me when I heard the news because I saw it. Ronald Reagan

was such a wonderful speaker and he could ad lib because he was an actor and he would never have allowed that. He would have caught himself and he would have made a joke about it. But he didn't. He didn't know anything was wrong."[4]

On August 26, 1991, ABC ran the George C. Scott made-for-television movie *Finding the Way Home*, originally titled *Mittlemann's Hardware*. It had been filmed the previous November in and around Denton, Texas. Scott plays Max Mittlemann, the owner of a once thriving hardware store. Faced with a declining business, plus medical and financial problems, Mittlemann suffers a form of psychological amnesia and disappears one day, leaving no trace of his whereabouts, and a wife (Beverly) to pick up the pieces. He surfaces in a camp of illegal migrant workers and finds a contentment there that he thought he had forever lost.

Beverly called Scott "a fabulous actor and very easy with me. When I did the movie with him he sat in his trailer and played computer games constantly. That's all he did. They bought him a computer and he played games. So there wasn't a lot of conversation with him. I didn't understand computers and he didn't need me to understand because he was fascinated with the games he was playing in this trailer. Ah, but he was a very giving actor which, to me, is a good actor. George C. Scott will give 100 percent to you and that was just lovely. It made it wonderful. He would go over lines with you. He really cared. He was a caring man—a caring actor. I was just absolutely thrilled that I could say somewhere in my career that I had worked with George C. Scott. The film was one of the highlights of my acting career."[5]

Over the next couple of years, Beverly filmed a guest spot on *P.S. I Luv U* and worked on her first animated film, *The Wish That Changed Christmas*, based on a story by Rumer Godden called "The Story of Holly and Ivy." Beverly furnished the voice of Mrs. Shepherd. Others in the cast included Paul Winchell and Jonathan Winters.

Beverly also filmed another pilot, *Camp Wilder*, which didn't sell but was broadcast in September 1992 before the start of the new season. She also made an appearance in a proposed feature film that showed great promise, *King B: A Life in the Movies*, which was loosely based on Roger Corman. The film never saw release.

After 36 years, Beverly was reunited with Roger Corman, the man who had starred her in five of his feature films during the mid- to late–1950s, on *The Haunted Symphony*. It went into production on March 26, 1993, in Russia. And like every other Corman film she worked in, it was yet another wild experience that she could have written a screenplay about for Roger to film.[6]

It all started with Beech Dickerson, an actor and friend of Roger's, who attended the ceremony when Beverly received her star on the Hollywood Walk of Fame. "Beech is the kind of man that keeps his friends," Beverly revealed. "He really got Roger and me back together again, because I hadn't seen Roger for many years. Beech called me and said, 'We're going to take Roger out for his birthday,' and I said, 'Okay.' So, once a year we take Roger out to lunch. Roger keeps saying he's going to hire me, but he never does."[7]

Beverly arrived in Moscow on Thursday, April 15, 1993. She was temporarily put up in a hotel room, which, she remarked in a journal she kept during the shoot, was no bigger than her bathroom in Los Angeles. She was told that she would be picked up at 9:15 A.M. on Friday for wardrobe fittings and that shooting would commence on Saturday the 17th. The film's schedule called for six-day work weeks from 9 A.M. to 9 P.M., with Sundays off. Beverly was told she would be moving to an apartment that Saturday for the duration of her stay.

When she arrived at the Mosfilm Studio the following morning, she was amazed at the size of it and remarked that it had to be twice the size of MGM. Wardrobe and wig fittings went well but Beverly couldn't find shoes that fit without pinching so she ended up wearing her moccasins under her gowns whenever she could get away with it.

Beverly was also surprised to find that the average salary in Moscow at that time was around $10 U.S. a month. The crew members on this picture made $25 a week — a small fortune for them. She also found that apartments were all owned by the state and were rent-free. Residents would be responsible for their utilities. However, all the apartment buildings were run-down and dirty. No effort was made to beautify the grounds with flowers, shrubs, etc. According to Beverly's diary (April 17, 1993), "Apartments are subsidized. When one becomes available, you stand in line and wait to get it[.] [I]f you don't, you live with two or three other families."

The first night Beverly tried to wash her dinner dishes, the faucet stuck while the water was running and then burst, flooding the kitchen. Finally someone from the film crew managed to find a man in the building who had to remove part of the wall in order to get at the shut-off valve.

Beverly wondered why her bedroom had large rugs covering the walls. She soon discovered that the walls did not have any insulation and that the outside dampness would leach through, leaving a horrible damp smell. She had a very hard time sleeping because of the damp and the odor.

The Mosfilm Studios were just as bad. Many of the windows were broken and it was always cold. Nearly all the scenes in the film were shot on indoor sets; even town streets were interiors.

The plan was to shoot three to four script pages a day. But on the very first day of filming, the shoot was cancelled because the director of photography's house had been broken into and valuable camera equipment had been stolen. Beverly used the free day to unpack and go shopping for staples. Later she and director David Tausik went over some new script changes that Beverly said watered down her character, Carlotta, too much for her liking. She and David agreed to play the character as originally written.

Tausik had enormous problems to overcome, the biggest of which was communication. Since most of the crew only spoke Russian, Tausik had to rely on a translator to make himself understood. Beverly recalls, "The director was an American — that was it. He had an interpreter — there were three interpreters on the set — and everybody else spoke Russian. The line producer and the assistant director spoke some English.

"David would say to the interpreter, 'Tell the director of photography that I want the camera to go over there and then we're going to put....' David would explain it to her in detail and she would turn to the d.p. and say in three words what David had spent ten minutes explaining. 'How the hell did she explain everything I said?' David would say. 'There's no way!' So it was very difficult. The director had his ideas but nobody understood what his ideas were because you only heard it from the interpreter."

These communication difficulties also extended to personal egos. "David would have the whole scene lit and then he would change his mind and decide to light it a different way. Then the d.p. would be very upset as it was very hard to light this picture and David didn't like some of the d.p.'s lighting. It was very frustrating because there was just a total lack of communication. It was very, very, very hard. The d.p. would want to do it this way and it would get lit and then David would say, 'But the action is going to be here.' Then the d.p. would say, 'Oh, but that's not where I have it lit, I have it lit over here.' So it was always very difficult to do.[8]

The actor who played the baron (Lev Prigunov) was Russian. "They had to dub everything he said because his accent was very, very thick. He spoke English but Russians speak in a different cadence than we do. They go up instead of down and it's very difficult so every Russian actor had to be dubbed."[9]

Beverly had a problem with the makeup woman they had assigned to her. "She was an apprentice," Beverly said. "and learning ... but not on me she won't." Beverly tolerated it for two days, then she finally spoke up. "She was sweet," Beverly remarked. "but, after all, it was my face up on the screen!" Ekaterina Ivanova, who headed up the makeup department, took over after that.

Most of the cast was a pleasure to work with — except Ben Cross. "When I first came in, Ben Cross started telling me all about Carlotta — my character — and I said, 'Ben, I'm quite aware of what I'm going to do with Carlotta and no, I don't agree with you on this and I do think that....' He looked at me and that was it. He left me alone. He was going to tell me what Carlotta was and who she was and how to play her. I had decided that this was not what I was going to do at all. I was very capable of playing Carlotta. I knew *exactly* what I was going to do with Carlotta."[10]

There were, however, still some problems as Beverly related, "At one point I wasn't sure if this thing was ever going to get finished because there was so much arguing. There were so many arguments between David and Ben Cross — screaming arguments: 'You don't know what you are doing. This is the way you should do it.' Oh God!"

At one point, it looked like Roger might have to intervene but as Beverly recalled, "No, everybody left Roger alone. Everyone felt that they were on their own. Roger had given everybody this job and that was it. No one wanted to tell him things were not going well because at one point I said, 'Well, get Roger over here and let him direct this damn thing if everybody is so upset with David!' And they said, 'Oh, no, no, no! We'll work it out.'"[11]

> People are in tears because they're screaming and carrying on and I'm trying to muddle through all this. Come on, I've been through worse! I just sort of sat there and said, "Well, let it go." Everybody's nerves were twisting tighter and tighter; always making more out of the situation than it actually was. It happens during every shoot. I just sat back there and said, "It'll be fine. It'll all get done." I was more concerned about what I was going to eat! "Was anybody ever going to get me my cereal?"[12]
>
> There was a tremendous power play going on from the beginning. It all got done and we were on time. It turned out fine. But in the middle of this shooting, we thought we were never going to make it.[13]

And then, one day, the studio caught fire.

> It was on the 13th of May. The studio caught fire and nobody knew where the fire was coming from. We tried to get out but the studio was just jammed full of smoke. The Russians said, "It's all right. It's not burning. It's just smoke. It'll be okay." But we said, "Well, this is a wooden structure here and we'd better get out."
>
> There was no way to get out except the fire escape — we were on the second floor. So we got out onto the fire escape — which was falling apart. It was all rusted and we thought, "Well, okay. This is just swell! It's rusted and if we all stand on it, it may just collapse altogether. But let's go anyway." So we started down the steps and we hung on and it started to creak and groan but we got down.
>
> The fire was in another section of the studio and eventually the firemen came. In Russia they take a long time to do anything. They finally put the fire out. It was really bad in Ben's room so I guess that's where it started. He had burned something before — he had a candle and he had

burned his drapes. So we figured he had lit another candle and burned down the rest of the studio because he wasn't very happy with a lot of things.

They moved him to a different room and then they finally got his original room aired out. They put him back and told him not to leave the candle on the windowsill next to the drapes because that was really a no-no! He said he wouldn't do that any more. Thank God, the fire was very small and it was put out fairly quickly. We went back to work but it smelled pretty bad.[14]

Beverly really wasn't prepared for the state Russia was in after the collapse of the USSR. Everything was in disrepair or neglected altogether. Food was terrible and limited to a few very basic staples. What was available was also very expensive due to massive inflation. The weather also seemed to be in revolt that year. "When I got there, it was very cold. It was so cold and it was April! Then it got very warm. Then it turned cold again — and snowed!

We went on location and it snowed. All the scenes were shot indoors except for the last two days. We shot those scenes at a castle that was owned by a baroness. It was taken by the Communists during the Russian Revolution of 1917. Later, it was turned into some kind of men's club and she was never able to get it back. It was a magnificent place, a huge beautiful castle with a lake and gorgeous property.

We almost thought we would have to leave the castle because we were doing the swordfight outside and it started to rain. It was also bitter cold. We were sitting in this castle and someone looked outside and the snow started to come down and then it turned into a blizzard! We were getting ready to leave when the snow stopped just as suddenly as it had started and then the sun came out. Now it was too sunny because we had filmed some of the scenes when it was very dark and we had to wait for the sun to go behind the clouds. We'd stand out there and try to act. We had these big coats on and they'd say, "Okay, let's go!" and we'd be shivering while trying to say our lines. It was impossible![15]

Corman was doing another picture at Mosfilm immediately after *The Haunted Symphony* ended: *Burial of the Rats*, based on the short story by Bram Stoker. He wanted Beverly for that film too.

I read the script, and I thought it was not the best script I had ever read. It also had a lot of T&A in it. But the thought of working in this studio with rats — I just couldn't do it. There was no way that I would work in this dirty studio with those rats. *The Haunted Symphony* was lovely with lovely clothes and you had a feeling of cleanliness even though you weren't clean. But to work where everybody's looking like the Wrath of God and writhing on the floor with rats by the billions — I said, "Nope. I don't think so."[16]

We did use some trained rats in one scene in *Haunted Symphony* and one got away. So we don't know where that rat is. He's some place in that studio — together with a lot of other rats who live there.[17]

They thought I'd be wonderful in *Burial* in the role of the leader of this group of women. But I just couldn't do it. It was hard enough in Russia but not with rats, too. So I turned it down. But I suggested to Roger that what he should do is make everybody think this is a woman who has all these rats under her control and then at the very end, when she goes crazy, reveal her to really be a man.

Roger had a lot of faith in David Tausik to send him over to Russia by himself. [Tausik had] only directed one other picture before this one. But Roger gives a lot of people breaks. He does it because he get them cheap, but who cares? No one else is going to give you those kind of breaks. Roger knows that, so that's fine. It's nice to know Roger never changes. He's the same as he's always been. Even though he wasn't there, it's still a Roger Corman film. I've done so many pictures for him, I just fit right in![18]

Once again, Beverly had to try to get more work on television after her return from Russia. She made a guest star appearance on *Friends* ("The One with All the Poker") playing Aunt

24. The Haunted Symphony, *Russia and Roger Corman—Together Again* 169

Alice Hirson, Beverly and Ellen DeGeneres in a scene from the *Ellen* episode "She Ain't Friendly, She's My Mother" (November 8, 1995).

Iris, a poker-loving relative of series regulars Courteney Cox and David Schwimmer. She is called upon to teach "the girls" how to play the game in order to win a bet with "the boys." But most of Beverly's scenes were subsequently cut. The network called it "time constraints." Beverly recalled that during the taping of the episode, she was so nervous about her ignorance of the game that she failed to deal one of the girls any cards!

Beverly also made an appearance on *Ellen* ("She Ain't Friendly, She's My Mother") where she plays Evie, a friend of Ellen's mother and a fellow bridge player. She taped the show on October 6, 1995. Three of the show's writers approached Beverly after the taping to tell her how delighted they were with her delivery of their lines. This is normally a rare compliment for an actor to receive but Beverly was often thanked by a show's writing staff for her performance.

Then, on December 13, 1995, *Variety* announced, "Beverly Garland signed to play mom of Lois Lane in *Lois and Clark—The New Adventures of Superman* series. Harve Presnell plays her dad."

25. A Hollywood Survivor

In 1990, Beverly's son James had married. Beverly worried about the marriage.

When he met her, she was a very domineering woman. But then I thought, "well, maybe he's marrying his mother because I'm probably a domineering woman also." Although, as Jimmy once said to me, "Mother, it's okay to say 'no' to me." He studied psychology so I know where he's coming from. My way of bringing up my children — and especially Jimmy — was to practically give them everything they wanted and to spoil them terribly. They probably have turned out being like, "What! I have to face this? Where's my mother because she makes everything okay!" "Oh, your dog died? Here's another one!" So I thought it was so funny when he said, "It's okay to say 'no' to me."

But, then again, it was my son and I adore him so and if he thought this marriage was what he wanted, I thought it was better to keep my mouth shut. No matter what you say to your children, it means absolutely nothing after they get to be 15. After 15, they lie! They pretend that they're listening but they're not. They're cooked and you might as well take the turkey out.

So, if that's what he wanted, no matter what I would have said to him would not have made it any better. It would have upset him. What good would it have done? He'd made up his mind. The best thing for me was to go along and I was wonderful to her.

I adored Carrington's first husband. I mean, I just adored him and that marriage just fell by the wayside. But I'm not married to them so I see them differently. I see them as a person that's got problems or they're sweet, or they're this, or they're that, and I can embrace them as they leave.

Jimmy met her at college. Jimmy is very — how can I put it? "I want it *right now*!" Instead of saying, "Well, maybe..." he says, "*I want it now*! I gotta have it. I just gotta have it. I can't think 'til I have it! I gotta have it!" His friend said he wanted this model boat. I said, "Jimmy, you don't need a boat. You've got all this stuff, you don't need a boat, too." Jimmy said, "I've gotta have that boat. I really like that boat. I mean, the boat would look good!" This went on for five days until finally his friend said, "Get the boat!" But Jimmy never lets up. He will not let up until he gets what he wants. He will not think until he gets it. That's how he was about her. He made up his mind.

I also think what happened was that he made up his mind and he knew it was wrong but he thought it would work. I think way back in his mind he thought, "What am I doing? But I've already told her and I'm afraid to get out."

It was the same with Carrington. The night before her wedding she was in my kitchen crying, "I don't know, Mommy. I don't know." I said, "Carrington, I'm going to tell you something. You know we've invited 250 people to come to this wedding. You just walk down the aisle and when you get there you say, 'I can't do this,' and we'll have a party! Who cares? We've already got the food and the place. We'll have a party. You don't have to get married." I meant that. But she got scared and thought, "Maybe it's just me." But it wasn't. She knew. There was something telling her not to do it. I said to her, "I don't care. It doesn't make any difference to me. But I don't want you to get married if you don't want to get married." But she went ahead with it. And she didn't stay married very long either.[1]

In Jimmy's case, the problem went much deeper than just a poor marriage choice. Beverly explained:

> It was about nine years ago (1995) and Jimmy was going to Outward Bound, as I recall. He wanted to go to Outward Bound so badly. This is a tough thing if you've ever done it. It's like going through Army basic training — crawling under this fallen log and climbing trees. They leave you overnight in the forest. And just before he left, he said to me, "I want to tell you something. I'm gay." And I said, "Okay. That's okay. Fine." Then he left and he didn't say anything to his daddy.
>
> We all had this suspicion about James and there were times we'd say, "Do you think he could be gay?" "No!" "Ah, maybe." "You think so?" "Yep!" But it was in our heads. It was always there. There were times it would pop into our heads. We asked everybody, "You think so? I don't ... no."[2]
>
> I think Jimmy was probably starting to wonder at that point and that he was kind of moving in that direction and she was a very difficult, difficult girl. He should never have married her. He graduated from college and married her the same day. Graduated in the morning and married in the afternoon. It doesn't work. It was not the right thing to do. But he was away from home and he had a lot going on in his head.
>
> So the best thing in the world was to break up that marriage and let it go. They had no children so that was okay. Maybe he just wanted to prove something, but I don't know.[3]
>
> I said to Fillmore, "Jimmy is coming home in two weeks and I need to tell you something. I want you to remember how you felt about Jimmy and what you thought when you saw him the last time he was here — before he went to Outward Bound — and then keep that in your mind." Fillmore said, "Okay, I've got it in my mind." And I said, "Because I'm just going to tell you now that Jimmy tells me that he's gay. Now, the way he was before he left for Outward Bound is exactly the same person on Tuesday that he was on Monday. So keep that in your mind. You don't have to say anything to me. Just think about it." He did and he just treated it beautifully. Fillmore was wonderful with it. I just thought I needed him to understand that the boy wasn't changed. He's the same boy that he was when he was sitting here yesterday as he is sitting here today. So, don't forget that. Fillmore later said to me, "That made a lot of sense to me." So Daddy was wonderful with it.
>
> I think deep down I always had an inkling. Everybody kind of said that in their minds and then quickly dismissed it. My only problem with being gay was that I was terribly concerned he might get AIDS; that he might get sick. That's the only concern I had. That was the only thing that weighed on my heart. That there was the chance. You know, there's not a lot of chance that maybe you're going to get cancer — you don't think about that so much. Naturally, your children could get cancer or they could lose a limb or something. But that's probably not going to happen. But when you are gay, then you worry about that and that's what worried me. I just didn't want Jimmy to get sick. That was my big problem and, of course, that has not happened. He's in a committed relationship. He's been in this relationship for nine years and they are really good together.
>
> I'm sorry that every mother doesn't have a gay son because it's just the most wonderful thing you could ever have. They are just the best. He's very sensitive and he's just a sweetheart. So, that lifestyle does not bother me. That's okay. You are what you are and I really believe that you are born that way. I certainly didn't bring Jimmy up to be gay. I brought him up just like every other little boy and this is what he is. I think that it's in a gene that happens to be there and you have to accept that.
>
> I've seen so many boys whose families have rejected them and thrown them out of the house. I think it is just so sad. So, so sad. I'm for gay rights and I always will be and I make no apologies for that. That's how I look at it and that's how I feel about it. As far as I'm concerned, to have a gay son is really quite delightful.[4]

Meanwhile, Beverly was looking forward to playing Lois Lane's mother Ellen Lane in *Lois and Clark — The New Adventures of Superman*. She felt that being cast as Ellen might have had something to do with her last series:

One of the producers of *Scarecrow and Mrs. King* also produced *Lois and Clark—The New Adventures of Superman* but I don't know if this had anything to do with why I was asked to play Lois' mom. I never asked him. I loved the part because they wrote me as an ex-alcoholic which was really wonderful for me. They gave Ellen a whole underbelly of who and what she was. I thought it was just great that they brought it out: "I'd love to have a drink but I just don't think...." "No, Mother! You'd better not!" I loved that part. It was wonderful.

It was also a wonderful relationship between Teri Hatcher and her mother — which was just charming. That was so much fun for me. I really didn't have that on *Scarecrow and Mrs. King*. I wish I did have it then. My scenes with Kate Jackson were wonderful scenes but you didn't have a real strong background about who this woman was. This was why I was always asking if we could do something with Dotty. But nobody would go that way and I think a lot of it had to do with Kate. The show was about Kate and don't forget it.

I just think that Lois' mother was so much more developed — yet Lois and her mother were very opposite. Lois would roll her eyes at her mother. Mrs. Lane was very flamboyant. She was a completely different character than Mrs. King's mother. Dotty West was a homebody. Whereas, Lois' mother was out there doing her thing. She dressed glamourously and thought she was pretty darn good. She thought that everybody should listen to her opinions. That didn't happen but it gave me a character with a background and a history. Give me something, even if it's just a second on the screen!

On *Scarecrow and Mrs. King* they wouldn't do that. I really argued and even had my agent talk to them about it. I really tried to have them write her in such a way that you saw this woman as a whole person instead of just walking in and out. I thought it was important but it didn't happen. But I think you finally saw it on *Lois and Clark*. It was entirely different. It wasn't that I didn't like the *Scarecrow and Mrs. King* character. I just wished that they had rounded her out. Kate Jackson wouldn't give that character what she needed. I think she had a lot of insecurity.

Teri Hatcher also had a rough time because she was young. She was doing her best. She was adorable, just adorable. But I think Teri was not "Well, this is my show and everybody else has to sit back."[5]

Beverly's first appearance on *Lois and Clark—The New Adventures of Superman* was on December 17, 1995, in the episode "Home Is Where the Hurt Is." In it, Ellen's ex-husband Professor Sam Lane (Harve Presnell) is creating cyborgs in his secret laboratory. The episode was part one of a two-parter. The second half, titled "Never on Sunday," aired on January 7, 1996.

Thinking back on the series, Beverly believed that the leads worked well.

I think Teri and Dean Cain were just wonderful together and she was so cute. Of course, I liked it before she cut her hair to pieces. I liked her with that little Dutch Boy hair; that was Lois Lane to me. Of course, she wanted to get away from that, which she did.

Teri really wasn't difficult to work with on this show. She was very much into herself and there was a lot of insecurity there from her. I can remember so many times she'd cry and carry on. She wasn't happy and I just didn't get into it.

I'm very funny on a set. I don't become your best friend, but I'm there and I tell what I think. However, I certainly don't ever take over. It's not my show and I just do my best. I try to be there for you if you need it. But I don't become your bosom buddy either. That's just how I am. So I did my job.

Teri got down to a size one [from weight loss]. I don't know but I think she was very stressed-out. I don't know if she was a happy camper or what, but she just got thinner and thinner until she got to the point where she was wearing a size zero. She was thin. People used to say that she had an eating disorder but I never saw that. I don't know whether she was bulimic. There were rumors that she was but I never saw it so I have no idea. She was so pretty but she was so very thin and then she cut her hair very short. And she would never take her picture with you. I brought my camera on the set one day and just said, "I want to take my picture with you. Some-

Lois Lane (Teri Hatcher) and her mom Ellen Lane (Beverly) from *Lois & Clark: The New Adventures of Superman*. This photograph was used as a prop in Lois' apartment.

body take our picture!" That's the only picture I have because I never had any publicity pictures with her—*ever*! "Not with me!" Kate Jackson was the same. What is it about me? Nobody wants to have their picture taken with me?

The still photographer on *Lois and Clark* said Teri was ridiculous. He said Teri would "x" out all her photos. She wouldn't allow anything out. That's absolutely true. She'd always find something wrong with every photo taken on the set.

Beverly enjoyed working with Dean Cain. "Dean was the stepson of Director Christopher Cain, who I worked with on *Sixth and Main*. His stepfather was wonderful. Dean is just the kindest, nicest guy. They're both just good people."[6]

Lois and Clark—The New Adventures of Superman featured Beverly's character in four more episodes between February 1996 and July 1997. Then, during the week of January 13, 1997, a bit of television history took place when CBS-TV's *Diagnosis Murder* revisited an unsolved TV episode murder from 24 years earlier. That in itself would not seem unusual if not for the fact that *Diagnosis Murder* wasn't on the air then. What the show did was combine an episode from CBS-TV's *Mannix* series ("Little Girl Lost," October 7, 1973) and offer a forensic solution to the one case *Mannix* couldn't solve.

Another first was the uniting of the *Mannix* episode's original cast, which included Mike Connors (Mannix), Julie Adams, Pernell Roberts, and Beverly Garland, with the star of *Diagnosis Murder*, Dick Van Dyke. New scenes alternated with flashback footage from the *Mannix* episode. "That was so much fun," she said. "I loved the whole idea of it. In the earlier show, I had kind of a Southern accent. But in the second one, I realized that my Southern accent really became more pronounced. I watched it and I thought, 'You're a little too Southern there, honey. Tone that down a little.'

"It was wonderful to work with Mike Connors again because we hadn't worked together for a long, long time. We all had a great time. It all went together so well going back and forth from the original broadcast to the new one. It was one of the best."[7]

Beverly's husband Fillmore had an entirely different take on Beverly's performance. "When you look at her career ... she did a show called *Mannix* and then they decided many years later that they'd bring it back. It was a great idea. Then Beverly showed me the original *Mannix* episode and I thought, 'My God! This is a wild lady. No wonder I married her!' That was done a few years after we met. But to see her walk...!

"I remember I was over at Bill Hayes' house where he was having a party. Bill was Beverly's manager and we weren't married at the time. There was a little flight of stairs to an upper level. She walked up about three steps and I thought, 'Oh God. Look at that!' She was wearing a silk dress. She walked up these steps and that silk dress just clung in the right way.... The same thing with this *Mannix*. I looked at that and her hair was very long and blonde. I thought she just looked great."[8]

Lee Goldberg, one of the two writers who wrote *Diagnosis Murder*'s "Hard-Boiled Murder," remarked on his website, "[W]hen she showed up on the set the first day ... she had the character and her accent down cold. It was uncanny ... as if she'd played it just yesterday instead of [24] years earlier. I'm glad I had a chance to meet her and work with her."[9]

Galvanized by her recent return to the live stage and her success in *The Gin Game*, Beverly again trod the boards in the Sacramento Theatre Company's February 16, 1997, presentation of *Love Letters* by A. R. Gurney. Once again, the cast consisted of only two actors and her partner this time out was Troy Donahue. "When my publicist Pamela Sharpe said to me, 'They want you to do *Love Letters* with Troy Donahue,' I said, '*Troy Donahue*? My God, he's ten years old!' He was such a lovely man. He was dyslexic and he had a very hard time with a lot of the lines. So the two of us worked hard but he was wonderful in it."[10]

After a short vacation to Santa Fe, New Mexico, Beverly reprised her *Love Letters* role opposite William Windom at her hotel's convention center in North Hollywood on May 14 and 15, 1997, for Women in Show Business, an organization that helps raise funds for underprivileged children. Beverly then toured Alaska for the National Tour Brokers Association.

It was also in the spring of 1997 that Beverly made a "guest voice" appearance on the first two of three episodes of *The Angry Beavers*. The episodes were "The Mighty Knothead" in which she was the Raccoon Princess, and "Open Wide for Zombies" in which she was the Swamp Witch.[11] Then on July 19, an episode of *Spider-Man* ("The Haunting of Mary Jane Hudson") aired on Fox-TV with Bev "guest-voicing." Her voice could also be heard around this time in a series of Milky Way candy bar commercials when she crooned, "Chocolate, caramel ... and beyond!"

Just before filming her last episode of *Lois and Clark* in April 1997 ("The Family Hour"), Beverly filmed a two-part show on *7th Heaven* for the WB Network. Starring Stephen Collins and Catherine Hicks, the popular syndicated series focused on a minister's family. Beverly's guest appearance in "Dangerous Liaisons" dealt with the minister's wife (Hicks) who was trying to cope with the news that her widower father (Graham Jarvis) was now seeing another woman, Ginger (Garland). As expected, she was not happy with the news and was anything but cordial to her father's new love.

Beverly made a total of nine appearances on *7th Heaven*, including two double episode shows between May 1997 and February 2004. Because this show was also an Aaron Spelling production, and because Beverly had made so many other appearances on Spelling productions over the years, the question arose if this association put her on the short list when casting for Ginger took place. "I don't know if Aaron Spelling had anything to do with me getting the part of Ginger — although Aaron and I go back a thousand years to when he and I were actors at the Players Ring Theatre. I will never know. It would be nice if it was."

When Graham Jarvis died on April 16, 2003, Beverly didn't know if she'd ever be on *7th Heaven* again. "Graham passed away and so what are they going to do with Ginger? I don't know if they'll bring her back. They have fifty million characters on that show. I've never seen a show with so many people. Half the kids that started out on the show aren't there any more because they wanted to go to college. A lot of them didn't want to do this any more. Some wanted to do other shows and it got to be difficult for them. Now the show's writer has written another series so this might be the last year. She may not want to continue with *7th Heaven*. Her new series hasn't sold yet but she thinks it will."

Regarding Stephen Collins, who played the Rev. Eric Camden on the show, Beverly said, "[He's] wonderful. He's an easy, easy guy who's interested in lots of things. He's a writer—he's written a couple of books. I think he has absolutely no sex appeal, but that's what I think. I don't think he's a sexy man. I know he's playing a minister but you can have a sexy man playing the part and have people go, 'Oh God! Wow!' But Stephen is a sweet guy and a nice, nice man. One of those really nice actors."

In Beverly's last appearance on the show, "Two Weddings, an Engagement, and a Funeral," "I only did a phone conversation. When I walked on the set, Collins was walking off the set and he said, 'Hi. How are you? I don't know if this is going to be our last show or our last season or what. There's my stand-in and he's going to read my lines.'

> Well, to me — and I could be very wrong and it's probably wrong — but when you come on the set and I'm going to be doing a telephone conversation with you, I would be there and do the conversation with you. Now you're not going to see me — I know that — but the way I say the lines is completely different from the way my stand-in is going to say the lines. He's — just — going — to — say — the — lines. I'm going to say them much differently. To make your performance a really good performance, it is my responsibility to be on the set and give you those cues, give you those lines. Because when I give them to you, your lines might be fuller and better because you are working with the actor that you're talking to on the phone.
>
> I'm sorry but that's what I think. I was disappointed in him that he left and said, "My stand-in will read the lines.' Of course, it was a short scene; I understood that. But still, I think that you as an actor have the responsibility to help other actors. You have to work as a team. That's what it's all about, I think. Because he left and the stand-in is just that, a stand-in, he can't read. He can't act. So Stephen disappointed me. Bad form, Stephen Collins."[12]

Beverly had sympathy for Catherine Hicks. "She's a very easy, cute kid and it's been a very difficult show for her because she has a little girl and her husband is a special effects makeup man who works a lot. She can't spend enough time with her little girl. So she's always torn." When Beverly did the show, Catherine was down to working two days a week so she could be with her child.[13]

Beverly's character on the show had to contend with a husband who was developing Alzheimer's Disease. "One of the directors, who directed many of the episodes of *7th Heaven*,

7th Heaven explored the devastating effects of Alzheimer's disease in the episode "Consideration" (December 10, 2001). Left to right: Graham Jarvis, Beverly, Catherine Hicks and Stephen Collins.

had a family member — I think it was his mother — that had the disease and he always wanted to do a show about it. So it was very close to his heart.

They did a fabulous job with it, I think. Graham was wonderful in it. Very few shows are going to tackle this subject. I think it was just fabulous that they decided to do that."

It will always remain a mystery to me why Beverly was not nominated for an Emmy by the show's producers for her incredible performance in the episode "Consideration" (December 10, 2001). Anyone viewing this show cannot help but notice what a gifted actress Beverly is.

Thinking back on those shows, Beverly had to credit Graham Jarvis and his own battle with cancer. "I think the producers of the show did know that Graham had cancer but he was fighting it. He was really working hard to fight the disease and maybe they felt, well, if he does pass away, at least we're started this whole thread about Alzheimer's; we can use that. The last show that we were supposed to film, he never did. He got so sick that he couldn't. They had to write him out. But he was thrilled to work. He loved to work and he was a very good actor. I called him and his nurse put him on the telephone. He tried to speak but he couldn't. I said, 'Hi, sweetheart. How are you doing?' His responses were slurred and his nurse finally took the phone away, so I really didn't get to talk to him. Later I learned that he died the next day. I thought he was a terrific guy."[14]

After filming the first two *7th Heaven* episodes in 1997, Beverly made an appearance on ABC-TV's short-lived series *Teen Angel*. In "The Un-Natural," she played Beatrice, the deceased wife of Jerry Van Dyke; she is called back to Earth by the Teen Angel (Mike Damus) to cheer up her husband on what would have been their fortieth wedding anniversary.[15] The show aired on February 6, 1998.

Beverly also filmed "The Other Mother" for CBS-TV's *The Simple Life*, starring Judith Light. The plot revolved around a pending TV interview between Light and her mother, played by Florence Stanley. Her mother wants no part of the interview so Light has to hire an actress to play her mother.

Within the time Beverly accepted the role on *The Simple Life* and the day of the taping (approximately one week), there were three rewrites and, while the taping was in progress, yet more. Beverly blamed it all on poor writing.

> The jokes today are just crap. I hate it. It's scraping the bottom of the barrel. Toilet humor has been around since the beginning; we don't have to talk about it on television.
>
> What's with that bull/cow joke? My God — are we not more sophisticated than that? I don't get it. That's where I come from on this. I don't think we need that base humor. Bathroom jokes have become commonplace.
>
> Those who say, "Well, you have such a thing about sexuality in America! You don't really talk about anything." Well, I see a lot of European films and I don't see any of this garbage. Maybe I'm not seeing the "right" European films. I don't think you need it. Do you really need to see men at the urinal? Is that important to the scene? Do you need to see the girl talking to her boyfriend whose sitting on the toilet?
>
> I just think there is so much wonderful humor that is not being tapped. As wonderful as Mel Brooks is with his 2000-year-old man, we don't have anything like that now. It is so funny and it doesn't involve going to the john or talking about bulls and cows.
>
> But then, you've got to be a hell of a good writer and maybe you aren't. So you get this kind of humor. Good writers don't need this but bad writers don't have anywhere else to go.[16]

The direction on *The Simple Life* was also a disappointment to Beverly. "Sitcoms today are very different. The directing is so different. 'Do it loud!' 'Do it faster.' 'Don't be as excited.' 'Be calmer.' 'Pick it up!' What kind of directing is this? You'd better damn well know what you're doing because directors don't have time to direct. When I filmed *The Simple Life*, the director didn't direct anything. He told you to go faster, or sit down, or pick it up. 'Don't be so intense.' 'Play it sweeter.' Or 'Not so sweet.' I remember the young man who played the public relations guy. The director said to him, 'Don't be so intense.' 'Play it down.' Now, I thought he was wonderful. I loved it when he played it that way.

But they didn't like it."[17] *The Simple Life* lasted for seven weeks (June 3 to July 8, 1998) before it was cancelled.

While still working on *7th Heaven*, Beverly tried her hand at recording audio books. In 1997, she recorded a story for "Carolyn G. Hart Presents: Malice Domestic Volume 4 — An Anthology of Original Mystery Stories in the Tradition of Agatha Christie." The story Beverly narrated was "Killer Fudge" by Kathy Hogan Trocheck. Other actors in the set included Meredith MacRae, Jamie Farr and Susan Anspach.[18]

In October 1997, Beverly made a return to radio when she joined the California Artists Radio Theatre (C.A.R.T.), under the direction of Peggy Webber. Webber began her radio repertory stage productions in 1984; since then, she has gathered the cream of Hollywood talent to record broadcasts which are heard on radio stations around the world.[19] Beverly's first two shows were "Your Loving Son, Nero" (as Agrippina, with Louis Nye as her son, the mad Emperor Nero) and Louisa May Alcott's "Little Women" as Marmee, the mother of the March family. Since then, Beverly worked on several of the company's productions — the last in 2007 when she appeared in "Ruggles of Red Gap" by Harry Leon Wilson.

Beverly had her second series on-screen wedding on *7th Heaven* when she and Graham Jarvis tied the knot during the filming of the episode "The Home of the Brave" in September 1998. A few weeks earlier (August 17), her daughter Carrington was married (a second time) during a ceremony at her parents' house.

Beverly and Fillmore spent Thanksgiving week in New York City to shop, take in some Broadway plays, and see the Thanksgiving Day Parade.

On March 10, 1999, Fillmore Crank, Beverly's husband of nearly 39 years, died of liver cancer. He had complained of having flu-like symptoms less than two months prior, but his cancer remained undetected until just a few weeks before his death. "I have to say that Fillmore never bored me," Beverly said of her beloved husband. "He always had something interesting to say. He was very well read and very politically sharp."

> It was a very good, good marriage. I am not a very easy person to get along with. I can be really kind of touchy at times. I think that's part of me and how I am. I'm an actress and, as Fillmore used to say, "I didn't marry you because you were bright or pretty or whatever. I married you because I adore you and it didn't make any difference to me." It didn't make any difference how I was as long as I loved him. That was all he cared about. So it was good. It was a good marriage and we had good kids.
>
> When Carrington got married, he wasn't looking good to me. We spent Thanksgiving in New York City and when we got back, we went to the Grand Canyon in Arizona. He wanted to take me there because I'd never seen it. Then he took me to the base where he had gone into the Army Air Corps during the Second World War, and he showed me this funny little town where he and Barbara lived when they got married. We had a wonderful time. He got to visit all the places he hadn't seen in a long time.
>
> Then in late January, he thought he had the flu and he just didn't feel good. His doctor thought he had hepatitis and so he started treating him for it — which really wasn't treating him at all — and he kept feeling worse and worse. But Fillmore would never talk about his illness because he was a Christian Scientist. He really never told me what it was that was making him so sick. I don't think he had any pain. It got so that he couldn't eat anything. He didn't want to eat anything because it made him terribly uncomfortable.
>
> There were very few outward signs — he didn't lose any weight. Finally one morning, he said, "You've just got to call the doctor because I'm not getting any better." A very good friend had died several months before and Fillmore said to me, "I think I'm going to end up like Hal." I knew what he was telling me. He was telling me he wasn't going to make it.
>
> The doctor told me to bring him in. He could see right away that something was wrong and

Fillmore had a test on his liver and they found this big mass that was absolutely inoperable. Most liver cancer that people get comes from another source and it goes into your liver. We took him to U.C.L.A. and they told us he had primary liver cancer and that there was nothing they could do about it. They said they could begin chemotherapy and that it might give him three months more. But Fillmore said, "No, I don't want to do that. I'm not going to do that to myself and my family."

So we came home and by this time Fillmore was not eating at all. He ate popsicles—that's about all. He stayed in bed. He felt awful and I said to him, "Maybe we ought to go back to U.C.L.A. and see if they can build you up. Maybe then we can think about doing the chemotherapy." But he was so weak. By this time he had lost more weight. So we took him back to the hospital and all they did was put him on IV because he was starting to dehydrate. But he just got weaker. He was so unhappy. Finally all the family said, "Just get him out of here. Just bring him home."

We bought a hospital bed and put him in Carrington's room but he only lasted not quite a week. We had a hospice nurse there and she was very nice. She came in on March 10, in the morning, and she said to me, "I've done a lot of this hospice work and I can tell you, he'll probably go on Friday." We said, "Okay." And then she left and he died about an hour later. He just couldn't make it.

I would have hated to have him go through all that chemotherapy. There was no chance of curing him or prolonging it for a year. It might have only given him three months at most and, maybe if you were lucky, a little longer but that's all. Maybe I'm a fatalist, maybe I should have done that, but everyone talked about it—the whole family sat down—and we all felt this was the right thing to do. Fillmore felt that way, too.

If it was me, that's what I would like to do. I'd like to go as easy as I could go. I don't want to suffer and I didn't want him to suffer. Chemo can be really horrendous. It just wasn't right. I knew Fillmore enough to know that he was so against hospitals. He just had to go on his own terms and that's how it was.

We had a wonderful service for him in a little church where Carrington had gotten married [First Christian Church] and people got up and talked about him. Lots of people came; all the hotel staff and his old friends—people he knew from his school and college days. There were also a lot of my friends and people from the NTBA as well as contractors that Fillmore had worked with. It was really lovely. After the church service, we had a huge reception at the hotel.

We had him cremated. I always said to him, "Where do you want to be buried?" But he'd never want to talk about it. Finally, at the end—about a week or so before he died—he said, "I think I'd like to be cremated. I'd like to have my ashes sprinkled over the hotel and over Catalina and Newport." I said, "Okay." Well, we thought about that for a long time and we went to Forest Lawn and we got an urn that looks like a book and I have it in my house. I still have it there. I've never spread his ashes.

You never really get over it. You're okay if you don't talk about it. I miss him so much. I'm good at it. I go out there and I do my thing but way down deep inside.... That's why I don't talk about it very much, because I don't really realize how much I miss him 'til I begin to talk about how he died.

Fillmore was the best and it's amazing how many people loved this man. You can't replace Fillmore. He just is irreplaceable. He was a special person, very special. He was a good daddy and a good provider. He was fun. I used to say to him, "You just have made me so happy." At least I said that enough times to him so I think he knew that. I had such a good life with him. I just hope I made his life happy, too.[20]

26. Fifty Years in Show Business

Eight months after her husband's death, Beverly found herself the very proud grandmother of Tula Pajeau Goodman, who was born on November 9, 1999, to Carrington and Carlos Goodman. Tula had the honor of having a restaurant named for her when the Beverly Garland Holiday Inn opened Tula's California Café and Coffee Room in 2005.

Beverly was eager to get back to work to help her cope with Fillmore's passing. An opportunity presented itself to join the cast of the popular ABC-TV daytime drama *Port Charles*. The soap opera was produced by the same people who were behind ABC's long-running *General Hospital*. Beverly was offered the role of Estelle, the mother of Rachel (Kimberlin Brown). Rachel had spread the word that her mother was deceased but she was actually confined to a mental institution.

Beverly's first appearance on the show was on April 7, 2000—after almost turning down the part.

> I originally didn't want to do *Port Charles* because I was hesitant to do a soap. I felt it might be a lot of work and I was worried that I wouldn't be able to remember my lines. But the gal who played my daughter, Kimberlin Brown, was so good to me. She would say, "Okay. As soon as you get out of makeup, let's go over the lines." And so we did. She was very willing to do that. We ran them, which was what I needed. Graham Jarvis and I used to do that all the time on *7th Heaven* and our scenes got better and better. The more you run your lines, the better your scenes are; the better you get.
>
> I liked the character of Estelle. The reason I did it was because I loved the character. She was crazy, she was nuts and I like to do that. I looked like the Wrath of God half the time because I didn't have any makeup on. But I thought it would be fun being a crazy woman on a soap. Why not? If you're going to do a soap, you might as well have something going. So I did it. Unfortunately, Kimberlin Brown left the show and they didn't know what the hell to do with the mother. Kimberlin wanted to see if she could get a starring role in another show but she didn't get it. Since then, I understand she's back in *General Hospital*.
>
> They were left with me and didn't know what to do so I think they wrote in that I had a boyfriend and I was traveling around the world. I never got anywhere. I'm still her mother; I'm still crazy; but I'm getting older.
>
> I loved Estelle. The wedding, though, was a hard thing for me because it was my first day on the set. But Kimberlin was fabulous. What a good girl she was to work with me.

According to Beverly, she and Kimberlin used to play a game to see how many scenes they could finish in one take. And, she was amazed at some of the cast members' responses to working with her. "This one actor came up to me after a scene we did and said, 'Oh, that scene was so good. I have to tell you, working with you I've learned so much in just these few scenes we've done together. I can't tell you how wonderful—how blessed I am—to have been able to work with you.' That blew my mind.

"Another actor that I had a scene with was surprised when I reacted to him. In the scene, he does something and I say, forcibly, '*Stop that!*' After the scene ended, he said, 'Wow, you're really into this part. I never knew that you were going to be as intense and as good as you were. Wow! That was a wild scene. Thank you.' Well, what the hell else was I supposed to do? Isn't that what we're here for?"[1]

At 74, Beverly was thrilled to still be working. To be on two television shows in recurring roles was a special achievement. She would also make a guest appearance on CBS-TV's *The Guardian* in an episode titled "Indian Summer" (October 30, 2001), and was a contestant for her favorite charity, the East Valley Y.M.C.A., on the "TV Moms Special Edition" of NBC's *The Weakest Link* on April 28, 2002. Beverly also probably holds the record for being the first contestant on the show to be thrown off while in the lead! She explained what happened.

> We rehearsed and Ted Andrew, who was the show's coordinator, said, "Now you write down who you think is the weakest and should be thrown off." And all the mothers said, "We can't do that, we're TV mothers!" So Ted said, "Oh, all right. Put my name down." So we all put his name down.
>
> Now, when it came to do the show, we were all waiting off stage to be introduced. I said, "Listen, girls. If you can't figure out anybody to put down, if it upsets you too much, put my name down. I don't mind." I said that because everybody was afraid to put somebody's name down. So I thought, "If you're upset, put my name down. It's all right with me." And they all said, "Good," and they did! I was doing very well and could have continued but all they remembered was what I had said and they didn't want to put each other's names down. The host of the show, Ann Robinson, said, "But Beverly was doing very well." She asked Pat Crowley, "Why did you put Beverly's name down?" Pat said, "Because she said I could put it down." "Oh," Ann replied. "Okay. Goodbye, Beverly—you *are* the Weakest Link!" I was on that show for only a second and a half!"[2]

Beverly did earn $10,000 for the Y.M.C.A. However, had she not been tossed off so soon, she probably would have won a lot more.

The Y.M.C.A. of East Valley also instituted the Fillmore P. Crank Distinguished Service Award in honor of Fillmore, a board member who had done a lot for the organization over the years. This is an award which is given yearly. The award is a bronze plaque engraved with drawings of Fillmore during different stages of his life: a small boy, a USC track star, a lieutenant in the U.S. Army Air Corps, and a businessman.

Beverly was also honored by the Pacific Pioneer Broadcasters with an award. The mayor of Los Angeles, Richard Riordan, and the members of the Los Angeles City Council declared January 19, 2001, Beverly Garland Day. The council's proclamation read, in part: "Beverly Garland is a great star of Film, Television, and Theatre whose tremendous talent is matched only by her tremendous heart. She is the very essence of dynamic talent, class, kindness, civility, business acumen, and indefatigable commitment to family, community, and country."

Beverly was inducted into The Pacific Pioneer Broadcasters Hall of Fame where she took her place with such previous honorees as Milton Berle, Bob Hope, Betty White, Bing Crosby, Sid Caesar and Dick Van Dyke. Among those who gathered to honor Beverly were emcee Tom Hatton of CBS Radio and president of the Pacific Pioneer Broadcasters, as well as Mike Connors, Roger Corman, Troy Donahue, Peter Graves, Joe Campanella, William Windom, Jane Kean, and Kimberlin Brown. Beverly also received the well wishes of members who couldn't attend. Among the letters were those of Fred DeCordova, Betty White, and Dick Van Dyke.

For as far back as the early 1990s, Beverly had been making occasional appearances at various Western, horror, and science fiction genre conventions. In June 2002 she was a guest of honor at the Palm Springs Film Noir Festival and a couple of years later at the Fifth Annual Williamsburg Film Festival in Virginia. Beverly was also a featured writer for *The North Hollywood News* with her own monthly column "The View," which began appearing in 1998.

Having starred in several low-budget films for Roger Corman during her very long career, Beverly fully understood the importance of helping young people who were hoping to make their mark in the film industry. Sometimes, an aspiring young filmmaker can live as close as next door. Beverly was glad to help out. "My neighbor down the street came up to my house and said, 'I'm doing this all by myself. It's my money; I wrote it; I'm filming it and I'm directing it.' I've known Lisa Stoll since she was knee-high to a grasshopper and she asked if I would play the mother and I said, 'Sure.' So I did. From what she tells me, everybody liked it. She sent it to every film festival in existence. It's kind of a weird film, though. She did it all in digital video. It's not a bad little film.

"There are times when I look good and others where I say, 'Oh my God! Where's the light?' But years from now I'll look back on it and say, 'Not bad.' Although I doubt I'll ever say, 'I looked good then.' I played the mother and I had a good part in it. The script was all right, it was just kind of strange. It was hard to understand in parts. There's a lot of the boy thinking and the boy walking and doing a lot of thinking. Too much thinking!"³

Lisa Stoll had gotten her master's degree in cinematography from the American Film Institute and had worked as a director of photography in features, documentaries, shorts, music video and commercials. She had tried her hand at writing, editing and even producing in addition to her work behind the camera. However, she always wanted to try her hand at directing. "I didn't even know if I could; I had no experience at all," Lisa confessed.

She had tried to pitch one of her scripts to a studio with the idea of directing it herself, but they only wanted the screenplay and planned using their own in-house director. Lisa decided to write a script that could be filmed on a low budget and would be easy to shoot. On the way back from the pitch meeting, Lisa had the entire concept for *If* mapped out in her head before she got home. "When I started this project," Lisa explained, "cloning and stem cell research was a very hot topic in the media. So I listened to a lot of television and radio

Beverly with writer-producer-director Lisa Stoll at the Los Angeles premiere of *If* in 2003.

discussions and learned that some people thought that if someone were to be cloned, they wouldn't have a soul; that they weren't really people. I was really interested in exploring a relationship between twins and that if one of them was cloned, would they still have that bond as twins and could that clone have a bond with his mother? This is what I wanted to explore through these characters."

After drafting her sister Kimberly Rowe and good friend Jesse Hlubik as the film's leads Jennifer and Josh, as well as several professional actors in supporting roles, Lisa needed an accomplished actress to play the mother, Katherine. She recalled,

> I sat down to write the whole script, and then I was interested in finding other actors to play the characters that were in the story. The mother was going to be a really critical role and it was my mother who was the first one to say, "What about Beverly?" because she lived next door to my mom. It was the house I grew up in and while I hadn't seen Beverly for a while, I thought she would be great. But I wasn't sure if she would be interested. Then, since I hadn't seen her in quite a while, that she might be too old. Also, I had never really talked to her in a professional sense. My relationship with Beverly centered around the fact that I grew up with her kids. I spent more time at Beverly's house than at my own because I was really good friends with her daughter Carrie and her son Jim.

The opportunity to approach Beverly about this project occurred soon after when Lisa was out getting her mother's mail. "I saw Beverly in her car pulling up into her driveway and she saw me and stopped to chitchat with me. When I saw her, I thought she looked great. We continued talking and catching up about her kids and that's when I said, 'Hey, Beverly. I'm doing this small independent film and I'm doing this out of my own pocket and is this something you might be interested in.' So she said, 'Come up to the house and we'll talk about it. It sounds interesting.' So I did. We talked about how the project evolved and the story and Beverly agreed to come on board."

Stoll got a friend to invest $12,000 and Lisa put up $6,000 of her own money. Keeping costs down, Lisa got her cast to work under a Screen Actors Guild Experimental Contract agreement, which, in effect, would defer their pay until the film sold. Because this was such a small production, Lisa was able to shoot at many locations without a permit. Interiors were done at friends' and relatives' houses and apartments; one of the cast got his doctor to allow the crew to film in his offices in exchange for a small walk-on role. The chambers of an L.A. Superior Court judge — who just happened to be a close relative of the director's — temporarily became a lawyer's office.

Lisa also got a friend to shoot some footage in rural Minnesota during a snowstorm and she had Jesse Hlubik and his brother shoot some second unit footage in New York City. "That was kind of exciting," Lisa said, "because Jesse and his brother look alike so I was able to play on the double image and cloning of Josh and also the city lights and chaos of New York City. But I also got all these locations for free. Another location was this cool abandoned factory. Jesse and I went there and hopped the fence and filmed a lot of really good footage of him in this industrial factory that was now run-down. It was real guerrilla filmmaking — get in, shoot it, and get out before we got into trouble!"

Lisa remembered one other location shoot when she was working with her sister and Beverly. "There was another time when I was shooting downtown with Beverly. This was during the driving scene through an area that has a lot of graffiti. I liked that kind of gritty wall art as a backdrop. We got there really early to film this scene. Lo and behold, one half-hour into the shoot, another film crew came — a really big production. So we moved one street down and one hour later, the same film crew moved down to where we were. We all laughed, saying, "What are the odds?" I'd been down there a million times and I had never seen anyone filming. The one day we show up...! We moved again and the crew kept following us for the rest of our time there."

Some homeless shelters in downtown Los Angeles substituted for a Russian backdrop at the film's end. (With an $18,000 budget, a filmmaker today has to get really creative.) *If* took two years — on and off — to shoot due to her actors' schedules. Whenever they had free time to devote to her project, they worked. Post-production took another year with Lisa doing all the editing and special effects herself. The only jobs she had to contract out were the sound effects and music score.

Lisa was very proud that she completed the project on budget and that what she set out to accomplish, she did. She remarked that she worked on so many films that never got finished or never got off the ground because of one setback or another. She had resolved that she wouldn't be one of those filmmakers. Thinking back on the film, Lisa said it was a complete thrill to direct Beverly.

> I never thought in my wildest dreams that that would every happen. I was really fortunate that I was able to spend a lot of time with Beverly talking about the story and her character. We had time to develop her character and have that dialogue, raise questions and really explore Katherine in depth.
>
> The back story of Katherine was that she and her husband had twins and when they were in their first month after birth (they were male and female — paternal twins), the son (Josh) died of S.I.D.S.— Sudden Infant Death Syndrome. This event was so tragic for this couple that the husband was willing to do anything to get his son back. He was even willing to go so far as to clone his son.
>
> Katherine was a religious woman who didn't want to go down that road. It was against her moral beliefs. So it created such tension that the marriage started to fall apart because of this unfortunate death. Katherine decided to leave her husband and took her daughter (Jennifer) with her.
>
> The movie starts 26 years later when Josh is drawn to Los Angeles and he doesn't even understand why. It's because of his twin-ship with his sister that he always felt he was missing a part of himself. So when he arrives in L.A., and Katherine sees Josh for the first time. She's in denial because of her beliefs and she flat-out rejects him.
>
> I think Beverly was able to convey Katherine's inner struggle between her nurturing side as a mother wanting to bond with that child that she never got to develop a relationship with, and coming to grips with the fact that he is a cloned version of that child and not being able to reconcile the difference. So she is really struggling with this dilemma. Is Katherine just going to sever her relationship with him again and act like he doesn't exist or is she going to come to terms with her religious beliefs and put that aside so that she can allow herself to love this child?
>
> I think Beverly really understood the dynamics of that and what I was interested in exploring. As a result, since a lot of it was already hashed out prior to filming, it made it a lot easier once we started the cameras rolling. Beverly was fully engaged in her scenes. It just made my job a lot easier because she was so professional. You could ask her to do the take 26 times and she would just come out and give it her all every single time. We still had an ongoing, open dialogue on the set where she was always glad for feedback and was always interested in knowing if I was happy with what she was doing.
>
> There were a couple of times when we had issues with a neighbor's dogs barking and we had to do Beverly's take a couple of times. At first I think she thought it was something that she was doing and I had to clarify that it was actually a sound issue and that what she was doing was just wonderful. She was bang on but the problem was that the sound was unusable.

Beverly had been scheduled for four days but her work on the film was always based on when she would be available. "One day," Lisa recalled, "Beverly came in and she had a puffy swollen red eye and I knew that she was very self-conscious about her eye and she was concerned about it. I assured her that we would light it and shoot it so that no one would see her eye and how red and puffy it was. She was such a trouper. She said, "Okay, kid. Let's just go with it." That's how professional Beverly was. She was willing to shoot the scenes despite the situation. A lot of times, actors would ask that their scenes be rescheduled. We could have easily done that but Beverly insisted, "We're here and you've got your crew so let's go with it." She was just amazing and I was really thankful for that type of commitment to the project."

Lisa premiered *If* in the 2003 Tambay Film Festival and later held a second premiere in Los Angeles. The film received very good reviews. One reviewer, Bob Ross of *The Tampa Tribune*, noted, "Beverly Garland, a Hollywood veteran, looks terrific while playing a difficult character...."

Lisa had very fond memories of Beverly and the Cranks.

What I remember the most about Beverly is that she was always full of life no matter if she was hosting a party or it was just the two of you chitchatting. But she was always very bubbly and very honest about her opinion or what she thought. She was very frank in that sense.

I used to spend a lot of time up at the Crank house. I would play with her kids or spend the night during the weekend when I was just a little kid and we had slumber parties. The one thing I always remembered is we would ask Beverly to scare us. We would tell her, "Come in and scare us." We'd ask her this at dinner time and later when we were all hunkered in our sleeping bags, drinking hot chocolate, watching scary movies, we would forget. But Beverly would come flying in and would roar or growl loudly and we would get so scared and scream and hide under the blankets. That was always fun because we never knew what Beverly was going to do. It was always like "The Fun Zone" over at the Cranks.

Jimmy and I loved horror movies so we'd stay up late — actually all night long — and watch horror movies and we would rate them. We devised this whole rating system which was based on certain criteria like — if the woman fell while running away from the monster or if she ripped her dress, then it would get points. You know, all those clichéd things about a horror film.

The Cranks were so gracious. They would always invite me to their family functions. The Cranks always had these big family gatherings, whether it was Christmas, Thanksgiving or someone's birthday party, so I was always part of those gatherings.

But one of my favorites was summertime out at Newport Beach. I really have fond memories of all those times that we went down there. The Cranks would rent a beach house on Balboa Island and there were usually a couple of families that would spend the summer down there. Summer days down at Newport Beach were spent hanging out on the beach, sailing, running around playing games. Beverly would spend the day reading or playing backgammon. She loved to play and taught me how to play. It was a lot of fun.

When I was younger I never really realized how big a star Beverly was because I always saw her as a second mother and I was always hanging out with her kids. There were times when people would come up and ask her for her autograph. I always thought that was cool. Occasionally Carrie and I would go down to the set with Beverly and watch her tape a television show. That was very exciting. It really opened my eyes when I saw her acting with all those other big stars.

When we were teenagers, Carrie and I got to work on a movie called *Roller Boogie* which Beverly starred in along with Linda Blair. They needed a lot of extras to roller skate in the background during the roller rink scenes and Carrie and I were hired. We thought that was great. I was thrilled to think I was going to get paid to skate around all day long! The cast and crew were really nice and the director, who lived down the street, would often give us a lift to the set.

When we were kids, Beverly would take Carrie, Jim and me to the movies. Sometimes she would drop us off or sometimes she would join us. We saw *Star Wars* and waited over two hours on line to see the film, filled with excitement and anticipation at what we were going to see.

Beverly went with us to see *Halloween*, a horror film. She was sitting next to me. I'll never forget how her hands were gripping the chair's arm rests, digging her nails in as she was watching the movie and every time something scary would happen up on the screen, she would let out this blood-curdling scream and then we'd scream, too. We were all scared and we'd hold each other's hands. It was really a great experience to be in the movie theater and see Beverly just as scared as we were! Then later, as an adult, to think back and say, "Wow, that was great! Beverly was in all those Roger Corman movies and she was like the 'Queen of Scream' and to think that she herself was so engrossed in the movie *Halloween* and got scared to the point where she would scream. It just showed that Beverly enjoyed being part of the audience as much as she enjoyed being an actress herself."[4]

Two months after the Tambay Film Festival, Beverly was back on the Warner Bros. studio lot filming her last made-for-television movie, *Christmas Vacation 2: Cousin Eddie's Island Adventure*, on June 12, 2003. In it, she plays Eddie's (Randy Quaid) Aunt Jessica and Uncle Nick's (Ed Asner) wife. Aunt Jessica is caught having an affair with the pool cleaner. She's in her seventies and the pool cleaner is more than 45 years her junior.

In 2003, once some cruise lines had started specialty cruises to attract customers, Beverly was hired by two of these lines — Crystal Cruises and Celebrity Cruises — to give lectures on "Making Cent$ as an Actress" and another on the leading men she worked with in film and television. Beverly said, "I talked to my girlfriend Jane Kean and asked her, 'How do you get on these cruises?' She gave me a name of this woman and I called her and talked to her. Than I sent an outline about what I was going to talk about as well as a video tape I had done and some photos. I was then put on the tour circuit. Both Crystal and Celebrity cruises wanted me so I did both. I had a wonderful time on both cruises and I wish I could have done more."[5]

On October 24, 2003, Beverly was invited by the University of Oklahoma College of Fine Arts to a 40th Anniversary screening of *Stark Fear* and to honor Oklahoma University film professor Ned Hockman (who directed the film) and Beverly (who — according to the university's press publicity — "pioneered leaving Hollywood to work on independent films").

> They called me and asked me to go back because they were doing a big thing of Ned Hockman and they wanted me to come. When I got the letter I said no, I wasn't going to come because, I said to myself, "It was the most god-awful movie I had ever done in my life." But I changed my mind and told them I would go. As it turned out, Ned Hockman landed up in the hospital so he couldn't come.
>
> Of course they're very proud of Ned Hockman at the college. I went to the event at the university and they showed the movie and I was glowing. "Let me tell you about Ned Hockman," I said. "Let me tell you how wonderful it is for me to be here." I was fabulous. I kept my mouth shut and I was their girl. I knew I had to do that and I did it. I was a good girl. I was wonderful. I had everyone in tears at the end, I'm sure.
>
> Then when I saw the movie again, I thought to myself, "You know, it isn't a bad movie." But it took me 40 years before I could get to that point. So, I guess, I should see these things 40 years after they're made to appreciate them.
>
> The director on the picture tried but we knew he didn't know what he was doing. Skip Homeier, Ken Tobey and I said, "He doesn't know what he's doing. We're from Hollywood — what does he know? He only teaches, he doesn't do. We do!" And it ended up with Skip directing.
>
> But none of that came up during the reunion 40 years later. Skip didn't come. I don't know where Skip is now. I don't know if they asked him or not but he never came. I think he probably would have ended up liking the movie, too.
>
> Of course, when you see a movie with a whole college and the whole town behind it — loving it — you say, "Well, okay. I'll go along with that. I guess 300 people are right. What do I know? So you try to see it through their eyes and it's okay now.[6]

On Monday, April 5, 2004, Beverly was a guest speaker at Santa Monica College's Mary Pickford Speakers Series. The lectures took place at the Academy of Entertainment & Technology. In their description of guest speaker Beverly Garland, it was noted that she "helped pave the way for many of today's strong female roles."

Back in November of 2000, a trading card series called *Twilight Zone—The Next Dimension* was issued with a limited edition worldwide of 8,000 sequentially numbered boxes. Each of the boxes contained two autographed guest star cards. Some of the featured stars were Burt Reynolds, Jack Klugman, Suzanne Lloyd, Don Rickles, Jeanne Cooper, William Shatner and Beverly Garland. Four years later, Beverly recorded a story for "The Twilight Zone Radio Dramas" hosted by Stacy Keach. The dramas were broadcast on WGN — The Voice of Chicago on Saturday nights at midnight. Beverly's episode was "Uncle Simon" in which she played Barbara Polk and Peter Mark Richman was Uncle Simon. The original broadcast was heard on June 26, 2004. Since then, the series was sold as a CD set commercially.

When the 2004 Valley International Film Festival (which exposes independent writers and filmmakers to industry experts) held its first annual awards gala dinner, among those honored were Joseph Campanella, who was inducted into the USA Television Hall of Fame, and Beverly, who received the Chairman's Award.

One of Beverly's last public appearances was on April 2, 2006, at the Long Beach Playhouse when she appeared in a one-woman show titled "Beverly Garland's First 50 Years in Show Business." The show consisted of Beverly's remembrances as well as a video presentation encapsulating her 50-year career in films, television and the stage. Among those who attended the show and reception afterwards were Lee Meriwether and Patricia Neal.

Farewell to Television's First Lady

Several years ago, Beverly said that she was feeling exceptionally well. However, she did have an appointment for a physical with her doctor. During the examination he took chest x-rays and one of the x-rays showed a seed-sized spot on her lung. The doctor explained what the options were, but he closed the door and said to her, "You're not leaving until you agree to have this operated on and removed because we can get it all out and you'll be fine." Beverly said to herself, "Okay. He knows what's best," and she had the operation. It was cancer and it was removed. Beverly went for regular examinations after the operation and she remained cancer-free.

Beverly's longtime friend and fan club president Carl Del Vecchio recounted what happened during the last two years of her life.

I called Beverly on January 1, 2008, to wish her a Happy New Year, and I noticed her voice was not right. She was not sounding the way Beverly normally sounded. I became very concerned. So I called her son James at the hotel and he explained that what she was experiencing was cognitive and neurological degeneration. It came on very suddenly and they did whatever they could. She went to several specialists. Supposedly, they even performed some procedures that were termed "invasive." But they could not determine what was wrong.

It did tend to progress very, very quickly. What James told me that seemed peculiar was that when he talked to his mother directly — face to face — he didn't often get a good response from her. However, talking to her on the telephone, she seemed much more lucid. It just seemed very odd that talking on the telephone, she would be more responsive.

When I called Beverly after that, I could tell there was definitely further degeneration. She was worse off and eventually she died on December 5, 2008.

I [got together with] Beverly on Mother's Day, May 2006. She had been complaining about having flu-like symptoms that she just couldn't get over for a while before our meeting. She was also wearing flat casual sandals and said that these were the only shoes that she felt comfortable wearing lately. When I was with her she seemed fine. There was no problem that I could detect and she seemed totally lucid.

The last thing Beverly did was for C.A.R.T. — "Ruggles of Red Gap" — and that was in March 2007. So this progression probably started little by little but probably actually got much worse at some point after this radio performance.

I had called Beverly in January 2008 because that was the anniversary of when we first met 42 years ago, in 1966. That's when I immediately noticed that something was very wrong with Beverly. If you made a transcription of our conversation and read it, the responses made perfect sense. But to hear it, that was not Beverly. The way she was speaking, it was not her. She would respond to you rather than talk with you. When I said, "Beverly! It's Carl Del Vecchio," she replied, "Carl — Del — Vecchio," as if she was trying to place the name. The voice I heard was not her normal speaking voice. There was definitely something wrong. During subsequent conversations talking to Beverly, it was obvious that her illness was getting worse and worse.

Beverly's daughter Carrington called me the night of December 5, 2008, to tell me that Beverly had passed away earlier that day. All the family was by her side. During our short conversation, Carrington said at the end that Beverly couldn't speak and that she couldn't move her hands.

I had asked Jimmy when I spoke to him, "Is it Alzheimer's?" He said the doctors really didn't know what it was. It's just that this progression — this neurological and cognitive degeneration — came on very, very fast. None of the doctors who examined Beverly apparently had seen anything like that before. They had never seen it come on so quickly. There was no explanation for it."[1]

Beverly was cremated. There was a memorial service at the Beverly Garland Holiday Inn in North Hollywood on Friday, December 12, 2008. Several hundred people attended—fellow actors, family and admirers of her long career.[2]

On January 25, 2009, Beverly was given a memorial tribute during the 15th Annual Screen Actors Guild Awards.

Epilogue

Beverly was once asked to describe herself—both on and off screen—and this is what she had to say.[1]

I think she's a very energetic woman. She's a Libra so she weighs everything. I think that she's a woman who is very easy to know but you don't really know her. She kind of keeps to herself. She is very outgoing but really that isn't her. She is really very much inside herself. She makes friends very easily but she is kind of a loner — very much a loner — who doesn't really share her whole life with a lot of people as she does with four or five really good friends. She needs people but she's comfortable in her own skin.

I think she is a very, very giving person, and I think that if there is ever a problem, she blames herself. "It's always my fault. I did it. It's my fault. Don't worry about it. I did it."

Beverly Garland, the actress, is much more flamboyant; she's out there. She can talk and walk and do and if she had to do any kind of personal appearance, she girds herself up and she does it. She does it well. She's never late. She knows her lines. She knows what she's doing. On the set, she's very much into herself. She doesn't talk to anybody particularly. She just dedicates herself to the work that day and nothing else interferes. She handles it well. She can handle any kind of acting well. She doesn't mind being down and dirty — in fact, that's what she likes. She has tremendous energy. She gets along with everybody. She's not a player.

As an actress, when it's lunch time, she eats around 11 o'clock in the morning and then she goes to her trailer and takes a nap. She doesn't go out to lunch with you. I can remember on one show I was sitting in a car — it was a convertible, I think — and they said, "You don't have to stay. We can get your stand-in." I said, "No. I'll stay. You're lighting the scene and it's fine." And I immediately went to sleep. I can go to sleep just like that. I can sit in a chair and in five minutes I can be asleep.

I'm a very closed person but nobody really knows that because I give the impression that I'm very open. But I keep mostly to myself a lot.

When Beverly was asked what her greatest regret might have been, she said,

When I started in the business, I was so afraid when I went to New York. I was all by myself and I didn't know what to do or where to go. I had no one to talk to. I think maybe I should have pursued that more. Then, I think, maybe what I should have done was tried to get a role on the Broadway stage.

I think my career could have gone much further if I hadn't married Fillmore. I think that maybe it would have been good for me to do *The Miracle Worker* on Broadway. I think my career would have gone a different way. Whether or not that would have been good for me, I don't know. But I think I could have been a bigger actress. I really do think I could have won an Academy Award with the right part.

I think that I pulled back on my career because I made that decision that my family came first and my career was second. If I hadn't done that, I think my career would have gone much further.

Now I can't really say that was a failure. But I think that I would have had a different career if I had done that. But I made choices in my life and the choices I made were the choices I stuck to and my life has been wonderful.

I've been blessed with a wonderful husband and I've been blessed with wonderful children. I've had a career that's spanned fifty years and more. There are not a lot of people out there that have had that kind of career.

I'm a survivor and I'm proud of all that. It might have been different if I had made different choices along the road. But I didn't because what was important to me were the choices I made. That was much more important to me than the career. But the career might have been different.

I look at an actress like Elaine Stritch and I see so much of me in her. But she took the road that I didn't take and that is not the road that I really wanted because if it had been what I really wanted, I would have done it. And when I sat down with my alter ego, I made the choice that I knew was right for me. I knew that.

But it would have been fun to be the other choice.

Afterword
by Peggy Webber

To begin at the beginning, I have to tell you that I worked in 1949 for Jack Webb and the various shows he produced before and after *Dragnet* on the radio. I worked with Jack as an actor even earlier, when he was a struggling freelance actor himself. One of the writers who worked with him was a very fine dramatist, James Moser. I had been given the role of Jack Webb's Ma Friday on the radio *Dragnet*, along with dozens of other characters that Jim Moser and Jack chose to keep, from the true stories taken from the Los Angeles police files.

One day, Jim Moser departed from the police plays and wrote an audition script for Jack about a doctor which was broadcast during a summer hiatus. Jack had introduced Richard Boone to his little band of "mimes" a few months earlier. Dick Boone did a few small radio roles with us. He had never done radio and latched onto me to give him some clues for the live broadcasts of the *Dragnet* shows. When we did the audition show *The Doctor* over NBC, Boone played that title role.

Shortly thereafter, I went to Japan to marry a doctor with the Atomic Bomb Casualty Commission. (He became famous, after we were married, for discovering radiation cataracts and did extensive pioneer work in the formative years of laser surgery.) When I returned to Hollywood after breaking contracts with a number of shows to stay in Japan, at the request of my husband, Jack had saved a starring part in his new *Dragnet* television series for me. It was the second show to be filmed, with Jack directing, and it was a role I had done very successfully on radio — a young Mexican woman who steals a baby from L.A. County Hospital when her newborn dies.... It was a huge success and I received excellent press and several offers for contracts the next day after it played coast to coast on NBC-TV. Television was relatively new at that time.

I was back in Japan when it played, awaiting the birth of my own first child. However, during the month I was back in Hollywood, Jim Moser gave a Christmas party. Jack and Julie Webb and all the gang were there. I spoke with Jim and I reminded him of the radio audition show *The Doctor* which played on NBC. Now that I was married to a doctor, I could give him my "inside views" of what the series could entail for TV. Jim Moser said, "Oh, it would be too bloody to put on television." I laughed at that and said people were hungry to know what doctors were doing. It was customary in the day [1951] not to expect much explanation from physicians and surgeons regarding their private medical practices. My own mother had had a hysterectomy a couple of years earlier with a fine surgeon, but he would not discuss what he had discovered or why the surgery was necessary or anything of that nature that one would expect today from one's own doctor. I kept talking to Jim and said, "By all means if you do it, get Richard Boone to play the doctor, because he looks unlike any movie star and would be believed." He also was a thoroughly good actor.

Well, I received a letter from Jim Moser about two years later when I was living in Durham, North Carolina, while my husband finished his residency at Duke University and I was expecting my second child. I was seven months along. Jim wrote, "I took your advice and turned *The Doctor* into a TV series and we are going to 'wing it' in a couple of weeks. I hope you can come back and do the lead in the first show with us." I wrote him back that I was seven months along in my pregnancy and the airlines would not let me fly at seven months. He wrote back that he was sorry. When I saw the show, it starred Beverly Garland and Lee Marvin. I had never heard of Beverly. We had a stock company of actors in radio and we all were like a family, we knew each other. But Beverly was marvelous and pretty and Lee Marvin was an actor with my agent, Meyer Mishkin, who introduced me to Lee before I was married, saying to him, "Lee, meet Peggy Webber. She will be one of the next biggest female stars in Hollywood." Of course, I left and was gone for most of the next four years. I flew back a few times and did some TV. Ironically, I co-starred with Lee in a live hour-long show on CBS and shortly thereafter my doctor husband and I bought a house that turned out to be right next door to Lee Marvin. Lee, who also worked on Jack Webb's early radio series, would inevitably introduce me to his friends at parties, etc., as the actress who played opposite him in his first TV film, *Medic*. He remembered my performances from *Dragnet* TV and confused me in his mind with Beverly.

So, jump ahead about forty years, and I was on a dais with Beverly Garland, and honoring William Windom. Windom was living in the lower bedroom of my house in Hollywood Hills and he was appearing regularly on about fifty of my early C.A.R.T. shows which played on NPR, etc.

Ironically, it turned out that Beverly had introduced Bill Windom to his wife. And as she spoke about this, I realized that we knew many of the same people and later in the Green Room we spoke briefly. I was presenting C.A.R.T. shows at the Hollywood Roosevelt Hotel before a live audience and invited her to play some key roles in shows we did from there.

One that stands out was the role of Marmee in *Little Women* which starred Shelley Long, John Astin, JoAnne Worley, Kathleen Freeman, Nancy Cartwright, William Windom, Janet Waldo, Cornelia O'Herlihy and Bairbre Dowling. Beverly was warm and gracious in the role, the best Marmee anyone could wish for, a joy to work with and quick to adapt, a thorough pro.

We worked on shows for a number of years until in 1999 I mentioned to my stock company that we would not be able to appear at the Roosevelt any longer. The management had sold it to an overseas company and the theater was to be destroyed. Beverly suggested that I move the company to her hotel and work out of the Little Theatre there. She spoke to the Holiday Inn management and they gave us the space for little or nothing. We had free parking in those days and from time to time Beverly herself would hostess with tea and coffee and other goodies to accompany our rehearsals.

One time I told her of the story with Jim Moser and she looked me straight in the eyes and said, "I owe you for everything!"

Once she played the Mother of Nero, Agrippina, in a comedy with Louis Nye titled "Your Loving Son, Nero." Nye as Nero was trying to kill his mother in the true spirit of the royal Romans of that ancient period. But like the Road Runner, she kept escaping all of his machinations. Bev played Ava Gardner in our radio production of "The Man with Bogart's Face" starring Rich Little. In "Ruggles of Red Gap" with Michael York, she played a singer from the Yukon who becomes a widow and moves to a small Western town. There she meets an earl from England and marries him, becoming the "Lady" of the village. She played a French woman in a show called "The Seven Layered Arsenic Cake of Madame La Farge" where she co-starred with William Windom and Louis Nye. David Warner narrated these stories (beginning with the Nero tale), alternately with Roddy McDowall. Beverly also played the aunt in "Jane Eyre." On our regular 90-minute shows, Beverly would narrate and act as hostess for me and for C.A.R.T. She did over a dozen of our shows.

We were the last company she worked with as an actress. She would often take a few of us to dinner after the shows at her restaurant, Tula's. It is named for her granddaughter. A huge picture is on one wall at the entrance of the five-year-old smiling child.

Beverly was always considerate and had no affectation. She was a joy to be around and had a great sense of humor.

I will always miss her.

Hollywood, California

Peggy Webber *is a veteran actress of movies and television. Her first love is radio, where she began her career at age 11. She is the founder and executive director/producer of the California Artists Radio Theatre (known as C.A.R.T.), which can be heard nationwide.*

Appendix I:
The Television Credits

Series Start	*Title*	*Role*
September 20, 1949	*Mama Rosa*	Nina
October 15, 1957	*Decoy*	Casey Jones
September 17, 1962	*Stump the Stars*	Herself
September 14, 1964	*The Bing Crosby Show*	Ellie Collins
September 27, 1969	*My Three Sons*	Barbara Douglas
October 3, 1983	*Scarecrow and Mrs. King*	Dotty West
April 7, 2000	*Port Charles*	Estelle Reese

RECURRING ROLES ON A SERIES

January 15, 1959	*Yancy Derringer*—"The Fair Freebooter"	Coco LaSalle
April 16, 1959	*Yancy Derringer*—"The Wayward Warrior"	
January 31, 1977	*Mary Hartman, Mary Hartman*	Cookie LaRue
November 5, 1982	*Remington Steele*—"Thou Shalt Not Steele"	Abigail Holt
April 5, 1983	*Remington Steele*—"The Sting of Steele"	
December 17, 1995	*Lois & Clark: The New Adventures of Superman*—"Home Is Where the Hurt Is"	Ellen Lane
January 7, 1996	*Lois & Clark: The New Adventures of Superman*—"Never on Sunday"	
February 11, 1996	*Lois & Clark: The New Adventures of Superman*—"I Now Pronounce You..."	
October 6, 1996	*Lois & Clark: The New Adventures of Superman*—"Swear to God, This Time We're Not Kidding"	
December 15, 1996	*Lois & Clark: The New Adventures of Superman*—"T'was the Night Before Mxymas"	
June 14, 1997	*Lois & Clark: The New Adventures of Superman*—"The Family Hour"	
May 12, 1997	*7th Heaven*—"Dangerous Liaisons" Part 1	Ginger
May 19, 1997	*7th Heaven*—"Dangerous Liaisons" Part 2	
May 11, 1998	*7th Heaven*—"Girlfriends"	
November 2, 1998	*7th Heaven*—"And the Home of the Brave"	
December 13, 1999	*7th Heaven*—"Forget Me Not"	
December 10, 2001	*7th Heaven*—"Consideration"	
May 13, 2002	*7th Heaven*—"Holy War" Part 1	
May 20, 2004	*7th Heaven*—"Holy War" Part 2	
February 23, 2004	*7th Heaven*—"Two Weddings, an Engagement and a Funeral"	

Series Start	Title	Role
Unaired or Unsold Pilots		
1959	*The Man*	Louise Fox
1961	*Russell*—"Night of the Wrangler"	Bonnie
1963	*Calhoun*—"The County Agent"	Nan Sloane
1974	*The Cowboys*	Mrs. Andersen
1975	*Joe & Sons*	Estelle
December 6, 1981	*Judgment Day*	Vicki Connors
July 4, 1990	*Bean Pole*	Margaret
Guest Appearances		
August 10, 1950	*The Lone Ranger*—"The Beeler Gang"	Laura Lawson
November 10, 1952	*Hollywood Playhouse* (a.k.a. *Hollywood Opening Night*)—"Thirty Days"	
September 13, 1954	*Medic*—"White Is the Color"	Estelle Collins
September 15, 1954	*The Lone Wolf*—"Pursuit"	Nancy Trout
September 30, 1954	*Lux Video Theater*—"Meet Jo Cathart"	Mary Lou Matthews
November 29, 1954	*Big Town*—"Hot Car Murder"	
December 9, 1954	*Four Star Playhouse*—"Bourbon Street"	Julie Cranston
December 31, 1954	*City Detective*—"Man Down, Woman Screaming"	Jeanne
January 22, 1955	*The Star & the Story*—"The Lie"	Laura Kent
January 26, 1955	*The Millionaire*—"Millionaire Carl Nelson"	Clara Nelson
March 24, 1955	*Four Star Playhouse*—"Night at Lark Cottage"	Lucille
March 31, 1955	*Lux Video Theater*—"My Name Is Julia Ross"	Julia Ross
May 21, 1955	*Damon Runyon Theater*—"Tobias the Terrible"	Deborah Weems
May 26, 1955	*Lux Video Theater*—"Thunder on the Hill"	Valerie
June 12, 1955	*Pepsi Cola Playhouse*—"Woman in the Mine"	Claire Walkowsky
July 7, 1955	*Lux Video Theater*—"The Creaking Gate"	Joyce Williams
August 5, 1955	*Soldiers of Fortune*—"The Lady and the Lion"	Elizabeth Marlowe
August 5, 1955	*Schlitz Playhouse of Stars*—"Too Late to Run"	
September 16, 1955	*Science Fiction Theatre*—"The Negative Man"	Sally Torens
November 8, 1955	*Navy Log*—"Family Special"	Sally
November 27, 1955	*Frontier*—"Cattle Drive to Casper"	Sarah Garvey
[no date] 1955	*Studio 57*—"Waterhole"	
January 7, 1956	*The Star & the Story*—"The Point of Honor"	Soledad
January 28, 1956	*The Star & the Story*—"Payment in Kind"	Aimie Preston
February 3, 1956	*State Trooper*—"Rodeo Roughhouse" (a.k.a. "Killer on Horseback")	Elli Austin
February 17, 1956	*Science Fiction Theatre*—"The Other Side of the Moon"	Katey Kersten
March 11, 1956	*Front Row Center*—"The Morals Squad"	Ann Kubichek
April 6, 1956	*Crusader*—"A Deal in Diamonds"	Ilona
April 26, 1956	*Four Star Playhouse*—"Touch and Go"	Maxine
June 14, 1956	*Four Star Playhouse*—"Second Chance"	Holly
August 2, 1956	*Climax!*—"Throw Away the Cane"	Jean
September 27, 1956	*Climax!*—"The Fog"	Shirley Connors
October 24, 1956	*Ford Theater*—"Measure of Faith"	Maria
October 25, 1956	*Wire Service*—"The Johnny Rath Story"	Elaine Rath
December 14, 1956	*Zane Grey Theater*—"Courage Is a Gun"	Dr. Ellen Kimberly
December 14, 1956	*Chevron Hall of Stars*—"One Way Flight"	Anne
January 17, 1957	*Lux Video Theater*—"To Have and Have Not"	Marie Browning
January 23, 1957	*O'Henry Playhouse*—"The Reformation of Calliope"	
February 25, 1957	*Wire Service*—"Profile on Ellen Gale"	Ellen Gale

Guest Appearance	Title	Role
June 27, 1957	Climax!—"A Taste for Crime"	Daisy
August 4, 1957	The Web—"Hurricane Coming"	
September 30, 1957	Alcoa Goodyear Theater—"Silhouette of a Killer"	Ellen
October 29, 1957	Bell Telephone Time—"The Other Van Gogh"	Johanna Van Gogh
October 31, 1957	Playhouse 90—"Edge of Innocence"	Gay Sherman
July 25, 1958	The George Fisher Show	Herself
August 4, 1958	It Could Be You	Herself
January 9, 1959	Walt Disney Presents: Tales of Texas John Slaughter—"Killers from Kansas"	Amanda Barko
January 23, 1959	Walt Disney Presents: Tales of Texas John Slaughter—"Sundown at Sandoval"	Amanda Barko
March 11, 1959	Trackdown—"Hard Lines"	Dora Crow
March 12, 1959	Zane Grey Theater—"Hanging Fever"	Margaret Waiston
May 20, 1959	The Millionaire—"Millionaire Louise Benson"	Louise Benson
July 10, 1959	Rawhide—"Incident of the Roman Candles"	Jennie Colby
October 9, 1959	Man from Blackhawk—"Logan's Policy"	Sarah Marshall
November 13, 1959	Walt Disney Presents: The Nine Lives of Elfego Baca—"Move Along, Mustangers"	Susanna O'Brien
November 20, 1959	Walt Disney Presents: The Nine Lives of Elfego Baca—"Mustang Man, Mustang Maid"	Susanna O'Brien
December 16, 1959	Hawaiian Eye—"Shipment from Kihei"	Rena Harrison
January 1, 1960	Twilight Zone—"The Four of Us Are Dying"	Maggie
February 27, 1960	Perry Mason—"The Case of the Mythical Monkeys"	Mauvis Meade
March 10, 1960	Zane Grey Theater—"A Small Town That Died"	Ruth Clarke
March 14, 1960	Riverboat—"Three Graves"	Nora James
March 29, 1960	Laramie—"Saddle and Spur"	Terry Blake
May 9, 1960	Tales of Wells Fargo—"Pearl Hart"	Pearl Hart
May 14, 1960	Wanted: Dead or Alive—"Prison Trail"	Sally Lind
September 6, 1960	Coronado Nine—"The Widow of Kill Cove"	Doris Denny
October 19, 1960	Hong Kong—"Freebooter"	Irene Vance
December 6, 1960	Coronado Nine—"Remember the Alamo"	Ann Chapman
December 13, 1960	Stagecoach West—"The Storm"	Sherry Hilton
December 13, 1960	Thriller—"Knock Three-One-Two"	Ruth Kenton
December 16, 1960	Michael Shayne—"Murder and the Wanton Bride"	Elaine Barstow
February 11, 1961	Checkmate—"Between Two Guns"	Jean
April 5, 1961	Dangerman—"Bury the Dead"	Jo Harris
May 18, 1961	Zane Grey Theater—"Jericho"	Amy Schroeder
May 21, 1961	Asphalt Jungle—"The Nine-Twenty Hero"	Caroline
September 28, 1961	Dr. Kildare—"Twenty-Four Hours"	Julia Dressard
October 2, 1961	The Jan Murray Show—"Charge Account"	Herself
November 6, 1961	87th Precinct—"Killer's Payoff"	Nancy Johnson
January 7, 1962	Bus Stop—"Summer Lightning"	Janie
February 13, 1962	Dick Powell Theater—"Seeds of April"	Alma Parsons
May 1, 1962	Cain's Hundred—"The Left Side of Canada"	Jeanette
June 13, 1962	Kraft Mystery Theater—"In Close Pursuit"	Louise Viaur
October 4, 1962	The Nurses—"The Walls Came Tumbling Down"	Ginny Nemets
November 1, 1962	Dr. Kildare—"Hastings Farewell"	Susan Hastings
November 8–9, 1962	By the Numbers	Herself
November 23, 1962	Rawhide—"Incident at Sugar Creek"	Marcie
December 26, 1962	Going My Way—"A Saint for Mama"	Marsha
February 22, 1963	Rawhide—"Incident of the Gallows Tree"	Della Locke
February 23, 1963	Sam Benedict—"Image of a Toad"	Jan Fielding
April 22, 1963	The Dakotas—"The Chooser of the Slain"	Katherine Channing

Television Credits

Guest Appearance	Title	Role
May 18, 1963	*Gunsmoke*—"The Odyssey of Jubal Tanner"	Leah Brunson
June 9, 1963	Celebrity Home Showcase KTLA Ch 5	Herself
October 29, 1963	*The Fugitive*—"Smoke Screen"	Doris Stillwell
November 1, 1963	*The Farmer's Daughter*—"The Stand-In"	Rep. Ellen Jory
November 13, 1963	*The Eleventh Hour*—"What Did She Mean By Good Luck?"	Mary Stone
January 14, 1961	March of Dimes Telethon	Herself
May 7, 1964	*Kraft Suspense Theater*—"Charlie, He Couldn't Kill a Fly"	Jeanne Kling
May 8, 1964	*The New Steve Allen Show*	Herself
June 12, 1964	*The Intelligent Parent*	Herself
October 26, 1964	*What's This Song?*	Herself
January 16, 1965	*The Hollywood Palace*	Herself
September 13, 1965	*A Man Called Shenandoah*—"The Onslaught"	Kate
September 16, 1965	*Laredo*—"Lazyfoot, Where Are You?"	Aggie
[no date] 1965	*I'll Bet*	Herself
January 1–7, 1966	*PDQ*	Herself
January 18, 1966	*The Gypsy Rose Lee Show*	Herself
February 19, 1966	*The Loner*—"Incident in the Middle of Nowhere"	Dolores
April 26–27, 1966	*Insight*—"A Thief Named Dismas"	Julia Weston
September 12, 1966	*The Newlywed Game*	Herself (with Fillmore Crank)
November 5, 1966	*Pistols 'n' Petticoats*—"The Ross Guttley Story"	Ross Guttley
[no date] 1966	*Chain Letter*	Herself
January 29, 1967	*Walt Disney Presents: Gallagher Goes West*—"Tragedy on the Trail" (Part 3)	Mrs. Carlson
February 5, 1967	*Walt Disney Presents: Gallagher Goes West*—"Trial By Terror" (Part 4)	Mrs. Carlson
May 21, 1967	*Insight*—"The Dog That Bit You"	Jean
September 15, 1967	*Judd for the Defense*—"The Deep End"	Dorothy Shaw
November 17, 1967	*The Wild Wild West*—"The Night of the Cut-Throats"	Sally Yarnell
January 1, 1968	*Gunsmoke*—"The Victim"	Lee Stark
January 20 & 27, 1968	*Mannix*—"Deadfall"	Edna Restin
April 7, 1968	*The Mothers-in-Law*—"Jealousy Makes the Heart Grow Fonder"	Audrey Fleming
June 16, 1968	*Insight*—"Don't Elbow Me Off the Earth"	Shirley
January 13, 1969	*Gunsmoke*—"Time of the Jackals"	Leona
February 24–28, 1969	*Lucky Pair*	Herself
March 14, 1969	*The Wild Wild West*—"The Night of Bleak Island"	Celia Rydell
April 22, 1969	*Lancer*—"The Devil's Blessing"	Clara Dunbar
September 29, 1969	*Here's Lucy*—"Lucy Goes to the Air Force Academy" (Part 2)	Secretary
February 2, 1970	*Gunsmoke*—"The Badge"	Claire Hollis
February 20, 1970	*Insight*—"The Day God Died"	Nancy
March 25, 1970	*Then Came Bronson*—"The Mary R"	Beth
July 27–31, 1970	*The Name Game*	Herself
November 25, 1971	CBS Thanksgiving Parade Jubilee	Herself
[no date] 1971	*Betty White's The Pet Set*	Herself
January 29, 1972	*Insight*—"Why Don't You Call Me Skipper Anymore?"	Kay Ward
May 25, 1972	*The Tonight Show*	Herself
September 12, 1972	*Marcus Welby, M.D.*—"A Fragile Possession"	Roberta Kingsley
October 19, 1972	*Mod Squad*—"The Eye of the Beholder"	Ellie Cord
November 14, 1972	*Temperatures Rising*—"R-X Love"	Claudia

Guest Appearance	Title	Role
January 17, 1973	*Owen Marshall, Counselor at Law*—"Sometimes Tough Is Good"	Mrs. Varni
February 12, 1973	*The Rookies*—"Three Hours to Kill"	Pat Whitfield
March 21, 1973	*Cannon*—"Deadly Heritage"	Cecilia Thatcher
March 26, 1973	*Hollywood's Talking*	Herself
May 7–11, 1973	*Baffle*	Herself
June 22, 1973	*Hollywood's Talking*	Herself
September 23, 1973	*The New Perry Mason*—"The Case of the Prodigal Prophet"	Laura Lee
October 7, 1973	*Mannix*—"Little Girl Lost"	Stella Carter
November 16, 1973	*Love, American Style*—"Love and the Big Top"	Maria Lombardi
December 10–14, 1973	*The Match Game*	Herself
[no date] 1973	*Hollywood's Talking*	Herself
February 6, 1974	*Doc Elliott*—"A Small Hand of Friendship"	Bonnie Ames
March 25, 1974	*Medical Center*—"The World's a Balloon"	Kay
November 15, 1974	*Planet of the Apes*—"The Interrogation"	Wanda
December 5, 1974	*Ironside*—"The Over-The-Hill Blues"	Andrea Reynolds
February 5, 1975	*Kung Fu*—"Battle Hymn"	Theresa Hobart
February 10, 1975	*Medical Center*—"The Invisible Wife"	Madeline Stockwood
August 4–8, 1975	*Showoffs*	Herself
October 6–10, 1975	*Showoffs*	Herself
October 14, 1975	*Marcus Welby, M.D.*—"To Live Another Day"	Nancy Zimmer
November 15, 1975	*The Mary Tyler Moore Show*—"Lou Douses an Old Flame"	Veronica Ludlow
February 2–6, 1976	*Cross-Wits*	Herself
April 5–9, 1976	*Cross-Wits*	Herself
April 26–30, 1976	*Break the Bank*	Herself
June 21–25, 1976	*Break the Bank*	Herself
October 12, 1976	*Switch*—"The Argonaut Special"	Nancy Thomas
January 9 & 16, 1977	*The Six Million Dollar Man*—"Death Probe"	The Secretary
April 17, 1977	*Lanigan's Rabbi*—"Say It Ain't So Chief"	Molly Franks
April 17, 1977	*The Nancy Drew Mystery*—"The Mystery of the Fallen Angels"	Thelma
November 25, 1977	*The Partridge Family—My Three Sons Thanksgiving Reunion*	Barbara Douglas
December 24, 1977	*The Tony Randall Show*—"Case: The Silvia Needleman Experience"	Sylvia Needleman
April 23, 1979	*How the West Was Won*—"The Slavers"	Hannah
April 30, 1979	*The Miss U.S.A.—Miss Universe Pageant*	Herself
December 12, 1979	*Charlie's Angels*—"Cruising Angels"	Pat Justice
June 27, 1980	*A Time for Love*	Herself
June 1980	VTV Value Television	Herself
November 23 & 30, 1980	*Trapper John, M.D.*—"Girl Under Glass"	Mrs. Kaufman
December 10, 1980	*Enos*—"Blue Flu"	Judge Cantwell
January 29–30, 1981	*The Young and the Restless*	Kay Chancellor
August 15, 1981	*Greatest Heroes of the Bible*—"Abraham's Sacrifice"	Sarah
December 15, 1981	*Hart to Hart*—"The Hart-Break Kid"	Real Grandma
January 19, 1982	*Flamingo Road*—"Heatwave"	Louise Stone
April 1, 1982	*Magnum P.I.*—"Three Minus Two"	Florence Russell
October 24, 1982	*Matt Houston*—"The Good Doctor"	Mrs. Chapman
December 1982	*Romance Theater*—"Gamble on Love"	Kitty
September 25, 1983	*Insight*—"The Day Everything Went Wrong"	Rita
April 30–May 4, 1983	*Celebrity Hot Potato*	Herself

Guest Appearance	Title	Role
May 10, 1983	*Woman to Woman*	Herself
November 16, 1984	*Today*	Herself
November 19–23, 1984	*Family Feud*	Herself
[no date] 1984	*Celebrity Hot Potato*	Herself
January 23, 1985	*Hotel*—"New Beginnings"	Alice Korman
February 16, 1985	*Dance Fever*	Herself
March 16, 1985	*Finder of Lost Loves*—"Surrogates"	Lucy Rowens
July 15–19, 1985	*All-Star Blitz*	Herself
October 17, 1985	*Hour Magazine*	Herself
November 25–29, 1985	*Alive & Well*	Herself
December 26, 1985	Hollywood Christmas Parade	Herself
April 12, 1986	*Crazy Like a Fox*—"Rosie"	Liz Wellington
October 10, 1986	*Fame, Fortune & Romance*	Herself
[no date] 1987	Mother-Daughter Pageant	Herself
February 2, 1989	*Heartbeat*—"Prison"	Alma
[no date] 1990	*The New Match Game*	Herself
January 25, 1991	*Sons and Daughters*—"Throw Mama from the Terrain"	Marcy
December 7, 1991	*P.S. I Luv U*—"Where There's a Will, There's a Dani"	Emma
December 1991	*The Wish That Changed Christmas*	Mrs. Shepherd
[no date] 1991	*Primetime Live*—"King of the B's"	Herself
September 17, 1992	*Camp Wilder*—"Bad Influence"	Grandma
March 2, 1995	*Friends*—"The One with All the Poker"	Aunt Iris
October 25, 1995	*A&E Biography*—"Lon Chaney, Jr."	Herself
November 8, 1995	*Ellen*—"She Ain't Friendly, She's My Mother"	Eva
February 13, 1997	*Diagnosis Murder*—"Hard-Boiled Murder"	Stella
May 8, 1997	*A&E Biography*—"Fred MacMurray"	Herself
July 19, 1997	*Spider-Man*—"The Haunting of Mary Jane Watson"	Miranda Wilson
January 30, 1998	*Teen Angel*—"Back to DePolo"	Grandma
February 6, 1998	*Teen Angel*—"The Un-Natural"	Grandma
April 26, 1998	*The Angry Beavers*—"The Mighty Knothead"	High Priestess
May 29, 1998	*Masters of Fantasy*—"Roger Corman"	Herself
June 17, 1998	*The Simple Life*—"The Other Mother"	Other Mother
November 14, 1998	*The Angry Beavers*—"Open Wide for Zombies"	The Swamp Witch
November 13, 1999	*The Angry Beavers*—"Practical Jerks"	Unseen Foe
October 2, 2000	*Celebrity Homes*—"Down-Home Homes"	Herself
October 30, 2001	*The Guardian*—"Indian Summer"	Pamela Vries
[no date] 2001	*Drive-In Movie Memories*	Herself
May 18, 2002	*It Conquered Hollywood—The Story of American International Pictures*	Herself
October 5, 2005	*TV Land Confidential*—"Writing, Rehearsing and Recording"	Herself

Appearances Missing Airdates

About Faces
Your First Impression
The New Stump the Stars
It Takes Two
Truth or Consequences
Kid Talk
You Don't Say
It's Your Bet
Win, Lose or Draw
The Al Jarvis Show
The Merv Griffin Show
Take 30
The New Steve Allen Show
Together: With Shirley and Pat Boone
People Are Talking in the Afternoon
Nashville Now

Appendix II: The Film and Made-for-Television Movie Credits

D.O.A. (1950)

CAST & CREDITS: Released April 21, 1950; 83 minutes; Black & White; A Harry M. Popkin Production; Released through United Artists; Director: Rudolph Maté; Producer: Leo C. Popkin; Associate Producer: Joseph H. Nadel; Executive Producer: Harry M. Popkin; Screenplay: Russell Rouse & Clarence Greene; Music: Dimitri Tiomkin; Director of Photography: Ernest Laszlo; Editor: Arthur H. Nadel; Art Director: Duncan Cramer; Set Director: Al Orenbach; Wardrobe: Maria Donovan; Makeup: Irving Berns; Assistant Director: Marty Moss; Sound: Mac Dalgleish and Ben Winkler; Technical Advisor: Edward F. Dunne, M.D.

Edmond O'Brien (Frank Bigelow); Pamela Britton (Paula Gibson); Luther Adler (Majak); Beverly Campbell [Garland] (Miss Foster); Lynn Baggett (Mrs. Philips); William Ching (Halliday); Henry Hart (Stanley Philips); Neville Brand (Chester); Laurette Luez (Marla Rakubian); Jess Kirkpatrick (Sam); Cay Forrester (Sue); Fred Jaquet (Dr. Matson); Lawrence Dobkin (Dr. Schaefer); Frank Gerstle (Dr. MacDonald); Carol Hughes (Kitty); Michael Ross (Dave).

SYNOPSIS:

FRANK BIGELOW: "I want to report a murder."
HOMICIDE CAPTAIN: "Sit down. Where was this murder committed?"
FRANK BIGELOW: "San Francisco, last night."
HOMICIDE CAPTAIN: "Who was murdered?"
FRANK BIGELOW: "I was."

Frank Bigelow (Edmond O'Brien), an income tax expert and notary, leaves for a vacation in San Francisco. After a night of parties and night clubs, he feels sick and goes to a hospital for an examination. The doctor gives him a shocking diagnosis: He has been poisoned. This poison has no apparent physical effects other than mild nausea but eventually it is fatal and there is no known antidote. With only a couple of days to live, Bigelow sets out to find his killer.

REVIEWS: *The Hollywood Reporter* (December 23, 1949): "United Artists has a first-rate exploitation entry in the Harry Popkin presentation, *D.O.A.*... Edmond O'Brien, in a most unusual role, delivers a dominating performance throughout. The supporting cast, made up largely of newcomers, is excellent and [a standout performance is] registered by Beverly Campbell [Garland]...." *Variety* (December 23, 1949): "An unusual story twist and good exploitation values brighten the box office out for *D.O.A.*" *Los Angeles Examiner* (December 24, 1949): "With an ingenious gimmick that really pays off in excitement, *D.O.A.* is without doubt the most unusual suspense melodrama of the year." *Hollywood Citizen News* (December 24, 1949): "An engrossing melodrama ... *D.O.A.* may not be subtle, but it is a wholly suspenseful film..." *L.A. Daily News* (December 27, 1949): "*D.O.A.* ... is another one of those whodunits with more than its share of mayhem." *Film Daily* (December 27, 1949): "Rudy Maté here has rendered a drama of furious excitement, resourcefully and imaginatively narrated." *Cue* (May 6, 1950): "[A]lmost unbearably tense homicidal melodrama ... a vivid, literate and intelligent whodunit — one of the best."

A Life of Her Own (1950)

CAST & CREDITS: Released October 1950; 108 minutes; Black & White; Released through MGM; Director: George Cukor; Producer: Voldemar Vetluguin; Screenplay: Isobel Lennart; Music: Bronislau Kaper; Conductor: Johnny Green; Director of Photography: George Folsey; Art Directors: Cedric Gibbons, Arthur Lonergan; Film Editor: George White; Sound: Douglas Shearer; Set Director: Edwin B. Willis; Associate Set Director: Henry W. Grace; Montage Sequence: Peter Bullbusch; Lana Turner's Gowns: Helen Rose; Hair Styles Designed By: Sydney Guilaroff; Makeup: William Tuttle.

Lana Turner (Lily Brannel James); Ray Milland (Steve Harleigh); Tom Ewell (Tom Caraway); Louis Calhern (Jim Leversoe); Ann Dvorak (Mary Ashlon); Barry Sullivan (Lee Gorrance); Margaret Phillips (Nora Harleigh); Jean Hagen (Maggie Collins); Phyllis Kirk (Jerry); Sara Haden (Smitty); Hermes Pan (Lily's Dance Partner); Carol Brannan (First Model); Tom Seidel (Bob Collins); John Crawford (Photographer); Richard Anderson (Second Hosiery Man); Kathleen Freeman (Peg); Whit Bissell (Rental Agent); Beverly Campbell [Garland] (Girl at Party).

SYNOPSIS: Small town girl Lily Brannel James (Lana Turner) comes to New York City looking to start a career in modeling and gets embroiled in a forbidden love affair.

REVIEWS: Variety (August 16, 1950): "A Life of Her Own ... doesn't have especially bright prospects, even among the [female] trade, where it will have most of its appeal." Independent Film Journal (August 12, 1950): "A rather familiar and routine version of the adultery triangle..." Film Daily (August 15, 1950): "It is a good woman's picture and all effort to sell it should be directed along those lines." Citizen News Hollywood (September 16, 1950): "As long as the 'slick' magazine serial and the soap opera retain their sway over the imagination of most people, pictures like A Life of Her Own will appeal to a tremendous audience." Cue (October 14, 1950): "[A]ll the plush and polish can't turn this gushing goo into a substantial drama."

Strictly Dishonorable (1951)

CAST & CREDITS: Released July 6, 1951; 86 minutes; Black & White; Released through MGM; Writer-Producer-Directors: Melvin Frank and Norman Panama; Based on the play by Preston Sturges; Music: Lennie Hayton; Original Operatic Scene: Mario Castelnuovo Tedesco; Opera Sequences Staged by Vladimir Rosing; Director of Photography: Ray June; Art Directors: Cedric Gibbons and Hans Peters; Film Editor: Cotton Warburton; Sound: Douglas Shearer.

Ezio Pinza (Augustino Caraffa); Janet Leigh (Isabelle Perry); Millard Mitchell (Bill Dempsey); Gale Robbins (Marie Donnelly); Maria Palmer (Countess Lili Szadvany); Esther Minciotti (Mme. Maria Caraffa); Silvio Minciotti (Uncle Nito); Arthur Franz (Henry Greene); Kathleen Freeman (organist at movie theater); Beverly Campbell [Garland] (Girl).

SYNOPSIS:
ISABELLE: "What are we supposed to do?"
GIRL: "We walk on. He sings. He fights. We walk off."
ISABELLE: "Well, ah ... How close can I stand to him?"
GIRL: "At your age? About 20 miles!"

Opera singer Augustino Caraffa (Ezio Pinza) has to marry a young Southern woman, Isabelle Perry (Janet Leigh), to avoid marriage to a grasping countess (Maria Palmer), being disowned by his traditional mother (Esther Minciotti), and the ruination of his career by the tabloid press.

REVIEWS: *The Hollywood Reporter* (June 29, 1951): "[A] smart, attractive entertainment package — a show that will do nicely in the sophisticated city spots and draw better than average elsewhere." *Variety* (July 4, 1951): "[A]n amusing celluloid treatment of the loves and life of a romantic opera star back in the speakeasy days." *Saturday Review* (July 1951): "[W]hatever your feelings about the April-November romance, there's a lot of fun in it." *L.A. Herald Express* (August 23, 1951): "Mildly risqué and containing some bright dialogue, *Strictly Dishonorable* rates as amusing and romantic froth."

Fearless Fagan (1952)

CAST & CREDITS: Released September 1952; 78 minutes; Black & White; Released through MGM; Director: Stanley Donen; Producer: Edwin H. Knopf; Screenplay: Charles Lederer; Music; Rudolph G. Kopp; Director of Photography: Harold Lipstein; Art Directors: Cedric Gibbons and Leonid Vasian; Film Editor: George White; Sound: Douglas Shearer; Set Directors: Edwin B. Willis and Fred Maclean; Special Effects: A. Arnold Gillespie; Hair Styles: Sydney Guilaroff; Makeup: William Tuttle.

Janet Leigh (Abby Ames); Carleton Carpenter (Private Floyd Hilston); Keenan Wynn (Sergeant Kellwin); Richard Anderson (Captain Daniels); Ellen Corby (Mrs. Ardley); Barbara Ruick (Nurse); John Call (Mr. Ardley); Robert Burton (Owen Gilman); Wilton Graff (Colonel Horne); Parley Baer (Emil Tauchintz); Budd Jaxon (Private Silvera); Alvy Moore (Private Thomson); Paul Burke (Private Hawkins); Jim Moloney (Private Ross); William Pullen (Gann); Mae Clarke (Telephone Operator); Beverly Campbell [Garland] (Smudgeface Wac); William Campbell (Voice); Gregory Walcott (M.P. at Gate); Fearless Fagan (Himself).

SYNOPSIS: Floyd Hilston (Carleton Carpenter), a circus performer, has a huge problem on his hands when he is drafted into the U.S. Army and has to find a home for his partner — a full-grown lion named Fearless Fagan.

REVIEWS: The Hollywood Reporter (July 7, 1952): "A wonderful combination of hilarity and poignancy ... a rib-tickling sure-fire comedy ideally suited for the family trade." Variety (July 9, 1952): "Metro has concocted a novel, funny comedy meller here.... [It] looms as a sturdy grosser." Time (August 4, 1952): "[A] merry little romp, with the lion's share of the acting honors going to Fagan." Saturday Review (September 6, 1952): "Though Fearless Fagan does have its moments of cuteness, for the most part it stays on its course of simple humor..." Hollywood Citizen News (September 17, 1952): "A completely enchanting comedy..." Los Angeles Times (September 13, 1952): "A serious note is injected when Fagan escapes, is wounded by Wynn and, crazed with pain, attacks his master. But this is straightened out satisfactorily so as not to interfere too much with the comedy motif." Los Angeles Examiner (September 13, 1952): "[H]ilariously funny and perfectly beguiling, plus very, very touching and highly romantic all at the same time..."

Problem Girls (1952)

CAST & CREDITS: Released May 1953; 70 minutes; Black & White; Released through Columbia Pictures; Director: E. A. DuPont; Writers-Producers: Aubrey Wisberg and Jack Pollexfen; Music: Albert Glasser; Piano Solo: Herman Wasserman; Director of Photography: John L. Russell, Jr.; Film Editor: Fred Feitshans, Jr.; Sound: Jack Lilly; Assistant Director: Chris Beute; Dialogue Director: David Chantler; Wardrobe: Marie Donovan; Photographic Effects: Jack Rabin; Makeup: Harry Thomas; Working Title: The Velvet Cage.

Helen Walker (Miss Dixon); Ross Elliott (John Page); Susan Morrow (Jean Thorpe); Anthony Jochim (Prof. Richards); James Seay (Max Thorpe); Marjorie Stapp (Bella); Roy Regnier (Dr. Manning); Eileen Stevens (Mrs. Kargen); Tom Charlesworth (Mr. Clammerley); Beverly Garland (Nancy Eaton); Joyce Jameson (Peggy Carstairs); Nan Leslie (Claire Harris); Joyce Jarvis (Valerie Creighton); Mara Corday (Dorothy Childers); Tandra Quinn (Judith); Norma Eberhardt (Louise); Eric Colmar (Intern); Merritt Stone (Photographer); Walter Bonn (Mr. Carstairs); John Deer (Henderson); Gladys Kingston (Miss Fanshaw); Juney Ellis (Miss Tippins).

SYNOPSIS: While awaiting his certification to practice, a young psychology teacher, John Page (Ross Elliott), takes a job at a school for the troubled daughters of rich patrons and makes some startling discoveries about the teaching staff.

REVIEWS: The Hollywood Reporter (March 11, 1953): "[A]n incredible little yarn so divorced from reality as to become ludicrous. Most of the characters are thoroughly unpleasant..." Variety (March 11, 1953): "Direction of E. A. DuPont manages to endow a fair amount of suspense in the proceedings. Generally grim atmosphere of the yarn is further accented by varied psychopathic tendencies of the pulchritudinous students." Motion Picture Herald (March 14, 1953): "The settings and characteristics are most depressing but may appeal to those who prefer productions that present an air of mystery and intrigue." Hollywood Citizen News (May 14, 1953): "[It's] rather on the ludicrous side, story-wise..." L.A. Examiner (May 14, 1953): "[A] group of beautiful but warped students in the school whose machinations are worthy of Bela Lugosi. Fortunately for the audience, they can act as well as be attractive on the screen."

The Neanderthal Man (1953)

CAST & CREDITS: Released July 1953; 77 minutes; Black & White; A Global Production; Released through United Artists; Director: E. A. DuPont: Writer-Producers: Aubrey Wisberg and Jack Pollexfen; Music: Albert Glasser; Director of Photography: Stanley Cortez; Art Director: Walter Koestler; Film Editor: Fred Feitshans; Sound: Robert Roderick; Costumes: Jack Masters; Makeup: Harry Thomas.

Robert Shayne (Prof. Clifford Groves); Joyce Terry (Jan Groves); Richard Crane (Dr. Ross Harkness); Doris Merrick (Ruth Marshall); Beverly Garland (Nola Mason); Robert Long (George Oakes); Tandra Quinn (Celia); Lee Morgan (Charlie Webb); Eric Colmar (Buck Hastings); Dick Rich (Sheriff Andy Andrews); Robert Easton (Danny); Frank Gerstle (Mr. Wheeler); Anthony Jochim (Skeptical Naturalist); Marshall Bradford (Conference Chairman); William Fawcett (Dr. Fairchild).

SYNOPSIS: Professor Clifford Groves (Robert Shayne), dismissed by his colleagues for his unorthodox theories about primitive and modern man, sets out to prove that his research is relevant. He believes that modern man still retains the characteristics of his long-distant past. Conducting a series of experiments, Groves transforms a common cat into a saber-tooth tiger. All that remains is for the scientist to perform the same experiment on himself to ultimately prove his theory—one way or another.

REVIEWS: The Hollywood Reporter (June 3, 1953): "It's an overlong, dull conversation piece that will make the weakest type of programmer." Variety (June 3, 1953): "Subject-wise, The Neanderthal Man offers an imaginative-enough scientific premise, but as developed here emerges as nothing more than a somewhat distasteful Jekyll and Hyde–type yarn..." L.A. Daily News (July 11, 1953): "Actually, this inhabitant of the Paleolithic era wasn't a really bad-looking chap, as prehistoric men go, but what the makeup men did to the professor would turn the stomach of the Java Man, who preceded the Neanderthal..." L.A. Examiner (July 11, 1953): "[A] rather fantastic opus with a pseudo scientific premise..." L.A. Times (July 11, 1953): "It doesn't seem as if anybody need prove that man has never completely lost his primitive instincts, but Prof. Groves appears to think such a demonstration necessary."

The Glass Web (1953)

CAST & CREDITS: Released 1953; 81 minutes; Black & White; Released through Universal-International; Director: Jack Arnold; Producer: Albert J. Cohen; Screenplay: Robert Blees and Leonard Lee; Based on a novel by Max Simon Ehrlich; Director of Photography: Maury Gertsman (3-D); Art Director: Bernard Herzbrun; Film Editor: Ted J. Kent; Sound: Leslie I. Carey and Robert Pritchard; Makeup: Bud Westmore; Hair Stylist: Joan St. Oegger; Gowns: Bill Thomas; Assistant Director: Joseph E. Kenney.

Edward G. Robinson (Henry Hayes); John Forsythe (Don Newell); Marcia Henderson (Louise Newell); Kathleen Hughes (Paula); Richard Denning (Dave Markson); Hugh Sanders (Stevens); Jean Willes (Sonia); Harry O. Tyler (Jake); Clark Howat (Bob Warren); Paul Dubov (Other Man); John Hiestand (Announcer); Bob Nelson (Plainclothesman); Dick Stewart (Everett); Jeri Lou James (Barbara Newell); Duncan Richardson (Jimmy Newell); Jack Kelly (First Engineer); Brett Halsey (Lew); Kathleen Freeman (Mrs. O'Halloran); Beverly Garland (Sally).

SYNOPSIS: Researcher Henry Hayes (Edward G. Robinson) and writer Don Newell (John Forsythe) who work for a weekly TV crime series, are being blackmailed by a TV actress (Kathleen Hughes) and then become prime suspects when she is murdered.

REVIEWS: The Hollywood Reporter (October 13, 1953): "[A]nother good picture that doesn't need 3-D and ... may only be hampered by the eye glass nuisance." Variety (October 13, 1953): "A satisfactory murder-mystery ... and properly valued direction by Jack Arnold make for an okay unfoldment of the melodramatics." Hollywood Citizen News (December 31, 1953): "A good suspense film.... [There's] nothing startling or novel in any classification, with the exception, perhaps, of the acting department..."

Bitter Creek (1954)

CAST & CREDITS: Released February 21, 1954; 74 minutes; Black & White; A Westwood Production; Released through Allied Artists; Director: Thomas Carr; Producer: Vincent M. Fennelly; Screenplay: George Waggner; Music: Raoul Kraushaar; Director of Photography: Ernest Miller; Art Director: James West; Film Editor: Sam Fields; Sound: Charles Cooper.

Wild Bill Elliott (Clay Tyndall); Carleton Young (Quentin Allen); Beverly Garland (Gail); Claude Akins (Vance Morgan); Jim Hayward (Dr. Prentiss); John Harmon (A.Z. Platte); Veda Ann Borg (Whitney); Dan Mummert (Jerry Bonner); John Pickard (Oak Mason); Forrest Taylor (Harley Pruett); Dabbs Greer (Sheriff); Mike Ragan (Joe Venango); Zon Murray (Second Rider); John Larch (Gunman); Joe Devlin (Pat Cleary); Earl Hodgins (Charles Hammond); Florence Lake (Mrs. Hammond); Jane Easton (Oak's Girl).

SYNOPSIS: Clay Tyndall (Wild Bill Elliott) arrives in the town of Bitter Creek seeking the man who murdered his brother. He soon suspects rancher Quentin Allen (Carleton Young) who believes he can outwit Tyndall by showing indifference. Tyndall falls for Allen's fiancée Gail (Beverly Garland). When Gail starts to show interest in Tyndall as well, Allen's jealousy begins to surface, leading the two men to the ultimate showdown.

REVIEWS: The Hollywood Reporter (March 4, 1954): "Given a solid, logically developed screenplay and an excellent supporting cast, Bitter Creek is easily the best Wild Bill Elliott oater in some years." Variety reviewer Whit (March 4, 1954): "Waggner's script ... strikes quality western territory, the usual clichés abandoned for fresh action which sees a multitude of realistic gun fights." Variety reviewer Brog (March 17, 1954): "This is [a] good example of a western feature turned out on a moderate budget. Logical story motivation and action, excellent performances by an above-average cast and expert direction give familiar ingredients the punch needed for its market." Film Daily (March 16, 1954): "Opening in a blaze of gunfire ... Bitter Creek shows promise in the opening frames, but thereafter never quite gets out of the 'adequate oater' classification." L.A. Times (March 9, 1954): "Westerns are looking for new angles and Bitter Creek has found a natural. Though the theme is blasé and the plot thick, story is all tied in with character study and motive, so that the picture is absorbingly human and appealing, making it one of the top westerns of the year. The whodunit angle helps out the suspense."

The Miami Story (1954)

CAST & CREDITS: Released May 3, 1954; 75 minutes; Black & White; Released through Columbia Pictures; Director: Fred F. Sears; Producer: Sam Katzman; Story and Screenplay: Robert E. Kent; Music: Mischa Bakaleinikoff; Director of Photography: Henry Freulich; Art Director: Paul Palmentola; Film Editor: Viola Lawrence; Set Director: Sidney Clifford; Assistant Director: Charles S. Gould;

Special Effects: Jack Erickson; Sound: Josh Westmoreland.

Barry Sullivan (Mick Flagg); Luther Adler (Tony Brill); John Baer (Ted Delacorte); Adele Jergens (Gwen Abbott); Beverly Garland (Holly Abbott); Dan Riss (Frank Alton); Damian O'Flynn (Chief Martin Belman); Chris Alcaide (Robert Bishop); Gene D'Arcy (Johnny Loker); George E. Stone (Louie Mott); David Kasday (Gil Flagg); Tom Greenway (Charles Earnshaw).

SYNOPSIS:
HOLLY ABBOTT: "Stay right there, Mr. Flagg. No matter how much you take off, my gun will keep you covered nicely!"

The citizens of Miami hire reformed racketeer Mick Flagg (Barry Sullivan) to rid the city of organized crime influence. Flagg, posing as the head of a Cuban syndicate, goes after the head of the Miami mob, Tony Brill (Luther Adler).

REVIEWS: The Hollywood Reporter (March 31, 1954): "A tense, hard-hitting melodrama, easily Sam Katzman's best production to date." Variety (March 31, 1954): "Suspenseful melodrama with good b. o. prospects..." Saturday Review (May 8, 1954): "[A] lively melodrama." Los Angeles Times (April 8, 1954): "[T]ruth to tell, the tale seems more doctored than documentary.... It's a bang-up gangster yarn..." Los Angeles Examiner (April 8, 1954): "The film, although packed with violence and bad characters, may stir up a storm in cities around the country and do some good while entertaining the customers, too." Hollywood Citizen News (April 1954): "A tough little tale, taut with tension..."

The Rocket Man (1954)

CAST & CREDITS: Released April 1954; 79 minutes; Black & White; A Panoramic Production; Released through 20th Century–Fox; Director: Oscar Rudolph; Producer: Leonard Goldstein; Screenplay: Lenny Bruce and Jack Henley; Based on a story by George W. George and George F. Slavin; Music Lionel Newman; Director of Photography: John Seitz; Art Director: George Patrick; Film Editor: Paul Weatherwax; Sound: Eugene F. Grossman; Costume Design: Travilla; Makeup: Louis Hippe; Assistant Director: Henry Weinberger; Set Director: Glen Daniels.

Charles Coburn (Mayor Ed Johnson); Spring Byington (Justice Amelia Brown); George Winslow (Timmy); Anne Francis (June Brown); John Agar (Tom Baxter); Emory Parnell (Big Bill Watkins); Stanley Clements (Bob); Beverly Garland (Ludine); June Clayworth (Miss Snedley); Don Haggerty (Officer O'Brien).

SYNOPSIS: Timmy (George Winslow), an orphan with a vivid imagination, receives a special gift from a benevolent alien: a ray gun that, when fired at a person, forces him to tell the truth. Timmy and his ray gun help to uncover small town political corruption.

REVIEWS: The Hollywood Reporter (April 28, 1954): "[A] warm, unpretentious little comedy, with a touch of fantasy added, that seems a natural for the family trade." Variety reviewer Whit (April 28, 1954): "This tale of a small boy and his magic space gun is strictly for the programmer trade." Variety reviewer Gros (May 5, 1954): "The current juve fad for science fiction on TV is the probable reason for this 79-minute item.... Film is low-budget in every department including scripting and thesping and doesn't add up as adequate supporting fare."

The Desperado (1954)

CAST & CREDITS: Released June 1954; 79 minutes; Black & White; A Silvermine Production; Released through Allied Artists; Director: Thomas Carr; Producer: Vincent M. Fennelly; Screenplay: Geoffrey Homes [Daniel Mainwaring]; Based on a novel by Clifton Adams; Music: Raoul Kraushaar; Director of Photography: Joe Novac; Art Director: James West; Film Editor: Sam Fields; Sound: John Kean; Assistant Director: Melville Shyer; Set Director: Vin Taylor; Dialogue Director: Stanley Price; Continuity: Mary Chaffee.

Wayne Morris (Sam Garrett); James Lydon (Tall Cameron); Beverly Garland (Lauren Bannerman); Rayford Barnes (Ray Novack); Nestor Paiva (Capt. Thornton); Dabbs Greer (Jim Langley); Roy Barcroft (Martin Novack); John Dierkes (Sgt. Rafferty); Florence Lake (Mrs. Carmeron); Dick Shackleton (Pat Garner).

SYNOPSIS: In the early 1870s, Texas is being run like a police state by its governor, E. J. Davis. Two young men — Tall Cameron (James Lydon) and Ray Novak (Rayford Barnes) — try to flee the oppression by heading out on the open road. They meet up with Sam Garrett (Wayne Morris), a killer with a price on his head. It isn't long before the uneasy relationship starts to crack and friendship turns to betrayal.

REVIEWS: *The Hollywood Reporter* (June 16, 1954): "The exciting thing about it is that all its characters act like real people." *Variety* reviewer Neal (June 17, 1954): "[A]n okay entry from Allied Artists for the giddyapper fans." *Variety* reviewer Brog (June 23, 1954): "[An] interestingly developed, if somewhat dragged out, western drama."

Two Guns and a Badge (1954)

CAST & CREDITS: Released September 12, 1954; 68 minutes; Black & White; Released through Allied

Artists; Director: Lewis D. Collins; Producer: Vincent M. Fennelly; Screenplay: Dan Ullman; Music: Raoul Kraushaar; Director of Photography: Joe Novac; Art Director: James West; Film Editor: Sam Fields; Sound: John K. Kean; Assistant Director: Melville Shyer; Second Assistant Director: Fritz Collings; Set Director: Vin Taylor; Continuity: Mary Chaffee; Special Effects: Ray Mercer.

Wayne Morris (Jim Blake); Beverly Garland (Gail Sterling); Morris Ankrum (Sheriff Jackson); Bill Phipps (Dick Grant); Damian O'Flynn (Wilson); Henry Rowland (Jim Larkin); Roy Barcroft (Bill Sterling); Stanford Jolley (Allen); Bob Wilke (Moore); Chuck Courtney (Val Moore); John Pickard (Sharkey); Gregg Barton (Outlaw).

SYNOPSIS: Jim Blake (Wayne Morris) rides into a town and is mistaken by the sheriff (Morris Ankrum) for a gunman he had summoned to help fight the ever-increasing lawlessness. Blake sees this as an opportunity to make up for his past life of crime and accepts the sheriff's offer to make him a deputy. There is also another reason why Blake is willing to stay: Gail Sterling (Beverly Garland), the pretty daughter of a local rancher. However, she is engaged to rancher Dick Grant (Bill Phipps), whom her father (Roy Barcroft) is grooming to take over the business.

REVIEWS: *The Hollywood Reporter* (September 10, 1954): "This is a routine oater with a little too much dialogue and soul-searching to do more than merely get by in the western market." *Variety* (September 15, 1954): "While long on dialog, in its action scenes there's plenty of punch." *Film Daily* (September 21, 1954): "[T]here's more than enough ridin' and shootin' to satisfy the most avid bang-bang fan.... [T]he stand out performance is turned in by Beverly Garland, who we suspect has a lot of legit training to her credit, [and] should emerge as one of the studio's best actresses in months to come." *Kinematograph Weekly* (September 10, 1959): "Popular cast, wholesome atmosphere."

Killer Leopard (1954)

Cast & Credits: Released August 22, 1954; 70 minutes; Black & White; Released through Allied Artists; Writer-Producer-Director: Ford Beebe; Music: Marlin Skiles; Director of Photography: Harry Neumann; Art Director: David Milton; Film Editor: John C. Fuller; Sound: Ralph Butler; Set Director: Joseph Kish; Special Effects: Ray Mercer; Makeup: Edward Polo; Assistant Director: Edward Morey, Jr.; Continuity: John Banse.

Johnny Sheffield (Bomba); Beverly Garland (Linda Winters); Barry Bernard (Pulham); Donald Murphy (Fred); Leonard Mudie (Barnes); Smoki Whitfield (Eli); Russ Conway (Maitland); Rory Mallinson (Deevers); Harry Cording (Saunders); Charles Stevens (Gonzales); Roy Glenn (Daniel); Bill Walker (Jonas).

SYNOPSIS: American screen star Linda Winters (Beverly Garland) travels to Africa in search of her husband Fred (Donald Murphy), who had to flee the United States when it was discovered that he had embezzled money from the company where he worked. Winters enlists the aid of Bomba (Johnny Sheffield) to help her find her missing spouse in the hope she can convince him to give himself up.

REVIEWS: *Motion Picture Exhibitor* (1954): "A routine entry in the 'Bomba of the Jungle' series, this offers the usual thrills and animal fights. The players give adequate performances."

New Orleans Uncensored (1955)

CAST & CREDITS: Released April 20, 1955; 75 minutes; Black & White; Released through Columbia Pictures; Director: William Castle; Producer: Sam Katzman; Screenplay: Orville H. Hampton; Based on a story by Lewis Meltzer; Music: Mischa Bakaleinikoff; Director of Photography: Henry Freulich; Art Director: Paul Palmentola; Film Editors: Gene Havlick and Al Clark; Sound: Josh Westmoreland; Special Effects: Jack Erickson; Set Director: Sidney Clifford; Assistant Director: Leonard Katzman.

Arthur Franz (Dan Corbett); Beverly Garland (Marie Reilly); Helene Stanton (Alma Mae); Michael Ansara (Zero Saxon); Stacy Harris (Scrappy Durant); Mike Mazurki (Mike); William Henry (Joe Reilly); Michael Granger (Jack Petty); Frankie Ray (Deuce); Edwin Stafford Nelson [Ed Nelson] (Charlie); Judge Walter B. Hamlin (Wayne Brandon); Ralph Dupas, Al Chittenden, Joseph L. Scheuering, Victor Schiro, Howard L. Dey (Themselves).

SYNOPSIS: Dan Corbett (Arthur Franz) hopes to start a log-hauling business after his release from the Navy. To make the money to buy a boat to begin his new venture, he gets a job as a longshoreman in the Port of New Orleans and quickly suspects that the mob is involved in some insurance scams. He offers to help the police by leading the authorities to the proof they need to convict the racketeers, headed up by Zero Saxon (Michael Ansara).

REVIEWS: *The Hollywood Reporter* (February 16, 1955): "It contains too many long dialogue scenes that explain the obvious, too many montage shots of café signs that fail to stimulate the imagination, too many courtesy closeups of New Orleans' public officials." *Variety* reviewer Brog (February 16, 1955): "The entertainment ... is only fair at best.... [T]he two femmes, Beverly Garland and Helene Stanton, both have some good moments but are generally lost in the material..." *Variety* reviewer Neal (February 16, 1955): "Showing up best is Beverly Garland, who falls for Franz after her own husband (William Henry) is murdered when he tries to leave the gang and branch out on his own." *Mirror News* (April 22, 1955): "[J]ust an *On the Waterfront* with a southern accent — only not so good."

The Go-Getter (1955)

CAST & CREDITS: Released 1955; 78 minutes; Black & White; A Pacific Coast Pictures Production; Released through Globe Releasing Corp.; Directors: Leslie Goodwins and Leigh Jason; Producer: Charles Maxwell; Associate Producer: Andy C. Burger; Screenplay: Charles Maxwell and Earl Baldwin; Music: Bill Gillette; Director of Photography: Charles Straumer.

Hank McCune (Henry R. "Hank" McCune); Hanley Stafford (Lester Mayberry); Thurston Hall (Mr. Higgins); Ray Collins (J.P. Miller); Beverly Garland (Peggy); Andrew Tombes (Mr. Symington); Mary Treen (Miss Wellington); Gene Roth (Head File Clerk); Arthur Q. Bryan (The Handyman); Maurice Cass (Elderly Professor); Ellen Corby (The Maid); Douglass Dumbrille (Dr. Baker); Tom Powers (Miller's Business Partner); Veola Vonn (A Clerk); Charles Maxwell; Howard Wright.

SYNOPSIS: Facing the loss of funds from their only patron, the board of directors of a rural college pin all their hopes on the school's least-likely-to-succeed student Henry (Hank McCune) landing a high-paying job in Los Angeles to prove that their teaching staff still produces successful alumni.

REVIEWS: *The Daily Cinema* (March 9, 1959): "A very slender central story line supports a series of gags here, some old, some new. These gags are put over by a reasonably competent cast."

Sudden Danger (1955)

CAST & CREDITS: Released January 5, 1956; 65 minutes; Black & White; Released through Allied Artists; Director: Hubert Cornfield; Producer: Ben Schwalb; Screenplay: Daniel B. Ullman and Elwood Ullman; Based on a story by Daniel B. Ullman; Music: Marlin Skiles; Director of Photography: Ellsworth Fredricks; Art Director: David Milton; Set Director: Clarence Steensen; Film Editor: William Austin; Sound: Charles Schelling; Recorder: Ralph Butler; Production Manager: Allen K. Wood; Assistant Director: Austen Jewell; Continuity: Kathleen Fagan; Wardrobe: Bert Henrikson: Makeup: Paul Malcolm. Working title: *Calculated Risk*

Bill Elliott (Doyle); Tom Drake (Curtis); Beverly Garland (Phyllis); Dayton Lummis (Wilkins); Helene Stanton (Vera); Lucien Littlefield (Dave); Minerva Urecal (Mrs. Kelly); Lyle Talbot (Woodruff); Frank Jenks (Kenny); Pierre Watkin (Caldwell); John Close (Duncan); Ralph Gamble (Dr. Hastings).

SYNOPSIS: Police Detective Doyle (Bill Elliott) suspects that the owner of a sportswear company, who appears to have committed suicide, was actually murdered. Suspicion falls on the woman's son Curtis (Tom Drake), even though he is blind. Several factors seem to support Curtis' guilt, including an insurance policy, most of which was going toward an experimental eye operation that might restore his sight. The operation is performed and is successful. However, Curtis keeps his regained sight a secret while he and his fiancée Phyllis (Beverly Garland) hunt for his mother's true killer.

REVIEWS: *The Hollywood Reporter* (December 13, 1955): "[It's] not flawless but it's as good as the average mystery.... Beverly Garland ... gives a better than routine performance in a routine role." *Variety* (December 13, 1955): "It's a lower-case melodrama that, through good performances, direction and writing, does a better job of meeting entertainment demands than the average supporting film fare."

The Desperate Hours (1955)

CAST & CREDITS: Released October 1955; 112 minutes; Black & White; VistaVision; A William Wyler Production; Released through Paramount Pictures; Producer-Director: William Wyler; Associate Producer: Robert Wyler; Screenplay: Joseph Hayes; Music: Gail Kubik; Director of Photography: Lee Garmes; Art Directors: J. McMillan Johnson and Hal Pereira; Film Editor: Robert Swink; Sound: Hugo Grenzbach and Winston H. Leverett; Set Decorators: Sam Comer and Grace Gregory; Costumes: Edith Head; Makeup: Wally Westmore; Assistant Directors: Charles C. Coleman and Hilton A. Green; Second Unit Director: John Waters.

Humphrey Bogart (Glenn Griffin); Fredric March (Dan C. Hilliard); Arthur Kennedy (Deputy Sheriff Jesse Bard); Martha Scott (Eleanor Hilliard); Dewey Martin (Hal Griffin); Gig Young (Chuck Wright); Mary Murphy (Cindy Hilliard); Richard Eyer (Ralphie Hilliard); Robert Middleton (Sam Kobish); Alan Reed (Detective); Bert Freed (Tom Winston); Ray Collins (Sheriff Masters); Whit Bissell (FBI Agent Carson); Ray Teal (State Police Lt. Fredericks); Beverly Garland (Miss Swift); Paul E. Burns (Chef); Edmund Cobb (Mr. Walling); Ann Doran (Mrs. Walling); Ralph Dumke (Co-worker); Pat Flaherty (Dutch); Joe Flynn (Motorist); Helen Kleeb (Miss Wells); Louis Lettieri (Bucky Walling).

SYNOPSIS: Three escaped prisoners, headed up by Glenn Griffin (Humphrey Bogart), invade the home of a suburban family and hold them hostage to evade a police search.

REVIEWS: *The Hollywood Reporter* (September 14, 1955): "The public will go for *The Desperate Hours* in a big way and so will the exhibitor. It's both a money picture and an artistic picture." *Variety* (September 14, 1955): "[A]n expert adaptation of the novel..." *Hollywood Citizen News* (October 13, 1955): "[E]xcellent production, superbly directed by William Wyler.... The cast is well chosen." *Los Angeles Times* (October 13, 1955): "[O]ne of the most exciting experiences ever offered in a motion picture theater." *Cue* (October 8, 1955): "Despite the film's resemblance to scores of other movie melodramas with a similar criminals-invade-home-and-hold-family-hostage formula (six this season alone), [the] film packs a terrific punch, mainly ... because of a fine script, slick production and extraordinary realistic performances..."

The Steel Jungle (1956)

CAST & CREDITS: Released March 31, 1956; 86 minutes; Black & White; Released through Warner Brothers; Writer-Director: Walter Doniger; Producer: David Weisbart; Music: David Buttolph; Conducted by Maurice DePackh; Director of Photography: J. Peverell Marley; Art Director: Leo K. Kuter; Film Editor: Folmar Blangsted; Sound: Stanley Jones; Assistant Director: Don Page. Working Title: *I Died a Thousand Times*.

Perry Lopez (Ed Novak); Beverly Garland (Frances Novak); Walter Abel (Warden Keller); Ted De Corsia (Steve Madden); Kenneth Tobey (Dr. Lewy); Allison Hayes (Mrs. Archer); Leo Gordon (Lupo); Stafford Repp (Beakeley); Kay Kuter (Stringbean); Ralph Moody (Andy Macklin); Bob Steele (Dan Bucci); Gregory Walcott (Guard Weaver).

SYNOPSIS: Ed Novak (Perry Lopez) is a small-time bookie who believes that loyalty to the mob is more important than the loyalty he owes to his pregnant wife Frances (Beverly Garland). That loyalty leads him to withhold evidence from the court and he is convicted. While in prison, Novak comes to a painful realization that will change the course of the rest of his life.

REVIEWS: *The Hollywood Reporter* (February 29, 1956): "This is a pretty good cops and robbers programmer." *Variety* (February 29, 1956): "[It] does an okay job of showcasing the newer faces of Perry Lopez and Beverly Garland."

Swamp Women (1956)

CAST & CREDITS: Released October 1956; 70 minutes; Eastman Color; A Woolner Brothers Production; Released through Favorite Films Corporation; Director: Roger Corman; Producer: Bernard Woolner; Story and Screenplay: David Stern; Music: Willis Holman; Director of Photography: Fred West; Film Editor: Ronald Sinclair; Sound: Ben Winkler. Alternate titles: *Swamp Diamonds* and *Cruel Swamp*.

Beverly Garland (Vera); Carole Mathews (Lt. Lee Hampton); Touch Conners [Mike Connors] (Bob Matthews); Marie Windsor (Josie); Jil Jarmyn (Billie); Susan Cummings (Marie); Jonathan Haze (Charlie); Ed Nelson (Police Sergeant).

SYNOPSIS:

VERA: "This stinking swamp water stinks!"

Police lieutenant Lee Hampton (Carole Mathews) is sent to prison to infiltrate a group of female inmates who know the whereabouts of a cache of stolen diamonds. Hampton arranges for the escape of the women (Beverly Garland, Marie Windsor and Jil Jarmyn) in the hope they will lead her to the loot.

REVIEWS: *Variety* (October 25, 1956): "Only meager entertainment is dished out.... Pic's chief asset is its exploitable tag..." *Los Angeles Examiner* (October 25, 1956): "I'll say this much for the three gang women—they're impressively mean dames, particularly Beverly Garland." *Mirror News* (October 26, 1956): "On almost every count, *Swamp Women* is badly done and preposterous." *Los Angeles Herald* (October 25, 1956): "Miss Garland proves to be a mean article with an automatic."

Gunslinger (1956)

CAST & CREDITS: Released October 1956; 77 minutes; Pathe Color; Widescreen; Released through American Releasing Corp.; Producer-Director: Roger Corman; Associate Producer: David Kramarsky; Screenplay: Charles B. Griffith and Mark Hanna; Music: Ronald Stein; Director of Photography: Fred West; Set Director: Harry Reif; Film Editor: Charles Gross; Assistant Director: Bartlett A. Carre; Choreographer: Chris Miller. Working Title: *Yellow Rose of Texas*.

Beverly Garland (Marshal Rose Hood); John Ireland (Cane Miro); Allison Hayes (Erica Page); Jonathan Haze (Jake Hayes); Martin Kingsley (Mayor Gideon Polk); Margaret Campbell (Felicity Polk); Chris Alcaide (Deputy Joshua Tate); Chris Miller (Tessie); Bruno VeSota (Zebelon Tabb); William Schallert (Marshal Scott Hood); Dick Miller (Pony Express Rider); Aaron Saxon (Nate Signo).

SYNOPSIS:

MARSHAL ROSE HOOD: "You're not bad, you're just no good."

When her husband Scott (William Schallert) is murdered, Rose Hood (Beverly Garland) puts on his marshal's badge and goes after his killer. However, the marshal's murderer has hired a professional gunslinger (John Ireland) for protection.

REVIEWS: *The Hollywood Reporter* (July 30, 1956):

"[It's] quite a startling western in which the avenging marshal is a woman and in which the woman not only doesn't end in a clinch with her lover but winds up shooting him dead.... Miss Garland and [Allison] Hayes are good as the feuding ladies from different sides of the tracks." *Variety* (July 30, 1956): "With such a twist to the conventional western plot, this Roger Corman production should get its share of playing time attention in the program market."

It Conquered the World (1956)

CAST & CREDITS: Released 1956; 71 minutes; Black & White; A Sunset Production; Released through American International Pictures; Producer-Director: Roger Corman; Executive Producer: James H. Nicholson; Story and Screenplay: Lou Rusoff; Music: Ronald Stein; Director of Photography: Fred West; Art Director: Karl Brainard; Film Editor: Charles Gross; Sound: Al Overton; Special Effects: Paul Blaisdell; Production Manager: Lou Place; Makeup: Larry Butterworth.

Peter Graves (Dr. Paul Nelson); Beverly Garland (Claire Anderson); Lee Van Cleef (Dr. Tom Anderson); Sally Fraser (Joan Nelson); Russ Bender (Brigadier General James Pattick); Jonathan Haze (Pvt. Manuel Ortiz); Dick Miller (Sgt. Neil); Taggart Casey (Sheriff N.J. Shallert); Paul Habor (Floyd Mason); Karen Kadler (Ellen Peters); Charles Griffith (Dr. Pete Shelton); Marshall Bradford (U.S. Secretary Platt); Thomas E. Jackson (George Haskell); David McMahon (General Carpenter).

SYNOPSIS:

> CLAIRE ANDERSON: "So that's what you look like! You're ugly, horrible.... You think you're going to make a slave of the world? I'll see you in Hell first!"

Dr. Paul Nelson (Peter Graves) heads up a U.S. military satellite project. A former colleague, Dr. Tom Anderson (Lee Van Cleef) is secretly in radio contact with an inhabitant of the planet Venus who claims it is one of the last of its kind. Gaining control of the military satellite, the alien uses it to come to Earth. Although Anderson believes he is helping the alien, the Venusian is in reality part of a vanguard who plan to take over Earth.

REVIEWS: *The Hollywood Reporter* (August 30, 1956): "[The movie] provides the kind of science fiction thrills its younger fans will expect and enjoy. There is even a moral to the story, that any tyrant, no matter how beneficial he seems, is bad in the end." *Los Angeles Examiner* (August 30, 1956): "This garish scarecrow comes from Venus and tries to take us over.... The picture essays a philosophical inquiry into the danger of bypassing human self-help and our basic nature to improve the race..." *Variety* (August 30, 1956): "For a low-budget programmer, this flying saucer pic is a definite cut above the normal fare.... Miss Garland is a promising young actress as well as a looker..."

Curucu, Beast of the Amazon (1956)

CAST & CREDITS: Released October 1956; 75 minutes; Eastman Color; Released through Universal-International; Writer-Director: Curt Siodmak; Producers: Richard Kay and Harry Rybnick; Associate Producers: Edward B. Barison and Jeffrey Mitchell; Music: Raoul Kraushaar; Director of Photography: Rudolf Icsey; Second Unit Photography: Jack Mills; Art Director: Pierino Massenzi; Film Editor: Terry Morse; Sound: Hans Olson and Hal Gordon; Special Effects: Howard A. Anderson; Wardrobe: Oscar Nelson; Animal Handler: Antonio Valenca.

John Bromfield (Rock Dean); Beverly Garland (Dr. Andrea Romar); Tom Payne (Tupanico); Harvey Chalk (Father Flaviano); Larri Thomas (Vivian, the Dancer); Wilson Viana (Tico); Sergio de Oliveira (Captain of Police).

SYNOPSIS: Dr. Andrea Romar (Beverly Garland) travels to Brazil to study native methods of shrinking heads. It is her hope that a formula can be developed from this research that will aid doctors in shrinking cancerous tumors so that they can be safely removed. Heading up the expedition is plantation owner Rock Dean (John Bromfield), who is trying to learn why his native workers are deserting the farms. They discover that a monster they call Curucu is terrorizing the Indians.

REVIEWS: *The Hollywood Reporter* (October 26, 1956): "[A] Brazilian-made jungle thriller with considerable interest despite a familiar plot and situations.... Bromfield and Miss Garland manage to give the picture authenticity..." *Variety* (October 26, 1956): "Femme star Beverly Garland attacked by a large boa constrictor, a water buffalo stampede, sights of a giant spider, and the carnivorous piranha fish are some of the scenes that will mean more on the scare side than the pic's title monster." *Showmen's Review* (November 3, 1956): "Bromfield acts his role with heroic aplomb and Miss Garland ... makes her role convincing." *Our Sunday Visitor* (October 28, 1956): "Academy Awards are usually given for great performances in excellent films. I wonder if any award will ever be given for a tremendous performances in a weak film. If so, I'd like to here and now nominate Miss Garland.... You just can't laugh at this well-edited but overdone adventure film merely because of the integrity and credibility of her performance. She plays her role as if she actually believed it — and this takes a lot of skill and faith in this picture. Any actress can do a good job in a great role. Few can do a truly convincing job in a poor one. Garland has made the ludicrous credible. This girl can act."

Naked Paradise (1956)

CAST & CREDITS: Released 1957; 68 minutes; Pathe Color; A Sunset Production; Released through American International Pictures; Producer-Director: Roger Corman; Executive Producer: James H. Nicholson; Screenplay: Charles B Griffith and Mark Hanna; Music: Ronald Stein; Director of Photography: Floyd Crosby; Property Master: Karl Brainard; Film Editor: Charles Gross; Sound: Robert Post; Assistant Director: Lou Place; Makeup: Curly Batson. Reissue title: *Thunder Over Hawaii*.

Richard Denning (Duke Bradley); Beverly Garland (Max MacKenzie); Lisa Montell (Lanai); Dick Miller (Mitch); Leslie Bradley (Zach Cotton); Jonathan Haze (Stony Gratoni); Johnny Kieoni (Kieoni); Carol Lindsay (Luau Dancer).

SYNOPSIS: Duke Bradley (Richard Denning) owns a small boat and agrees to take a group of tourists on a pleasure cruise of the beautiful Hawaiian islands. Among the passengers are Zack Cotton (Leslie Bradley), his girlfriend Max Mackenzie (Beverly Garland), Stony (Jonathan Haze) and Mitch (Dick Miller). However, these "tourists" turn out to be anything *but*.

REVIEW: *The Hollywood Reporter* (February 18, 1957): "[A] straight adventure story with no attempt at being anything else, but it is blessed with some magnificent Hawaiian backgrounds that are authentic and well utilized, good performances and writing.... Miss Garland shows again that she can do important dramatic work when she has the chance." *Variety* (February 18, 1957): "Corman helms his characters convincingly and all principals come up with above-average performances.... Miss Garland in particular is a standout..."

Not of This Earth (1957)

CAST & CREDITS: Released April 1957; 67 minutes; Black & White; Released through Allied Artists; Producer-Director: Roger Corman; Screenplay: Charles B. Griffith and Mark Hanna; Music: Ronald Stein; Director of Photography: John Mescall; Production Manager: Lou Place; Film Editor: Charles Gross; Sound: Phil Mitchell; Property Master: Karl Brainard; Key Grip: Charles Hannawalt; Special Effects: Paul Blaisdell; Makeup: Curly Batson.

Paul Birch (Paul Johnson); Beverly Garland (Nadine Storey); Morgan Jones (Officer Harry Sherbourne); William Roerick (Dr. Frederick W. Rochelle); Jonathan Haze (Jeremy Perrin); Roy Engel (Sgt. George Walton); Anna Lee Carroll (Woman from Davanna); Barbara Bohrer (Waitress); Tamar Cooper (Nurse Joanne Oxford); Pat Flynn (Officers Simmons); Harold Fong (Specimen); Gail Ganley (Teenage Girl); Dick Miller (Joe Piper); Ralph Reed (Teenage Boy).

SYNOPSIS: In a California city, a series of horrible murders have police totally perplexed. Bodies are being found completely drained of blood. As the number of victims mounts, a man (Paul Birch) with black glasses and carrying a metal briefcase visits a local clinic, insisting that the nurse on duty, Nadine Storey (Beverly Garland), give him an immediate transfusion. Nadine refers him to Dr. Rochelle (William Roerick). Placing the doctor under hypnosis, the man in black, who calls himself Johnson, agrees to let the doctor study his abnormal blood. Johnson also insists that Nadine move into his house to give him his daily transfusions. Nadine soon makes a horrifying discovery.

REVIEWS: *Variety* (March 27, 1957): "It plays off at a regulation pace with attention to chills and thrills.... Mixed up in the action is attractive and competent Beverly Garland." *The Hollywood Reporter* (March 21, 1957): "[A] slightly above average production for this kind of picture. Miss Garland, especially, does very well by some surprisingly good humor that is part of the Griffith-Hanna script."

Badlands of Montana (1957)

CAST & CREDITS: Released May 1957; 75 minutes; Black & White; Regalscope; A Regal Films Inc. Production; Released through 20th Century–Fox; Writer-Producer-Director: Daniel B. Ullman; Associate Producer: Herbert E. Mendelson; Music: Irving Gertz; Director of Photography: Frederick Gately; Art Director: Dave Milton; Film Editor: Neil Brunnenkant; Sound: Ralph Butler; Set Director: Morris Hoffman; Property Master: Chester Duncan; Assistant Director: Harold E. Knox; Wardrobe: Norman Martien; Makeup: Emile LaVigne. Working title: *Lonesome Guns*.

Rex Reason (Steven Brewster); Beverly Garland (Susan Hammer); Emile Meyer (Henry Harrison Hammer); Keith Larsen (Rick Valentine); Margia Dean (Emily Branton); Stanley Farrar (Jake Rayburn); Rankin Mansfield (Doc Travis); William Phipps (Walt Branton); Lee Tung Foo (Ling); Ralph Peters (Sammy Fielding); Robert Cunningham (Paul Johansson); Russ Bender (George Johannson); John Pickard (Vince Branton); Roydon Clark (Posse Member); Ralph Sanford (Marshal); William A. Forester (Bledsoe); Paul Newlan (Marshal); Jack Kruschen (Cavalry Sergeant); Larry J. Blake (Outlaw); Elena Da Vinci (First Girl); Helen Jay (Second Girl); John Lomma (Bank Teller); William Tanner (Outlaw); George Taylor (Bank Teller).

SYNOPSIS: Mayoral candidate Steven Brewster (Rex Reason) is unjustly accused by his rival of attacking Emily Branton (Margia Dean). He is severely punished and forced to flee the town. While on the run, Brewster stumbles upon the hideout of a gang of bandits headed up by Henry Hammer (Emile Meyer) and falls in love with his daughter Susan (Beverly Garland). Brewster joins the gang with some surprising turns of events as a result.

REVIEWS: *The Hollywood Reporter* (May 2, 1957): "[I]t makes a good story. Ullman has peopled his tale with interesting characters and enough action so this interest is sustained. The cast is interesting and Ullman has given more time than usual in such a picture to seeing that the romantic elements are properly handled. Reason and Miss Garland make a good romantic couple..." *Variety* (May 2, 1957): "Beverly Garland is attractively excellent..."

COMMENT: During a western film convention (Memphis Film Festival 1999) several years ago, star Rex Reason recalled what happened when he and Beverly shared the podium during a question and answer session.

Beverly was sitting next to me. It was my turn to answer a question and the host asked, "Of all the actresses you kissed, who was your favorite?" Oh boy! I thought for a long time trying to remember and finally I said that I really didn't know. At that moment Beverly turned to me, suddenly grabbed the back of my head and leaned over to place a very long and sexy kiss onto me that I will never forget. Arms flailing, I didn't want to hold her nor push her away. I was caught completely off guard. After she released me, the host laughingly said, "I guess we have the answer." For the rest of the day, when passing Beverly I would give her a high sign letting her know she did a great job for the fans.

Later, I was told by a few fans that they never saw as red a face as mine after that Beverly Garland kiss. That day, I walked away with an unforgettable memory of a very special person.

I miss her and she is missed by many.

The Joker Is Wild (1957)

CAST & CREDITS: Released October 1957; 126 minutes; Black & White; VistaVision; Released through Paramount; Director: Charles Vidor; Producer: Samuel J. Briskin; Screenplay: Oscar Saul; From a book by Art Cohn; Based on the life of Joe E. Lewis; Music: Walter Scharf; Director of Photography: Daniel L. Fapp; Art Directors: Hal Pereira and Roland Anderson; Set Decorators: Sam Comer and Grace Gregory; Film Editor: Everett Douglas; Sound: Harold Lewis and Charles Grenzbach; Assistant Director: C. C. Coleman, Jr.; Special Effects: John P. Fulton; Costumes: Edith Head; Dances Staged by Josephine Earl; Hairstyles: Nellie Manley; Makeup: Wally Westmore. Re-release title: *All the Way*.

Frank Sinatra (Joe E. Lewis); Mitzi Gaynor (Martha Stewart); Jeanne Crain (Letty Page); Eddie Albert (Austin Mack); Beverly Garland (Cassie Mack); Jackie Coogan (Swifty Morgan); Barry Kelley (Captain Hugh McCarthy); Ted de Corsia (Georgie Parker); Leonard Graves (Tim Coogan); Valerie Allen (Flora); Hank Henry (Burlesque Comedian).

SYNOPSIS: A biopic on the life of club entertainer Joe E. Lewis (Frank Sinatra), who runs afoul of the mob, and his efforts to overcome the effects of a terrible injury received as a result.

REVIEWS: *Show Business* (August 20, 1957): "The film is colorful, amusing, honest and touching. It is full of jokes, dancing, girls, music, gangsters, backstage life.... Beverly Garland and Jackie Coogan give fine performances." *Variety* (August 28, 1957): "It has some good, dramatic story material. Oscar Saul's screenplay builds splendidly and is peppered with some bright and sharp dialog.... Beverly Garland ... works well as Albert's wife." *The Hollywood Reporter* (August 28, 1957): "There is a great deal of comedy and drama in this account and Sinatra handles all of it beautifully, giving one of his finest performances. Beverly Garland is capable as Mack's wife." *Mirror News* (September 26, 1957): "[A] hard, sardonic, sometimes sad look at the life and times of one of America's café comic greats. Eddie Albert makes a sympathetic Austin Mack. Beverly Garland is sharp as Mack's wife." *Los Angeles Times* (September 26, 1957): "The film must be classed as a modernly realistic biography—the type that assumes to tell all, without too much concern about the sympathy aroused by its main real-life character. Most interesting in the support.... Eddie Albert is ... first class as the loyal piano player with Lewis. Beverly Garland does a capable character as his wife."

Chicago Confidential (1957)

CAST & CREDITS: Released October 1957; 75 minutes; Black & White: A Peerless Production; Released through United Artists; Director: Sidney Salkow; Producer: Robert E. Kent; Screenplay: Raymond T. Marcus; Based on a book by Jack Lait and Lee Mortimer; Music: Emil Newman; Director of Photography: Kenneth Peach; Art Director: Albert D'Agostino; Film Editor: Grant Whytock; Sound: Al Overton; Set Director: Herman Schoenbrun; Assistant Director: Milton Carter; Property Master: Max Frankel; Wardrobe: Bernice Pontrelli and Einar Bourman; Script Supervisor: John Franco; Makeup: Lee Greenway.

Brian Keith (District Attorney Jim Fremont); Beverly Garland (Laura Barton); Dick Foran (Artie

Blaine); Beverly Tyler (Sylvia Clarkson); Elisha Cook, Jr. (Candymouth Duggan); Paul Langton (Capt. Jake Parker); Anthony George (Duncan); Douglas Kennedy (Ken Harrison); Gavin Gordon (Alan Dixon); Jack Lambert (Smitty); John Morley (Mickey Partos); Benny Burt (Hallop); Mark Scott (Evans); Henry Rowland (Milt the Bartender); George Cisar (Tomkins); Asa Maynor (Betty); Jean Dean (Marion); Sharon Lee (Chorus Girl); Phyllis Coates (Helen Fremont); Lynn Storey, Nancy Marlowe, Helen Jay, Linda Brent ("B" Girls); Thomas Browne Henry (Judge); Dennis Moore (Jury Foreman); Bryon Keith (TV Announcer).

SYNOPSIS: Illinois State Attorney Jim Fremont (Brian Keith) uncovers evidence of an attempted mob takeover of a union when he investigates the murder of the union's treasurer, a crime for which the organization's president, Blane (Dick Foran), has been charged. Freemont enlists the aid of Blane's girlfriend Laura (Beverly Garland) to uncover the truth.

REVIEWS: *The Hollywood Reporter* (August 19, 1957): "Miss Garland — one of the best young actresses in Hollywood — contributes a good portrait." *Variety* (April 30, 1957): "Pic serves its purpose for the intended market and carries enough interest for okay reception by program audiences. Beverly Garland provides ... interest as Dick Foran's fiancée..." *Mirror News* (October 17, 1957): "The action is fast [and the] acting is generally competent." *L.A. Examiner* (October 18, 1957): "The picture occasionally makes an interesting documentary point as when it touches on corruption and the shakedown of union members by the mobsters." *Los Angeles Times* (October 18, 1957): "Miss Garland, gone brunet for this picture, and perfecting her performance with every picture, is quite good as a been-around-and-insulted-by-experts young lady."

The Saga of Hemp Brown (1958)

CAST & CREDITS: Released September 26, 1958; 80 minutes; Eastman Color; Widescreen; Released through Universal-International Pictures; Director: Richard Carlson; Producer: Gordon Kay; Screenplay: Robert Creighton Williams; Story: Bernard Girard; Music: Herman Stein; Director of Photography: Irving Glassberg; Art Director: Robert Smith; Film Editor: Tony Martinelli; Sound: Ralph Brown; Set Director: John Austin; Unit Manager: Edward Dodds; Assistant Director: Gordon Mclean; Wardrobe: Bill Thomas; Hairstylist: Edith House; Makeup: Jack Kevan; Camera: Phil Lathrop; Operator: Lloyd Ward; Script Supervisor: Luanna Sherman; Assistant Directors: Robert Pierce and Roy Vaughn. Working title: *The Return of Hemp Brown*.

Rory Calhoun (Hemp Brown); Beverly Garland (Mona Langley); John Larch (Jed Givens); Russell Johnson (Hook); Fortunio Bonanova (Serge Bolanos); Allan Lane (Sheriff); Trevor Bardette (Judge Rawlins); Morris Ankrum (Bo Slauter); Addison Richards (Army Colonel); Charles Boaz (Alf Smedley); Tom London (Floyd Leacock); Francis McDonald (Oldtimer); Theodore Newton (Murphy); Marjorie Stapp (Mrs. Ford); Yvette Vickers (Amelia Smedley); Victor Sen Yung (Chang);

SYNOPSIS: Wrongly suspected of a payroll robbery that resulted in some deaths, cavalry officer Hemp Brown (Rory Calhoun) receives a dishonorable discharge. Hemp is certain that a man named Jed Givens (John Larch) is responsible. Enlisting the help of a traveling circus performer's assistant, Mona Langley (Beverly Garland), Hemp sets out to find Givens and clear his name.

REVIEWS: *The Hollywood Reporter* (August 12, 1958): "You can take it as an almost unfailing dramatic axiom that a good western has one plot, while a bad western has half a dozen. On this basis, Gordon Kay's production *The Saga of Hemp Brown* is in every sense an A Picture." *Variety* (August 12, 1958): "Although [it] contains some divertingly off-beat plot ideas, it is basically a budget western that will have to depend for its success on the strength of Rory Calhoun as the star. Calhoun plays it mostly taciturn, but Miss Garland has dignity as well as allure."

The Alligator People (1959)

CAST & CREDITS: Released July 1959; 73 minutes; Black & White; CinemaScope; Released through 20th Century–Fox; Director: Roy Del Ruth; Producer: Jack Leewood; Executive Producer: Robert L. Lippert; Screenplay: Orville H. Hampton; Story: Charles O'Neal and Orville H. Hampton; Music: Irving Gertz; Director of Photography: Karl Struss; Art Director: Lyle R. Wheeler and John Mansbridge; Film Editor: Harry Gerstad; Sound: W. Donald Flick; Set Decorators: Joseph Kish and Walter M. Scott; Production Manager: Herbert E. Mendelson; Property Master: George Westenhiser; Special Effects: Fred Etcheveiry; Script Supervisor: Mary Coleman; Wardrobe: Ollie Hughes and William McCrary; Hairstylist: Eve Newing; Makeup: Dick Smith.

Beverly Garland (Joyce Webster aka Jane Marvin); Bruce Bennett (Dr. Eric Lorimer); Lon Chaney, Jr. (Mannon); George Macready (Dr. Mark Sinclair); Frieda Inescort (Mrs. Lavinia Hawthorne); Richard Crane (Paul Webster); Douglas Kennedy (Dr. Wayne MacGregor); Bill Bradley (Patient); Hal K. Dawson (Train Conductor); Dudley Dickerson (Train Porter); John Frederick (Male Nurse); Vince Townsend, Jr. (Butler); Lee Warren (Male Nurse); Ruby Goodwin (Maid).

SYNOPSIS: Dr. Mark Sinclair (George Macready) has developed a serum from alligators which allows humans to repair damaged body parts. One of his patients is Paul Webster (Richard Crane) who was near death after an airplane accident but was miraculously cured by Sinclair's treatment. However, on his wedding night Paul realizes something has gone very wrong and he abandons his bride Joyce (Beverly Garland) to return to the clinic for help. Joyce traces her husband back to his family home in the Louisiana bayou in search of answers but finds only a deeper mystery.

REVIEWS: *Variety* (August 1959): "Equipped with well motivated lines, Miss Garland turns in a fine performance." *Motion Picture Herald* (August 8, 1959): "[A] compactly-told terror tale..." *Los Angeles Times* (August 28, 1959): "This one is strictly from the swamps." *L.A. Examiner* (August 27, 1959): "A fairly well executed story." *Kinematograph Weekly* (August 27, 1959): "[An] artful 'believe it or not' approach adopted by the scriptwriter makes the bizarre hokum [easy] to swallow.... Beverly Garland meets emotional needs.... Arresting story, versatile cast..."

Gunfight at Sandoval (1961)

CAST & CREDITS: Two episodes of TV's *Walt Disney Presents: Tales of Texas John Slaughter* combined for European theatrical release; 72 minutes; Color; A Walt Disney Production and Release; Director: Harry Keller; Producer: James Pratt; Writers: Frank D. Gilroy and Maurice Tombragel; Music: Franklyn Marks, Joseph Dubin and Stan Jones; Director of Photography: William Snyder; Art Director: Marvin Aubrey Davis; Film Editors: Robert Stafford and Stanley Johnson; Sound: Robert Cook.

Tom Tryon (Texas John Slaughter); Beverly Garland (Mrs. Barko); John Anderson (Sgt. Duncan MacGregor); John Daheim (Private Jeff Clay); Lyle Bettger (Al Barko); Judson Pratt (Captain Cooper); Don Haggerty (First Outlaw); Lane Bradford (Second Outlaw); Christopher Dark (Reed); Robert F. Hoy (Jim); Dan Duryea (Dan Trask); Ann Doran (Mrs. Chadwick); Robert Foulk (Pitts); Henry Wills (Brown); Norma Moore (Adeline Harris).

SYNOPSIS: In "Killers from Kansas," the first of the two episodes, Texas John Slaughter (Tom Tryon) and a fellow ranger are in the middle of a bank transaction when the bank is robbed by the Barko Gang, headed up by Mrs. Barko (Beverly Garland). In the second episode, "Showdown at Sandoval," Slaughter captures Mrs. Barko, who refuses to explain why she was trying to combine forces with bandit Dan Trask (Dan Duryea) even though she faces death.

Stark Fear (1963)

CAST & CREDITS: Released January 1963; 86 minutes; Black & White; A Burke-Hockman-Swain Production; Released through Ellis Films. Director: Ned Hockman (and Skip Homeier, uncredited); Producers: Joe E. Burke, Ned Hockman, and Dwight V. Swain; Associate Producer: Carl G. Stevenson; Music: Johnny Williams; Music Conductor: Lawrence V. Fisher; Director of Photography: Robert E. Bethard; Art Director-Set Director: Marcus Fuller; Assistant Director: Robert E. Rogers; Sound: John Pierce; Wardrobe: Joan McCrary; Hairstylist: Roy Long; Makeup: Melvin Parlow; Script Supervisor: Daniel Chichester; Key Grip: Cloy Webb; Gaffer: Les Tannehill; Dialogue Coach: Charles Suggs. Working titles: *The Hate Within* and *Brink of Love*.

Beverly Garland (Ellen Winslow); Skip Homeier (Gerald Winslow); Kenneth Tobey (Cliff Kane).

SYNOPSIS: To help her unemployed husband Gerald (Skip Homeier) get out of debt, Ellen Winslow (Beverly Garland) takes a job with a local businessman, Cliff Kane (Kenneth Tobey). Instead of being pleased, jealous Gerald berates her and then abandons her. Unable to understand his behavior, but assuming it is a matter that they can resolve, Ellen sets out to find him. Her search leads her to Gerald's Texas hometown where she soon discovers that his jealousy is the least of his problems — and hers as well.

Twice Told Tales (1963)

CAST & CREDITS: Released October 30, 1963; 119 minutes; Technicolor; An Admiral Pictures Production; Released through United Artists; Director: Sidney Salkow; Writer-Producer: Robert E. Kent; Based on Stories by Nathaniel Hawthorne; Music: Richard LaSalle; Director of Photography: Ellis W. Carter; Art Director: Franz Bachelin; Film Editor: Grant Whytock; Sound: Lambert E. Day and Alfred R. Bird; Set Director: Charles S. Thompson; Property Master: Irving W. Sindler; Special Effects: Milton Olsen; Script Supervisor: Jean Dowling; Production Manager: Joseph Small; Assistant Director: Al Westen; Costumes: Marjorie Corso and Tom Welch; Hairstylist: Jane Shugrue; Makeup: Gene Hibbs; Casting Director: Ralph Acton; Still Photographer: Madison Lacy; Grip: Sam Bishop; Music Editor: Edna Bullock. Working title: *The Corpse-Makers*.

"Dr. Heidegger's Experiment": Vincent Price (Alex Medbourne); Sebastian Cabot (Dr. Carl Heidegger); Mari Blanchard (Sylvia Ward).

"Rappaccini's Daughter": Vincent Price (Dr. Rappaccini); Brett Halsey (Giovanni Guasticonti); Abraham Sofaer (Prof. Pietro Baglioni); Joyce Taylor (Beatrice Rappaccini); Edith Evanson (Lisabetta).

"House of the Seven Gables": Vincent Price (Gerald Pyncheon); Beverly Garland (Alice Pyncheon); Richard Denning (Jonathan Maulle); Jacqueline De Wit (Hannah); Floyd Simmons (Mathew); Gene Roth (Cab Driver).

SYNOPSIS: Three tales by Nathaniel Hawthorne are adapted for the screen. In "Dr. Heidegger's Experiment," Dr. Carl Heidegger (Sebastian Cabot) discovers a liquid which can restore youth and even raise the dead, and learns a terrible lesson when he gives the miraculous drug to his friend (Vincent Price) and restores his beloved fiancée (Mari Blanchard) to life.

In "Rappaccini's Daughter," Dr. Rappaccini (Vincent Price) is determined to protect his daughter (Joyce Taylor) from the ills of the world by turning her body into one that is poisonous to the touch. What he doesn't anticipate is his daughter falling in love.

In "House of the Seven Gables," Gerald Pyncheon (Vincent Price) returns home to the House of the Seven Gables after a long absence, bringing his wife Alice (Beverly Garland). She discovers that the house hides a treasure and a vengeful ghost.

REVIEWS: *Variety* (September 13, 1963): "Package is highly exploitable and any goose-pimple merchant can proceed on promotion on premise that this is one of the season's better scarers." *New York Post* (May 28, 1964): "[C]lumsily directed, indifferently acted, unconvincing and oh so tedious." *New York Daily News* (1964): "3 Stars. Good supporting casts and effective backgrounds bolster the production." *New York Times* (September 1963): "Vincent Price, not content with his systematic cinematic massacre of Edgar Allan Poe, has added Nathaniel Hawthorne to his repertory. Brett Halsey, Beverly Garland, Sebastian Cabot and Richard Denning play Hawthorne as if he were just another B-picture hack, while Mr. Price parodies the material with his usual smirk. Luckily, he hasn't yet discovered Melville..." *The Daily Cinema* (February 10, 1967): "Best of the three stories is, of course, the famous 'House of the Seven Gables.'... But, in fact, each has its merit as an intriguing 'shocker'..."

Pretty Poison (1968)

CAST & CREDITS: Released September 18, 1968; 89 minutes; Deluxe Color; A Lawrence Turman Films–Molino Production; Released through 20th Century–Fox; Director: Noel Black; Producers: Marshal Backlar and Noel Black; Executive Producer: Lawrence Turman; Screenplay: Lorenzo Semple, Jr.; Based on the novel *She Let Him Continue* by Stephen Geller; Music: Johnny Mandel; Director of Photography: David Quaid; Art Director: Jack Martin Smith; Production Designer: Harold Michelson; Set Director: John Mortensen: Film Editor: William Ziegler; Sound: Dennis Maitland; Assistant Director: Roger Rothstein; Unit Production Manager: Jack Grossberg; Special Effects: Ralph Winigar and Billy King; Key Grip: Robert War; Gaffer: Richard Falk; Costume Design: Ann Roth; Hairstylist: Willis Hanchett; Makeup: Robert Jiras; Property Master: Joseph Caracciolo; Second Assistant Director: Martin Danzig. Working title: *She Let Him Continue*.

Anthony Perkins (Dennis Pitt); Tuesday Weld (Sue Ann Stepanek); Beverly Garland (Mrs. Stepanek); John Randolph (Azenauer); Dick O'Neill (Bud Munsch); Clarice Blackburn (Mrs. Bronson); Joseph Bova (Pete); Ken Kercheval (Harry Jackson); Don Fellows (Detective); Parker Fennelly (Night Watchman); Tim Callahan (Plainclothesman); George Fisher (Burly Man); William Sorrells (Cop at Beanery); Dan Morgan, Mark Dawson, Gil Rogers (Men at Police Station); John Randolph Jones, Maurice Ottinger (Highway Policemen); Tom Gorman (First Detective); Bill Fort, Ed Wagner (Cops); George Ryan's Winslow High Steppers (Marching Band).

SYNOPSIS: Dennis Pitt (Anthony Perkins), a man with a history of mental illness, befriends a young woman, Sue Ann (Tuesday Weld). When he tells her he is a CIA agent on assignment, Sue Ann sees him as a way to free herself from her overbearing mother (Beverly Garland).

REVIEWS: *The Hollywood Reporter* (September 17, 1968): "Lawrence Turman's production might well have been this year's *Bonnie & Clyde*. It is not. What makes the film the more disappointing are the flashes of vestigial promise which remain on the screen. There will be a coterie who will covet the film, for those moments and for the attempt, ignoring the whole. General audiences will simply note that the film ambles prettily in many directions from scene to scene without ultimate aim." *Variety* (September 1968): "Miss Garland [is] (excellent in her portrayal of a casual, but not unloving mother).... Despite some moments of excellence, film goes too much off the track, leaving 20th Century–Fox with an uphill selling chore." *Boston Herald* (September 1968): "The portrayal of the mother by Miss Garland is outstanding, just suggesting caricature to the right degree. For the suspense and horror fans, this is made to order. The film doesn't depend solely on the excellent performances and good direction of the running action, but has added emphasis in the cutting and the fresh work of the camera." *The Miami Herald* (February 26, 1969): "*Pretty Poison* is an unusual suspense film in which psycho-boy meets psycho-girl. It's a simple but shattering horror story, with the horror angel insinuating its way slowly and then hitting

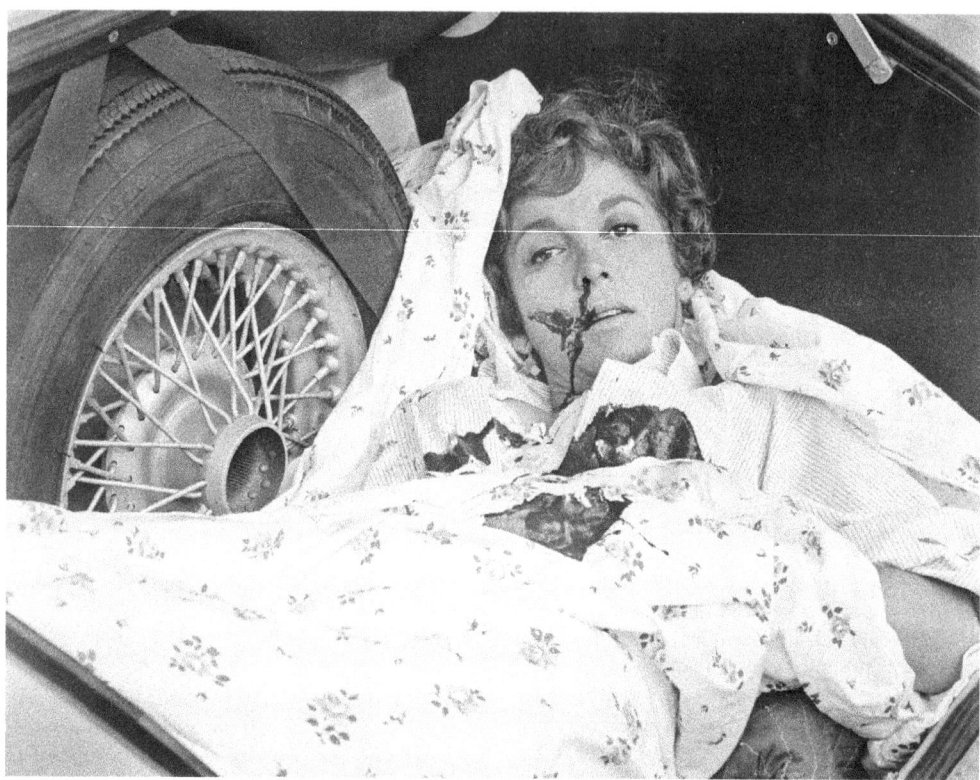

20th Century–Fox decided to cut this scene of the murdered Mrs. Stepanek (Beverly) from the final print of *Pretty Poison* (1968). It was deemed too violent due to the recent assassinations of Robert Kennedy and Martin Luther King, Jr.

with the force of a trip-hammer." *Today's Cinema* (March 7, 1969): "Quite suspenseful, once it gets going, as a study of unbalanced minds it could go well in selected cinemas. Beverly Garland provides striking support as [Weld's] waspish mother." *Time* (no date): "The nicest, nastiest crime film to come out of Hollywood in years." *The New Yorker* (no date): "It may be the beginning of a clean, direct, and new kind of American filmmaking."

The Mad Room (1969)

CAST & CREDITS: Released April 30, 1969; 93 minutes; Pathe Color; Released through Columbia Pictures; Director: Bernard Girard; Producer: Norman Maurer; Screenplay: Bernard Girard and A. Z. Martin; Based on a Screenplay by Reginald Denham and Garrett Fort; From the play *Ladies in Retirement* by Edward Percy and Reginald Denham; Music: David Grusin; Director of Photography: Harry Stradling, Jr.; Art Director: Sidney Litwack; Film Editor: Pat Somerset; Sound: Charles J. Rice, James Z. Flaster and Arthur Piantadosi; Set Director: Sid Clifford; Assistant Director: Rusty Meek; Costumes: Moss Mabry; Hairstylist: Virginia Jones; Makeup: Ben Lane. MPAA Rating: M.

Stella Stevens (Ellen Hardy); Shelley Winters (Mrs. Armstrong); Skip Ward (Sam Aller); Carol Cole (Chris); Severn Darden (Nate); Beverly Garland (Mrs. Racine); Michael Burns (George); Barbara Sammeth (Mandy); Jenifer Bishop (Mrs. Ericson); Gloria Manonn (Edna); Lloyd Haynes (Dr. Marion Kincaid); Lou Kane (Armand Racine).

SYNOPSIS:

MRS. RACINE: "I pledge one free massage and all the benefits that go with it."

After spending several years in a mental institution for the murder of their parents, Mandy (Barbara Sammeth) and her brother George (Michael Burns) are released under the custodial care of their older sister, Ellen Martin (Stella Stevens). Ellen has found a job as a companion to a wealthy widow, Mrs. Armstrong (Shelley Winters), and feels their return will jeopardize her plans to marry the stepson (Skip Ward) and heir of her employer if the widow learns about the siblings' crime.

REVIEWS: *The Hollywood Reporter* (March 1969):

"This psychological chiller should bring as many people to the box office as it will goose bumps to the skin, which is quite a few. There are minor sub-plots in the film which fit very nicely, such as Beverly Garland's drunk character search for her husband who she feels has run off with Miss Winters. Miss Garland is as fine an actress as there is around and draws a gem of a performance. Girard ... simply sets his camera on her ... and lets her do the rest." *Variety* (March 1969): "[W]eak story which pretends to be a psycho-suspense yarn, but it has actually all been seen before.... Beverly Garland ... has one good scene where she shows up drunk at a party and tells everything she knows." *New York Times* (March 1969): "First-rate whodunits are rare, so we can hail Columbia Pictures for *The Mad Room*—a fine suspense-shocker.... Here, after a long, dry spell, is a dandy of a chiller that is original, civilized, well played, exquisitely directed and scenic. Threading it all is a current of electric tension that triggers a jolting surprise and a hair-raising post script. Beverly Garland has a fine drunken monologue toward the end in a scene that seemingly snaps the tension but actually heralds the terror." *The Independent Film Journal* (March 18, 1969): "Better-than-average evening of gruesome entertainment.... Beverly Garland is pretty good..."

Cutter's Trail (1970)

CAST & CREDITS: Original Airdate: February 6, 1970; 90 minutes; Color; CBS-TV; Director; Vincent McEveety; Producer: John Mantley; Teleplay: Paul Savage; Music: John Parker; Director of Photography: Richard Batcheller; Art Director: Albert Heschong; Film Editor: Howard A. Smith; Sound: Bud Alper; Assistant Director: Paul Nichols.

John Gavin (Ben Cutter); Manuel Padilla, Jr. (Paco Avila); Marisa Pavan (Angelita Avila); Beverly Garland (Maggie); Joseph Cotten (Gen. Spalding); Nehemiah Persoff (Santillo); J. Carrol Naish (Froteras); Shug Fisher (Tuttle); Ken Swofford (Clay Wooten); Victor French (Alex Bowen); Robert Random (Kyle Bowen); Robert Totten (Thatcher); Tom Brown (Orville Mason); Steve Falk (D.W. West).

SYNOPSIS: Marshal Ben Cutter (John Gavin) chases a gang of Mexican bandits after they burn down his town. He befriends a young boy, Paco (Manuel Padilla, Jr.), and his mother (Marisa Pavan) who, along with the other inhabitants of a Mexican village, are being terrorized by the bandits.

REVIEWS: *The Hollywood Reporter* (February 10, 1970): "[A] disappointing and slow-moving hour and a half with its stereotyped stalwart hero, a touch of *Shane* and revenge-bent bad guys. The script ... was flawed ... and wasted actors Joseph Cotten, Nehemiah Persoff, J. Carrol Naish and Beverly Garland." *Variety* (February 10, 1970): "[T]elefilm creates a stark mood, has a realism about it that makes the hardness of life believable, makes the sentimental ending that much more touching."

Say Goodbye, Maggie Cole (1972)

CAST & CREDITS: Original Airdate: September 27, 1972; 90 minutes; Color; ABC-TV; An ABC Circle Films Production; Director: Jud Taylor; Producers: Leonard Goldberg and Aaron Spelling; Associate Producer: Robert Monroe; Teleplay: Sandor Stern; Music: Hugo Montenegro and Bradford Craig; Song: "Learn to Say Goodbye" Sung by Dusty Springfield; Director of Photography: Tim Southcott; Art Director: Tracy Bousman; Film Editor: Bill Mosher; Sound: Glen Anderson; Set Director: Don Webb; Assistant Director: Fred Giles; Property Master: Bob Henderson; Costumes: Evelyn Caruth and Robert Fuca; Wardrobe Design: Nolan Miller and Madeline Sylos; Makeup: Gene Hibbs and Howard Smit; Hairstylists: Sherry Wilson and Joyce Morrison; Casting: Bert Remsen; Script Supervisor: Doris De Herdt; Production Managers: Phil Bondelli and Norman Henry.

Susan Hayward (Dr. Maggie Cole); Darren McGavin (Dr. Lou Grazzo); Michael Constantine (Dr. Sweeney); Michel Nichols (Lisa Downey); Dane Clark (Hank Cooper); Beverly Garland (Myrna Anderson); Jeanette Nolan (Mrs. Downey); Maidie Norman (Nurse Ferguson); Richard Anderson (Dr. Ben Cole).

SYNOPSIS: After the death of her husband, research doctor Maggie Cole (Susan Hayward) begins working at an inner city clinic and becomes emotionally involved with a teenage girl dying from Leukemia.

REVIEWS: *Variety* (September 27, 1972): "The soap opera-like overtones were ever apparent in the handling of the title role.... Pilots tend to make for rather unsatisfying made-for-TV movie fare ... and *Maggie Cole* was no exception to that rule." *TV Guide* (date unknown): "[The] strong veteran cast includ[es] Beverly Garland..."

The Weekend Nun (1972)

CAST & CREDITS: Original Airdate: December 20, 1972; 90 minutes; Color; ABC-TV; A Miller-Milkis Production; Director: Jeannot Szwarc; Producers: Thomas L. Miller and Edward K. Milkis; Teleplay: Ken Trevey; Music: Charles Fox; Director of Photography: Ronald W. Browne; Art Director: William L. Campbell; Film Editor: Rita Roland. Working title: *Matter of the Heart*.

Joanna Pettet (Sister Mary Damian aka Marjorie Walker); Vic Morrow (Chuck Jardine); Ann Sothern

(Mother Bonaventure); James Gregory (Sid Richardson); Beverly Garland (Bobby Sue Prewitt); Kay Lenz (Audree Prewitt); Michael Clark (Rick Seiden); Tina Andrews (Bernetta); Judson Pratt (Priest); Lynn Borden (Connie); Marion Ross (Mrs. Crowe); Stephen Rogers (Arlen Crowe); Ann Summers (Administrator); Barbara Werle (Sister Gratia).

SYNOPSIS: Catholic nun Sister Mary Damian (Joanna Pettet) also works as a probation officer and becomes more and more embroiled in the frightening world of her juvenile charges.

REVIEWS: *The Hollywood Reporter* (December 20, 1972): "Occasionally sloppy camerawork, awkward cutting and a tendency to caricaturize life-style detract from an absorbing plotline and an interesting cast.... Beverly Garland has a small, cliché part as Audree's neglectful, loose-living mother." *Variety* (December 20, 1972): "Touchy subject is handled by director Jeannot Szwarc with taste and sincerity as Miss Pettet tackles fictional role based on real-life story..."

The Voyage of the Yes (1973)

CAST & CREDITS: Original Airdate: January 16, 1973; 90 minutes; Color; CBS-TV; The New CBS Tuesday Night Movies; A Fenady Associates–Bing Crosby Productions Production; Director: Lee H. Katzin; Producer: Andrew J. Fenady; Teleplay: William Stratton; Music: Richard Markowitz; Song "El Condor Pasa" Sung by Desi Arnaz, Jr., and Mike Evans; Director of Photography: John A. Alonzo; Production Design: Stan Jolley; Assistant Director: Herb Greene; Technical Advisor: Hilyard M. Brown; Film Editors: Michael Karr and Melvin Shapiro.

Desi Arnaz, Jr. (Cal Markwell); Mike Evans (Orlando B. Parker); Beverly Garland (Agatha Markwell); Skip Homeier (Arnold Markwell); Scoey Mitchell (Pretty); Della Reese (Opal Parker); Dick Powell, Jr. (Dick Stanwood); Steven Marlo (Lt. Matthews); Ed McCready (Peter Reed); Steve Franken (Doctor); Ben Wright (Philip Blemsley); Beulah Quo (Nurse).

SYNOPSIS: Teenagers Cal Markwell (Desi Arnaz, Jr.) and Orlando B. Parker (Mike Evans) decide to sail a 26-foot-long sailboat from California to Hawaii.

REVIEW: *Variety* (January 16, 1973): "Two young guys — one white and one black — from opposite backgrounds is central tale of the watery CBS Tuesday night movie. Miss Garland [gives strong support]."

Unwed Father (1974)

CAST & CREDITS: Original Airdate: February 27, 1974; 90 minutes; Color; ABC-TV; A Wolper Production; Director: Jeremy Paul Kagan; Producer: Stan Margulies; Executive Producer: Lawrence Turman; Teleplay: W. Hermanos; Story: Carol McKean and W. Hermanos; Music: Jerry Fielding: Director of Photography: Jules Brenner; Art Director: Howard E. Johnson; Film Editors: Patrick Kennedy and John Levin.

Joseph Bottoms (Peter); Kay Lenz (Vicky Simmons); Beverly Garland (Estelle); Kim Hunter (Judy Simmons); Joseph Campanella (Scott Simmons); Willie Ames (Gum); William Bassett (Principal); William Hansen (Judge); Gina Alvarado (Mrs. Howell); Ed Bernard (Butler); Michelle Art (Donna); Richard Gilliland (Jeff); Jane Hill (Gloria); Joan Crosby (Waitress); Michael Talbot (Corey); Marni Alexander (Karen).

SYNOPSIS:

ESTELLE: "People shouldn't be allowed kids after 25. I mean, babies take more out of you than a crash diet."

The teenage father (Joseph Bottoms) of an unborn child fights the child's mother (Kay Lenz), her parents (Kim Hunter and Joseph Campanella) and his own mother (Beverly Garland) in the courts for sole custody of his child, whom the mother wants to put up for adoption.

REVIEWS: *The Hollywood Reporter* (February 27, 1974): "[A] charming little picture.... Beverly Garland turns in a great performance as Bottoms' beer-drinking slovenly mother." *Variety* (February 27, 1974): "Beverly Garland turns in a solid job..."

The Healers (1974)

CAST & CREDITS: Original Airdate: May 22, 1974; 90 minutes; Color; NBC-TV; A Warner Brothers Television Production; Director: Tom Gries; Producer: John Furia, Jr.; Associate Producer: Sid McCoy; Executive Producer: Jerry Thorpe; Teleplay: John Furia, Jr., and Howard Dimsdale; Music: David Shire; Director of Photography: Jack Woolf; Art Director: Walter Scott Herndon; Film Editor: Michael A. Hoey; Sound: Charles Haggin.

John Forsythe (Dr. Robert Kier); Pat Harrington, Jr. (Joe Tate); Katherine Woodville (Claire Parlini); Season Hubley (Ann Kilmer); Anthony Zerbe (Dr. Albert Scanlon); Beverly Garland (Laura Kier); John McIntire (Dr. Ernest Wilson); Lance Kerwin (Kennedy Brown); Michael C. Gwynne (Dr. Anton Balinowski); Shelly Juttner (Nikki Kier); Christian Juttner (Vince Kier); Ellen Weston (Barbara).

SYNOPSIS: Dr. Robert Kier (John Forsythe) and his staff at a medical research institute battle diseases and cope with funding problems, internal rebellion and a myriad of other difficulties that arise in the running of the hospital.

REVIEWS: *Variety* (May 1974): "Anthony Zerbe and Beverly Garland are too skilled not to make something of the scraps the script threw them — but the whole effort was in vain." *Variety* (May 24, 1974): "It's not possible for the viewer to become involved in this sterile affair which drags along sluggishly despite an attempt to give it a hustle-bustle air as though the fate of mankind is being settled every moment of every day. Frankly, these doctors are a bore..."

Where the Red Fern Grows (1974)

CAST & CREDITS: Released June 21, 1974; 97 minutes; Deluxe Color; Released through Doty-Dayton; Director: Norman Tokar; Producer: Lyman D. Dayton; Associate Producer: Hubie Kerns; Executive Producer: George Ellis Doty; Screenplay: Douglas C. Stewart and Eleanor Lamb; Based on the novel *Where the Red Fern Grows* by Wilson Rawls; Music: Lex de Azevedo; Songs: The Osmonds; Sung by Andy Williams; Director of Photography: Dean Cundey; Production Design: Michael Devine; Film Editor: Bob Bring; Sound: Richard Pitstick, John Post and Samuel C. Crutcher; Special Effects: Richard Albarn; Wardrobe: Ellen Prince; Hairstylist and Makeup: Anna Sugano; Assistant Director: William White; Property Master: Roger Pancake; Script Supervisor: Kathleen Newport; Animal Trainer: Harold "Butch" Packer; Production Coordinator: Gary Simpson; Production Assistant: Gilda Stratton.

James Whitmore (Grandpa); Beverly Garland (Mother); Jake Ging (Father); Lonny Chapman (Sheriff); Stewart Petersen (Billy); Jill Clark (Alice); Jeanna Wilson (Sara); Bill Thurman (Sam Bellington); Bill Dunbar (Ben Kyle); Rex Corley (Rubin Pritchard); John Lindsey (Rainie Pritchard); Garland McKinney (Mr. Pritchard); Robert Telford (Station Master); Charles Seat (Carl Brown); Roger Pancake (Shopkeeper); Marshall Edwards (Preacher).

SYNOPSIS: A young boy, Billy (Stewart Petersen), works and saves all his earnings so that he can purchase two coon hounds and train them to hunt raccoons for the coveted gold cup first prize in the annual Coon Hunt Contest.

REVIEWS: *Variety* (October 30, 1974): "Performances are generally fine, with Garland reaffirming her status as one of the screen's underrated actresses. Although not ideally cast as a pioneer lady, she nevertheless brings an understated emotional urgency to every moment she is on screen." *Los Angeles Times* (October 30, 1974): "[A] gentle family film about a boy growing up during the Depression in the Oklahoma Ozarks and his close-knit, hard-working, loving family. Beverly Garland is weathered and caring as the mother." *TV Guide* (date unknown) (Judith Crist): "It has a very good performance by Beverly Garland and enough sentimentality to delight lovers of *Lassie*." *Los Angeles Herald-Examiner* (October 31, 1974): "[S]creenplay from Wilson Rawls' novel is sometimes a little stilted but compensates by being unpretentious.... [D]irection does not force the pace or push for any profound statement."

Deadly Volley (1975)

CAST & CREDITS: Original Airdate: January 27, 1975; 90 minutes; Color; ABC-TV; ABC's Wide World Mystery.

Beverly Garland (Team Owner); William Beckley (Linc); Sam Chew, Jr. (Barry); Peter De Anda (Russ); Leslie Evans (Fran); Lee Kroeger (Noelle); Marian Cargo (Connie); Cheryl Miller (Arlene); Charles Knox Robinson (Ted).

SYNOPSIS: A professional tennis team owner (Beverly Garland) is nearly murdered. The police investigate and find that everyone on the team had sufficient motive. However, there is one other possibility: the ghost of a tennis pro who probably had the greatest motive of them all.

Airport 1975 (1974)

CAST & CREDITS: Released October 1974; 107 minutes; Color; Released through Universal; Director: Jack Smight; Producer: William Frye; Executive Producer: Jennings Lang; Screenplay: Don Ingalls; Based on the Novel by Arthur Hailey; Music: John Cacavas; Director of Photography: Philip Lathrop; Art Director: George C. Webb; Set Director: Mickey S. Michaels; Film Editor: J. Terry Williams; Sound: Melvin M. Metcalfe and Robert Hoyt; Costumes: Edith Head; Assistant Director: Alan Crosland; Stunt Coordinator: Joe Canutt; Second Unit Director: James Gavin; Camera: Rex Metz; Technical Advisor: Captain Donald McBain; Special Effects: Ben McMahan; Script Supervisor: Betty A. Griffin; Production Managers: Lloyd Anderson and Ben Bishop.

Charlton Heston (Alan Murdock); Karen Black (Nancy Pryor); George Kennedy (Joe Patroni); Efem Zimbalist Jr. (Captain Stacy); Susan Clark (Helen Patroni); Helen Reddy (Sister Ruth); Linda Blair (Janice Abbott); Dana Andrews (Scott Freeman); Beverly Garland (Mrs. Freeman); Roy Thinnes (Urias); Sid Caesar (Barney); Myrna Loy (Mrs. Devaney); Ed Nelson (Major John Alexander); Nancy Olson (Mrs. Abbott); Larry Storch (Glenn Purcell); Martha Scott (Sister Beatrice); Jerry Stiller (Sam); Norman Fell (Bill); Conrad Janis (Arnie); Eric Estrada (Julio); Christopher Norris (Bette); Gloria Swanson (Herself).

SYNOPSIS: A midair collision between a private plane and a 747 jetliner kills or critically injures the pilots and forces a 747 stewardess (Karen Black) to try to fly the plane until a trained pilot (Charlton Heston) can be brought on board to take over.

REVIEWS: *The Hollywood Reporter* (October 11, 1974): "Universal has produced another entertaining, self-congratulatory formula-made epic, confident of a large audience fascination with multiple jeopardy." *Los Angeles Times* (October 18, 1974): "*Airport* generated plenty of suspense and was lots of fun; *Airport 1975* is too much a rehash to seem anything but mechanical and finally silly in its predictability." *Newsweek* (November 4, 1974): "This sequel to the financial blockbuster *Airport* doesn't have a wing and a prayer." *Time* (November 4, 1974): "It is to be wished that everyone in the film would go away—violently—and that catastrophe movies would molder with them."

Sixth and Main (1977)

CAST & CREDITS: Released September 1977; 104 minutes; Color; A Cain Ragan Rogers Production; Released through National Cinema; Writer-Producer-Director: Christopher Cain; Associate Producer: Jim Ragan; Executive Producer: Jerry Rogers; Music: Bob Summers; Director of Photography: Hilyard John Brown; Film Editor: Ken Johnson: Sound: Robbie Robinson; Sound Effects: Jack May and Bill Wistrom; Assistant Directors: Cal Roberts and Tom Evans; Costumes: Gwen Capetanos; Makeup: Leonard Drake: Song "6th & Main" Sung by D' Mitch Davis; Script Supervisor: Patricia Tooke; Property Masters: Tom Kakos and Jim Dultz.

Leslie Nielsen (John Doe); Roddy McDowall (Skateboard); Leo Penn (Doc); Beverly Garland (Monica Cord); Gammy Burdett (Peanut); Joe Maross (Adair); Bard Stevens (Mr. Carlsburg); Martin St. Judge (Prophet of Doom); Ken Johnson (Doorman); Bill Erwin (Derelict); Sharon Thomas (Tina); Phylis Flax (First Lady); Vera Lockwood (Mrs. Allison); Lisa Todd (Young Lady); Ancel Cook (First Bum); Arnold Stoltz (Second Bum); Edwin Mills (Third Bum).

SYNOPSIS: John Doe (Leslie Nielsen), a successful screenwriter who gave up fame and fortune for the streets of Los Angeles, meets socialite Monica (Beverly Garland), who is unaware of John's past and determined to rehabilitate him.

REVIEWS: *The Hollywood Reporter* (August 31, 1977): "Director Chris Cain ... handles actors well and obtains excellent production values from numerous locations. However, the plot seems rather schizoid. The film waffles between wonderfully naturalistic scenes and whole passages filled with overwrought idealistic notions.... *6th and Main* plays like a Frank Capra movie sprinkled with four-letter words. Beverly Garland has the thankless task of playing [a] rather despicable character.... To her credit, Garland manages to soften the character somewhat..." *Variety* (August 31, 1977): "[A] very professionally made low-budgeter.... The film is earthy without being vulgar..."

Roller Boogie (1979)

CAST & CREDITS: Released December 21, 1979; 103 minutes; Technicolor; An Irwin Yablans Production; Released through United Artists; Director: Mark L. Lester; Producer: Bruce Cohn Curtis; Associate Producer: Joseph Wolf; Executive Producer: Irwin Yablans; Screenplay: Barry Schneider; Story: Irwin Yablans; Music: Bob Esty; Musical Numbers Staged by David Winters; Director of Photography: Dean Cundey; Art Director: Keith Michl; Film Editor: Howard Kunin; Sound: Anthony Santa Croce; Assistant Director: Dan Allingham; Makeup: Gigi Williams; Roller Skating Camera Operator: Daniel Pearl.

Linda Blair (Terry Barkley); Jim Bray (Bobby James); Roger Perry (Roger Barkley); Beverly Garland (Lillian Barkley); Jane Alice Brandon (Judy); Kimberly Beck (Lana); Stoney Jackson (Phones); Albert Insinnia (Gordo); Jimmy Van Patten (Hoppy); Mark Goddard (Thatcher); Sean McClory (Jammer/Bumper); Patrick Wright (Sgt. Danner); Dorothy Meyer (Ada); M.G. Kelly (J.D.); Chris Nelson (Franklin); Shelley Golden (Mrs. Potter); Bill Ross (Goon #1); Carey Fox (Goon #2).

SYNOPSIS: Terry Barkley (Linda Blair), a gifted teenage music major, and her boyfriend Bobby James (Jim Bray), an Olympic skater hopeful, band together with other skaters to save their favorite roller rink from demolition by ruthless shopping mall developers.

REVIEWS: *Variety* (December 6, 1979): "Beverly Garland is on target in her caricature of a desperately with-it Bev Hills matron." *The Hollywood Reporter* (December 10, 1979): "Performances are acceptable, with Beverly Garland taking top comedic honors for her hilarious portrayal of Blair's mother." *Los Angeles Times* (December 21, 1979): "[D]rive-in fun made by people who knew exactly what they were doing."

It's My Turn (1980)

CAST & CREDITS: Released October 24, 1980; 91 minutes; Metrocolor; A Raystar Production; Released through Columbia Pictures; Director: Claudia Weill; Producer: Martin Elfand; Associate Producer: Norman Gan; Executive Producer: Jay Presson Allen; Screenplay: Eleanor Bergstein; Music: Patrick Williams; Title Song Sung by Diana Ross; Music: Michael Masser; Lyrics: Carole Bayer Sager; Production Designer: Jack De Govia; Director of Photography: Bill Butler; Set Directors: Linda De Scenna and Geoff Hubbard; Film Editors: Byron "Buzz" Brandt, Margorie Fowler and James Coblintz; Sound: Pat Somerset and Jeff Bushelman; Assistant Directors: Michael Genne and Ron Frantzvog; Casting: Jane Jenkins; Costumes Designer: Ruth Meyer; Costumes: Cynthia Bales and Eddie Marks; Hairstylists: Damion Grill, Diane Pepper and Martin Samuels; Makeup: Lee Harman; Unit Production Manager: Bob Schneider; Location Manager: Nancy Zearfoss; Still Photographer: Mel Traxel. Working title: *The Perfect Circle*.

Jill Clayburgh (Kate Gunzinger); Michael Douglas (Ben Lewin); Charles Grodin (Homer); Beverly Garland (Emma); Steven Hill (Jacob); Teresa Baxter (Maryanne); Joan Copeland (Rita); John Gabriel (Hunter); Charles Kimbrough (Jerome); Roger Robinson (Flicker); Jennifer Salt (Maisie); Daniel Stern (Cooperman); Diane Wiest (Gail); Ronald C. Frazier, Edwin J. McDonough, Toshi Toda (Professors); Robert Ackerman (Good Will Man); Noah Hathaway (Homer's Son); Marilyn Gates (Homer's Daughter); Raymond Singer (Rabbi).

SYNOPSIS: A math professor (Jill Clayburgh) meets and falls in love with Ben, an ex–baseball player (Michael Douglas), at her father's (Steven Hill) wedding to Ben's mother (Beverly Garland).

REVIEWS: *The Hollywood Reporter* (October 16, 1980): "[A] rather hit and miss romantic comedy which acts adult but like most puppies lacks the teeth necessary for any real bite.... Beverly Garland is especially good as Clayburgh's new stepmother." *Variety* (October 16, 1980): "A wonderfully witty yet realistic look at love relationships.... [A] cut above most of the romantic comedies ... of late." *Star-Ledger* (October 24, 1980): "[W]hat should be a charming and engrossing look at post-feminist American mores is in fact a rather chaotic star vehicle for two actors whose egos far outweigh their talents." *People Weekly* (October 1980): "After the glut of wretched horror films this year, it's our turn, finally, for a romantic, witty, intelligent love story."

Life, Liberty and Pursuit on the Planet of the Apes (1981)

CAST & CREDITS: Original Airdate: 1981; 93 minutes; Two episodes of TV's *Planet of the Apes* combined for release as a feature; Color; CBS-TV; Directors: Arnold Laven and Alf Kjellin; Producer: Stan Hough; Writers: Barry Oringer and Richard Collins; Based on the novel *Planet of the Apes* by Pierre Boulle; Music: Lalo Schifrin; Music Editor: Kenneth Hall; Special Effects: L.B. Abbott; Makeup: Al Schultz; Stunt Coordinators: Paul Stader and Glenn R. Wilder.

Roddy McDowall (Galen); Ron Harper (Alan Virdon); James Naughton (Pete Burke); Mark Lenard (Urko); Booth Colman (Zaius); Jacqueline Scott (Kira); Martin E. Brooks (Leander); Michael Strong (Travin); Jamie Smith-Jackson (Arna/Girl); David Naughton (Dr. Stole); Diana Hale (Brigid); Phil Montgomery (Jordo); Ron Stein (Human); Raymond Mayo (Human/Lafer); Beverly Garland (Wanda); Anne Seymour (Ann); Norman Burton (Yalu); Harry Townes (Dr. Malkhus); Lynn Benesch (Susan); Lee Delano (Gorilla Officer); Eldon Burke (Peasant Ape); Ron Stein (Gorilla Leader); Wayne Foster (Gorilla Lieutenant).

SYNOPSIS: In "The Surgeon," Galen (Roddy McDowall) tries to sweet-talk fellow ape Kira (Jacqueline Scott), into surgically removing a bullet from his human friend Virdon (Ron Harper). In "The Interrogation," Wanda (Beverly Garland), a scientist, wants to experiment on captured human Pete Burke (James Naughton) using an ancient book she found on brainwashing.

This Girl for Hire (1983)

CAST & CREDITS: Original Airdate: November 1, 1983; 90 minutes; Color; CBS-TV; An Orion TV Production; Director: Jerry Jameson; Executive Producer: Barney Rosenzweig; Associate Producer: P.K. Knelman; Teleplay: Terry Louise Fisher and Steve Brown; Story: Barbara Avedon, Barbara Corday and Barney Rosenzweig; Based on a Character Created by Clifford and Jean Hoelscher; Music: Bruce Broughton; Director of Photography: Robbie Greenberg; Art Director: David M. Haber; Film Editor: Gregoria Prange; Sound: John Asman; Set Director: Ethel Robins Richards; Costume Designer: Betsy Heimann; Hairstylist: Stephen Robinette: Makeup: John Norin; Property Master: Ray Jeffers; Assistant Directors: Alan Crosland and Mary Ellen Canniff; Casting: Diane Dimeo; Stunts: Ron Stein; Location Manager: John Warren; Script Supervisor: Joyce Webb.

Bess Armstrong (B.T. Brady); Celeste Holm (Zandra Stoneham); Cliff De Young (Lt. Phil Hansen); Hermione Baddeley (Edwina Gaylord); Scott Brady (Mitch Dillon); Howard Duff (Wolfe Macready); Jose Ferrer (Harrison Wooly); Beverly Garland (Evan Picard); Roddy McDowall (Manfred Hayes); Percy Rodriguez (Jonathan Eastman); Ray Walston (Abner Litto); Elisha Cook, Jr. (Eddie the Newsman).

SYNOPSIS: When writer Harrison Wooly (Jose Ferrer) is murdered, B.T. Brady (Bess Armstrong)— a private investigator Wooly had hired for an assignment — takes on the case to determine who murdered him and finds that just about everyone he knew hated him and could be a suspect.

REVIEWS: *Variety* (November 3, 1983): "[A] stylishly executed whodunit, a takeoff of those mysteries of the 1940s..." *The Hollywood Reporter* (October 31, 1983): "Tele-features have been flirting with a role reversal 1940s-derived woman detective for a couple seasons now, but none of them have worked thus far — including this one.... A colorful array of supporting characters and suspects bolster the film's appeal. Among them are ... Beverly Garland..."

The World's Oldest Living Bridesmaid (1990)

CAST & CREDITS: Original Airdate: September 21, 1990; 96 minutes; Color; CBS-TV; A Hearst Entertainment and Accent III Production; Director: Joseph L. Scanlan; Producer: Christopher Morgan; Co-Producer: Janet Kovalcik; Executive Producer: Donna Mills; Teleplay: Janet Kovalcik; Music: Jay Gruska; Director of Photography: Craig Denault; Film Editor: Michael A. Hoey; Production Manager: Dennis Chapman; Executive in Charge of Production: Ken Gord; Assistant Directors: David Smith and Karen Hall; Casting: Pamela Basker and Sue Swan. Filmed in Toronto and London.

Donna Mills (Brenda Morgan); Brian Wimmer (Alex); Beverly Garland (Brenda's Mother); Winston Rekert (Brian); Art Hindle (Roger); Laura Press (Sheila); David Gardner (Frank); Gary Reineke (George); Kathie Griffin (Interviewee #2); Mark Wilson (The Best Man); Colin Mochrie (Outdoor Bar Waiter); Gordon Woolvett (Rodney).

SYNOPSIS: A lawyer (Donna Mills) is beginning to come to grips with her unmarried status until she hires a handsome male secretary (Brian Wimmer).

REVIEW: *Variety* (September 21, 1990): "This telefilm is pure fluff. The cast handles the material quite well especially the sassy Beverly Garland as the lawyer's mum, who keeps asking, 'How's the sex?' It's kind of hokey stuff that takes some unbelievable turns, all in the name of romance. The character's complete reversal is a bit mystifying and probably insulting to career women who are not morose at the thought of being single."

Finding the Way Home (1991)

CAST & CREDITS: Original Airdate: August 26, 1991; 100 minutes; Color; ABC-TV; A Peter K. Duchow Enterprises Production; Director: Rod Holcomb; Producers: Peter K. Duchow, Rod Holcomb and Scott Swanton; Teleplay: Scott Swanton; Based on the novel *Mittelmann's Hardware* by George Raphael Small; Music: Lee Holdridge; Director of Photography: Neil Roach; Production Design: Anthony Cowley; Film Editor: Paul Rubell; Sound: Stacy Brownrigg; Set Director: Susan Mina Eschelbach; Costume Design: Vincent Lapper and Dottie Vielle. Working title: *Mittelmann's Hardware*.

George C. Scott (Max Mittelmann); Beverly Garland (Arlene); Joseph Alcala (Luis); Christine Baumann (Karina); Joe Berryman (Ernie); Julie Carmen (Elena); Raul V. Carrera (Older Trujillo Brother); Julio Cedillo (Hector); Dina Chavez (Rosa); Hector Elizondo (Ruben); Eddie Flores (Miguel); Geoff Graza (Younger Trujillo Brother); Al Gonzalez (Martin); Jerry Haynes (Doctor); David Hussey (Cliff); Willie Minor (Guard); Matthew Posey (Inspector); Anthony Ramirez (INS Officer); Sylvia Rawley (Grandmother); Richard Reyes (Carlos).

SYNOPSIS: Suffering from amnesia after a car accident, hardware store owner Max Mittelmann (George C. Scott) is befriended by Mexican migrant workers. Meanwhile, his wife Arlene (Beverly Garland) is left with the business and mounting debt, along with trying to find her missing spouse.

REVIEWS: *The Hollywood Reporter* (August 26, 1991): "*Home* isn't so much a story as it is a message hammered home via a telefilm. Here the point is to say something 'important,' something 'big' about the human condition. This results in sterile theatrics and highfalutin speeches. Pity, since the fine photography by Neil Roach and the admirable acting of George C. Scott and Hector Elizondo are not enough to save *Home*. Preachy and full of pious pronouncements, *Finding the Way Home* isn't so much a telefilm as it is an overwrought, sociopolitical slogan. Though it claims a solid crew of performers, *Home* isn't where the heart is." *Variety* (August 12, 1991): "George C. Scott turns in a mighty [performance] as a 60-year-old Texan, whose hardware store and marriage both are sliding. Having lost his wallet, his memory and his way following an auto accident, Max ends up in a Mexican migrant workers camp. Back at home, Max's wife, beautifully played by Beverly Garland, worries briefly about her husband's disappearance, then gets to work salvaging the hardware store."

Hellfire (1993)

CAST & CREDITS: Released to Showtime Networks Inc./video 1995; 85 minutes; Color; A Concorde-New Horizon Picture Corp. Production; Released through Concorde-New Horizon Picture Corp.; Director: David Tausik; Producer: Roger Corman; Co-Producer: Anatoly Fradis; Associate Producers: Felix Kleiman, Tara McCann, Craig J. Nevius and Amy Segal; Screenplay: Beverly Gray, David Hartwell and Tara McCann; Music: Vladimir Komarov and Bruno Louchouarn; Director of Photography: Yevgeni Korzhenkov; Production Design: Ilya Amursky; Film Editors: Brian L. Chambers and Mike Jackson; Sound: Alexey Artykovich; Property Master: Ron Durrant; Special Effects: Rafael Shatkow; Makeup:

Ekaterina Ivanova; Costumes: Nelly Fomina; Production Manager: Jon Kuyper; Assistant Director: Alexander Zelenkov. Aka *Haunted Symphony; Blood Song; Roger Corman Presents: Hellfire*.

Ben Cross (Marius Carnot); Jennifer Burns (Gabrielle Apollinaire); Beverly Garland (Carlotta); Doug Wert (Julian); Lev Prigunov (Baron Jean Octavie); Vladimir Kuleshov (Tristan); Ekaterina Kednikova (Yvette); Irina Latchina (Young Carlotta); Aleksandr Pyatkow (Constable); Yelena Bardina (Louise); Yelena Kostina (Celeste); Vladimir Vozhenikov (Archbishop).

SYNOPSIS: In 19th century France, Gabrielle (Jennifer Burns), the great-niece of a controversial composer, inherits his estate 40 years after his execution for heresy. Not long after her arrival at her great-uncle's home, Gabrielle discovers what she thinks is her uncle's unfinished masterwork and hires a local choirmaster, Marius (Ben Cross), to complete it. Both are unaware that it is actually a satanic pact in which measures can only be added after the choirmaster, under the uncle's influence, commits murder. When this symphony is completed, it will permit the souls of Gabrielle's uncle Baron Octavie (Lev Prigvnor) and Carlotta (Beverly Garland), his lover, to take over the bodies of Marius and Gabrielle — granting them immortal life.

Death Falls (1996)

CAST & CREDITS: Released 1996; 88 minutes; Color; An AAA Enterprises Production; Director: June Samson; Producer; Van Scarboro; Co-Producer: Hamish Gibson; Executive Producer: Joseph N. Trimarchi; Screenplay: Buck Flower and John Goff; Music: Bob Summers; Director of Photography: Dennis Dulzell; Art Director: Christopher Amy; Set Director: Hector Lopez; Film Editors: Ken Johnson and Lisa Yesko; Sound: Edward L. Moskowitz; Special Effects: Robert Calvert; Hairstylist & Makeup: Barbara Gotschall and Laini Thompson; Casting: Maureen A. Arata and Barbara Claman; Stunts: Ray Saniger and Michael Stevenson; Property Master: Gerald Wade. Working title: *Stallions*.

Rip Torn (Dub Farley); Roberts Blossom (Hals Johnson); Beverly Garland (Mae Baxter); Jeffrey Combs (Lonnie Hawks); Kaz Garas (Sheriff Perrin); John Hammil (Courter); Dennis Fimple (Griff); Gailard Satain (Hearse Driver); James Short (Roger Hawks); Nancy Parsons (Nurse); Jerry Lane (Trapper); Carrington Garland (Barmaid); Brad Keehn, Gary D. Bierend (Security Guards); Wesley Maddox (Man at Staging Area).

SYNOPSIS: Unwilling to spend what little time he has left in a hospital, Hals Johnson (Roberts Blossom) gets his friend Dub Farley (Rip Torn) to help him escape. During the attempt, the duo incurs the wrath of a police officer who follows them back to their hometown in the mountains and enlists the aid of a local posse to track down the two men — including a sworn enemy of the pair, Lonnie Hawks (Jeffrey Combs).

If (2003)

CAST & CREDITS: Premiered on April 26, 2003, at the Tambay Film & Video Festival; 87 minutes; Color; A Space Dawg Production; Director of Photography-Writer-Producer-Editor-Director: Lisa Stoll; Co-Producer: Andrew Roa; Associate Producers: Brenda Beck, Jesse Hlubik; Executive Producer: Jan Corey; Music: Helen Simmins-McMillin; Sound: Peggy McAffee; Visual Effects: Bruce Wright.

Beverly Garland (Katherine); Jesse Hlubik (Josh); Kimberly Rowe (Jennifer); Andrew Roa (Gus); Sewell Whitney (Michael); Jack Knight (Robert).

SYNOPSIS: Josh (Jesse Hlubik) has a love-at-first-sight reaction to Jennifer (Kimberly Rowe), but her mother Katherine (Beverly Garland) will not allow the relationship to continue because Josh is actually a clone of her dead son.

REVIEW: *Tampa Tribune* (April 2003): "In her debut as a writer-director, filmmaker Lisa Stoll shows visual imagination and storytelling skill with *If*, a romantic science fiction mystery bolstered by original ideas and strong performances.... Beverly Garland, a Hollywood veteran[,] looks terrific while playing a difficult character. Despite a low budget, Stoll maintains high production values.... [It is] an admirable independent effort..."

Christmas Vacation 2: Cousin Eddie's Island Adventure (2003)

CAST & CREDITS: Original Airdate: December 20, 2003; 83 minutes; Color; NBC-TV; A Elliot Friedgen & Company-National Lampoon Production; Released through Warner Bros. Television; Director: Nick Marck; Producer: Elliot Friedgen; Writer-Executive Producer: Matty Simmons; Music: Nathan Furst; Director of Photography: Ron Schmidt; Art Director: Jim Wardell; Sound: Todd Grace and Rudi Pi; Assistant Director: Michael Otis Ropert; Production Coordinator: Carol Kravetz; Casting: Kim Orchen; Visual Effects: Rick Cortes.

Randy Quaid (Eddie Johnson); Fred Willard (Professor Doomitz); Edward Asner (Uncle Nick); Beverly Garland (Aunt Jessica); Miriam Flynn (Catherine Johnson); Kate Bradley (Paige); Jake Thomas (Third Johnson); Rodger Bumpass (Lab Visitor); Eric Idle (English Victim); Maya Quin (Airplane Hostess); Angela Bennett (Doomitz's Assistant);

Dana Barron (Audrey Griswold); Sal Catalano (Taxi Driver).

SYNOPSIS: Cousin Eddie (Randy Quaid) loses his job at a nuclear facility to a monkey. Convinced that Eddie might sue, his boss offers to send him and his family to a South Pacific island for Christmas. Eddie's Uncle Nick (Ed Asner) joins the family and tells his nephew that he's divorcing Eddie's Aunt Jessica (Beverly Garland) because she left him for their pool cleaner — some 45 years her junior.

Chapter Notes

Chapter 1

1. Pacific Pioneers, "Guest Speaker, Beverly Garland," September 4, 1997.
2. Interview: October 26, 1997.
3. Ibid.
4. James A. Fessenden, "Beverly's Struggle to Become an Actress," *The Beverly Garland Club: Plain & Fancy #1*.
5. Interview: October 1997.
6. Ibid.
7. Ibid.
8. Ibid.
9. Ibid.
10. Ibid.
11. Ibid.
12. Ibid.
13. Ibid.
14. Ibid.
15. James A. Fessenden, "Our Bev...by Her Dad," *The Beverly Garland Club: Plain & Fancy #1*.
16. Interview: October/November 1997.
17. Ibid.

Chapter 2

1. Interview: October/November 1997.
2. Norman Boyd, "Interview with director Caradoc Rhys," source unknown.
3. James A. Fessenden, "Beverly's Struggle to Become an Actress," *The Beverly Garland Club: Plain & Fancy #1*.
4. Interview: October/November 1997.
5. Ibid.
6. Ibid.
7. Ibid.
8. Beverly's home addresses in Phoenix: Rte 1 Box 1391 and 310 West Grenada.
9. "Miss Garland ... who was in Phoenix for public appearances on behalf of ... [*Stump the Stars*] ... recalled that when she came here from California as a freshman, she had just recovered from a bout of pneumonia which had caused her to lose her hair. As a result, she had to wear a scarf ... until her hair grew back." "North High Visited by TV Personality," *The Mustang Roundup*, March 8, 1963.
10. Interview: October/November 1997.
11. Ibid.
12. Ibid.
13. Ibid.
14. Ibid.
15. Ibid.
16. Ibid.
17. The play was written by Leo Sanders and performed at the North Phoenix High School on Friday, February 27, 1942. Beverly played Pat. Event was sponsored by The Girl's League and The Boy's Alliance.
18. Interview: October/November 1997.
19. "A talented young lady whose ambition is to become a really great actress and who is fast becoming a veteran on our stage is Beverly Fessenden. She gave a fine performance in *Quiet Wedding* [as Janet Royd]." *Heart of the City* (April 28 to May 8, 1943) playbill, "Who's Who in the Cast."
20. According to one local news source, Philip E. Matthews, "a soldier stationed at Luke Field landed the male lead [Dallas Chaytor] in the production." The notice went on to say that *Quiet Wedding* was "anything but quiet and depicts in a rollicking manner the trials and foibles that sometimes attend a modern wedding."
21. *The Women*, a three-act comedy by Clare Booth, consisted of 44 cast members with 12 scenes. Beverly played Jane. Demand for tickets was so great, the production — which was originally scheduled for a six day run from April 11 to April 16, 1944 — was extended for another four nights.
22. Interview: October/November 1997.
23. Ibid.
24. National Honor Roll — Fifty-two students made the list that year (1945) from North Phoenix High School. Students were selected based on the following formula: 60 percent for grades; 20 percent for citizenship; 20 percent for comprehensive test grades and those who ranked in the upper 15 percent of their class.
25. Interview: October/November 1997; *The Beverly Garland Club Journal* (various issues).
26. Ibid.
27. Ibid.
28. Ibid.
29. Ibid.
30. Ibid.

Chapter 3

1. Interview: October/November 1997.
2. One of the first theatre-restaurant entertainment experiences, The Earl Carroll Theatre, opened its doors in Los Angeles in 1938. During World War II, Earl Carroll held weekly dances on Sundays for men and women in uniform, sponsored by the Hollywood Guild Canteen.
3. Interview: October/November 1997.
4. Ibid.

5. Ibid.
6. Ibid.
7. Ibid.
8. Ibid.
9. Ibid.
10. Ibid.
11. Ibid.
12. The play ran from June 2 to June 7, 1947. "Top supporting honors go to Beverly Campbell, Laguna actress who plays Lady Bonita Towyn." *Los Angeles Times*, June 5, 1947.
13. *The Beverly Garland Club Journal #6* (Fall 1977).
14. Interview: October/ November 1997.
15. Ibid. Beverly left on August 3, 1947, for the east coast. Beverly's great aunt lived at 24 Ludlow Road, Westport, Connecticut. Beverly spent two to three months in Connecticut. During her stay, Beverly modeled scarves for a Westport textile company. Some of the ads appeared in *Vogue Magazine*.
16. Ibid.
17. Ibid.
18. Ibid.
19. Ibid.
20. Ibid.
21. *Outward Bound* ran from February 25 to February 29, 1948. "His [director Wes Densmore] casting was well nigh perfect even though he took certain liberties with the author's original conception as in the placing of Beverly Campbell in the role of Mrs. Cliveden — Banks. This part is usually played by a very much older woman.... In *Outward Bound* she [Garland] creates a woman of depth with more than the normal complement of unpleasant attributes.... It was a performance to remember." Jack Taylor, "Small but Enthusiastic Crowd Attends Opening of Playhouse's Best," *South Coast News*, February 26, 1948. "My greatest plaudits must go to Beverly Campbell. In the past, pretty girls who seem to swarm about the Playhouse have aroused my old-world gallantry to the point of dulling my critical sense.... But it is with icy objectivity that I say that Miss Campbell is as accomplished an actress as can be found anywhere." Archer Jones, "Curtain Time," *The Laguna Beachcomber*, February 28, 1948.
22. Interview: October/November 1997.
23. Ibid.
24. "Holiday Stage Ends 2nd Successful Season," *Southern California Beachcomber*, September 1948.
25. Interview: October/November 1997. *She Loves Me Not*— Comedy by Howard Lindsay (June 28–July 3, 1948): "Beverly Campbell, heretofore, seen as a brittle minx, did the Dean's daughter with charm and a sweetness that was delightful." Jack Taylor, "Sock & Buskin," *South Coast News*. *Goodbye Again*— A Comedy by Allan Scott and George Haight (July 5–10, 1948): "Beverly Campbell is satisfying as Julia's talkative sister." "Tustin View's Funny Face," Source Unknown; "Beverly Campbell scored ... as the prissy sister." *The Coastline Dispatch*, July 1948. *The Spider*— A Mystery by Fulton Oursler and Lowell Bretand (July 19–24, 1948): "Beverly Campbell was properly distraught as one of the suspects." Jack Taylor, "Holiday Stage Offers *Spider* This Week," *South Coast News*, July 1948; "Beverly Campbell filled this picture for needed feminine relief in a cast in which the men outnumbered the women four to one. Miss Campbell has the promise of a fine actress." *Spider* Provides Audience with Thrills at Tustin," Source Unknown, July 1948. *Life with Father*— A Comedy Adapted by Howard Lindsey and Russel Crouse (July 26–31, 1948): "Don Quinn as the oldest son and Beverly Campbell as the visitor to the Day household coordinated their efforts to give the play its most hilarious laughs. These two young actors show great promise." Kirk, "*Life with Father* Good Entertainment," Source Unknown. *I Remember Mama*— Adapted by John Van Druten (August 9–14, 1948): "Miss Campbell is youthfully effective, composing her part with ease in a difficult duo-role as the narrator and senior daughter." Don Johnson, "Mary Finney Lauded for Part on *I Remember Mama* on Tustin Stage, *Santa Ana Register*, August 1948; "As the narrator in the person of Mama's literary daughter Katrin, Beverly Campbell scored magnificently. Her sweet freshness and self-assuredness were a pleasure to witness. The role was difficult with a heavy demand on emotion which Miss Campbell executed excellently." R. E. F., "*Mama* Delights Audience at Holiday Stage," Source Unknown, August 1948.
26. Interview: October/November 1997.

Chapter 4

1. "Happy Birthday"—The National Touring Company opened Pasadena Civic Auditorium Lo Bera Theatre, Los Angeles.
2. Interview: October 1997.
3. Interview: October 26, 1997 — "Rudolph Mate was a wonderful director but you couldn't understand him because of his thick accent."
4. Interview: October 1997.
5. Editor — Henry Hart, Interview: October 26, 1997.
6. Interview: October/November 1997.
7. Ibid.
8. Ibid.
9. Ibid.
10. Pacific Pioneers Guest Speaker: Beverly Garland, September 4, 1997:
Years ago, Mickey Rooney was doing another Andy Hardy film and I went out on an interview. The man says to me, "Yeah. Ahem. You'll be fine." I thought, "My God. I don't have to read? I can't believe that! I don't have to read anything?" He says, "No. You'll be fine. It's okay. Bye!"
As I started out the door, he said, "Oh, by the way, you go to Western which I just told you about." He had told me that. "And," he added, "the girl is Southern." "Okay. Fine," I said "So I go to Western and they put me in this wonderful chiffon dress and this picture hat and gloves. The bus pulls up and we go to Selznick on the back lot. All these girls are on the bus. The bus stops and everybody gets off the bus. I'm the last one off the bus and my line is "I'm so glad to be here." I remember I'm Southern. So I get off the bus and I say, "Yeah, Well I wanna tell ya, I done glad to be hair!" The director said, "WHAT did you say?" and I repeated my line.
You see I had heard *Amos & Andy* (on the radio) all my life and I wasn't good at Amos, but I was great at Andy! They did call me that night and asked me if I could come in again. They had decided to redo the scene and that the girl was no longer Southern. It was years before I ever knew how a Southern lady talked."
11. Interview: October/November 1997. "Mama Rosa's Boarding House" (Monday 7 P.M. KTLA), 13 episodes: "Situation comedy flows easily as a result of a good scripting job by Betty Mears and well-handled theatrical direction by Eugenis Deliguard. Performers appeared perfectly adjusted to parts ... staffers did a fine job on sets." *Variety*, September 20, 1949.
12. Interview: October/November 1997.

13. Ibid.
14. Ibid.
15. Ibid.
16. *Heaven Can Wait*— Laguna Beach Playhouse, June 27–July 3, 1950. *Clutterbuck*— Laguna Beach Playhouse, July 1951.
17. Interview: October 26, 1997. The Player's Ring, a 150-seat theatre, was located at 8351 Santa Monica Boulevard in Los Angeles.
18. "Laud Beverly Campbell In Top Portrayal," Source Unknown, 1950.
19. Interview: October/November 1997.
20. Ibid. Beverly (as Beverly Campbell) also made a 41-minute in-house film for the Retail Clerks Union in 1951 titled *A Watch for Joe*. In 1952 Beverly (as Beverly Campbell) appeared as a grocery cashier in a 30-minute color featurette, "The Magic Wheel — The History of the National Cash Register Company."

Chapter 5

1. *Red Rainbow* (opened May 5, 1952): "The only redeeming feature about the production are the performances of three members of the cast. Beverly Campbell, Hans Josef Schumm, and Thayer Roberts." Tom Coffey, *L.A. Mirror*; "The Red Rainbow which opened at the Beaux Arts Theatre last night deserves superlatives — it is superlative. Plaudits are due Beverly Campbell for her portrayal of the actress who learns her father was responsible for sabotage." Wylie Williams, *Citizen News*, May 6, 1952; "Cast is competent. Especially impressive [is] ... Beverly Campbell a pretty girl who plays an actress." George Jackson, *L.A. Herald & Express*, May 6, 1952; "Amazingly enough three cast members manage to wade through the morass of words and Fagan's inept direction to give creditable performances. They are ... and Beverly Campbell as a rising legit star." *Variety*, May 7, 1952; the highest priced tickets for the play were $3.00. *Thieves Paradise* (opened May 27, 1952): "I doubt that its stay at the Beaux Arts will be long or profitable." Patterson Greene, *L.A. Examiner*.
2. Interview: October 26, 1997. Beverly recalled one poodle in particular, a little black male named "Beau":

My father was very keen on raising dogs and he would take them to obedience school so they were all well-trained. One of my father's dogs was Beau. Beau was extremely well-trained and he loved to dress up. I did a lot of publicity pictures with him. He would wear his dark glasses, a hat, and hold a pipe in his mouth. We'd put him on a float in the pool and he would float around. He was so funny. I took him to New York when I did "Decoy" and, because it rained a lot in New York, I had bought him a red plaid plastic raincoat with red plastic booties — because he loved to wear shoes. When I got to my apartment in New York City, I took him out in his new raincoat and he was so excited. The apartment building had its own doorman and as we stepped out into the street, Beau saw a dog walk by wearing a Black Gabardine rain-coat. Then he saw another dog with a Black Gabardine raincoat and he sat down as if to say, "I am NOT going to walk around New York in a Red Plaid Plastic Raincoat! I'm not going to do it!" and he wouldn't budge! In New York City at that time, dog owners had to curb their pets. So I showed him the gutter and told him that he had to go there and he said, "Okay," and did it there every day. The next day I took him to work with me and on the way home we walked up to Saks — In those days they had a pet department — and I bought him a Black Gabardine raincoat with a little red hankie, and he thought it was just the best. He walked everywhere in his raincoat.

One morning it was raining and I put on his raincoat and took him across the street to Central Park. You weren't allowed to let your dogs off the leash in the park. Now this as at 5:30 A.M. because I had to get up early to go to work. So he ran and he came back and a policeman saw us and said, "I'm sorry but you can not let your dog off the leash in the park." And I said, "I am so sorry, but he's looking for his galosh." The policeman said, "What?" I said, "He's looking for his galosh." He said, "What do you mean he's looking for his galosh?" I said, "Beau," and he came over to me and he had three galoshes on and the policeman looked at him and I said, "Beau — Fetch!" and he ran and came back with his little red galosh in his mouth. The policeman shook his head and said, "I don't believe this. I've gotta tell you lady, I am not going to give you a ticket."

Beau was so funny. You know, you could take him anywhere. You could say, "sit and stay," and you could leave him there for four hours and he would never move until you came back and gave him a command. He was so well trained and he won a lot of trophies and ribbons. He was probably the best-behaved dog I've ever seen.

After I came back from New York I had Beau for a long time but eventually I gave him back to my mother when my father died because she was alone. She had Beau for several years but then he got very, very ill and eventually she had to have him put down. It broke our hearts because we all loved that dog.

3. Interview October 26, 1997.
4. Ibid.
5. Ibid.
6. *The Glass Web*, 1st sneak preview held Thursday, September 17, 1953, at the Picwood Theater, Westwood, California — previewed the film both in 2-D and 3-D.

SUMMARY OF PREVIEW CARDS

	2-D Screening	3-D Screening
Outstanding	10	11
Excellent	40	31
Very Good	89	75
Good	26	70
Fair	21	35
TOTAL	186	222

Some of the preview cards asked: "Which scenes did you dislike?" Answers included: "When they threw everything at you just to prove it was in 3-D."; "The glasses give me a headache."; "It could have been done without the 'gimmicks' in 3-D."; "The 3-D hurtling objects — unnecessary."

7. Interview: October/November 1997.
8. M.L., *The Hollywood Reporter*, March 4, 1954.
9. Interview: October 26, 1997.
10. Ibid.
11. Ibid.
12. Ibid.
13. Ibid.
14. Ibid.
15. Ibid.
16. Ibid.
17. Ibid.
18. Ibid.
19. "The Play's the Thing," *The Player's Ring*. May 1953.
20. Interview: October/November 1997.

21. Ibid.
22. Roger Corman, "Pacific Pioneers Honor Beverly Garland," taped January 19, 2001.
23. Interview: October/November 1997.
24. Ibid.
25. Ibid.

Chapter 6

1. *The Beverly Garland Club Journal* (various issues) and several taped interviews from 1980 through 1997.
2. Ibid.
3. Ibid.
4. Ibid.
5. Ibid.
6. Ibid.
7. Ibid.
8. Ibid.
9. Ibid.
10. Ibid.
11. Ibid.
12. Ibid.
13. Ibid.

Chapter 7

1. *The Beverly Garland Club Journals* (various issues) and several taped interviews from 1976 through 1997.
2. Ibid.
3. Ibid.
4. Ibid.
5. Ibid.
6. Ibid.
7. Ibid.
8. Ibid. "Miss Garland continues to show increasing stature as a promising young actress, as well as a looker." *Variety*, "It Conquered the World."
9. "*Not of This Earth* purchased for filming by Roger Corman Productions." *Variety*, "*Not of This Earth*," January 23, 1956; "Beverly Garland signed for starring role in Roger Corman's *Not of This Earth*." *Variety*, June 1, 1956.
10. *Not of This Earth* completed post-production in August 1956.
11. Interview: California 1980. "*Georgia Peaches* aka *Follow That Car* (1980), part of Vivian Stark played by Sally Kirkland." *Not of This Earth* interviews: 1976 to 1997.
12. Carl Del Vecchio, "Interview with Paul Blaisdell," *The Beverly Garland Club Journal #8 C*, 1979.
13. *The Star and the Story* (also known as *Rheingold Theater*): "The Lie"—January 22, 1955; "Point of Honor"—January 7, 1956; "Payment in Kind"—January 28, 1956; *Four Star Playhouse*: "Night at Lark Cottage"—March 24, 1955; "Touch and Go"—April 26, 1956; "Second Chance"—June 14, 1956; *Climax!*: "Throw Away the Cane"—August 2, 1956; "The Fog"—August 27, 1956; *Wire Service*: "The Johnny Rath Story"—October 25, 1956; "Profile on Ellen Gale"—December 17, 1956; *Science Fiction Theater*: "The Negative Man"—September 16, 1955; "The Other Side of the Moon"—February 17, 1956; Pilot Episode: "State Trooper"; "Rodeo Roughhouse" (aka "Killers on Horseback")—February 3, 1956; *The George Sanders Mystery Theatre*: "The Call"—October 1956.

Chapter 8

1. *The Beverly Garland Club Journal* (various issues) and several taped interviews between 1976 and 1997.
2. Ibid.
3. Ibid.
4. Ibid.
5. Ibid.
6. Ibid.
7. Ibid.
8. Ibid.
9. Ibid.
10. Ibid.
11. Ibid.
12. Interview: October 26, 1997.
13. Beverly recalled her impressions of the show's star, Mercedes McCambridge during an interview conducted in May 2004: "She was very tough — her voice, especially, but she always had a toughness about her that made me uncomfortable. I thought she had a great voice. She always seemed to get the parts that I thought I could do. I thought I was prettier and I thought I could do just as good a job as she could. I also didn't think I was quite as rough and tough as she was."
14. Mike Connolly, "Rambling Reporter," *The Hollywood Reporter*, December 21, 1956.
15. *Los Angeles Herald Examiner*.

Chapter 9

1. "Hedda Hopper Names Top Film Finds of 1956," *L. A. Times*, January 6, 1957.
2. "Hollywood Today" with Sheilah Graham, *Citizen News*, January 8, 1957.
3. Interview: September 8, 1995.
4. Warner Bros. (1944); directed by Howard Hawks; edited by Christian Nyby; screenplay by William Faulkner; O'Brien / Bogart played Harry "Steve" Morgan; Garland/Bacall played Marie "Slim" Browning; teleplay by S. H. Barnett.
5. Interview: October 26, 1997.
6. Beverly flew to Philadelphia first, where, along with her *It Conquered the World* co-star Peter Graves, she attended the grand opening of The Sheraton Hotel—a 22-story building housing one thousand rooms at a cost of $1.6 million. Other celebrities on hand for the opening festivities included Alice Faye, Ginger Rogers, June Lockhart, Eddie Fisher, George Jessel, Phil Harris, Joe E. Brown, Toots Shor and Gypsy Rose Lee, among others. Following a tour of the hotel, Beverly, Peter Graves, and tennis pro Jack Kramer headed for Camden, New Jersey, with journalist Jimmy Starr (*L.A. Herald & Express*, March 8, 1957) to take in some of the city's restaurants and night clubs. "As gentle snow flakes drifted down, adding a dazzling sparkle to the miles of vari-colored neon on Broadway, Beverly Garland, Bunny Cooper, Gene Nelson and I piled into a warm taxi and headed for Greenwich Village where we found that delightful comedienne Kaye Ballard at the Bon Jour." Jimmy Starr, *Los Angeles Herald & Express*, March 15, 1957; *Variety*, April 16, 1957, interview.
7. Pacific Pioneers, "Guest Speaker, Beverly Garland," September 4, 1997.
8. Just before she began filming *Chicago Confidential*, Beverly became god-mother to John and Ann Lupton's daughter, Rollin. The Luptons were old friends of Beverly's. At the time, John was the star of ABC-TV's *Broken Arrow*.
9. *Climax!* had previously televised an adaptation of Robert Louis Stevenson's story on July 28, 1955. The teleplay was written by Gore Vidal and also starred Michael Rennie. Other cast members included Cedric Hardwicke, John Hoyt and Mary Sinclair.

10. "The record shows that out of roughly two hundred television roles [as of May 1959], Miss Garland has played the villain or heavy in at least 70% of them, a scandalously high figure." Donald Freeman, "Female Villainy—Without Sneers," *The San Diego Union*, May 29, 1959.
11. Interview: November 1, 1997.
12. "Beverly filmed *The Other Van Gogh* for 'Bell Telephone Time' as Johanna Van Gogh. Harry Townes plays Vincent's brother, Theo." Source unknown, May 27, 1957. "Garland had femme lead in 'Hurricane Coming' segment of series, *The Web*. The Kay Lenard teleplay goes before the cameras, Thursday [June 6]." *Variety*, June 4, 1957.
13. "Miss Garland looked like the 'before' of a permanent wave commercial but blew up a storm of her own with the competing males ... telefilm has enough good production values to overcome the slight story and keep the looker from fishing in other channels." Helm, "The Web—Hurricane Coming," *Variety*, July 31, 1957.
14. Interview: November 1, 1997.
15. Playhouse 90: "The Edge of Innocence" went into production on July 26, 1957. The show also starred Teresa Wright and Lorne Greene and was produced by Andre de Toth and Berne Gilers. Teleplay was directed by Arthur Hiller.

Chapter 10

1. "We were talking to Beverly Garland and found out why summer TV has her all over the dial. She made 15 [sic] TV pictures in the past three years with about half going into re-run. So you mix all those repeats into the new lot and there are more Beverly Garlands on TV than test patterns." Leo Guild, "On the Air," *The Hollywood Reporter*, July 18, 1957.
2. "Pyramid Productions had been producing *Big Story* and *Treasury Men* at the time they signed Beverly Garland to star in *Decoy*." Walter Ames, *Los Angeles Times*, March 27, 1957.
3. *Billboard*, May 20, 1957.
4. Pacific Pioneers, "Guest Speaker, Beverly Garland," September 4, 1997.
5. *The Hollywood Reporter*, July 25, 1957.
6. Beverly's first day on the set of *The Saga of Hemp Brown* was August 22, 1957.
7. Beverly sublet her apartment at 904 Westmount Drive, West Hollywood, California, during the time she filmed *Decoy* in New York City. Interview: September 8, 1995.
8. "Beverly Garland Confidential," *The Beverly Garland Club Plain & Fancy #6*.
9. "Letter from Beverly Garland," *The Beverly Garland Club Plain & Fancy #3*.
10. Beverly Garland, "*Decoy* Saved My Life."
11. Ibid.
12. Interview: September 8, 1995.
13. Ibid.
14. Ibid.
15. Ibid.
16. Ibid.
17. Ibid. "*Decoy* has outfitted me with a basic wardrobe, but I still use some of my own clothes." Beverly Garland, "Beverly Garland Confidential," *The Beverly Garland Club Plain & Fancy #3*.
18. Interview: September 8, 1995.
19. Boots Lebaron, "What Other Cop Measures Up to This One," *L.A. Times*, April 6, 1958. "Beverly admitted once that in the episode when Casey Jones posed as a Coney Island shimmy dancer ["First Arrest"] she was 'embarrassed doing that scene.'" *The Beverly Garland Club Plain & Fancy # 8, 9*.
20. Interview: September 8, 1995.
21. Ibid.
22. Ibid.

Chapter 11

1. "On All Channels," *Variety*, March 28, 1958.
2. "Letter from Beverly Garland," *The Beverly Garland Club Plain & Fancy #6*.
3. "Fan Fare," *New Californian*, February 3, 1983.
4. The show's executive producer was Don Sharpe. Beverly had guest starred on two previous Don Sharpe Productions, *Four Star Playhouse* (1955): "Night at Lark Cottage" and *Star and the Story* (1956): "Payment in Kind."
5. "Beverly Garland is slated for a new Goldstone-Tobias package to be titled *Lady Pirate*." *The Hollywood Reporter*, December 16, 1958. "There's a series in the planning stages for Beverly. Title: *Lady Pirate*." *TV Guide*, January 1959.
6. Allen Rich, *Listening Post & TV Review*, 1958/1959.
7. Interview: November 1, 1997.
8. Dwight Newton, "A Crank in the Office," *San Francisco Examiner*, February 7, 1963.
9. Interview: November 1, 1997.
10. *The Beverly Garland Club Journal* (various issues).
11. Ibid.
12. Ibid.
13. Ibid.
14. Ibid.
15. Ibid. "Equipped with well motivated lines, Miss Garland turns in a fine performance." Glen, *Variety*.
16. Interview: June 1980.
17. *Rawhide*: "Incident at Sugar Creek" (November 23, 1962), "Incident of the Gallows Tree" (February 22, 1963).
18. Interview: November 1, 1997.
19. "It was Rod Cameron himself who insisted Beverly Garland by cast as the femme lead in two initial segments of his *Coronado 9* series. Call it sentimental or superstition, but Bev vis-à-vis'd Rod in the pilots of his *State Trooper* and *City Detective*—and you know what a big bundle he made from those series." Hank Grant, "On the Air," *The Hollywood Reporter*, May 19, 1959.
20. Interview: May 11, 2004.
21. Beverly also starred in "Remember the Alamo" (original airdate: December 6, 1960).
22. *Elfago Baca* was a 10 episode series. The titles of Beverly's two episodes were "Elfago Baca and the Mustangers." The second episode was titled "Mustang Man, Mustang Maid."
23. Interview: November 1, 1997.
24. "Temper and Talent," *The Sunday Star Bulletin*, September 4, 1960.
25. *The Beverly Garland Club Journal #6 c*, 1978.

Chapter 12

1. "Letter from Beverly Garland," *The Beverly Garland Club Plain & Fancy #7*; "Beverly Garland Confidential," *The Beverly Garland Club Plain & Fancy #8, 9*.

2. Rod Serling wrote the teleplay of "The Four of Us Are Dying" based on the story written by George Clayton Johnson.
3. "Beverly boarded for Tokyo. During a lay-over in Honolulu, she contacted some of our very dear friends and had a wonderful surprise visit." James A. Fessenden, "Dad Says," *The Beverly Garland Club Plain & Fancy #8*, 9.
4. *Rogue for Hire* was an unsold series from J. Gross and Philip Kasne, producers who had been behind the early 1950s series, *The Lone Wolf* starring Louis Hayward (Beverly had appeared in one episode, "Pursuit") among others. Apparently, six episodes had been filmed, however, only one — "Operation Jaguar" — survived (cast unknown). There is no evidence that Beverly ever filmed an episode while in Japan. "As regards the American episodes of *Rogue for Hire*, movie stunt pilot Paul Mantz contributed some sequences about which it was reported in June 1959 that 'several episodes have been completed.'" "At the end of 1959, Gross and Kasne axed the project, [Jerome] Thor being summoned back from Japan where he was shooting sequences for *Rogue for Hire*. A statement claimed 'the American-made films were not approved, and did not get a sale.'" Unfortunately, the websites from which this information was drawn did not credit any sources other than a reference to stunt pilot, Paul Mantz, who supposedly was involved in the flying sequences for this series. As per two online sources: www.78rpm.co.uk; www.jitterbuzz.com/man_1959_08.html.
5. "Letter from Beverly Garland," *The Beverly Garland Club Plain & Fancy #8*, 9.
6. *The Beverly Garland Club Journal*.
7. Dave Jampel, "In Tokyo," *Variety*, October 21, 1959.
8. Hank Grant, "On the Air," *The Hollywood Reporter*, November 4, 1959.
9. James A. Fessenden, "Dad Says," *The Beverly Garland Club Plain & Fancy #8*, 9.
10. "Letter from Beverly Garland," *The Beverly Garland Club Plain & Fancy #8*, 9.
11. Interview: November 1, 1997.
12. Ibid.
13. "*Danger Man*, an ITC Production with each episode filmed in a different locale here and abroad, makes its debut April 5 over CBS-TV network under co-sponsorship of Brown & Williamson Tobacco and Kimberly-Clark Corp. Ralph Smart is producer and also directs several segments. Other directors include Charles Friend, Peter Graham Scott, and Seth Holt. Among stars in episodes are Mai Zetterling, Lois Maxwell, Beverly Garland, Robert Fleming, Moira Lister, Hermione Baddeley and Ronald Howard." "Danger Man Bows on CBS-TV April 5," *The Hollywood Reporter*, February 10, 1961.

Chapter 13

1. "Beverly Garland cast by producer Herb Hirschman in feminine lead in 'The Case of the Mythical Monkeys' segment of CBS-TV's *Perry Mason*." *The Hollywood Reporter*, January 5, 1960. (Beverly's secretary in the show was Louise Fletcher who went on to win an Oscar in *One Flew Over the Cuckoo's Nest*). "Beverly Garland has been signed by producer Hal Hudson to star opposite Dick Powell in segment of Four Star — Dick Powell's *Zane Grey Theater* ... and filming begins next week [February 1] at Four Star's Television." *The Hollywood Reporter*, January 22, 1960. "Darren McGavin checks back into Revue [Productions] today as star of the *Riverboat* series after a two-week absence caused by flu and an auto accident. He begins filming the 'Plague Town' [*sic*] episode with Beverly Garland." *Variety*, February 10, 1960. Beverly plays a woman doctor in this episode which aired as "Three Graves."
2. Paul Baessler, "Bev Isn't Waiting for Work," *Los Angeles Examiner*, week of March 27, 1960.
3. *The Hollywood Reporter*, March 21, 1960. "Teleflex [*Pearl Hart*] penned by producer Nat Holt." *Variety*, March 22, 1960.
4. "TV's Beverly Garland Is Tired of Just Jobs — Ready to Starve," Hal Humphrey, *L.A. Mirror News*, May 23, 1960.
5. Producer of *Playhouse 90* from 1956 to 1961 (also director). *The Miracle Worker*, a three-act play by William Gibson was adapted from his 1957 *Playhouse 90* teleplay of the same name. It was based on Helen Keller's autobiography, *The Story of My Life*.
6. Interview: California, 1980.
7. Ye Little Club: 455 North Canon, Los Angeles, owned by Marshall Edson and Michael Gaith. A 1957 advertisement read: "Ye Little Club swinging nightly with such beautiful people as Zsa Zsa Gabor, Dick Martin, Beverly Garland, the Macdonald Careys, the James Masons."
8. Interview: May 13, 2004. "Beverly Garland ... is marrying 38-year-old widower Fillmore Crank, wealthy builder. They will marry in Las Vegas in two weeks [May 23rd], going immediately to Honolulu for a month's honeymoon. Accompanying them on the honeymoon will be Crank's two children, Cathleen (15) and Fillmore, Jr. (12). When the bride and bridegroom return they will live on Mulholland Drive in one of the four homes the bridegroom owns." Louella O. Parsons, "Bev Garland to Marry Builder," *Los Angeles Examiner*, May 12, 1960. "Motion Picture and television actress Beverly Garland and wealthy widower Fillmore Crank ... were married at the home of a friend, Mrs. Corke Loew, by Justice of the Peace Oscar Bryan." "Beverly Garland Weds in Vegas," *Los Angeles Examiner*, May 25, 1960.
9. Fillmore had also dated Gisele MacKenzie before he met Beverly and recalled an unusual phone call he got from her one day in an interview on November 1, 1997: "Another girl that I dated and whom I liked a lot was Gisele MacKenzie. I remember one time I was working out at the house and I got a call from Gisele and she said, 'I don't think we ought to go out tonight,' and I said, 'Okay. What's the problem?' and she said, 'I'm going to get married.' And I said, 'I think that's a good idea. We don't need to go out.' A lot of times when you're a single guy, girls will jump at you to get somebody else off the dime. You go and you get a little involved, all of a sudden you get the 'Dear John.'" The man Gisele married in 1958 was orchestra leader Robert Suttleworth. Gisele MacKenzie died in 2003 of cancer. "The actress Beverly Garland, a close friend of McKenzie's, said, 'She could sing no matter where she was. She didn't have to have a piano, a violin or anything. She was on key and so brilliant that it just blew your mind.'" Tom Vallance, *The Independent*, September 16, 2003.
10. Interview: November 1, 1997.
11. Ibid.
12. Interviews: May 7, 8, 2004.
13. Interview: November 1, 1997.

Chapter 14

1. "The actress and her husband are owners of 'Desert Bel Air,' a posh forty acre housing development across

the street from Eldorado Country Club in Palm Desert ... designed by Richard Dorman, A.I.A. The plan of the house was derived from the early California ... rambling ranch type hacienda.... An H plan creates two patios ... enclosed on three sides by the house and in the front by a fence and high iron gate. The house has deep overhangs, rustic beams, sliding glass doors which lead to the outside patio and pool area, Mexican tile floors and cathedral ceilings. There are 2 bedrooms, a large kitchen with an open bar leading into the living room, a dining area between the entry and living room, small maid's room and an attractive den ... the master bedroom has a large dressing area and sunken marble shower that overlook a private patio." "Beverly Garland — Hollywood Actress — Desert Housewife," *Palm Springs Life* Vol. 5 #8 (April 1963).

2. Interview: November 1, 1997.
3. Charles Denton, *L.A. Examiner*, January 2, 1961.
4. *Variety*, January 27, 1961.
5. Hank Grant, "On the Air," *The Hollywood Reporter*, February 15, 1961.
6. Paul Baessler, *TV Weekly*, June 10–16, 1962.
7. Peter Francis "Beverly Garland," *Faces International* (Winter 1992).
8. Pacific Pioneers, "Guest Speaker, Beverly Garland," September 4, 1997.
9. "Twenty Four Hours": teleplay: E. Jack Newman; executive producer: Norman Felton; producer: Herbert Hirschman; director: Boris Segal. *Variety*, February 21, 1961.
10. Interview: November 1, 1997.
11. Interview: October 26, 1997.
12. "Fillmore told the author that he always knew when Beverly was going to be working late the following day because she would be in the kitchen long after dinner making his supper with precise instructions on how to cook it." Interview: May 4, 2004.
13. Filmed at Republic Studios, "A Rope for a Lady" co-starred Allison Hayes.
14. Dwight V. Swain was a freelance writer who reportedly had more than 30 films to his credit.
15. Ned Hockman was the president of the Oklahoma University Film Producers Association and was supposedly a former U.S. delegate to the Cannes Film Festival. Several of the film's principal crew were faculty members of the university. All took sabbaticals from the school to work on the film.
16. Cinematographer Carl Stevenson was a former U.S. Air Force officer who used to film rocket launches at Cape Canaveral.
17. Hockman apparently disappeared at some point in the production and never returned to the set. Skip took over and completed the filming himself.
18. Interview: June 1980.
19. "James A. Fessenden, 56, ... died Wednesday in an automobile crash near Riverside on U.S. 60. Fessenden, operator of a hearing aid business in Riverside, was driving west when his car collided with a vehicle.... Officers said [the other driver] was admitted to Riverside Community Hospital, seriously injured. The highway patrol said Fessenden's car appeared to have been on the wrong side of the road but that he could have been swerving to avoid a collision." "Beverly Garland's Father Dies in Auto Crash," Source Unknown, Friday, September 29, 1961.
20. Interview: October 26, 1997.
21. "Rhubarb the Cat Earns $100 a Day," Source Unknown, June 5, 1962. Glenn Smith was the cat's trainer.
22. Hank Grant, "Beverly Garland — Looks Mean Nothing," *TV Time*, June 5, 1962.
23. Interview: May 12, 2004.
24. Ibid.
25. *Stump the Stars* was taped at the CBS-TV Studios on Fairfax and Wilshire Boulevard in Hollywood, California.
26. Interview: May 12, 2004.
27. Ibid.
28. Ibid. "On every cruise they had a costume party. Sebastian's wife and I got into a pair of Sebastian's pants — the two of us — and Sebastian's shirt and the two of us came as Sebastian Cabot." Beverly Garland, Interview: May 13, 2004.
29. Interview: May 13, 2004.
30. *Variety*, August 15, 1962; *The Hollywood Reporter*, August 17, 1962.
31. *Radio Television Daily*, September 7, 1962; *The Hollywood Reporter*, November 7, 1962.
32. "Beverly Garland has been selected as special guest and hostess at the opening of the Christmas Seals Campaign kickoff ... will be on October 2nd with a ... breakfast to be served at the association's offices at 1670 Beverly Boulevard." "Here & There," *The Hollywood Reporter*, August 23, 1962.
33. Interview: May 12, 2004.
34. Harold Hefferman, "Beverly's Entrance Was Earth Shaking Event," *The Detroit News*, October 11, 1962.

Chapter 15

1. *The Beverly Garland Club Journal* #4 c, 1977.
2. *The Herald Examiner*, December 5, 1962.
3. *The Hollywood Reporter*, December 13, 1962. "Teen Age Trials," "The Ben Hunter Show," "You Don't Say," "The Jack Barry Show" (television); "Panorama Pacific" (radio).
4. *The Hollywood Reporter*, January 8, 1963.
5. "Travel Logs," *The Hollywood Reporter*, December 10, 1962.
6. P. M. Clepper, "Sometimes Acting Is Painful for Beverly," *St. Paul Pioneer Press*, December 16, 1962.
7. Wade H. Mosby, "Show Biz," *The Milwaukee Journal*, December 23, 1962.
8. www.jppatches.com/images/page89.htm; Interview: May 12, 2004.
9. Anthony La Camera, "Meet the Real Beverly Garland," *The Boston Sunday Advertiser*, February 17, 1963.
10. *The Beverly Garland Club Journal*.
11. *The Hollywood Reporter*, March 8, 1963.
12. "Beverly Garland is featured on *The Dakotas* at 7:30 P.M. Monday [April 22] and appears later the same day on *Stump the Stars* at 10:30 P.M." *L.A. Times*, April 21, 1963.
13. Interview; May 7, 2004. Carrington Crank was born on January 27, 1964.
14. Interview: November 1, 1997.
15. "Beverly Garland, whose *Decoy* series ... is still running in syndication, will be guest of honor today at a luncheon hosted by California Association of Private Investigators at the Statler Hilton Hotel." *The Hollywood Reporter*, June 21, 1963. The following month, Beverly was herself a defendant as reported by Eunice Field in "Tail of Woe," *TV Mirror Magazine*, July 1963, "Beverly Garland's pooch — half Shepherd, half African Lion Dog — wagged his tail and knocked down a neighbor's kid. Small claims court for Bev."
16. "She's Finally Getting a Chance to Laugh Out Loud," *TV Guide*.

17. *The Hollywood Reporter*, July 3, 1963.
18. "She's Finally Getting a Chance to Laugh Out Loud," *TV Guide*.
19. Harry Harris, "She Loves to Make a Fool of Herself," *The Philadelphia Inquirer*, June 23, 1963.
20. *The Beverly Garland Club Journal*.
21. "Stanwyck Regular in Jackie Cooper's 'Calhoun' Series." Hank Grant, "On the Air," *The Hollywood Reporter*, October 25, 1963. "Cooper rolls the pilot November 11th with three days of interiors and 19 days of exteriors, latter to be lensed in and near Las Cruces, New Mexico. Stuart Rosenberg will direct script by Merle Miller." *Variety*, October 28, 1963. Stuart Rosenberg was one of Beverly's producers on her *Decoy* series.
22. Interview: May 9, 2004.
23. Interview: May 7, 2004.

Chapter 16

1. *Variety*, March 25, 1964.
2. May 8, 1964.
3. *The Beverly Garland Club Journal*.
4. "Many a big name was saddened to read that fire has gutted Paul Levitt's Player's Ring Theatre here. So many prominent performers worked there early in their careers ... Beverly Garland." *L.A. Herald Examiner*, June 12, 1964.
5. *The Beverly Garland Club Journal*.
6. Ibid.
7. Interview: October 26, 1997.
8. *The TV Collector*, June/July 1985.
9. Eleanor Roberts, "Yes, Bing Does Sing on His TV Show—Der Bingle Puts Teen 'Daughters' at Ease," Source Unknown.
10. Interview: May 10, 2004.
11. Telephone Interview: 2001.
12. Interview: November 1, 1997.
13. Interview: October 26, 1997.

Chapter 17

1. Interview: May 8, 2004.
2. "The casts of *The Addams Family*, *Green Acres*, and *Petticoat Junction* are latest to join list of stars participating in the 19-hour Arthritis Foundation Telethon Spectacular Show on KTLA, March 5–6. Also set Agnes Moorehead, Beverly Garland, Pat Boone (and others) for featured performances written hourly segments. Begins 11 P.M. Saturday to 6 P.M. Sunday." *The Hollywood Reporter*, February 22, 1966.
3. Now called the John Anson Ford Amphitheatre, "The Pilgrimage Play Theatre" is one of the oldest performing arts venues in Los Angeles still in use since 1920. Located on a 45-acre, park-like setting on the east side of the Cahuenga Pass. The theatre seats over 1,400 and is open May through October every year.
Beverly recalled when she tried out for a role in a play at the theatre: "I remember I was out of a job and they were interviewing for Mary Magdalene at the Pilgrimage Theatre and I decided I'd see if I could get the part. They gave me the script and I read it and I said to one of the interviewers, 'Could you tell me how to pronounce this word?' she said, 'What?' I said, 'How do you pronounce this word?' She just chuckled and I thought, 'Okay. The hell with her.' So I get up. You have to speak very loud because it was a big round auditorium. I get up and shout, 'Hear Ye! Hear Ye! The Messa's coming!' All she had to do was tell me it was 'Messiah' and I could have gotten the part." Pacific Pioneers, "Guest Speaker, Beverly Garland," September 4, 1997.
4. Interview: May 7, 2004.
5. "Beverly Garland has been set for a regular role in Disney's frontier TV drama, *Gallegher Goes West*. Cast includes John McIntire, Jeanette Nolan, and Roger Mobley in the title role. Shooting resumes Monday with James Sargent directing from Maurice Tombragel's script. Ron Miller co-producers with Disney." *The Hollywood Reporter*, May 6, 1966.
6. Interview: November 1, 1997.
7. "Here & There," *The Hollywood Reporter*, June 20, 1966.
8. Interview: May 13, 2004.
9. Interview: May 7, 2004.
10. Ibid.
11. Margaret L. Lesher, "Reflections of an Actress," *The Contra Costa Times*, August 14, 1977.
12. *The Beverly Garland Club Journal*.
13. Interview: May 13, 2004.
14. *The Beverly Garland Club Journal*.
15. Ibid.
16. Ibid.
17. Interview: November 1, 1997.
18. Interview: November 21, 2010 (letter). Beverly and Kaye Ballard appeared in *Great to Be Alive* at the Las Palmas Theatre in Hollywood in 1956. This was a musical whodunit written by Walter Bullock, Sylvia Regan and Abraham Ellstein.
19. *The Beverly Garland Club Journal*. "Harry Bluestone (1907–1992): 85, a familiar figure on the Los Angeles musical scene for decades and a violinist who played with the Dorsey brothers ... Red Nichols bands. As a teenager, he traveled to Paris with a small jazz group to back up expatriate singer Josephine Baker. He came to L.A. in the late 1930s ... began working with radio and motion pictures orchestras." Obituary, *L.A. Times*, December 28, 1992.
20. *The Beverly Garland Club Journal #4 c*, 1977.
21. Interview: November 1, 1997.
22. Ibid.
23. *The Beverly Garland Club Journal #4 c*, 1977.
24. Interview: October 26, 1997.
25. Interview: California, 1980.
26. Interview: May 9, 2004.

Chapter 18

1. Arnold Hano, "If She Can Be Fred MacMurray's Wife, Why Can't I?," *TV Guide*, January 10–16, 1970.
2. Interview: November 1, 1997.
3. CBS-TV press release dated February 17, 1965, Ed Harmann quote.
4. "There will soon be twice as many widowers ... in television-land, ... on the three major networks shows. New widowers will join the ranks to replace last season's dropouts." Cynthia Lowry (AP Staff Writer), "Widowers in Vogue for New TV Season" Source Unknown.
5. Beverly's first appearance on *My Three Sons* was on the episode "The First Meeting."
6. Fred MacMurray's "temporary replacement" was the 6'2" dialogue coach on the series, Kathy Barrett.
7. *The Beverly Garland Club Journal*.

8. "When I arrived on the first day for my hair and makeup, they said to me, 'Now be sure you like your hair because you won't be able to change it for the entire season.' You couldn't change your hair style or color or anything." They gave Beverly a wig and on the first day she had this hair that had bangs and some little curls and she thought, "Gee, I look good!" A month later she said, "'I was screaming is there ANY WAY I can get rid of these damn curls?' 'No,' they said." Pacific Pioneers, "Guest Speaker, Beverly Garland," September 4, 1997.
9. Interview: May 7, 2004. Richard Garland died on May 24, 1969. He was 41 years old.
10. Interview: November 1, 1997.
11. Interview: November 1, 1997.
12. Original airdate: September 29, 1969.
13. Interview: June 1980. *The Beverly Garland Club Journal*. "A disappointing and slow moving hour and half with its stereo-typed stalwart hero ... and wasted actors Joseph Cotton, Nehemiah Persoff, J. Carroll Nash and Beverly Garland." John Gaff, *The Hollywood Reporter*, February 10, 1970. CBS-TV had ordered six scripts but a series never materialized.
14. Interview: November 1, 1997.
15. Ibid.
16. Ibid.
17. Interview: May 10, 2004.
18. Interview: May 7, 2004.
19. Interview: November 1, 1997.
20. Interview: May 8, 2004.
21. Interview: May 10, 2004.
22. Interview: November 1, 1997.
23. The San Fernando Valley earthquake occurred on February 9, 1971, at 6:01 A.M. and was measured at 6.5 magnitude. Ronald Reagan was governor of California at the time.
24. Fred Silverman worked at CBS-TV from 1970 to 1975.
25. Not even a mid-season move to Thursday nights at 8:30 P.M. was in time to save it.
26. Interview: May 10, 2004.
27. The night before the start of the parade, an eyewitness told the author, "Co-hosts Beverly Garland and Bob Crane were to meet with some CBS-TV executives in the lobby of their Philadelphia hotel. Crane was no where to be found. Everyone was wondering what happened to him when Beverly quipped, 'He's probably in someone's hotel room with his pants around his ankles.' Eventually Crane turned up — pants securely fastened for the time being." Crane was the star of CBS-TV's *Hogan's Heroes* (1965–1971). Yet another Fred Silverman casualty.

Chapter 19

1. Interview: November 1, 1997. Casey Stengel died in 1975 in Glendale, California.
2. Fillmore explained that the franchising with the Howard Johnson hotels or any of the major chains is that "They don't put any money into anything. The secret of their success is that they just skim off the top like an agent, and they get three to seven percent of everything you take in. Some of that is advertising. With Howard Johnson we were at three and a half percent — that's a lot of money. The hotel [in 1997, when this interview took place] was doing about eight million dollars a year. They send us about one million dollars a year in business, but we have to make up the difference." Interview: November 1, 1997.

3. Beverly played a joke on Fred MacMurray during the opening of the Beverly Garland Howard Johnson Motor Lodge Ceremony: "I was doing *My Three Sons* when the North Hollywood hotel opened. Fred MacMurray came to the opening and I remember I had a very revealing dress. It was black and it had knit and chiffon stripes from top to bottom so if you moved a certain way, your nipple hit the chiffon. I asked Fillmore, 'Should I wear this dress?' and, of course, he said, 'Oh, yes! Wear that dress!' People were fascinated watching me move and walk. Fred just couldn't keep his eyes off that dress. It was so funny because Fred was so prim and proper and he was so shocked. I thought it was great!" Interview: May 7, 2004.
4. Interview: May 7, 2004.
5. Ibid.
6. Ibid.
7. *The Beverly Garland Club Journal*.
8. Susan Hayward also made *Heart of Anger*, playing attorney, Jessie Fitzgerald. The made-for-TV movie/pilot also starred Lee J. Cobb and was directed by Don Taylor.
9. *The Beverly Garland Club Journal #2 c*, April 1976.
10. "She [Hayward] was sick during the production; she spent a lot [of] time in her dressing room and wasn't too communicative because she wasn't feeling well." Kevin Lee Minton, "Beverly Garland — An Interview" *Film Fax #46* (Aug.–Sept. 1994).
11. Interviews: June 1980 and May 10, 2004.

Chapter 20

1. *The Beverly Garland Club Journal #12 c*, 1983.
2. Peter Citron, "Cowboys Really Men in *Cowboys*," *Omaha World-Herald*, March 8, 1974.
3. Interview: May 11, 2004.
4. "Beverly Garland Says: I Want to Go Back to Playing Alcoholics and Wild Loose Women," *The Enquirer*, 1974.
5. *The Beverly Garland Club Journal*.
6. *The Beverly Garland Club Journal #4*.
7. Beverly's contract dated July 10, 1974, promised her at least eight days employment at a salary of $2,250 and a minimum of $3,000 guaranteed.
8. Pacific Pioneers Broadcasters, January 19, 2001.
9. Interview: May 11, 2004.
10. Ibid.
11. As of November 1975, one year after its general release, *Where the Red Fern Grows* had made over $6 million in domestic receipts.
12. Interview: New York City, 1976.
13. Interview: May 13, 2004.
14 *The Beverly Garland Club Journal #2 c*, April 1976.
15. *The Beverly Garland Club Journal*.
16. Interview: May 11, 2004.
17. David Cuthbert, "The Stars Gathered Here Too," *The Times Picayune* (New Orleans), February 12, 1975, (Beverly noted in the article "they cut one scene in the hospital...")
18. Pacific Pioneers, "Guest Speaker, Beverly Garland," September 4, 1997.
19. *The Beverly Garland Club Journal #2 c*, April 1976.
20. Interview: New York City, 1976.
21. Pacific Pioneers, "Guest Speaker, Beverly Garland," September 4, 1997.
22. Interview: November 1, 1997. Interview: May 13, 2004.

Chapter 21

1. Interview: May 13, 2004.
2. Interview: New York City, 1976.
3. *The Beverly Garland Club Journal #3 c*, 1976.
4. *The Beverly Garland Club Journal #4 c*, 1977.
5. *The Beverly Garland Club Journal #6 c*, 1978. Interview: May 7, 2004.
6. *The Beverly Garland Club Journal #5*.
7. Ibid.
8. *The Beverly Garland Club Journal #6 c*, 1978.
9. *The Beverly Garland Club Journal #4 c*, 1977.
10. Ibid.
11. Interview: November 1, 1997.
12. *The Beverly Garland Club Journal*.
13. *The Beverly Garland Club Journal #6 c*, 1978.
14. *TV Guide*, December 24, 1977.
15. *The Beverly Garland Club Journal*.
16. Ibid.
17. *The Beverly Garland Club Journal #6 c*, 1978.
18. *The Beverly Garland Club Journal #7 c*, 1979.
19. "We broke ground for a second tower in North Hollywood which will add an additional one hundred rooms and which was completed around Christmas [1979]. We had a total of two hundred fifty-five rooms with the addition of the second tower." Interview: June 1980.
20. Interview: May 7, 2004. Interview: California, June 1980.
21. Interview: California, June 1980.
22. Interview: May 10, 2004.
23. Interview: November 1, 1997.
24. Taped letter from Beverly Garland — February 1979.
25. Taped Letter from Beverly Garland — February 1979. Paige, Arizona, was used in numerous Hollywood films. Among them: *Planet of the Apes* (1968, 2000) and *The Greatest Story Ever Told* (1965). The 3-month average temperatures in Paige, Arizona: January: High 42, Low 24; February: High 51, Low 30; March: High 58, Low 36.
26. Interview: May 13, 2004.
27. Interview: June 1980.
28. Interview: November 1, 1997.
29. *The Beverly Garland Club Journal #9 c*, 1980.
30. *The Beverly Garland Club Journal #8 c*, 1979.
31. Ibid.
32. Interviews: May 7, 2004, May 8, 2004.
33. Interview: November 1, 1997.

Chapter 22

1. Anthony Zerbe and John Shea were originally announced but did not appear in the film. *Variety*, January 1980.
2. Interview: June 1980.
3. *The Beverly Garland Club Journal #9*.
4. *The Beverly Garland Club Journal*.
5. Interview: June 1980.
6. Interview: New York City, 1976.
7. *The Beverly Garland Club Journal #9 c*, 1980.
8. *The Beverly Garland Club Journal #10 c*, 1981.
9. Interview: May 11, 2004.
10. Interview: May 12, 2004.
11. *The Beverly Garland Club Journal #11 c*, 1982. The Cranks also spent a week touring England before returning to Los Angeles.
12. Letter from Beverly.
13. *The Beverly Garland Club Journal #11 c*, 1982. The cruises were sponsored by the Home Savings & Loan Association.
14. Audio Letter from Beverly, 1982.
15. Carolyn Jones died on August 3, 1983, of colon cancer.
16. Interview: November 1, 1997.
17. *The Beverly Garland Club Journal #11 c*, 1982.
18. *The Beverly Garland Club Journal #12 c*, 1983. Whomemoppers — a restaurant at Universal Studios where Beverly held the party talked about it for quite a while afterwards.
19. Letters sent to the nominating committee included: Joel Wachs, president, Los Angeles City Council; Peggy Stevenson, council president Pro Tempore City of Los Angeles; Vance Stickell, executive vice president of marketing, *Los Angeles Times*.
20. *The Beverly Garland Club Journal #12 c*, 1983.
21. Ibid.

Chapter 23

1. *The Beverly Garland Club Journal #12 c*, 1983. *The Sting of Steele* starred Stephanie's father, Efrem Zimbalist, Jr.
2. *The Rookies*: original airdate: February 12, 1973. "Three Hours to Kill": Beverly played Pat Whitfield, Kate Jackson, series regular, played Jill Danko.
3. Interview: May 11, 2004.
4. Ibid.
5. *The Beverly Garland Club Journal #12 c*, 1983.
6. *The Beverly Garland Club Journal #13 c*, 1984.
7. In the series opener, Amanda King (Kate Jackson) plays a divorced housewife and mother of two boys who lives with her mother, Dotty West (Beverly Garland) in suburbia. One day Amanda encounters secret agent Lee Stetson (Bruce Boxleitner) at a train station. Lee gives her a package to avoid it getting into an enemy agent's hands. Lee then tracks Amanda back to her home to retrieve the package and a clandestine working relationship — and later a romance — develops between the two with Amanda's mother being kept totally in the dark about her daughter's new "career."
8. *The Beverly Garland Club Journal #12 c*, 1983.
9. Ibid.
10. Beverly's daughter Carrington appeared as Young Agent in the first season episode, "A Matter of Choice."
11. Richard Turner, "Producers Out at Scarecrow Despite Success" *TV Guide*.
12. "Beverly Garland — A Busy Samaritan," *CBS Trade News*, July 31, 1984.
13. Beverly's son James was selected as a page for California Senator Hayaukua for several months in 1982. James was on his own in Washington, D.C., attending school in the early hours of the morning and then performing his duties as a Senate page for the rest of the day.
14. Vera Miles' last appearance, according to the International Movie Data Base, was in *Separate Lives* (1995).
15. Interview: May 11, 2004.
16. *The Beverly Garland Club Journal #13 c*, 1984.
17. News clipping April 27, 1985 — Source unknown.
18. "Patty Duke New SAG President," *Daily Variety*, November 6, 1985.
19. "Beverly Garland to Visit Juniata's Campus," *The Juniatian* Vol. 37 No. 14 (June 30, 1986).
20. The other Honorees included: Louis L'Amour,

James Arness, Fred MacMurray, Jock Mahoney, Fess Parker, Guy Madison and George Montgomery. Beverly was the only woman honored that year.
21. The final season of *Scarecrow and Mrs. King* was costing $850,000 per episode. The show was nominated for two Emmys in 1986 in music and costumes.
22. Interview: May 11, 2004.

Chapter 24

1. *The Beverly Garland Club Journal #4 c*, 1977.
2. Interview: May 10, 2004.
3. Interview: May 11, 2004.
4. Interview: May 12, 2004.
5. Interview: November 1, 1997.
6. Budget on the film was set at $2 million.
7. Interview: November 1, 1997.
8. Interview: May 13, 2004.
9. Interview: May 13, 2004. Beverly's diary entry, May 4, 1993: "The actor who plays the Baron (Lev Prigunov) makes a high salary for a Russian — one hundred fifty U.S. dollars per week."
10. Beverly's diary entry, April 24, 1993: "Jennifer Burns, who had been looking forward to working with Ben Cross, overheard him say she was 'terrible.' Has been going through hell to keep herself performing."
11. Interview: May 13, 2004.
12. Ibid.
13. Beverly's diary entry, April 21, 1993: "Ben and David's tension has dissipated. All seems much better. Crew loves Ben but he is such a typical actor — so involved in himself. So demanding with such charm — he is so into him. But he is bright — a good actor and very knowing and lets you know that he knows. He could eat you alive if you would let him. He leaves me alone. I have him buffaloed. They say Ben will finish 15th of May!"
14. Interview: May 14, 2004.
15. Beverly recalled: "There was one other little scene at the graveyard which was done in the Mosfilm Studio back lot at night." Interview: May 13, 2004.
16. Adrianne Barbeau eventually played the role.
17. Beverly noted in her diary that "the rats in Moscow were as big as small dogs. The Russian government tried poison but didn't work. Now they just shoot them but too many to make a difference."
18. During the summer of 1993, Beverly attended American Cinematique's salute to Roger Corman in Los Angeles. Among the other guests were Corman alumni Dick Miller and Jackie Joseph. Interview: May 13, 2004.

Chapter 25

1. Interview: November 1, 1997.
2. Interview: May 9, 2004.
3. Interview: May 12, 2004.
4. Ibid.
5. Interview: May 11, 2004.
6. Ibid.
7. Interview: May 12, 2004.
8. Interview: November 1, 1997.
9. "A Writer's Life: Beverly Garland" Saturday, December 6, 2008, http://www.leegoldberg.typepad.com
10. Interview: May 10, 2004.
11. The original title for this episode was "Voodoo Hoodoo," however, the network's lawyers thought there might have been some objections on religious grounds. So the show had to come up with a new title and re-shoot the opening credits to include it causing the episode to be delayed for several months while the corrections were completed in Korea where the animation cells were drawn.
12. Interview: May 11, 2004.
13. Ibid.
14. Ibid.
15. Beverly filmed another episode of *Teen Angel* titled "Back to DePolo" which aired one week earlier. The series only lasted 17 episodes before being cancelled.
16. Interview: November 1, 1997.
17. Ibid.
18. The book was published by Dove-New Star Publishing. Beverly later recorded two more books-on-tape stories in 2000: *The Greatest Mystery Stories of the 20th Century — Nine Sons* and *The Greatest Horror Stories of the 20th Century — Smoke Ghosts*.
19. www.calartistsradiotheatre.org. Many of these programs are available for purchase in MP3 or CD format. Beverly Garland also has guest appearances in "Call of the Yukon," "The October Country" and "Reno."
20. Interview: May 13, 2004.

Chapter 26

1. Interview: May 11, 2004.
2. Interview: May 12, 2004. *The Weakest Link*: episode title "TV Moms Edition" original airdate: April 28, 2002. "Moms" included: Beverly Garland, Pat Crowley, Karen Grassle, June Lockhart, Alley Mills, Janet Hubert, Jo Marie Payton and Carol Potter.
3. Interview: May 11, 2004.
4. Taped Interview: April 2011.
5. Interview: May 11, 2004.
6. Ibid.

Farewell to Television's First Lady

1. Interview: March 2011.
2. Donations in her memory were requested by the family to be made to the Motion Picture & Television Fund, P. O. Box 51150, Los Angeles, CA 90051; The Interval House Crisis Shelters & Centers for Victims of Domestic Violence, c/o The Beverly Garland Memorial Fund, P. O. Box 3356, Seal Beach, CA 90740.

Epilogue

1. Interview: May 12, 2004.

Select Bibliography

Books

Barabas, SuzAnne, and Gabor Barabas. *Gunsmoke: A Complete History and Analysis of the Legendary Broadcast Series with a Comprehensive Episode-by-Episode Guide to Both the Radio and Television Programs.* Jefferson, NC: McFarland, 1990.
Castle, William. *Step Right Up! I'm Gonna Scare the Pants Off America.* New York: Pharos Books, 1992.
Goldberg, Lee. *Unsold Television Pilots, 1955–1989.* Jefferson, NC: McFarland, 1990.
Lentz, Harris M., III. *Television Westerns Episode Guide: All United States Series, 1949–1996.* Jefferson, NC: McFarland, 1997.
Linet, Beverly. *Susan Hayward: Portrait of a Survivor.* New York: Atheneum, 1980.
Lucanio, Patrick, and Gary Colville. *American Science Fiction Television Series of the 1950s: Episode Guides and Casts and Credits for Twenty Shows.* Jefferson, NC: McFarland, 1998.
Warren, Alan. *This Is a* Thriller: *An Episode Guide, History and Analysis of the Classic 1960s Television Series.* Jefferson, NC: McFarland, 1996.

Periodicals

The Beverly Garland Club Journal, Issue Numbers 1–13.
The Beverly Garland Club Newsletters, dated 1979–2001.
Daily Variety, Los Angeles.
The Hollywood Reporter, Los Angeles.
Plain & Fancy, Journal of the Beverly Garland Fan Club, Issue Numbers 1–9, dated 1955–1960.
Variety, New York City.

Index

Numbers in ***bold italics*** indicate pages with photographs.
Titles in ***bold italics*** indicate films in which Beverly Garland appeared.

ABC Wide World of Mystery ("Deadly Volley") 124
"Abraham's Sacrifice" (*Greatest Heroes of the Bible*) 138–***139***
The Academy of Entertainment and Technology 187
Adams, Julie 173
Adler, Luther 34
Agar, John 82
Airport 1975 (1974) 121, 219–220
Albert, Eddie 53, 130–131
Alcoa—Goodyear Theater ("Silhouette of a Killer") 57–***58***
All the King's Men (1949) 27
Allen, Steve 15
Allied Artists 32, 34, 35, 39
The Alligator People (1959) 64–65, 87, 213–214
Allison, June 37
Altman, Robert 81
Alyn, Kirk 226
Amazon River 44
Ames, Walter 4
Amos & Andy 226
"And Then They Forgot God" (*Human Dimension*) 1
Anderson, Judith 38
Andrews, Dana 121
The Angry Beavers ("The Mighty Knothead"; "Open Wide for Zombies"; "Practical Jerks") 174
Ansara, Michael 35
Arboles Drive, Glendale, California 16, 19
The Arboretum, Arcadia, California 35
Arden, Eve 105
"Argonaut Special" (*Switch*) 130
Arliss, Anita 12, 16
Arnaz, Lucie 164
Arness, James 49, 90, 96, 138, 235
Arnold, Edward 226
Arnold, Jack 34
Arthritis Foundation Telethon 102, 232
Asner, Ed 125–***126***, 180
A.S.P.C.A. (American Society for the Prevention of Cruelty to Animals) 117
The Asphalt Jungle ("The Nine-Twenty Hero") 78, 79
Astin, John 132
Aunt Miriam 22
Auntie Mame (play) 56
Autry, Gene 116
Avalon, Frankie 99
Ayres, Lew 51, 52

Bacall, Lauren 56
"Back to DePolo" (*Teen Angel*) 235
"Bad Influence" (*Camp Wilder*) 165
"The Badge" (*Gunsmoke*) 95, 104, 105, 111, 124
Badlands of Montana (1957) 54, 211–212
Baessler, Paul 76, 230
Baker, Carroll 56
Balboa Island, California 20, 21
Ball, Lucille 96, 111
Ballard, Kaye 105, 228, 232
Bancroft, Anne 71, 72
Barbeau, Adrienne 235
Barnett, S.H. 228
Barrett, Kathy 232
Barris, Chuck 103
Barry, Gene 138
Barrymore, Ethel 38
"Battle Hymn" (*Kung Fu*) 125
Beanpole (pilot episode) 160
Beau ***55***, 227
The Beaux Arts Theatre, Los Angeles, California 32, 227
Beechwood Drive, Los Angeles, California 48, 49
"The Beeler Gang" (*The Lone Ranger*) 28
Belem Zoo, Brazil 45
Bell Telephone Time ("The Other Van Gogh") 57, 229
Bellamy, Ralph 51
Beltone Hearing Aids 32
The Ben Hunter Show 231
Bennett, Bruce 64
Bergman, Ingmar 53
Bergstein, Eleanor 144
Berry, Noah, Jr. 107
"Between Two Guns" (*Checkmate*) 76, 84, 133
Betz, Carl 104
The Beverly Garland Club 151, 153, 225
Beverly Garland Day, Los Angeles, California 181
Beverly Garland Holiday Inn 118, 180, 190
The Beverly Garland Howard Johnson Motor Lodge 118, ***129***, 136, 141, 160
Beverly Garland Motor Lodge, Sacramento, California 136–137
Beverly Garland's First 50 Years in Show Business 187
Beverly Garland's Pointe West Motor Lodge, Sacramento, California 137, 141
B.H.S. Productions, Inc. 79
Big Town ("Hot Car Murder") 38
Billingsley, Barbara 158
Bing Crosby Productions 94, 95
The Bing Crosby Show 3, 94–***97***, 98–100, 110, 135
Birch, Paul 49, 50
Bitter Creek (1954) 34, 205
Black, Noel 103
Blair, Linda 139–140
Blaisdell, Paul 50
Blake, Beverly 19
Blue River–BMI Records 105
Bluestone, Harry 105, 232
The Bob Crane Show 87
Bobby Sherman Enterprises 121
Bogart, Humphrey 35, 56
The Bon Jour, New York City, New York 228
Bond, Ward 75, 158
Boone, Richard 35, 36, 193, 194
Bottoms, Joseph 121
"Bourbon Street" (*Four Star Playhouse*) 36
Boxleitner, Bruce 138, 154, 157, 158, ***159***, 160, 234

Boyer Family 103
Bradley, Mayor 129
Brand, Neville 68, 100
Brazil, South America 42, 45, 46
Break the Bank 129
Bretand, Lowell 226
Bridges, Cindy 100
Bridges, Lloyd 100
The Broadway, Hollywood Boulevard, Los Angeles, California 59
Broadway, New York City, New York 22
Brodkin, Herb 82
Bromfield, John 42, 45, 46
Bronson Caves, Los Angeles, California 48
Brooks, Jim 125
Brosnan, Pierce **155**
Brown, Joe E. 228
Brown, Kimberlin 180, 181
Brown, Peter 100
Bruce, Lenny 34
Bryan, Oscar (Justice of the Peace, Las Vegas, Nevada) 230
Buckner, Brad 158
Bullock, Walter 232
Buono, Victor 148
Burbank on Parade (1985) 159
Burbridge, Margaret 112
Burial of the Rats (1993) 168
Burnes, Allan 125
Burns, Jennifer 235
Burr, Raymond 124
"Bury the Dead" (*Dangerman*) 70, 78
Bus Stop ("Summer Lightning") 81
Buttram, Pat 82
By the Numbers 84

Cabot, Kaye 133
Cabot, Sebastian 83–84, **85**, 87, 92, 133, 231
Cahn, Sammy 95
Cain, Christopher 133, 173
Cain, Dean 172, 173
Cain's Hundred ("The Left Side of Canada") 81
Calhoun (unsold pilot) 92, 232
California Artists Radio Theater 178, 189, 194
California Association of Private Investigators 231
California Studios 68
California Tourism Corporation 158
"The Call" (*The George Sanders Mystery Theater*—pilot) 228
Call of the Yukon (radio play) 235
Cameron, Rod 3, 32, 66, 229
Camp Wilder ("Bad Influence") 165
Campanella, Joseph 1, 82, 105, 107, 121, 137, 181, 187
Campbell, Beverly 24, 29, 226, 227
Campbell, Bill 20
Campbell, Bob 20, 21, 22, 31
Cannon ("Deadly Heritage") 120
Capital 149–150, 159

Carey, Macdonald 99
Carey, Philip 100
Carolyn G. Hart Presents: Malice Domestic Vol. 4 (audio book) 178
Carr, Tom 71, 76
Carr, Vickie 99
Carradine, David 125
C.A.R.T. *see* California Artists Radio Theater
Cartwright, Angela 158
"The Case of the Mythical Monkeys" (*Perry Mason*) 71, 124, 230
"Case: The Sylvia Needleman Experience" (*The Tony Randall Show*) 135
Cassavetes, John 56
The Castaways Restaurant **21**, 22
Castle, William 35
Catalina Island, California 20
Catskill Actor's Theatre (C.A.T.), Highland Lake, New York 162–163
Caulfield, Joan 108
The CBS Thanksgiving Parade Jubilee (1971) 115
Celebrity Cruises 186
The Chairman's Award 187
Chamberlain, Richard 78
Chaney, Lon, Jr. 64, 65, 87
"Charlie, He Couldn't Kill a Fly" (*Kraft Suspense Theater*) 94
Charlie's Angels ("Cruising Angels") 140
Checkmate ("Between Two Guns") 76, 84, 133
Cher 140
Chicago Confidential (1957) 57, 212–213, 229
"Chooser of the Slain" (*The Dakotas*) 89
Christian, Linda 73–74
Christian Scientist 178
Christmas Seals Campaign 84, 87, 231
Christmas Vacation 2: Cousin Eddie's Island Adventure (2003) 186, 223–224
City Detective ("Man Down, Woman Screaming") 32, 66, 229
The City of Los Angeles 5
Clayburgh, Jill 142
Clayton, Jan 83
Clements, Colin 12
Climax! ("The Fog"; "A Taste for Crime"; "Throw Away the Cane") 3, 53, 57, 228
Clutterbuck (play) 226
C'mon Along America ... There's a Better Way to Go 145–146
The Coach House 60
Coco Palms Hotel, Kauai, Hawaii 53
Coe, Fred 71
Cole, Julian 145
Cole, Tina 110, 140–141, 145, 152
Collins, Stephen 174–**176**

Colorado Street, Glendale, California 29
Columbia Pictures 40
Colway, Lorraine 72, 164
The Community Chest Show— Storytime (radio show) 15
Connelly, Joe 85
Connors, Mike 39, 105, 145, 173, 174, 181
Conrad, Robert 104
Conried, Hans 83
Conte, Richard 85
Coogan, Jackie 104, 132
Cook, Carol 164
Cook, Laird 164
Cooper, Ben 52
Cooper, Bunny 42, 52, 228
Cooper, Jackie 92, 232
Cooper, Jeanne 146–147, 152
Cooper, Ray 24, 25, 27, 137
Corman, Roger 4, 39–41, 46, 47, 48, 53, 60, 165–168, 181, 186, 228, 235
Coronado Nine ("Remember the Alamo"; "The Widow of Kill Cove") 66, 229
Cottage Grove Street, Glendale, California 9
Cotten, Joseph 58, 88, 233
The Cowboys (pilot, unaired) 120–121
Crain, Jeanne 28
Crane, Bob 82, 233
Crane, Richard 64
Crank, Carrington 80, 89, 92, 95, 99, 106–107, 112, 139, 145, 147, 152, 164, 170, 178, 179, 183, 185, 189–190, 234
Crank, Cathleen 74–75, 106
Crank, Fillmore 1, 4, 71–**73**, 74–75, 78, 82, 89, 101, 103, 108, 112, 114, 116–117, 125, 126–127, 128–129, 133, 136, 137–138, 139, 141, 143, 151, 158, 162, 164, 171, 174, 178, 179, 191, 231
Crank, Fillmore, Jr. ("Smoke") 74–75, 106, 114, 140–141
Crank, James (Jimmy) 1, 105, 106–107, 112, 117, 123–124, 130, 139, 145, 147–148, 152, 160, 170–171, 183, 185, 189–190, 234
Crank, "Smoke" *see* Crank, Fillmore, Jr.
Crawford, John 39
Crawford, Lorraine 39
Crazy Like a Fox ("Rosie") 160
Crosby, Bing 13, 85, 94–96, **97**, 98–100, 161
Crosby, Gary 99
Cross, Ben 167–168, 235
Cross Wits 130
Crouse, Russell 226
Crowley, Pat 235
"Cruising Angels" (*Charlie's Angels*) 140
Cukor, George 29
Culp, Robert 64
Curtis, Jamie Lee 132

Curtis, Tony 31
Curucu, Beast of the Amazon (1956) 41, 42, **43**, 47, 52, 57, 65, 210–211
Cutter's Trail (1970) 111–**113**, 217

The Dakotas ("The Chooser of the Slain") 89, 231
The Damon Runyon Theater ("Tobias the Terrible") 38
Damus, Mike 177
Dance Fever 158
Dangerman ("Bury the Dead") 69–70, 78, 230
Dark of the Moon 31
Davis, Bette 3, 17, 21, 22
Day, Dennis 99
"The Day Everything Went Wrong" (*Insight*) 102
"The Day God Died" (*Insight*) 102
Day of the Bad Man (1958) 56
The Day the Earth Moved (1974) 121–122
Dayton, Lyman 122, 123
"Deadfall" (*Mannix*) 105
"Deadly Heritage" (*Cannon*) 120
"Deadly Volley" (*ABC Wild World of Mystery*) 124, 219
Death Falls (1996) **164**, **223**
"Death Probe" (*The Six Million Dollar Man*) 131
De Carlo, Yvonne 98
Decision at Durango see ***Day of the Bad Man***
De Cordova, Fred 112, 181
Decoy—The Story of a New York Policewoman 1, 3, 56, 57, 59–60, **61**–62, 63, 73, 82, 83, 90, 227, 229, 232
"The Deep End" (*Judd for the Defense*) 104
Dehner, John 102
Del Ruth, Roy 64
Delta Queen 160
Del Vecchio, Carl A. 151, 189–190
Demarest, William 151
Demetrio, Anna 28
Denning, Richard 87
Densmore, Wes 226
"Desert Bel Air" Development 76, 230–231
Desilu-Gower Studios 95, 96
The Desperado (1954) 35, 206
The Desperate Hours (1955) 36, 208–209
"The Devil's Blessing" (*Lancer*) 107
Diagnosis Murder ("Hard-Boiled Murder") 173–174
Dickerson, Beech 152, 165
Disney, Walt 63, 74
D.O.A. (1950) 24, 25–26, **27**, 28–29, 56, 68, 202
Doc Elliott ("A Small Hand of Friendship") 121
Doctor in Spite of Himself (play) 12
Dr. Kildare ("Twenty-Four Hours"; "Hastings Farewell") 3, 76, **77**, 78, 87, 231

Dodd, Father 31
Dodd, Molly 31
"The Dog That Bit You" (*Insight*) 102
Don Fedderson Productions 108
Donahue, Troy 174, 181
Doniger, Walter 38
"Don't Elbow Me Off the Earth" (*Insight*) 102
Don't Take My Penny (play) 15
Dorman, Richard, A.I.A. 231
Doron, Oliphant 12
Dors, Diana 83, 84–**85**
Dorsey, Jimmy 95
Dortort, David 120
Doty, G. Ellis 122
Douglas, Barbara 4
Douglas, Diana 120
Douglas, Michael 142
Dove-New Star Publishing 235
Drake, Tom 76
Dru, Joanne 108
Duff, Howard 51
Duke, Patty 72, 158, 160
Duke-Astin, Patty see Duke, Patty

The Earl Carroll Theatre 18–19, 39, 225
The East Valley YMCA 181
Eastwood, Clint 65
"Edge of Innocence" (*Playhouse 90*) 58, 229
87th Precinct ("Killer's Payoff") 78
Eisenhower, Dwight D. 5, 76, 88
Eldorado Country Club 76, 231
The Eleventh Hour ("What Did She Mean By Good Luck?") 91
Ellen ("She Ain't Friendly, She's My Mother") **169**
Elliott, Wild Bill 34
Ellstein, Abraham 232
Emmy Award Nomination 36, 68
The Emmy Awards 5
The Empire State Building, New York City, New York 23
Englund, Robert 132
Episcopalian Church 31
Ever Since Eve (play) 12
Everett, Chad 89

Fagan, Myron 32
"The Fair Freebooter" (*Yancy Derringer*) 63
Fanny with the Cheeks of Tan (16mm) 145
Farewell to 59 Birthday Party 150
The Farmer's Daughter ("The Stand In") 3, 92, 95
Farrell, Glenda 99
Faulkner, William 228
Faye, Alice 228
Faylen, Carol 96, **97**
Fearless Fagan (1952) 31, 203–204
Fedderson, Don 108, 110
Fennelly, Vince 76
Fessenden, Amelia "Millie" 7, 8, 9, 10, 12, 13, 15, 16, 18, 19, 20, 32, 80–81, 101–102, 114, 123, 152

Fessenden, Beverly 14, 15
Fessenden, Bill 8
Fessenden, James A. 7, 8, 10, 12, 13, 14, 16, 18, 19, 20, 32, 80–81, 97–98, 225, 230, 231
Fessenden, William Pitt 5
Fessenden Family 103
The Fighting Lawman (1953) 32–34
Fillmore P. Crank Distinguished Service Award 181
Finders of Lost Loves ("Surrogates") 159
Finding the Way Home (1991) 165, 222
Finney, Mary 226
First Christian Church, Los Angeles, California 179
Fisher, Eddie 228
The Fisherette 20
The Fishing Lesson (16mm) 145
Flamingo Road ("Heatwave") 148
Fleming, Eric 25, 66
Fleming, Rhonda 105
Fletcher, Louise 230
"The Fog" (*Climax!*) 53, 228
Fontaine, Joan 99
Ford Theater ("Measure of Faith") 52
Forest Lawn Cemetery, Los Angeles, California 17
Forrest, Steve 102
Forsythe, John 34
"The Four of Us Are Dying" (*Twilight Zone*) 155, 230
Four Star Playhouse ("Bourbon Street"; Night at Lark Cottage"; "Second Chance"; "Touch and Go") 36, **51**, 228, 229
Four Star Productions 64, 76, 230
"A Fragile Possession" (*Marcus Welby, M.D.*) 118
Francisco, James 121
Franklin Marshall College, Pennsylvania 160
Franz, Arthur 35, 107
"Freebooter" (*Hong Kong*) 75
Freeman, Kathleen 29, 194
Friends ("The One with All the Poker") 168
Frontier ("Cattle Drive to Casper") 38
The Fugitive ("Smoke Screen") 91

Gallagher, Peter 138
Garland, Carrington see Crank, Carrington
Garland, Richard ("Chuck") 31, 34, 38, 39, 41, 42, 52, 64, 110, 233
The Garland Center 160
Garmore Productions 80
Gates, Nancy 41, 82
Gates, Phil 14
Gavin, John 111–**113**, 149
Geller, Stephen 103
General Mills Buc Wheats Cereal (TV commercial) 136

George, Anthony 84
The George Sanders Mystery Theatre (pilot) 228
Georgia Peaches (1980) 50, 228
Gershwin & Hart 21
Gertrude 88
Gethers, Steve 94, 95
Gibson, William 230
The Gin Game 162–163, 174
Ginger 14
Ginny Lee 14
Girard, Bernard 68, 94, 105–106
"Girl Under Glass" (*Trapper John, M.D.*) 145
Glad Wrap (TV commercial) 125
Glamour Preferred (play) 21
The Glass Web (1953) 34, 205, 227
Glendale, California 9, 14
The Glendale Center Theatre 29
Glendale Community College 17, 18, 20
The Go-Getter (1955) 38, 208
Gobel, George 99
Going My Way ("A Saint for Mama") 85, 87
Goldberg, Lee 174
The Golden Boot Award 160
Goldwaters Department Store 14
Gomez, Thomas 99
"The Good Doctor" (*Matt Houston*) 150
Goodbye Again 24, 226
Goodman, Tula Pajeau 180
Grady, Don 152
Graham, Sheilah 5, 56, 228
The Grand Hotel, Belem, Brazil 44
Grant, Hank 229, 230
Grant, Kathryn 99
Grassle, Karen 235
Graupe, Rehlein 18, 20, 21
Graves, Peter 49, 90, 181, 228
Great to Be Alive (play) 232
Greatest Heroes of the Bible ("Abraham's Sacrifice") 138–**139**
The Greatest Horror Stories of the 20th Century (audio book) 235
The Greatest Mystery Stories of the 20th Century (audio book) 235
Greene, Lorne 98, 228
Greene, Mike 89
Gregory, James 104
Grey, Virginia 34
Griffith, Charles B. 152
Grillo, Basil 94, 95
Grodin, Charles 142
Gross, J. 230
The Guardian ("Indian Summer") 181
Gunfight at Sandoval (1961) 214
Gunn, Moses 120
Gunslinger (1956) 4, 46, 47–48, 89, 209, 210
Gunsmoke ("The Badge"; "The Odyssey of Jubal Tanner"; "Time of the Jackals"; "The Victim") 95, 104, 105, 111, 124

Gurney, A.R. 174
Guy Madison Productions 71
Gypsy 122
The Gypsy Rose Lee Show 101–102

Hale, Nathan 29
Hale, Ruth 29
Hall, John, Jr. 60
Happy Birthday (play) 25, 226
"Hard-Boiled Murder" (*Diagnosis Murder*) 174
"Hard Lines" (*Trackdown*) 64
Harper, Ron 78
Harrington, Pat, Jr. 87
Harris, Phil 99, 228
Hart, Moss 29
"The Hart Break Kid" (*Hart to Hart*) 148
Hart to Hart ("The Hart Break Kid") 148
Hartmann, Edmund 108
Hatcher, Teri 150
Hatton, Tom 181
The Haunted Symphony (1993) see **Hellfire**
"The Haunting of Mary Jane Hudson" (*Spider-Man*) 174
Hausells, Keller 72, 74
Haver, June 108
Hawaii (Maui) 132
Hawaiian Eye ("Shipment from Kihei") 68
Hawks, Howard 228
Hayes, Allison 47, 48, 73–74, 231
Hayes, Bill 41, 174
Hayward, Louis 230
Hayward, Susan 118, 233
Head, Edith 53–54, 138
The Healers (1974) 121, 218–219
Heart of a City (play) 15
Heartbeat ("Prison") 160
"Heatwave" (*Flamingo Road*) 160
Heaven Can Wait (play) 227
Hellfire (1993) 165–168, 222–223
Hemingway, Ernest 56
Henderson, Florence 145
Here's Lucy ("Lucy Goes to the Air Force Academy — Part II") 111
Heston, Charlton 121
Hicks, Catherine 174–**175**, 177
Higgins, Bob 74
Highland Avenue, Los Angeles, California 151
Hill, Arthur 118, 142
Hill, Jenny 118
Hill, Steven 142
Hirschman, Herb 230
Hirson, Alice **169**
Hlubik, Jesse 183
Hockman, Ned 79, 186, 231
The Holiday Stage, Tustin, California 23–24, 32, 226
Hollywood Boulevard, Los Angeles, California 149
Hollywood Guild Canteen 226
The Hollywood Palace (1965) 99
The Hollywood Walk of Fame 5, 149–**152**, 153

Holt, Nat 230
Homeier, Skip 79–80, 186
Hong Kong ("Freebooter") 52, 75
Honorary Mayor of North Hollywood 120, 130
Hopkins, Miriam 25
Hopper, Hedda 5, 56, 57, 95, 228
Horace Mann Elementary School 9
Horton, Robert 96, 100
Hotel ("New Beginnings") 158
How the West Was Won ("The Slavers") 138
Howard, George 19
Howard Johnson Hotels 116, 233
Hubert, Janet 235
Hudson, Hal 230
Human Dimension ("And Then They Forgot God") 1
Hunt, Marsha 57
Hunter, Jeffrey 41, 52
Hunter, Kim 121
"Hurricane Coming" (*The Web*) 228
Hussey, Ruth 38

I Magnins 17
I Remember Mama 24–25, **26**, 226
If (2003) **182**–186, 223
"Image of a Toad" (*Sam Benedict*) 84
"In Close Pursuit" (*Kraft Mystery Theater*) 81
"Incident at Sugar Creek" (*Rawhide*) 81
"Incident in the Middle of Nowhere" (*The Loner*) 100
"Incident of the Gallows Tree" (*Rawhide*) 84, 229
"The Incident of the Roman Candles" (*Rawhide*) 65
"Indian Summer" (*The Guardian*) 181
Inescort, Frieda 64
Insight (Spanish) 123
Insight ("The Day Everything Went Wrong"; "The Day God Died"; "Don't Elbow Me Off the Earth"; "A Thief Named Dismas"; "Why Don't You Call Me Skipper Anymore?") 102
"The Interrogation" (*Planet of the Apes*) 123–**124**
"The Invisible Wife" (*Medical Center*) 125
Ireland, John 47
Ironside ("The Over-the-Hill Blues") 124
It Conquered the World (1956) 4, 48–49, 50, 210, 228
ITC Productions 230
It's My Turn (1980) 142–144, 220–221
Ivanova, Ekaterina 167

The Jack Barry Show 231
Jack Ingram Ranch, Topanga

Canyon, Los Angeles, California 33, 47
Jackson, Kate 154–*159*, 160, 172, 173, 234
Jameson, Joyce 235
Jane Eyre (radio play) 194
Janssen, David 52, *91*
Jarvis, Graham 174–*176*, 177, 180
Jasmine 122
"Jealousy Makes the Heart Grow Fonder" (*The Mothers-in-Law*) 105
Jergens, Adele 34
Jericho (Zane Grey Theater) 71, 78
Jessel, George 228
The John Anson Ford Amphitheatre 232
"The Johnny Rath Story" (*Wire Service*) 228
Johnson, Andrew 5
Johnson, George Clayton 155, 230
The Joker Is Wild (1957) 3, 53, *54*, *55*, 56, 59, 78, 138, 212
Jones, Carolyn 34, 96, 98, 149–150, 234
Jones, Catherine "Casey" 60
Jones, Morgan 49
Jordan, Bobby 226
Judd for the Defense ("The Deep End") 104
Judgment Day (unsold pilot) 148
June Mad (play) 19
Juniata College, Pennsylvania 160

Kaiser, Fr. Ellwood E. 102
Kappa Delta Kappa 14
Kasne, Philip 230
Katkow, Norman 100
Katzman, Sam 35
Kaufman, George 29
Kay, Richard 42
Kaye, Stubby 83, 92
Keach, Stacy 187
Kean, Jane 181, 186
Keith, Brian 57, 67, 102
Kelly, Gene 85
Kelly, Jack 32
"Killer Fudge" (short story) 178
Killer Leopard (1954) 35, 207
"Killers from Kansas" (*Walt Disney Presents: Tales of Texas John Slaughter*) 63–64
"Killer's Payoff" (*87th Precinct*) 78
King B: A Life in the Movies (1993) *165*
The King Family 99
Kirk, Phyllis 59
Kirkland, Sally 228
Kodak Theater, Los Angeles, California 151
KOY Radio 94
Kraft Music Hall (radio) 95
The Kraft Mystery Theater ("In Close Pursuit") 81
The Kraft Suspense Theater ("Charlie, He Couldn't Kill a Fly") 94
Kramer, Jack 228
KTLA-TV 226

Kulp, Nancy 102, 160
Kung Fu ("Battle Hymn") 125

"The Lady and the Lion" (*Soldiers of Fortune*) 38
Lady in the Dark (play) 21
The Laguna Beach Community Players 21, 23–24
The Laguna Beach Playhouse 29, 226
Lake Tahoe, California 122
Lamar, Heddy 89
L'Amour, Louis 234
Lancer ("The Devil's Blessing") 107
Landon, Michael 96
Lanigan's Rabbi ("Say It Ain't So, Chief") 132
Lansing, Robert 78, 102
Laramie ("Saddle and Spur") 71
Laredo ("Lazyfoot, Where Are You?") 100
LaRue, Cookie 131–132
LaSalle, Coco 63–64
Las Palmas Theatre, Los Angeles, California 105, 232
Lassiter, Louise 131
Las Vegas, Nevada 72, *73*
Laurie, Piper 139
The Lawyer (unsold story idea) 71
"Lazyfoot, Where Are You?" (*Laredo*) 100
Lear, Norman 131
Lee, Gypsy Rose 228
"The Left Side of Canada" (*Cain's Hundred*) 81
Leigh, Janet 29, 31
Leighton, Linda 82
Lenard, Kay 228
Lenz, Kay 121
Leonard, Margaret 60
Lester, Mark L. 140
Let's Put on a Play (play) 15
"A Letter to My Runaway Child" (45 rpm record) 105
Levitts, Paul 96, 232
Lewis, Elliot 81
Lewis, Jerry 83
"The Lie" (*Rheingold Theatre* a.k.a. *The Star and the Story*) 38, 228
Life, Liberty and Pursuit on the Planet of the Apes (1974) 221; see also *Planet of the Apes* ("The Interrogation")
A Life of Her Own (1950) 29–*30*, 202–203
Life with Father 24, 226
Light, Judith 177
Lincoln, Abraham 5
Lindsey, Howard 226
"Little Girl Lost" (*Mannix*) 105, 120, 173
Little Theatre of Glendale 11, 12
Little Theatre of Phoenix 15, 19, 94
Little Theatre of the Verdugos 11, 12

Little Women (radio play) 178, 194
Livingston, Barry 152
Livingston, Stanley 152
The Lo Bera Theatre, Los Angeles, California 226
Lockhart, June 228, 235
Loew, Corke 230
Logan, Joshua 25
Logan-Crank, Barbara 74
Loggia, Robert 66
Lois & Clark: The New Adventures of Superman 169, 171–*173*
The Lone Ranger ("The Beeler Gang") 28
The Lone Wolf ("Pursuit") 38, 230
The Loner ("Incident in the Middle of Nowhere") 100
Long, Richard 83
Long Beach, California 8
Long Beach Playhouse, Long Beach, California 187
Lopez, Perry 38
Lorre, Peter 57
Los Angeles City Council 181
Los Angeles County Hospital 35
Los Angeles Visitors and Convention Bureau 129
Los Angeles Visitor's Information Center 151
"Lou Douses an Old Flame" (*The Mary Tyler Moore Show*) 125–*126*
Love, American Style ("Love and the Big Top") 120
Love Letters (play) 174
"Lucy Goes to the Air Force Academy"—Part II (*Here's Lucy*) 111
Ludlow Road, Westport, Connecticut 226
Luke Field, Arizona 15
Lupton, Ann 228
Lupton, John 228
Lupton, Rollin 228
Lux Girls 36
Lux Video Theatre ("The Creaking Gate"; "Meet Joe Cathart"; "My Name Is Julia Ross"; "Thunder on the Hill"; "To Have and Have Not") 36, 56, 136
Lyn, Dawn 112, 152

Macbeth 38
Mack, Cassie 53, 54, *55*
MacKenzie, Gisele 230
MacMurray, Fred 56, 75, 108, *109*, 114–115, 135, 151, 152, 232, 233, 235
Macready, George 64
The Mad Room (1969) 105–106, 148, 216–217
Maddox, Pastor 11
Madison, Guy 235
The Magic Wheel (1952) 227
Magnum P.I. ("Three Minus Two") 150
Mahoney, Jock 63–64, 235
The Maker of Dreams (play) 12
Malden, Karl 138–139

Malone, Dorothy 98
Mama Rosa's Boarding House (1949) 28, 226
"The Man" (unsold pilot) 68
A Man Called Shenandoah ("The Onslaught") 100
The Man with Bogart's Face (radio play) 195
Mandel, Loring 95
Mannix ("Deadfall"; "Little Girl Lost") 105, 120, 173
Mansfield, Jayne 83
Mantley, John 111
March, Fredric 36
March Air Force Base, California **90**
Marcus Welby, M.D. ("A Fragile Possession"; "To Live Another Day") 118, 125
Martin, Ross 83, 104
Martindale, Virginia 108
Marvin, Lee 36, 84, 194
Mary Hartman, Mary Hartman 131–132, 146
Mary Pickford Speakers Series 187
Mary Pickford Studios, the Bronx, New York 59
The Mary Tyler Moore Show ("Lou Doses an Old Flame") 125
Mason, Johnny 16
The Match Game 120
Mate, Rudolph 226
Matt Houston ("The Good Doctor") 150
Matthews, Carole 39
The May Company 65
Mayo, Virginia 158
McBain, Ed 78
McCambridge, Mercedes 228
McCarthy, Kevin 159
McDevitt, Ruth 103
McDowall, Roddy 133, 148, 195
McGavin, Darren 230
McGoohan, Patrick 69
McGuire, Dorothy 38
McHugh, Frank 96, **97**
McIntire, John 232
Mears, Betty 226
"Measure of Faith" (*Ford Theater*) 52
Medford, Don 91
Medic ("White Is the Color") 35, 36, **37**, 68, 84, 135, 194
Medical Center ("The World's a Balloon") 125
Medina, Patricia 88
The Merv Griffin Show 158
MGM Studios 3, 28, 29, 31, 35, 52, 76, 78
The Miami Story (1954) 34, 35, 39, **40**, 57, 205–206
Michael Shayne ("Murder and the Wanton Bride") 76
"The Mighty Knothead" (*The Angry Beavers*) 174
Miles, Vera 158
Milky Way Candy Bar (TV commercial) 174

Milland, Ray 29
Miller, Dick 235
Miller, Merle 232
Miller, Ron 232
The Millionaire ("Millionaire Carl Nelson"; Millionaire Louise Benson") 38
"Millionaire Carl Nelson" (*The Millionaire*) 38
"Millionaire Louise Benson" (*The Millionaire*) 38
Mills, Allen 235
Mills, Donna 160
The Miracle Worker (play) 71, 72, 191, 230
The Miss USA Beauty Pageant (1979) 139
The Mission Inn, Riverside, California 32
Mobley, Roger 102, 232
Molière, J.-B.P. 12
Monte Carlo, Monaco 134
Montgomery, George 235
Morris, Wayne 32, 35
Morton, Greg 157, **159**
Moscow, Russia 147–168, 235
Mosfilm Studios 165–168, 235
Moser, James 35, 193
The Mothers-in-Law ("Jealousy Makes the Heart Grow Fonder") 105
"Move Along, Mustangers" (*Walt Disney Presents: The Nine Lives of Elfego Baca*) 66
Mowbray, Alan 226
Mulholland Drive, Los Angeles, California 230
"Murder and the Wanton Bride" (*Michael Shayne*) 76
Murray, Don 56
"Mustang Man, Mustang Maid" (*Walt Disney Presents: The Nine Lives of Elfego Baca*) 229
"My Brother's Killer" (*Decoy—The Story of a New York Policewoman*) 1
My Fair Lady (play) 56
My Three Sons 4, 75, 108, **109**–115, 140, 151, 158, 162, 233
"The Mystery of the Fallen Angels" (*Nancy Drew Mystery*) 132

Naked Paradise (1957) 53, 211
Nakowsky, Mrs. 15–16
Nancy Drew Mystery ("The Mystery of the Fallen Angels") 132
Nash, J. Carroll 233
The National Company 25
National Honor Roll Society
National Lampoon's Christmas Vacation 2 — Cousin Eddie's Island Adventure (2003) 186, 223–224
The National Tour Brokers Association 4, 128–129, 131, 145–146, 174
The National Touring Company 226

Navy Log ("Family Special") 38
The Neanderthal Man (1953) 32–**33**, 204–205
"The Negative Man" (Science Fiction Theater) 38, 228
Neiman, Irving G. 95
Nelson, Chris 162–163
Nelson, Ed 39, 125, 162–**163**
Nelson, Gene 228
Nelson, Patty 125
"New Beginnings" (*Hotel*) 158
New Orleans Uncensored (1955) 35, 57, 78, 125, 207–208
The Newlywed Game 103
Newman, E. Jack 100
Newport Beach, Newport, California 98, 122, 185
Nielsen, Leslie 133–134
"Night at Lark Cottage" (*Four Star Playhouse*) 228, 229
"The Night of Bleak Island" (*The Wild, Wild West*) 107
"The Night of the Cutthroats" (*The Wild, Wild West*) 104
"Night of the Wrangler" (*Russell*, unaired pilot) 76
"Nine Sons" (short story) 235
"The Nine-Twenty Hero" (*Asphalt Jungle*) 78
Niven, David **51**
Nolan, Jeanette 232
Nolan, Kathy 98
Noonan, Tommy 92
North Hollywood News 182
North Phoenix High School 14, 15
Not of This Earth (1957) 4, 48, 49–50, 211, 228
N.T.B.A. *see* The National Tour Brokers Association
The Nurses ("The Walls Came Tumbling Down") 1, 5, 82
Nyby, Christian 228

Oakland, California 228
O'Brien, Edmund 25, 56, 84
"The October Country" (short story) 235
"The Odyssey of Jubal Tanner" (*Gunsmoke*) 89
Official Films 59
On the Waterfront (1954) 35
Once in a Lifetime (play) 29
"One for the Birds" (*The Bing Crosby Show*) 99
"The One with All the Poker" (*Friends*) 168
"The Onslaught" (*A Man Called Shenandoah*) 100
"Open Wide for Zombies" (*The Angry Beavers*) 174
Osborne, Robert 144
O'Sullivan, Maureen 58
"The Other Mother" (*The Simple Life*) 177–178
"The Other Side of the Moon" (Science Fiction Theater) 38, 228
"The Other Van Gogh" **57, 229**

Out of the Frying Pan (play) 15
Outward Bound (play) 23, 226
"The Over-the-Hill Blues" (*Ironside*) 124
Over the Limit 159
Owen Marshall — Counselor at Law ("Sometimes Tough Is Good") 118

Pacific Federal Savings 151
The Pacific Pioneer Broadcasters 181
Paige, Arizona 138, 234
Palm Desert, California 89, 231
Palm Springs, California 72, 174
The Palm Springs Film Noir Festival 182
Panorama Pacific (radio show) 87
Pantomime Quiz see *Stump the Stars*
Paramount Studios 3, 96
Paris, France 134
Parker, Fess 76, 235
Parsons, Louella O. 5, 230
The Partridge Family — My Three Sons Thanksgiving Reunion (1977) 135
The Pasadena Civic Auditorium, Los Angeles, California 226
Patches, J.P. 88
"Payment in Kind" (*Rheingold Theater* a.k.a. *The Star and the Story*) 228, 229
Payton, Jo Marie 235
P.D.Q. 100
"Pearl Hart" (*Tales of Wells Fargo*) 71, 230
People Are Talking in the Afternoon 158
The Perfect Circle see **It's My Turn**
Perkins, Anthony 103–104
Perry Mason ("The Case of the Mythical Monkeys") 71, 95, 124, 230
Persoff, Nehemiah 233
Persuade Me (play) 29
Petersen, Stewart 123
Le Petite Restaurant, Los Angeles, California 102
Pevney, Joe 85
Phoenix, Arizona 8, 14, 15, 16
Pierrette 12
The Pilgrimage Play Theatre 232
Pinky (1949) **28**
Pinza, Ezio 29
Pistols 'n' Petticoats ("The Ross Guttley Story") 102–103
Plain & Fancy (Fan Club Journal) 225
Planet of the Apes ("The Interrogation") 123–**124**
Planet of the Apes (1968/2000) 234
The Player's Ring 29, 31, 32, 96, 175, 227, 232
Playhouse 90 ("The Edge of Innocence") 58, 136, 229

The Play's the Thing (play) 32, 34, 227
Pleshette, Suzanne 72
"Point of Honor" (*Rheingold Theater* a.k.a. *The Star and the Story*) 228
Polaroid Cameras (TV commercial) 136
Police Woman 62
Pollexfen, Jack 32
Port Charles 180–181
Potter, Carol 235
Powell, Dick 36, 37, 230
Powers, Marla 108
Powers, Stefanie 148
Presnell, Harve 169, 172
Pretty Poison (1968) 103–104, 215–**216**
Prigunov, Lev 167, 235
"Prison" (*Heartbeat*) 160
Problem Girls (1953) 32, 204
Proctor, Kay 55
"The Profile on Ellen Gale" (*Wire Service*) 54, 228
P.S. I Luv U ("Where There's a Will, There's a Dani") 165
Puerto Vallarta, Mexico 125
"Pursuit" (*The Lone Wolf*) 230
Pyramid Productions 57

Quaid, Randy 186
Queen of Armed Forces Day **90**
The Quiet Wedding (play) 15, 19
Quinn, Don 226

Radio and Television Women of Southern California 98
Radio KIEV 19
Radio KOY 15
Radio KYA 13
The Rainbow Players 19
Randall, Tony 135–136
Rastar Productions 142
Rawhide ("Incident at Sugar Creek"; "Incident of the Gallows Tree"; "Incident of the Roman Candles") 25, 65, 84, 87
Rawls, Wilson 122
Reagan, Nancy 164
Reagan, Ronald 5, 158, 164–165, 233
Reason, Rex 211–212
Red Rainbow 227
Regan, Sylvia 232
"Remember the Alamo" (*Coronado Nine*) 229
Remington Steele ("The Sting of Steele"; "Thou Shalt Not Steele") 150, 154–**155**
Rennie, Michael 57
Reno (radio play) 235
Republic Pictures 231
Retail Clerks Union 226
Reunion in Vienna (film test) 28
Revue Productions 230
Rheingold Theatre a.k.a. *The Star and the Story* ("The Lie"; "Payment in Kind"; "The Point of Honor") 28, 228, 229
Rhubarb 81, 231
Rhys, Caradoc 12
Rhythm Roundup — A South American Cruise 15
Richardson, Shirley 112–114, 130
Richmond, Peter Mark 81, 187
Ring Around the Ring (play) 31
Riordan, Mayor Richard 181
Riverboat ("Three Graves") 71, 230
Riverside, California 32
RKO-Pathé 54
Roberts, Pernell 173
Roberts, Thayer 227
Roberts, Wayne 76
Robinson, Edward G. 34
Robinson, Hubbell 71
The Rocket Man (1954) 35
Rockwood, Roy 35
"Rodeo Roughouse" a.k.a. "Killers on Horseback" (*State Trooper*) 221
Roerick, William 49
Rogers, Ginger 228
Roller Boogie (1979) 139–140, 144, 185, 220
Roman, Ruth 99
The Rookies ("Three Hours to Kill") 120, 234
Rooney, Mickey 226
Roosevelt Junior High School 10
"A Rope for a Lady" (*Jericho/Zane Grey Theater*) 78, 231
Rosenberg, Stuart 232
Rosenthal, Everett 56
"Rosie" (*Crazy Like a Fox*) 160
Ross, Jerome 95
"The Ross Guttley Story" (*Pistols 'n' Petticoats*) 102–103
Ross-Leming, Eugenie 158
Rowe, Kimberly 183
Rowlands, Gina 56
Royal, Dan 50
The Ruggles of Red Gap (radio play) 178, 189, 195
Rumplemeyers Restaurant, New York City, New York 59
Russell, Charles 76
Russell ("Night of the Wrangler," unaired pilot) 76
"R-X Love" (*Temperatures Rising*) 120
Ryan, Robert 57–**58**
Ryerson, Florence 12

"Saddle and Spur" (*Laramie*) 71
S.A.G. (Screen Actor's Guild) 24, 111
The Saga of Hemp Brown (1958) 58, 59, 213, 229
Saint, Eva Marie 38
St. Clair, Jim 14
"A Saint for Mama" (*Going My Way*) 55
St. John, Jill 150
Saints and Sinners Club 18
Salkow, Sidney 57, 87

Sam Benedict ("Image of a Toad") 84, 87
San Fernando State College 82
San Fernando Valley Earthquake 233
Santa Fe Springs Parade 102
Santa Monica Boulevard, Los Angeles, California 226
Santa Monica College 187
Say Goodbye, Maggie Cole (1972) 118
"Say It Ain't So, Chief" (*Lanigan's Rabbi*) 132
Say When Again 82
Scarecrow and Mrs. King 4, 154–160, 161, 171, 172, 234, 235
Schick-Sun 138
Schlitz Playhouse of Stars ("Too Late to Run") 38
Schroder, Jimmie 12
Schumm, Hans Josef 227
Science Fiction Theater ("The Negative Man"; "The Other Side of the Moon") 38, 228
Scott, George C. 165
Scott, Pippa 108
Scott, Zachary 51
Scottsdale, Arizona 14
Screen Actors Guild (S.A.G.) 24, 111, 160, 183
The Screen Actors Guild Awards 190
The Searchers (1959) 69
Sears Roebuck & Company 16
Seberg, Jean 56
Second Chance (play) 228
The Seduction (1982) 144
Segal, Boris 231
Selleck, Tom 150
Semple, Lorenzo, Jr. 103
Serling, Rod 68, 100, 230
The Seven Layered Arsenic Cake of Madame La Farge (radio play) 195
17 Barrel Street, New York City, New York 60
7th Annual Emmy Awards Ceremony 38
7th Heaven 174–***176***, 177, 180
Shadowcon VII (June, 1983) 155
Sharpe, Don 229
Sharpe, Pam 174
"She Ain't Heavy, She's My Mother" (*Ellen*) ***169***
She Let Him Continue (novel) 103
She Loves Me Not (play) 24, 226
Shea, John 234
Sheffield, Johnny 35
Sheldon, James 95, 232
Sher, Jack 100
Sheraton Hotel, Philadelphia, Pennsylvania 228
Sheridan, Ann 103
Sherman, George 67
Sherry, Diane 96, ***97***, 99
Sherry, William Grant 17, 21
Shigeta, James 99
Shor, Toots 228

"Showdown at Sandoval" (*Walt Disney Presents: Tales of Texas John Slaughter*) 63
Showtime Cable Network 160
"Silhouette of a Killer" (*Alcoa – Goodyear Theater*) 57–***58***
Silver Circle Cruise Line 148
Silverman, Fred 115, 233
Simon, Mayo 95
The Simple Life ("The Other Mother") 177–178
Sinatra, Frank 3, 53
Singer, Arthur 56
Siodmak, Curt 41, 42, 44, 45–46
The Six Million Dollar Man ("Death Probe") 131
Sixth and Main (1977) 133, 173, 220
Skag (unaired pilot) 138–139
"The Slavers" (*How the West Was Won*) 138
Small, Edward 57, 87
"A Small Hand of Friendship" (*Doc Elliott*) 120
Smart, Ralph 230
Smith, Glenn 81, 231
Smith, Martha ***159***, 160
Smith, William 100
"Smoke Ghosts" (short story) 235
"Smoke Screen" (*The Fugitive*) 92
Snow, Pat 9
S.O.A.R. Project 158
Soldiers of Fortune ("The Lady and the Lion") 38
"Sometimes Tough Is Good" (*Owen Marshall – Counselor at Law*) 118
Sons and Daughters ("Throw Mama from the Terrain") 164
Sothern, Ann 38
South America 42
Spelling, Aaron 149, 158, 159, 175
The Spider (play) ***24***, 226
Spider-Man ("The Haunting of Mary Jane Hudson") 174
Stack, Robert 21, 158
Stagecoach West ("The Storm") 76
Stallions see ***Death Falls***
"The Stand In" (*The Farmer's Daughter*) 92, 95
Stanley, Florence 177
Stanwyck, Barbara 29, 54
The Star and the Story a.k.a. *Rheingold Theater* ("The Lie"; "Payment in Kind"; "The Point of Honor") 38, 228, 229
Stark, Ray 143
Stark Fear (1963) 78–80, 164, 186, 214
Starr, Jimmy 228
State Trooper ("Rodeo Rough House" a.k.a. "Killers on Horseback") 66, 228, 229
The Steel Jungle (1956) 38, 209
Stengel, Casey 116, 217, 233
Stephens College, Columbia, Missouri 16
Sterling, Jan 81

The Steve Allen Show 87, 94
Stevens, Connie 98
Stevens, Stella 105, 122, 148
Stevenson, Carl 231
Stevenson, Peggy 234
Stewart, Jay 84
Stickell, Vance 234
"The Sting of Steele" (*Remington Steele*) 150, 154–***155***
Stokey, Mike 83, ***85***, 87, 92
Stoll, Lisa ***182***–186
"The Storm" (*Stagecoach West*) 76
Stout, Paul 157, ***159***
Strictly Dishonorable (1951) 29, 203
Stritch, Elaine 192
Studio 57 38
Stump the Stars 83–***85***, 87–89, 104, 133, 231
Sudden Danger (1956) 39, 208
Sullivan, Barry 34, 148
"Summer Lightning" (*Bus Stop*) 81
Summer Story Time 82
"Sundown at Sandoval" (*Walt Disney Presents: Tales of Texas John Slaughter*) 63, 214
"Surrogates" (*Finder of Lost Loves*) 159
Suttleworth, Robert 230
Swain, Dwight V. 79–80, 231
Swamp Women (1956) 39–41, 209
Swann, Francis 15
Switch ("The Argonaut Special") 130

Talbott, Gloria 12
Tales of Wells Fargo ("Pearl Hart") 71
Tambay Film Festival 186
"A Taste for Crime" (*Climax!*) 57
Tausik, David 166–167
Taylor, Rod 52, 75
Teen Angel ("Back to DePolo"; "The Un-Natural") 177, 235
Tehachapi Prison, California 20
Temperature's Rising ("R-X Love") 120
"Tempest in a Teacup" (45 rpm record) 105
Thatcher, Margaret 164
"A Thief Named Dismas" (*Insight*) 102
Thieves Paradise (play) 32, 227
This Girl for Hire (1983) 157, 221–222
Thomas, Larri 45
"Thou Shalt Not Steele" (*Remington Steele*) 150
3-D Process 34, 227
"Three Graves" (*Riverboat*) 11, 230
"Three Hours to Kill" (*The Rookies*) 120, 234
"Three Minus Two" (*Magnum P.I.*) 150
Thriller ("Knock Three-One-Two") 71, 76
"Throw Away the Cane" (*Climax!*) 3, 53, 57, 228

"Throw Mama from the Terrain" (*Sons and Daughters*) 164
A Time for Love (Telethon) 145
"Time of the Jackals" (*Gunsmoke*) 105
"To Have and Have Not" (*Lux Video Theater*) (1957) 56
"To Live Another Day" (*Marcus Welby, M.D.*) 125
"To the Moon, Alice" (Showtime Cable Network) 160
Tobey, Kenneth 79
"Tobias the Terrible" (*Damon Runyon Theatre*) 38
The Today Show 158
Together 158
Tombragel, Maurice 232
The Tony Randall Show ("Case: The Sylvia Needleman Experience") 135–136
Top Finds of 1956 56
Tormé, Mel 99
"Touch and Go" (*Four Star Playhouse*) **51**, 228
Towers, Constance 149
Townes, Harry 228
Toys for Tots 158
Trackdown ("Hard Lines") 64
"Tragedy on the Trail" (*Walt Disney Presents: Gallagher Goes West*) 102
Trans-Continental Films Productions 69
Trapper John, M.D. ("Girl Under Glass") 145
Trevor, Claire 38
"Trial by Terror" (*Walt Disney Presents: Gallagher Goes West*) 102
Trocheck, Kathy Hogan 178
Trotter, John Scott 95
Tula's California Café and Coffee Room 180, 195
Turner, Lana 29, 118, 123
Turney, Harold 24
Tustin, California 23–24
"TV Mothers Special Edition" (*The Weakest Link*) 181, 235
20th Century–Fox 28, 64, 123
"Twenty-Four Hours" (*Dr. Kildare*) 76, 231
26th Street Armory, New York City, NY 59
Twice Told Tales (1963) 87–**88**, **214–215**
Twilight Zone ("The Four of Us Are Dying") 68, 95, 100, 155
The Twilight Zone Radio Dramas 187
Twilight Zone—The Next Dimension 187
Two Guns and a Badge (1954) 35, 206–207
Tyron, Tom 63

UCLA 179
UCLA Medical Center 68
Uncle Simon (radio play) 187
United Artists 24
U.S. Army Air Corps 15
U.S. Senate Page 234
Universal-International 34, 46, 56, 58, 59
Universal Studios 4, 56, 58, 59, 128
University of Oklahoma 79, 80
University of Oklahoma College of Fine Arts 186
"The Un-Natural" (*Teen Angel*) 177
Unwed Father (1974) 2, 121, 218

The Vagabond House, Los Angeles, California 31
The Valley Home for Women, California 82
Valley International Film Festival (2004) 186
Van Cleef, Lee 32, 48, 49
Van Druten, John 226
Van Dyke, Dick 174, 181
Van Dyke, Jerry 177
Van Huesen, James 95
Van Patten, Dick 102
"The Victim" (*Gunsmoke*) 89, 90, 104
VOGUE Magazine 226
"Voodoo Hoodoo" (*The Angry Beavers*) 235
The Voyage of the Yes (1973) 120, 218

Wachs, Joel 234
Wagner, Robert 130–131, 148
"The Walls Came Tumbling Down" (*The Nurses*) 1, 82
Walt Disney Presents: Gallagher Goes West ("Tragedy on the Trail"; "Trail by Terror") 102, 232
Walt Disney Presents: Tales of Texas John Slaughter ("Killers from Kansas"; "Sundown at Sandoval") 63–64, 214
Walt Disney Presents: The Nine Lives of Elfego Baca ("Move Along, Mustangers"; "Mustang Man, Mustang Maid") 66
Wanda 123–**124**
Warner Brothers 3, 38, 56
Wasson, Craig 138
A Watch for Joe (1951) 227
Wayne, David 99
"The Wayward Warrior" (*Yancy Derringer*) 63
The Weakest Link ("TV Mothers Special Edition") 181, 235
The Web ("Hurricane Coming") 57, 229
The Weekend Nun (1972) 120, 217–218
Weill, Claudia 142
Weld, Tuesday 103–104
Welles, Orson 46

Wendkos, Paul 100
Westinghouse Group of Stations 59
Westmount Drive, West Hollywood, California 229
Westport, Connecticut 22–23, 226
Westport Inn, Connecticut 22
"What Did She Mean By Good Luck?" (*The Eleventh Hour*) 91
What's Going on America 98
What's This Song? 98
Where the Red Fern Grows (1974) 122–123, 132, 138, 219, 233
White, Betty 181
"White Is the Color" (*Medic*) 68
Whitman, James 122
"Why Don't You Call Me Skipper Anymore?" (*Insight*) 102
"The Widow of Kill Cove" (*Coronado Nine*) 66
The Wild, Wild West ("Night of Bleak Island"; "Night of the Cut-throats") 104, 107
Williams Field, Arizona 15
Williamsburg Film Festival 182
Winchell, Paul 165
Windom, William 81, 122, 174, 181, 194, 195
Windsor, Marie 39, 152
Winters, Jonathan 165
Wire Service ("The Johnny Rath Story"; "Profile on Ellen Gale") 54, 228
Wisberg, Aubrey 32
The Wish That Changed Christmas 165
Woman to Woman 158
The Women (play) 15
Women in Show Business 174
Woolworths 14
World War II 8, 14, 18, 226
"The World's a Balloon" (*Medical Center*) 125
The World's Oldest Living Bridesmaid (1990) 160, 222
Wright, Teresa 228
Wyler, William 36
Wyman, Jane **109**
Wynn, Keenan 94

Yancy Derringer ("The Fair Freebooter"; "The Wayward Warrior") 63
Ye Little Club, Los Angeles, California 72, 230
You Don't Say 100, 231
Young, Robert 118
The Young and the Restless 146–147
Your Loving Son, Nero (radio play) 178, 194

Zane Grey Theater 71, 78, 230
Zerbe, Anthony 121, 234
Ziegfeld Follies 18
Zimbalist, Efram, Jr. 102, **155**, 234
Zimbalist, Stephanie 150, **155**

www.ingramcontent.com/pod-product-compliance
Ingram Content Group UK Ltd.
Pitfield, Milton Keynes, MK11 3LW, UK
UKHW050535150426
5217IPUK00026B/1939